D1526316

INDIA'S POLITICAL ADMINISTRATORS
1919–1983

India's Political Administrators
1919–1983

DAVID C. POTTER

CLARENDON PRESS · OXFORD
1986

Oxford University Press, Walton Street, Oxford OX2 6DP
Oxford New York Toronto
Delhi Bombay Calcutta Madras Karachi
Petaling Jaya Singapore Hong Kong Tokyo
Nairobi Dar es Salaam Cape Town
Melbourne Auckland
and associated companies in
Beirut Berlin Ibadan Nicosia

Oxford is a trade mark of Oxford University Press

Published in the United States
by Oxford University Press, New York

British Library Cataloguing in Publication Data
Potter, David, 1931 Nov. 3-
India's political administrators 1919–1983.
1. Civil service—India—History—
20th century
I. Title
354.54006 JQ247
ISBN 0–19–821574–6

Library of Congress Cataloging-in-Publication Data
Potter, David C.
India's political administrators, 1919–1983.
Bibliography: p.
Includes index.
1. Civil service—India—History—20th century.
2. Colonial administrators—India—History—20th century. 3. India—Politics and government—1919–1947.
4. India—Politics and government—1947– . I. Title.
JQ246.P68 1986 354.54005 86–8801
ISBN 0–19–821574–6

Typeset by Hope Services, Abingdon, Oxon
Printed in Great Britain by
Billing & Sons Ltd
Worcester

FOR JENNIFER

Preface

THE origins of this book go back to the winter of 1960–1, when I spent six months in four rural districts of Rajasthan observing community development administrators at work. In viewing Indian administration from the bottom up, so to speak, I was struck particularly by two things. First, although many rural administrators seemed able enough and dedicated to the goals of the development plans, they appeared also to be heavily constrained, and sometimes virtually immobilized, by red tape; all public bureaucracies are necessarily bound by rules, of course, but the procedural controls within which these administrators had to work seemed exceptionally stultifying. Secondly, the head of the district administration appeared to preside over these people from a great height, only very occasionally appearing amongst them in the villages; he seemed to be concerned to ensure the maintenance of the rules yet he appeared not to be bound by them himself. He seemed to hold the key to the whole structure, and deserved closer attention.

Nearly all such heads of districts in Rajasthan, and indeed throughout India, were members of the Indian Administrative Service, or IAS. The IAS also held most of the key posts in administration at the state government level and also at the centre in New Delhi. When I went back to India in 1966–7, I devoted most of my attention to the IAS, interviewing many of them in four states—Bihar, Maharashtra, Rajasthan, and Tamil Nadu (then called Madras State), and also in New Delhi. Some of the results of that research are reported in this book. One of the things that stood out from that experience was that, unlike the earlier study of rural development administration when my attention was drawn up to the IAS district head and beyond, this time my attention was drawn backward in time. It was clear that in order to understand the IAS and the distinctive features of the administrative apparatus of the Indian state in which the IAS was lodged, it was necessary to go back to the way the British organized the administration of India earlier this century, and particularly to the way the Indian Civil Service, or ICS worked within the colonial state.

There certainly appeared to be an ICS tradition of administration, although it was difficult to discern its essential content. It also seemed reasonably clear that it had survived the end of colonial rule and remained important in independent India. But what was its essential content and why had it persisted (if it had?) I began to pursue these large questions in 1967 with work in the National Archives of India, New Delhi, and have continued to work on them intermittently since then, principally in relevant unpublished materials in the India Office Library and Records, London, and the Centre of South Asian Studies Archive, Cambridge University. I returned to India in 1983 to assess the extent to which the ICS tradition was still alive in the 1980s, talking with some IAS people whom I had met seventeen years previously, and who were by 1983 holding very senior positions either in state government or in the Government of India. The results of all these archival and field researches are summarized in this book. Although the study concentrates on explaining how and why the ICS tradition has persisted (and changed), it also suggests at least a partial explanation of the phenomena I encountered at the outset in the districts of Rajasthan.

Completing this study has taken a very long time, and many have helped along the way. It is a pleasure to acknowledge their assistance.

The research on which this study is based would not have been possible without grants from the following institutions and I am grateful for their assistance:

The London School of Economics and Political Science, for field research: Rajasthan, 1960–1;

The American Institute of Indian Studies, for field research: Bihar, Maharashtra, Madras, Rajasthan, New Delhi, Mussoorie, 1966–7;

The Nuffield Foundation, for field research: New Delhi, Rajasthan, Tamil Nadu, Mussoorie, 1983;

The Open University, for travel to India, 1983, and travel to archives in England.

I am indebted to the librarians and staff of the Centre of South Asian Studies, University of Cambridge, and in particular to Miss Mary Thatcher and Dr Lionel Carter; the India Office Library and Records, London, and in particular Dr Richard Bingle; the National Archives of India, New Delhi, and in particular Shri S. V. Desika Char; the Indian Institute of Public Administration Library, New Delhi; and the Lal Bahadur Shastri National Academy of Administration Library, Mussoorie, Uttar Pradesh.

In trying to understand the ICS tradition I have relied considerably on unpublished autobiographical memoirs and other papers by ICS men deposited by them or their descendants in the Centre of South Asian Studies Archive, Cambridge University, or the India Office Library and Records, London. I am grateful to the individual authors or their present-day representatives for allowing these valuable materials to be consulted and referred to in scholarly works. In three particular cases of European manuscripts in the India Office Library and Records from which I quote more than a sentence or two, I have sought and kindly been granted the necessary permissions, from Mrs B. M. D. Lee Warner for the Hume Papers, Mrs P. V. Lamarque for the Lamarque Papers, and Mr J. W. Orr for the Orr Papers.

Much of the material in the latter part of this book is based on personal interviews with Indian administrators, principally in Rajasthan, Maharashtra, Tamil Nadu, Bihar, New Delhi, and Mussoorie. With only rare exceptions, I have enjoyed their company immensely and learned much from them. It is no exaggeration to say that the whole thing would have been quite impossible without their help. It would be invidious to single out particular individuals here. It must suffice to say that those who helped the most are the eighty-seven ICS and IAS administrators identified in the bibliography as having been interviewed.

Many scholars in Britain, India, and North America have provided criticisms and helpful suggestions of earlier formulations of the argument advanced in this book. In particular I am indebted to Shriram Maheshwari, Kuldeep Mathur, and R. B. Jain of the Indian Institute of Public Administration, New Delhi, and the late B. S. Narula, also of the Institute, for drawing my attention to much I would have otherwise missed; C. P. Bhambhri of Jawaharlal Nehru University for the same reason; Mike Mahar of the University of Arizona who, on a train between Meerut and Muzaffarnagar, talked me into continuing with this project when I was on the verge of packing it in; the three scholars who asked the toughest and most fruitful questions when the argument was first outlined—W. H. Morris-Jones (University of London) at a conference in Paris, Hamza Alavi (University of Manchester) at a conference in Liverpool, Paul Brass (University of Washington) at a seminar in Vancouver; and the three who read and criticized the first draft manuscript—Richard Taub (University of Chicago), Frank Castles (Open University), and W. H. Morris-Jones. The responsibility for the final result is mine.

Cambridge University Press have kindly given permission to reproduce certain evidence reported in Chapter 2 that appeared previously in an article of mine in *Modern Asian Studies*. Similarly, other evidence in Chapters 2 and 5 has been reported previously in articles of mine in the *Indian Journal of Public Administration* and *Political Science Review*, and I am grateful to the Indian Institute of Public Administration and the University of Rajasthan respectively for permission to reproduce it here. I want to thank John Hunt, Project Officer (Cartographer) at the Open University, for ably drawing the maps, and Gloria Channing and Jo Doherty, also at the OU, for typing speedily and cheerfully several quite different drafts.

The dedication of this book hardly needs any explanation. She was around when it all began in Rajasthan, helped to keep it going over the years, and provided vital assistance and encouragement in the closing stages. I recall it all with love and gratitude.

Bedford, 1985

Contents

List of Tables

Abbreviations

AEO	Agricultural Extension Officer
ARC	Administrative Reforms Commission, Government of India
Cambridge Archive	Centre of South Asian Studies Archive, Cambridge University
CID	Criminal Investigation Department
CP	Central Provinces and Berar, a province in British India
CSP	Civil Service of Pakistan
Dept.	Department
DI	Deputy Inspector
DMK	Dravida Munnetra Kazhagam
EPW	*Economic and Political Weekly* (Bombay)
Ests.	Establishments Division, Home Department, Government of India
GOI	Government of India
IAS	Indian Administrative Service
ICS	Indian Civil Service
IIPA	Indian Institute of Public Administration, New Delhi
IJPA	*Indian Journal of Public Administration*, journal of IIPA
INA	Indian National Army, in the 1940s
IOL MSS Eur.	European manuscripts collection in the India Office Library and Records, London
IP	Indian Police, an élite all-India service in British India
IPS	Indian Police Service, successor to the IP in independent India
MAS	*Modern Asian Studies* (Cambridge)
MISA	Maintenance of Internal Security Act (1971)
MLA	Member of Legislative Assembly
MP	Madhya Pradesh
NAI	National Archives of India, New Delhi
NWFP	North West Frontier Province

PA	Personal Assistant
PAR	Department of Personnel and Administrative Reforms, Government of India
Rs	rupees
SDO	Subdivisional Officer, in a district
SP	Superintendent of Police
TS	Typescript
UP	United Provinces, a province of British India, later Uttar Pradesh in independent India

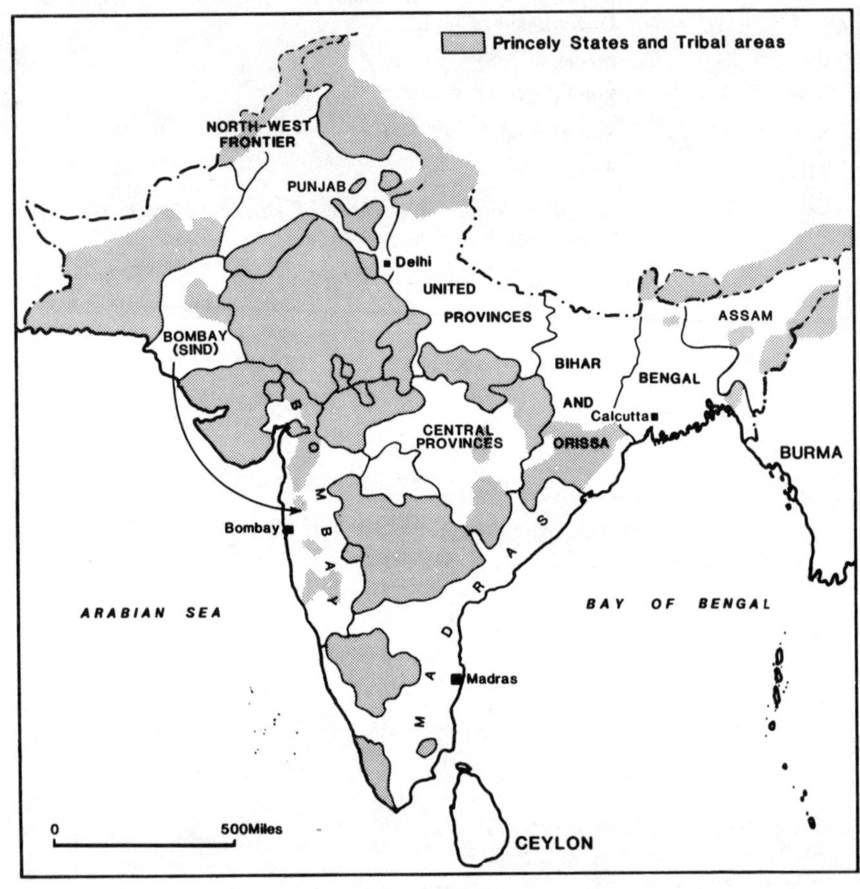

MAP 1. India *c*.1930

MAP 2. India *c.*1980

Introduction

MOST of the people who did the work of the colonial state in India were Indians. Although many administrators and soldiers were needed to govern and control a subcontinent the size of Europe containing about one-fifth of the world's population, very few were recruited in Britain by the imperial power in London. The rest had to be found cheaply in India. Pre-eminent among the administrators who could be sent from Britain were the men of the Indian Civil Service (ICS). They were trusted agents of the British Government recruited by the Secretary of State for India. They were placed in posts specially reserved for them in the districts and secretariats in each province and at the centre. In the secretariats they were responsible for handling questions of policy arising in India in a manner broadly consistent with the economic and strategic interests of the British Government. In the districts, even while overseeing the routine work of revenue collection and maintenance of law and order, they were inevitably engaged also in political work with local collaborators and others, nursing support structures and moving for advantage in fluid situations while never losing sight of imperial aims and requirements. Setting aside strategic posts for a special group of political administrators in this way had a profound influence on the entire structure of the colonial state and its administration.

Although much had changed by the early 1980s, this basic framework of administration was still in place. The ICS was succeeded by the Indian Administrative Service (IAS). When recruitment to the ICS stopped forever in the 1940s, recruitment to the IAS began. Over the years IAS men and women gradually moved in as ICS men moved up and then out. With the retirement of the last ICS man, Mr N. K. Mukharji, in March 1980 the handover was complete. Yet the IAS still held control posts in districts and secretariats. Although changes in the range of posts held by the IAS and the nature of their work reflected the changed orientation of the Indian state, their location and activities followed broadly the pattern set by the ICS in the 1920s and 1930s.

Such administrative continuity might be considered quite unremarkable. After all, public bureaucracies everywhere are notoriously slow to change, if left to their own devices. But here the case was different. The ICS was the instrument of the imperial power, and the leaders of the Indian National Congress had made it clear during their struggle for independence that they wanted to abolish the ICS and all it stood for. Jawaharlal Nehru was 'quite sure' in 1934 that 'no new order can be built in India so long as the spirit of the Indian Civil Service pervades our administration and our public services', it being therefore 'essential that the ICS and similar services must disappear completely'.[1] Yet when the British left in the 1940s, and the new Indian Government took over with Nehru as Prime Minister, ICS Indians (with their tradition) were invited to stay on. As an Indian journalist later remarked, 'this would be unbelievable were it not true', but Nehru and his colleagues sought to build 'a new India, a more egalitarian society . . . through the agency of those who had been the trained servants of imperialism—it is as if Lenin, on arrival in Russia, had promptly mustered the support of all the White Russians he could find.'[2]

In the years afterwards the ICS tradition not only survived, it prospered. In the spring of 1964 Nehru was asked at a private meeting with some friends what he considered to be his greatest failure as India's first Prime Minister. He reportedly replied 'I could not change the administration, it is still a colonial administration.'[3] Nehru then went on to elaborate his belief that the continuation of that colonial administration 'was one of the main causes of India's inability to solve the problem of poverty'. More recently his daughter, Mrs Indira Gandhi, 'had occasion to regret that her father had not seized the opportunity to overhaul our administration'.[4] Yet, although the Nehrus and many others have been critical, some have paid 'a high tribute to the [administrative] services established by the former British Government in India', claiming that 'those familiar with the difficulties encountered elsewhere in the world, particularly Africa, have been loud in their praises of the good fortune of India and Pakistan in taking over their respective shares of those services', and their 'good

[1] Nehru, J., *An Autobiography*, London, 1936, p. 445.

[2] Seminarist, 'Self before Service', *Seminar* 84 (1966), 13.

[3] Vittachi, T., 'Bureaucrats who won't lie down', *Guardian* (London), 10 Apr. 1978, 17.

[4] Singh, P., 'A Matter of Ambiguity', *Indian Book Chronicle*, 16 Mar. 1981, 106, as cited in LaPorte, R., *Public Administration Review*, 41. 5 (1981), 588.

judgement' in continuing them 'almost unchanged'.[5] As for Africa, however, one of the foremost experts on post-colonial administration in that part of the world has pointed out that 'perhaps the most difficult problem is the re-orientation of the administrative machine from its colonial outlook'.[6]

Although many have drawn attention to the general phenomenon, and then passed judgement on it, there has been no systematic attempt to try to explain how and why the colonial administrative traditions persisted without major change after the departure of the colonialists. This study aims to provide such an explanation for the Indian case. It tries to answer the following broad questions: what were the main features of the ICS tradition? To what extent have they persisted into the 1980s? How and why did they persist (if they did)? More especially, how and why did colonial administrators manage to survive the end of British rule in 1947? What have been the consequences for Indian politics and administration?

To describe the content of a tradition and explain its persistence presents certain conceptual problems. The first relates to how one conceptualizes the content of a tradition. Standard works on the nature of traditions rightly stress their immense complexity.[7] The literature on the British in India and the ICS mirrors this, referring unsystematically to a vast array of behaviour patterns, norms, and values. The conceptual framework used here to make the job of description manageable is inspired by the one used successfully by Armstrong in his analysis of another administrative tradition.[8] Following this lead, I identify the content of an administrative tradition as comprising (1) persons in an array of administrative positions (or 'posts') located within the structure of the state apparatus as a whole, (2) behaviour patterns, or methods of work, appropriate to the positions, (3) norms and values which can serve to legitimate the behaviour patterns and the positions. The identification of main features of the ICS tradition in Chapter 1 and again in Chapter 6 is in accordance with this formulation.

The essential point about any tradition, however, is that it has two aspects: one is content, the other is a process of reproduction. If the

[5] Coen, T., *The Indian Political Service*, London, 1971, p. 3.

[6] Kirk-Greene, A., 'New Africa's Administrators', *Journal of Modern African Studies*, 10. 1 (1972), 103.

[7] Shils, E., *Tradition*, London, 1981. Williams, R., *Culture*, London, 1981.

[8] Armstrong, J., *The European Administrative Elite*, Princeton, 1973.

content of an administrative tradition is not actively and continuously reproduced through time, then it will quickly break down. One of the lacunae in the relevant literature (to which we come shortly) is that there is no satisfactory explanation of how and why administrative traditions persist—no explanation of how this general process of reproduction works. The primary focus of this book is precisely on this aspect. I shall argue in this connection that such an explanation can be found by examining the detailed working of three necessary processes.

The first is *political support* for the structures, behaviour patterns, and norms and values of the tradition. The process of 'political support for an administrative tradition' is complex, and more will be said about it in due course. But two aspects need to be distinguished at the outset. One is the *agency* of power exercised by administrators within the state working actively to retain their tradition in the face of opposition. The other is the broad *structure* of state and class power in which the bureaucracy is located. The second process is *obtaining similar successors* on a continuing basis. This involves the steady replacement of retiring administrators by younger recruits similar in educational and class background and at least familiar with the principal norms and values of the tradition. This may appear at first glance a relatively straightforward matter but, as this study will attempt to show, replenishing the members of an administrative tradition on a steady basis can be surprisingly difficult for those engaged in the operation. The third process is *shaping successors* to the tradition. Shaping refers to deliberate attempts by experienced administrators to mould new recruits to the behaviour patterns of the tradition (and the norms and values implicit in such patterns). The most significant period when this occurs is during the first few years of service in a particular administrative group—during initial training and particularly (as I shall argue later) during the young recruit's first posting working with other administrators who 'carry the tradition'.

These three processes amount to both necessary and sufficient conditions for the reproduction of an administrative tradition. As long as there is political support for the administrative structure from the state leadership, as long as similar successors can be obtained on a continuing basis, and as long as these successors are shaped to the central norms and values of the tradition, then that is enough to reproduce an administrative tradition. There is nothing automatic about these processes. Some are tougher to maintain than others at different times. But all three are necessary.

The reproduction of the ICS tradition is examined in Chapters 2 to 5 of this book in accordance with the explanatory framework just outlined. It is not possible, within the confines of a study of this length, to give a detailed history of the whole process of reproduction from 1919 to 1983 paying attention continually to all three in the broadest sense. I have instead concentrated on particular aspects at different times. Nevertheless, the four chapters do indicate the overall nature of the process throughout the period.

Chapter 2 shows how all three conditions were met during the 1920s and 1930s. Evidence is advanced suggesting that obtaining suitable successors for the ICS during these two decades presented great difficulty for the imperial power and required its political support in the face of considerable opposition. The chapter also shows the working of the shaping process, paying particular attention to how Indian recruits acquired certain ICS norms and values. Chapter 3 concentrates mainly on how and why the ICS managed to survive the end of colonial rule in 1947. It also describes how the position of the new IAS successors was secured in the constitution. The analysis is bound up centrally with structure and agency aspects of political support. Chapter 4 deals with political support in the period 1950–83. It argues that the ICS/IAS as an institution did not fit easily into the new constitution, setting up tensions within the state that led to increasing criticism of the ICS tradition. The chapter examines how and why the tradition managed to survive during this period, concentrating on political support in relation primarily to attempts that were made from time to time to bring about administrative reform. Political support for the continued existence of the ICS/IAS as an institution was not enough. It was also necessary to ensure that IAS successors were steadily shaped to the norms and values of the tradition. Chapter 5 examines the shaping process during the period 1950–83, showing how certain gentlemanly and service class norms and values were passed on to new generations.

There is a potential difficulty with the argument being made here that structures, procedures, norms, and values in an administrative tradition remain 'similar' through time. At what point do structures, procedures, and norms stop being similar and start being different? Or, what is the break point between continuity and change? Clearly, structures, procedures, and norms are changing to some extent all the time. What one needs to determine is whether or not their 'central features' remain similar over a period of time. Unfortunately, identifying central features can be a hazardous business. The danger is to accept a common usage like 'traits that endure' and thereby become involved in the circular argument of identifying continuity as features that have continued. The danger recedes if one carefully identifies central features at one point in time, according to the sources appropriate to that time, and then repeats the exercise at another point in time, according to the (different) sources appropriate to that time. This is the approach I have adopted in Chapter 1 and then again in Chapter 6. (The sources used in this study are discussed at the end of the introduction.)

One other broad issue of method: how long must an administrative tradition remain similar before it becomes continuous? I suggest that sufficient time must elapse for at least two generations of persons to pass through a state structure. I adopt the perhaps generous standard of 30 years as the time interval between generations based on the consideration that the age difference between, say, an ICS father and his IAS son or daughter would be about 30 years on average. It, therefore, takes about 65 years for two generations of persons to enter, pass through, and retire, assuming notionally a career of entry between the ages of 21 and 24 and retirement between the ages of 50 and 55. Why two generations rather than one? This is based on the observation that one main aspect of the process of reproduction is an older generation selecting and shaping in its likeness a younger one. One generation being shaped by another may not be particularly noteworthy, but that generation in turn shaping a third, while structures, procedures, and norms remain similar, appears to me a sufficiently rigorous test of the continuity of a tradition. For this reason, a span of 65 years from 1919 to 1983 is used in this study.

That no such analysis has been attempted before is evident from a consideration of the general direction of other relevant studies. To do justice to the various literatures involved would require a very lengthy bibliographic essay, and that is not attempted here. It must suffice to locate this study in two literatures. One is the detailed work on India's top administrators past and present as part of comparative administration literature. The other is, much more broadly, all the work on the government and politics of India as part of the vast, rapidly growing, and theoretically stimulating literature of the nature of the state.

India's top administrators—ICS and IAS—have received a lot of detailed attention from historians and students of public administration, far too much in the eyes of Guha and others.[9] Certainly the ICS/IAS have been only a minuscule contingent in India's huge public bureaucracy, and, in many ways, other civil servants are as, or more, important—from professional experts like doctors and engineers to those indispensable people who sit behind counters in post offices and railway stations.[10] But the ICS tradition has major consequences for all other civil servants. That continues to be the main justification for studies such as this, even though studies of other civil servants at different levels are also needed and have begun to appear in increasing numbers lately—a welcome development.

Modern historians have given detailed and exclusive attention to the ICS in the later stages of British rule: Spangenburg for the late nineteenth century, Alexander for the early twentieth century, and Beaglehole and especially Ewing for the last two decades of the raj.[11] A number of other historical works on British administration in India, Misra for instance, give prominence to the ICS, and, in addition, there is the rich and still rapidly growing literature on the raj in the twentieth century, to which the so-called 'Cambridge school' has made such a notable contribution.[12] However all these valuable historical studies

[9] Guha, R. *et al.*, *Subaltern Studies: Writings on South Asian History and Society*, i, ii, iii, Delhi, 1982–4.

[10] It should perhaps be noticed that I use the term 'administrator' instead of others in common usage—'civil servant', 'public servant', 'bureaucrat'—when referring to the ICS and IAS. These terms have different meanings in scholarly works, although making such close distinctions here is not necessary. I prefer the term administrator for the ICS/IAS and others in the 'higher reaches', because they are especially involved with 'administration in its large sense', following Dubhashi (IAS, Karnataka), that is, 'the total effort to translate aspirations and ambitions, ideologies and ideals into policies, plans, programmes and projects and building up organizations and institutions to take charge of these plans and programmes, manning them with the personnel both competent and motivated and continuously leading, directing and coordinating their efforts so as to realise the objectives in view . . . .'. Dubhashi, P. R., *The Process of Public Administration*, Pune, 1980, p. 2.

[11] Spangenburg, B., *British Bureaucracy in India: Status, Policy and the ICS in the Late 19th century*, New Delhi, 1976. Alexander, H. M. L., 'Discarding the "Steel Frame": Changing Images among Indian Civil Servants in the Early Twentieth Century', *South Asia*, New Series, v (1982), 1–12 (based on his unpublished Ph.D. dissertation, University of Sydney, 1977: 'The Ruling Servants: The Indian Civil Service, 1878–1923'). Beaglehole, T., 'From Rulers to Servants: The Indian Civil Service and the British Demission of Power in India', *Modern Asian Studies* (hereafter *MAS*), 11. 2 (1977), 237–55. Ewing, A., 'The Indian Civil Service, 1919–1942', unpublished Ph.D. dissertation, Cambridge University, 1980.

[12] Misra, B. B., *The Bureaucracy in India: An Historical Analysis up to 1947*, London, 1971. Examples of the 'Cambridge School' are in Gallagher, J., Johnson, G., and Seal, A. (eds.), *Locality, Province and Nation: Essays on Indian Politics 1870–1940*, Cambridge,

end when the British go home. Low argued some time ago that 'there can be no doubt that the imperial era has left its legacies to the post-imperial period' and that it should be 'part of the historian's responsibility to discern what these are, how they came to be fashioned, and how they were carried over into the post-imperial era',[13] but no historian so far has taken up his challenge to discern what the administrative legacy was, and how it was carried over.

Most social scientists interested in Indian administrators have been similarly mesmerized by the date 1947, though from the other side of the divide. Nearly everyone makes some reference to the 'historical background' (and the 'colonial legacy'), but usually only as a preliminary to the main concerns, which start after independence. Taub's important study of the IAS in Bhubaneswar, Orissa, in the 1960s provides an illustration.[14] The main body of the work is focused on the structure of the IAS, who the officers are and why they joined, and various sources of strain identified by them in interviews, including those produced by the British legacy. There is a short preliminary chapter on ICS history, based mainly on older histories by former ICS men—Blunt, O'Malley, and Mason.[15] (Taub is aware that these subjective works portray a 'somewhat romanticized picture'; Blunt's book was actually written as propaganda to assist ICS recruitment in Britain in the 1930s, Mason's classic was intended as a tribute to his Service.) No connection is made between the early background chapter and the ICS legacies of centralized decision-making and generalized rigidity discussed later. This is not meant as

1973; Baker, C., Johnson, G. and Seal, A. (eds.), *Power, Profit and Politics: Essays on Imperialism, Nationalism and Change in Twentieth-Century India*, Cambridge, 1981. For a general guide to various 'schools' and literatures, Moore, R. J., 'Recent Historical Writing on the Modern British Empire and Commonwealth: Later Imperial India', *Journal of Imperial and Commonwealth History*, 4. 1 (1975), 55–76.

[13] Low, D. A., *Lion Rampant*, London, 1973, p. 217. There has recently been some suggestive general work along these lines, e.g. Morris-Jones, W. H. and Fischer, G. (eds.), *Decolonisation and After: The British and French Experience*, London, 1980, especially the essay by Miege, J.-L.; Moore, R. J. (ed.), *Tradition and Politics in South Asia*, Delhi, 1979, especially the essay by Cantlie; Anderson, B. R. O'G., 'Old State, New Society: Indonesia's New Order in Comparative Historical Perspective', *Journal of Asian Studies*, xlii. 3 (1983), 477–96; Mommsen, W. and Osterhammel, J. (eds.), *Imperialism and After*, London, 1986.

[14] Taub, R., *Bureaucrats under Stress: Administrators and Administration in an Indian State*, Berkeley, 1969.

[15] Blunt, E., *The ICS*, London, 1937. O'Malley, L., *The Indian Civil Service 1601–1930*, London, 1931, Mason, P. (pseud. Philip Woodruff), *The Men who Ruled India: The Founders*, London, 1953 and *The Men who Ruled India: The Guardians*, London, 1954.

criticism, because Taub's interests lay in the problems of the present, not in explaining where those problems came from. Other studies of the IAS adopt a similar perspective.[16] So do most of the major studies of other civil servants at different levels, such as Roy on agricultural development administration in Mehsana District (Gujarat), Varma on the Madhya Pradesh secretariat, Anter Singh on irrigation administration in Ganganager and Kotah districts, Chaturvedi on agricultural development administration in four Rajasthan districts, Mathur on Block Development Officers in Uttar Pradesh and Rajasthan, Muthayya and Gnanakannan on community development personnel in Kerala, Karnataka, and Tamil Nadu.[17]

Some studies of Indian administration have more to say about the legacies of the colonial past in relation to analysis of the administrative present, for example, Heginbotham on development administration in North Arcot District, Mook on the behaviour of subordinate administrators in agriculture and education departments in four Tamil Nadu districts, Kothari and Roy on conflicts between administrators and politicians in Meerut District, Tyagi on the civil service in Punjab State, Maheshwari and later Ray on the all-India services, Khanna on bureaucratic performance in the Indian Railways, and Sogani on the role of the Chief Secretary (with special reference to Rajasthan).[18] In all these studies, however, the ways in which the colonial legacy are handled offer no satisfactory explanation of why it is still prevalent in the present. Some give a descriptive history which fails to explain persistence (e.g. Tyagi); others explain the origins of certain aspects of

[16] e.g. Prasad, B., *The Indian Administrative Service*, Delhi, 1968; Bansal, P. L., *Administrative Development in India*, New Delhi, 1974.

[17] Roy, R., *Bureaucracy and Development: the Case of Indian Agriculture*, New Delhi, 1975; Varma, R. S., *Bureaucracy in India*, Bhopal, 1973; Anter Singh, *Development Administration*, Delhi, 1981; Chaturvedi, H. R., *Bureaucracy and the Local Community: Dynamics of Rural Development*, Bombay, Centre for the Study of Developing Societies, Monograph No. 2, 1977; Mathur, Kuldeep, *Bureaucratic Response to Development: A Study of Block Development Officers in Rajasthan and Uttar Pradesh*, Delhi, 1972; Muthayya, B. C. and Gnanakannan, I., *Development Personnel: A Psycho-Social Study across Three States in India*, Hyderabad, 1973.

[18] Heginbotham, S. J., *Cultures in Conflict: The Four Faces of Indian Bureaucracy*, New York, 1975; Mook, B., *The World of the Indian Field Administrator*, New Delhi, 1982; Kothari, S. and Roy, R., *Relations between Politicians and Administrators at the District Level*, New Delhi, 1969; Tyagi, A., *The Civil Service in a Developing Society*, Delhi, 1969; Maheshwari, S., 'The All-India Services', *Public Administration* (London), 49 (1971), 291–308; Ray, S., *Indian Bureaucracy at the Crossroads*, New Delhi, 1979; Khanna, K., *Behavioural Approach to Bureaucratic Development*, New Delhi, 1983; Sogani, M., *The Chief Secretary in India: A Study of his Role in State Administration in Rajasthan*, New Delhi, 1984.

the colonial legacy without explaining their continuation into the present (e.g. Heginbotham); others do make reference to reasons why the ICS survived in the 1940s but mainly in terms of Sardar Patel's important support at the time, e.g. Maheshwari. In none is there any conception of a continuing process, without which any attempt at explaining persistence (i.e. continuing legacy) remains incomplete.

There are two notable exceptions amongst scholars who work in the field of India's public administration. One is Braibanti, who has written extensively on the ICS tradition in both India and Pakistan. He certainly has never had any difficulty in travelling back and forth across 1947 in the course of his work. His general line on the ICS tradition is important, and may be said to comprise two aspects: firstly, that it was broadly speaking 'inevitable' in the traumatic circumstances of the 1940s that the structure and traditions of the ICS were retained;[19] secondly, that between 1947 and the 1960s the ICS tradition was gradually changed, indeed eventually transformed, by the coming of a new IAS ethos.[20] In this book I take issue with both these propositions, arguing that there was no inevitability about the reproduction of the ICS tradition—it had to be worked at constantly, even in the 1940s, and that essential features of the ICS tradition persisted without fundamental (or transforming) change into the 1980s.

The other notable exception is Subramaniam,[21] whose general theory of administrative systems in commonwealth countries both dismisses the moment of independence as a break point and speaks directly to the main issues raised in this book. His explanation for the persistence of India's distinctive type of administrative system relies centrally on the analysis of the continuing power of what he calls 'the derivative middle class'—a class formed initially in the special circumstances of colonial rule, which took over the state at the time of independence, and continued both to dominate the state and produce the people who filled higher posts in the administration. His explanation is not grounded in Marxism, although, as he says in his Preface, Marxism 'may be felt by the second remove'. I find Subramaniam's theory stimulating and accept his main contention that

[19] Braibanti, R., 'The Civil Service of Pakistan: A Theoretical Analysis', *South Atlantic Review*, 58 (1959), 258–304.

[20] Braibanti, R., 'Reflections on Bureaucratic Reform in India', in Braibanti, R. and Spengler, J. (eds.), *Administration and Economic Development in India*, Durham, NC, 1963, pp. 3–68. See also Braibanti, R. and Associates, *Asian Bureaucratic Systems emergent from the British Imperial Tradition*, Durham, NC, 1966.

[21] Subramaniam, V., *Transplanted Indo-British Administration*, New Delhi, 1977.

continuing class support (as a recruitment base) is necessary for the persistence of an administrative tradition, although I differ somewhat on how one conceptualizes that class and its dominant norms and values (in Chapter 1). On the broad issue of class support, however, this study fills out in a more detailed way for the Indian case Subramaniam's broader comparative formulation. I depart from Subramaniam by arguing that the class factor by itself does not explain administrative persistence. Knowing the class background of administrators does not mean that everything else necessarily follows. While not denying the importance of class, this study attempts to provide a more elaborate, empirically based explanation of the phenomena to which Subramaniam's important theory refers.

Such work by social scientists on the IAS forms part of a large and expanding literature on the role of top administrators in the public policy making of different societies. There has been increasing interest in the interaction between politicians and top administrators, their degree of influence in policy making, and their conflict or convergence in the process in, for instance, Crozier, Suleiman, Dogan, Aberbach, *et al.*[22] This research has had varied results, but on one finding they are all agreed: that administrators engage heavily in politics. As Muramatsu and Krauss said at the beginning of their 1984 article on bureaucrats and politicians in policy making in Japan, 'in the last few years, political scientists have discovered the bureaucracy and bureaucrats as political actors'.[23] To identify India's top administrators as political, as this study does also, should occasion less surprise now than it might have done some years ago.

In contributing to that growth point in the comparative administration literature, however, this study does depart from the dominant methodology employed in such studies. Such investigations normally use systematic sampling and survey techniques to learn about the social backgrounds of politicians and administrators, their perceptions of and attitudes towards each other, and their self-perceptions of their role in policy making and politics. Valuable as such studies can be, they are essentially ahistorical. They cannot explore effectively questions of

[22] Crozier, M., *The Bureaucratic Phenomenon*, Chicago, 1964; Suleiman, E., *Politics, Power and Bureaucracy in France: The Administrative Elite*, Princeton, 1974; Dogan, M. (ed.), *The New Mandarins of Western Europe: The Political Role of Top Civil Servants*, New York, 1976; Aberbach, J., Putnam, R., and Rockman, B., *Bureaucrats and Politicians in Western Democracies*, Cambridge, Mass., 1981.

[23] Muramatsu, M. and Krauss, E., 'Bureaucrats and Politicians in Policy Making: The Case of Japan', *American Political Science Review*, 78. 1 (1984), 126.

where such attitudes and perceptions come from, and how and why such political administrators have come to hold them. That is one of the main things this study attempts to do.

Another reason why an analysis of the reproduction of the ICS tradition has not been attempted before is that the subject falls between the dominant concerns of the principal theories of the state, both pluralist and Marxist. These theories have tended to direct the attention of scholars interested in the Indian state to areas of research other than the one explored here. Most studies of India's government and politics in the 1960s and 1970s, informed broadly by pluralist theory, tended either to concentrate on the political inputs of the plurality of groups, voters, and political parties as the motor of the political system, while seeing the outputs of the state bureaucracy as largely derivative, or to treat the state bureaucracy rather separately in fairly conventional public administration terms, while seeing political forces as vague environmental factors. Much useful research was done on party building, interest groups, and related matters (e.g. Weiner, Brass, the Rudolphs, Kothari, Kochanek) and on India's public administration (as reported in the issues of the *IJPA* and elsewhere), with Morris-Jones and Hanson being perhaps the two scholars who did most to connect politics and administration.[24] No such bifurcation of politics and state bureaucracy was evident in Marxist research on the nature of the state in South Asia (e.g. Alavi, Bettelheim, Sen, Moore, and numerous studies in the journal *Social Scientist*).[25] Their work was also fundamentally historical in conception. At the same time the principal Marxist preoccupation was to try to discern the dominant mode of production and the class character of the state.[26] The state

[24] Weiner, M., *Party Building in a New Nation: The Indian National Congress*, Chicago, 1967; Brass, P., *Factional Politics in an Indian State*, Berkeley, 1965; Rudolph, L. and Rudolph, S., *The Modernity of Tradition: Political Development in India*, Chicago, 1967; Kothari, R., *Politics in India*, Boston, 1970; Kochanek, S., *The Congress Party of India*, Princeton, 1968 and *Business and Politics in India*, Berkeley, 1974; Morris-Jones, W. H., *The Government and Politics of India*, 3rd edn., London, 1971; Hanson, A. H., *The Process of Planning: A Study of India's Five Year Plans, 1950–1964*, London, 1966.

[25] Alavi, H., 'The State in Post-Colonial Societies', *New Left Review*, 74 (1972), 59–81; Bettelheim, C., *India Independent*, New York, 1968; Sen, A., *The State, Industrialization and Class Formation in India: A Neo-Marxist Perspective on Colonialism, Underdevelopment and Development*, London, 1982; Moore, B., *Social Origins of Dictatorship and Democracy*, Boston, 1966, is a renegade work of great distinction, but I include it here because it is closer to Marxism than to other theoretical discourses; *Social Scientist*: monthly Journal of the Indian School of Social Sciences, Trivandrum, which has appeared regularly since 1972.

[26] An extended review of this literature is in Thorner, A., 'Semi-Feudalism or

was not seen as merely an instrument of class rule, but it did tend to be viewed as a single entity (with little in the way of internal contradictions or conflicts) and as essentially determined by the logic of its location within the class structure. Although valuable, Marxist work was long on theory, shorter on detailed empirical research relevant to it.

Recently the positions of both pluralists and Marxists have moved somewhat, partly in consequence of the important debates between them. Neo-pluralist theories have shifted attention more towards what is happening within the state, as external political forces are seen increasingly as less decisive in explaining the performance of the state. Nordlinger, for example, has theorized the democratic state as almost wholly independent of politically powerful groups in civil society.[27] Marxist theories have also been shifting their ground as regards the dependence of the state on class and the economic base. The state is now seen as more autonomous *vis-à-vis* these forces. Skocpol's conceptualization of the relative autonomy of the state is perhaps one of the most forceful early statements of this position.[28] These theoretical developments have helped to move social science research on the state in some new directions. Indeed, increased interest in relations between politicians and top administrators within the state, noticed earlier, is one manifestation of such a shift in pluralist theory. Marxists, also, are less inclined now to treat the state as a monolith driven entirely by class forces. Alavi, for instance, has drawn attention to conflicts and contradictions within states of 'peripheral capitalism' and Kraus and Vanneman make a sharp conceptual distinction between the power of the state and the power of the bureaucrats who staff it.[29]

This study contributes to existing pluralist studies of politicians and top administrators and their relative power within the state by examining these relations through time. More centrally, it contributes to an area of thought that Marxist theories surprisingly have neglected:

Capitalism: Contemporary Debate on Classes and Modes of Production in India', *EPW* xvii. 49 (1982), 1961–8; 50 (1982), 1993–9; 51 (1982), 2061–6.

27 Nordlinger, E., *On the Autonomy of the Democratic State*, Cambridge, Mass., 1981.

28 Skocpol, T., *States and Social Revolutions: A Comparative Analysis of France, Russia and China*, Cambridge, 1979.

29 Alavi, H., 'State and Class under Peripheral Capitalism', in Alavi, H. and Shanin, T. (eds.), *Introduction to the Sociology of the 'Developing' Societies*, London, 1982; Alavi, H., 'Class and State', in Gardezi, H. and Rashid, J. (eds.), *Pakistan: The Roots of Dictatorship*, London, 1983; Kraus, R. and Vanneman, R., 'Bureaucrats versus the State in Capitalist and Socialist Regimes', *Comparative Studies in Society and History*, 27 (1985), 111–22.

the reproduction of state forms through time. Therborn's work on state apparatuses in feudal, capitalist, and socialist societies is one of the very few that gives the process of reproduction primary importance.[30] His analysis, however, aims to explain how whole social formations are reproduced through time and what role the state plays in that general process; he has nothing to say about how the state itself, or a particular administrative tradition within it, is reproduced within that broader context.

Any successful explanation of the ICS tradition requires consideration of empirical evidence at local, regional, all-India, and even international levels over a 65-year period. Many historians and social scientists might object that broad all-India studies of this nature should not be attempted because India is such a large and complex society with so many important regional differences that there are few, if any, generalizations that hold. But the ICS (IAS) was an all-India service, linking the administration from the localities to the centre. To carve out a segment only for analysis—one region or district, for example—would have led to serious distortions. To minimize the problems of such a broad sweep of time and place I have focused specifically on the ICS and IAS, whilst arguing also that these two small services and their tradition held the key that locked the rest of India's large bureaucracy in place at different levels.

Even narrowing the analysis of the ICS tradition of administration quite drastically in this way still leaves immense problems of scope. As noted earlier, to describe the ICS tradition requires identifying positions, behaviour patterns, norms, and values. Behaviour patterns? Take an ICS district collector: he was responsible for all government action in that area, and thus had literally thousands of detailed enumerated powers. It is impossible to list them all here and describe what an ICS man did in relation to each one. Furthermore, details differed from province to province, from district to district, and changed over time. Individual ICS men also differed in what they did in relation to each aspect of the job. Even to give a detailed, minute by minute description of a day in the life of one ICS Collector would be a gigantic task, and very misleading. The problems are multiplied because the ICS and IAS not only occupied the post of District Collector but also held a wide variety of other posts elsewhere.

Most descriptions of administrative behaviour in India seek to

[30] Therborn, G., *What does the Ruling Class do when it Rules? State Apparatuses and State Power under Feudalism, Capitalism and Socialism*, London, 1978.

overcome these problems by paying attention chiefly to prescribed duties and functions attached to the main types of posts. Such descriptions can provide an overall idea of what administrators were supposed to do, but inevitably they leave out a great deal. Orr (ICS, Bihar and Orissa)[31] noticed this difference between what was prescribed and what he did when he worked in Bihar districts in the early 1940s: District and Subdivisional officers were 'inundated with detailed bureaucratic instructions on what had to be done in every department of administration . . . [but] they were never told how to carry out their duties as distinct from what their duties were'.[32] I think Orr is wrong to use the word 'never' here, but the general distinction he makes is valid and important. There is a further distinction. One way an ICS Collector carried out his manifold duties was to go on tours of inspection in the district. He also dealt with paper work, attended meetings, received visitors, presided at courts, and so on. What did an ICS man do? He did those things. But one can also ask: how did an ICS man do what he did? When he went on tour, for example, how did he inspect the jail or local revenue office, and what did he say to whom? There are few such descriptions in the existing literature on India's public administration. To get them requires a careful examination of tour diaries, letters to relations, and reliable memoirs. And even then, such descriptions can only be illustrations of broader trends in behaviour.

In this study there is frequent reference to this level of detail. In consequence, the stretch between the empirical evidence and the general argument is sometimes very long. But I have decided to include the detail, even though one rarely finds it in works of this scope, because it is only through such detailed descriptions and even anecdotes (even if one can cite only a few from the many that exist) that one can really get inside an administrative tradition. Analyses that rely only on more schematic formulations may be more tidy in appearance, but they can also be virtually unrecognizable to the administrators whose behaviour they purport to explain.

The detailed descriptions and anecdotes reported here about the ICS come from autobiographical accounts. Most of them come from unpublished archival material. The study also relies on evidence

[31] All ICS and IAS Officers will be identified in the text in terms of the provincial or state cadre to which they were permanently allotted. This distinctive administrative arrangement is discussed later.

[32] Orr Papers, IOL MSS Eur. F.180/22, TS p. 70.

obtained from interviews (by the author) of ICS and IAS men and women, unpublished government records, civil lists, and the more usual primary and secondary sources. Each type of source has strengths and weaknesses, and a word must be said about some of these.

Autobiographical reminiscences by older men of their experiences when young have several well-known drawbacks. Powers of memory decline as one gets older. Also, as Wadsworth (ICS, Madras) concedes at the beginning of his memoir, 'memories become blurred by the images of later days which lie over them'.[33] There is also a tendency to exaggerate the importance of one's own career, to emphasize successes and play down or bury failures. In addition, certain types of people are far less likely to write reminiscences, the disreputable, for example. Some of these drawbacks also apply to other forms of autobiographical material, such as old letters and tour diaries. Although spontaneous and contemporary, these are also subject to problems of misplaced emphasis and bias. Anyone who has written regular letters to parents, for instance, knows that they necessarily portray an edited version of the full range of one's activities from day to day. Personal diaries can be more helpful, but need not be. Despite such drawbacks, autobiographical materials, if used with care, do provide a most useful supplement to other forms of evidence. After going through a large number of such accounts, I have made use mainly of those that are extensive and informative, in that they contain exact dates and considerable detail. Letters home, diaries, and reminiscences clearly based on them, have been preferred to accounts apparently based only on memory. The obvious whitewashes are not difficult to spot and have been avoided.

Another major source is interview material. The analysis in Chapter 5 relies heavily on my interviews in 1966–7 with 65 young IAS men and women in Bihar, Madras (later Tamil Nadu), Maharashtra, and Rajasthan. The nature of the sample and other details are indicated in the chapter's introduction. I have also interviewed at various times a number of other IAS and ICS people, in some cases at length, and have watched them at work and relaxed with them socially. These experiences, which gave me much insight into the ICS and IAS, have had an important effect on this study as a whole. Unfortunately such experiences cannot be documented openly, due to promises of

[33] Wadsworth Papers, Cambridge Archive, TS p. 4.

confidentiality made at the time—most IAS men and women I know were still in government service in 1983. The use of vague references to anonymous interviewees as evidence is never very convincing, yet this study does rely on such evidence. The least unsatisfactory solution is to follow a practice used by Brass;[34] a code number is placed on each set of interview notes made by me at the time, and where I cite a particular remark or observation by a respondent, the source is identified by code and the notes are available on request for inspection by bona fide scholars. I also identify the names of those 65 respondents (and others I interviewed for this study) in the bibliography while ensuring that particular names cannot be traced to particular code numbers.

Finally, a word about civil lists: India Office Lists during the raj and official IAS Civil Lists since 1956 are most important sources for this study, and I have spent much time happily foraging in them. Forage one must, for they are not organized as one would like. The data in some of the tables, for example, were acquired by my going carefully, entry by entry, through the appropriate civil lists. One encounters problems when trying to classify individual entries in civil lists. Also, such lists were known occasionally to contain errors. It is most unlikely, however, that the data on the ICS and IAS in the lists are seriously awry. ICS and IAS people would not have allowed it. In the 1980s it was still 'the Bible'. It was still said, according to Saxena (IAS, UP), that 'in the house of an IAS officer one would find only three books—the railway timetable, because he is always on the move, a crime thriller because that is the only book he reads, and of course the civil list'.[35]

[34] Brass, P., *Language, Religion and Politics in North India*, Cambridge, 1974.
[35] Saxena, N. C., 'The World of the IAS', *Administrator*, xxvi. 1 (1981), 16.

I

Content of the tradition: 1919–1947

ADMINISTRATIVE traditions have two ingredients. One is *content* which is made up of structure, behaviour patterns, and norms and values. The other is a *process* that reproduces that content through time. This chapter concentrates on the content of the ICS tradition between 1919 and the end of colonial rule in terms of the structural aspects of location and movement, a characteristic behaviour pattern involving political work, and six norms and values that figure prominently in the collective identity of the ICS as gentlemen of the service class.

STRUCTURE: LOCATION AND MOVEMENT

Tracing the early career of one recruit immediately highlights distinctive features of the ICS framework in British India. Take Solomon, educated at Clifton and King's College, Cambridge.[1] He entered the ICS in 1926 and after a year of training in England arrived in the autumn of 1927 in the Province of Bihar and Orissa.[2] After a spell of district training, Solomon was posted to Shahabad District in charge of a portion of it as an SDO (Subdivisional Officer). Within a year he was transferred to Giridh Subdivision in Hazaribagh District, where he worked for nearly three years. His memoir (based on his tour diary of that time) gives details of his routine work in court as a magistrate and touring in the countryside inspecting subordinate Indian personnel engaged in the collection of revenue for the raj. During the time he was in Giridh (1929–32), however, Gandhi and the Indian National Congress launched the civil disobedience campaign, as part of their struggle for independence from British rule. Since Giridh was a lively centre for the campaign, Solomon as the

[1] The source for the account that follows is Solomon Papers, IOL MSS Eur. F.180/24, later published, in slightly amended form, in Solomon, S., *Memories, with Thoughts on Gandhi*, London (Counter-Point), 1983.

[2] The Province of Bihar and Orissa as shown on Map 1, *c.* 1930, was divided into two separate provinces in 1937.

Government's man in charge there was kept busy coping with it. As he says: 'Government encouraged District and Subdivisional officers to rally all those who could be counted on to withstand the popular tide.' An *aman sabha* (loyal assembly) was formed in a number of places including Giridh, and 'I threw myself wholeheartedly into the campaign'. In a letter home to his brother in London, he described one such *aman sabha* mass meeting, held on 1 December 1930. There were 'about 2,000 to 3,000 persons assembled', the Collector of the district, A. D. Tuckey (ICS, Bihar and Orissa), presided, 'and the Congress was well-condemned'. A loyal *Brahman* 'spoke eloquently on the side of law and order and I was deeply moved'. 'I also spoke in English'. A number of such meetings were held. Also, with the assistance of 'able and enthusiastic Indian officers under me', a regular *aman sabha* bulletin was produced as 'a special feature of our anti-Congress propaganda at Giridh'. We 'were unsparing in our onslaughts on Congress and Mahatma alike'. In one issue, when Gandhi kept 'prevaricating for some time about his attendance at the Round Table Conference in London, we broke into verse—in the vernacular script, of course—

Ghandhi par chahiye ne ratkna thicana,
Belayat jana, ne jana, jana, ne jana!

(No use relying on Gandhi, going to England, not going, going, not going!)' *Aman sabha* bulletins were scattered extensively throughout the Subdivision and were read out to crowds of villagers by headmen or scribes.

Early in 1932 Solomon went home on leave to England for eight months. On his return he was posted as SDO Gumla in Ranchi District, being transferred after a couple of months to Darbhanga, then again to Bettiah. In March 1935 he was posted to the provincial secretariat in Patna (it shifted to Ranchi in the hot weather) as Publicity Officer under the Chief Secretary, R. E. Russell (ICS, Bihar and Orissa). Solomon summarized his duties there simply as 'to explain to the press and people, and to defend, the policies and actions of Government'. In this capacity he carried on a running correspondence with the Congress daily newspaper the Patna *Searchlight*, edited by 'the very able Murlidhar Prasad', and under pseudonyms wrote weekly columns in the *Sentinel*, 'whose Muslim editor, Syed Mohiuddin-Ahmed, was most friendly to Government', and also the Patna daily *The Indian Nation*, whose editor, C. V. Rao, was a 'non-Congressman from South

India, and therefore more receptive to the Government point of view'. Solomon remarks that 'my personal relations with all these editors, even with Murlidhar Prasad of the *Searchlight*, remained harmonious throughout, for we never questioned one another's sincerity, and they knew I was essentially liberal (and Liberal) . . . '. He also arranged, in connection with the 1935 Jubilee, 'magic lantern shows' depicting scenes in the lives of the Royal Family and royal visits to India. He estimated at the time that nearly a million people in the Province, mostly villagers, attended these shows during the two years he held this post.

In 1937 Solomon went home on leave again, during which time he married. When he and Mrs Solomon returned at the end of the year, he was given charge as Collector and District Magistrate of his first District—Singhbum. However, he was there only a few months before being transferred in March 1938 to the now separate Province of Orissa, as Collector of Balasore District. During the two years he was there (until April 1940), he was much concerned with opium. Balasore was 'one of the blackest spots in the world map of opium consumption'. A Congress Ministry was in office in Orissa (and in Bihar and elsewhere), as a result of elections held in 1937 in accordance with the Government of India Act 1935, and this ministry 'resolved, as one of their first reforms, to introduce opium prohibition', beginning as an experiment with Balasore District. 'It fell on me, therefore, not only to implement this policy, but also to put forward the detailed plan which was to be approved by Government and have legislative effect.' Solomon went on to hold additional posts in both Bihar and Orissa at provincial and district levels until he left India in 1947.

Solomon's account illustrates the main features of ICS location and movement within the structure of the raj. Their location gave them formal overall control of the state structures at different levels. They were in positions to frame new rules when initiatives or changes in policy took place, for example, Solomon's work on opium in Balasore. They also were in positions to ensure that the basic rules of the raj were maintained, for example, Solomon's involvement in the administration of the law, the supervision of revenue collection, and his political work with the *aman sabha* in Giridh (roundly condemning the Indian National Congress and trying to win the support of village people for his 'side') and in the Bihar Secretariat (actively engaged through the press and in other ways in publicly defending the actions of government against opposition). Solomon's account also shows that members of the ICS were located at all levels of the administrative structure. Solomon started typically in a district at subdivisional level, then moved to the provincial secretariat, then back to the district. Other ICS men also worked for short periods for central government. Solomon's memoirs also reveal that ICS men moved frequently from one post to another; he, in fact, moved ten times in ten years.

The location of ICS men in control posts at all levels provided a framework of rule that obtained throughout British India. Table 1 gives the overall position for 1919 and 1938.

The first thing to notice is the overall size of the ICS. It was not just small, it was minute in relation to the state structures in which it was located. Table 1 shows there were 1,032 ICS men in British India (excluding Burma) in 1919, and 1,029 in 1938. They comprised only about ·001 per cent of all the persons employed by the colonial state in India; the 1931 Census counted about one million such persons in a population of 353 millions.[3]

Secondly, the ICS was truly an all-India service. Table 1 shows them located at all levels—in the districts as Collectors or SDOs, in each provincial headquarters in the secretariat or in some other leading capacity, and at the centre. Fourteen per cent were 'judicial', working permanently as judges in districts or, in a few cases, as judicial commissioner or High Court justices. A few 'Political' ICS men had been permanently seconded to the Foreign and Political Department of the Government of India in 1919, later (in 1938) the Indian Political Service; most of them were serving in princely states, not in British India.

Thirdly, Table 1 shows that roughly 50 per cent of the ICS in British India worked in the districts. The district was the basic unit of field administration in each province. The chief government officer in each district was variously known, in different regions, as District Magistrate, District Collector, District Officer (with reference to his overall co-ordinating role), and sometimes (particularly in backward areas) Deputy Commissioner. Increasingly since independence the generic title of Collector has been used. Henceforth in this study the person holding this office of head of the district will be identified as the Collector. As head of the magistracy, the police, land revenue, and general administration he had broad powers indeed. Most Collectors

[3] GOI Department of Commercial Intelligence and Statistics, *Statistical Abstract for British India from 1926–27 to 1935–36*, 1938.

Table 1. *ICS Location, 1919 and 1938*

Provincial cadre of ICS	District level		Judicial		Provincial level		Government of India		Totals	
	1919	1938	1919	1938	1919	1938	1919	1938	1919	1938
Assam	34	19	2	1	12	13	1	4	49	37
Bengal	70	81	29	34	45	42	16	20	160	177
Bihar (and Orissa)	50	59	13	15	28	27	14	10	105	111
Bombay (and Sind)	59	70	23	21	59	27	13	12	154	130
Central Provinces & Berar	36	36	7	10	19	17	18	12	80	75
Madras	80	78	23	19	37	45	10	17	150	159
Punjab	51	85	16	20	37	24	20	16	124	145
United Provinces	117	117	28	20	37	33	28	25	210	195
Totals: 1919	497 (48%)		141 (15%)		274 (27%)		120 (11%)		1032 (101%)	
Totals: 1938		545 (53%)		140 (14%)		228 (22%)		116 (11%)		1029 (100%)
+ 1919/1938 recruits									101	49
+ Political									62	43
+ Burma									123	116
Total ICS									1318	1237

Sources: Data compiled on the basis of classifying each entry in the relevant civil lists: *India Office List, 1921*, London, 1921, pp. 453–796; *India Office and Burma Office List, 1939*, London, 1939, pp. 249–654

Notes:

The recruits of 1919 and 1938 are not included in the main table because these young men had not yet arrived in India. ICS men serving in Burma are kept separate because Burma was no longer part of British India in 1938.

The North West Frontier Province did not have a separate ICS cadre in 1919 or 1938. ICS men there were in the Political Service.

The 1921 List is more reliable than the 1920 List and was used to obtain the figures for 1919. The 1939 Civil List gives the position as of early autumn 1938.

in British India were ICS men. In Bihar in 1938, for example, 13 of the 16 districts had an ICS Collector, the remaining three being temporarily covered by senior men from the provincial civil service (but in two of these three districts—Patna and Ranchi—there was an ICS 'presence' because ICS Commissioners of Divisions were there); 19 of the 23 districts in Madras and 13 of the 20 districts in Bombay had ICS Collectors.[4] In 1919[5] ICS coverage of Collectorships was rather more extensive, although even then it was still far from complete.[6] In addition to ICS Collectors, there were more junior ICS men who also worked and trained in districts, as SDO or in some other capacity, as did Solomon. Each Collector held the post for a fixed term, then moved on to be replaced by another; this contrasted with the position of most other subordinate civil servants, who stayed in the district indefinitely.

Fourthly, it can be seen from Table 1 that about one quarter of the ICS worked at provincial level. The framework of provincial rule was such that a few ICS men in each province could be deployed to achieve overall control of government. The Bihar Secretariat in 1938, for example, worked alongside the Governor and the Congress Ministry (accountable to the Bihar Legislative Assembly) to advise them on policy, exercise financial control, frame rules and principles of administrative procedure, direct all the executive departments of government, and so on. The phrase 'advise on policy' hardly captures the complexities of the relationship between the secretariat and a Governor or minister and more will be said about these relationships subsequently. One fact, however, needs to be stressed right away: the secretariat was separated from all the government departments and agencies containing technical experts and others who implemented policy in Bihar, the main departments being judicial, public instruction, police, forest, public works, civil medical, public health, jail, excise, registration, agriculture, industries, co-operatives, income tax, civil veterinary, and the archaeological survey. There was also a large and separate Land Revenue and General Administration Department

[4] The 1938 data reported here and subsequently in this section have been compiled from *Thacker's Indian Directory including Burma and Ceylon, 1938–9* (Calcutta), and from *The India Office and Burma Office List, 1939* (London).

[5] The 1919 data reported subsequently in this section have been compiled from *Thacker's Indian Directory, 1919* (Calcutta), and from *The India Office List, 1920* (London).

[6] In 1919 about 10% of Collectors were not ICS, e.g. in Bombay Province two of the 27 districts had non-ICS Collectors, in Madras Province it was four out of 25, in Bihar and Orissa four out of 21.

under a Board of Revenue. The secretariat comprised an 'office' of superintendents, clerks, stenographers, typists, and a few officers appointed for a fixed term only. In Bihar in 1938 there were only twelve officers in the secretariat; one Chief Secretary, six Secretaries, three Deputy Secretaries, and two Under Secretaries. Authority to act for 'government' rested with these twelve officers, not with the office. Any matter of consequence that required the 'approval of government'—and most such matters did—had to be cleared with secretariat officers and ministers. A small and separate secretariat, interposed between the political leadership and government departments, was an arrangement peculiar to colonial rule. It enabled a few officers to achieve overall control. For example, only eighteen ICS men worked at provincial level in Bihar in 1938. Two were in Government House—The Governor and his Principal Secretary; nine ran the secretariat—the Chief Secretary, four (of the six) Secretaries, two (of the three) Deputy Secretaries, and the two Under Secretaries; three headed the Land Revenue and General Administration Department; the remaining four were heads of important government departments outside the secretariat—Commissioner of Excise, Registrar of Joint Stock Companies, Director of the Industries Department, and Registrar of the Co-operative Department. ICS men were similarly deployed in other provincial governments in 1938, except that the Governors of Bengal, Bombay, and Madras were politicians sent out from Britain, not ICS men. Nor was this picture of ICS dominance of provincial level administration confined to 1938. It was present throughout the period. In 1919, for example, the Bihar Secretariat had a Chief Secretary and three Secretaries, all ICS men; Bombay Province's secretariat had a Chief Secretary and four Secretaries, all ICS; in Madras Province, there was similar ICS dominance of the secretariat, with four key posts outside it held by ICS men—Director of Industries, Registrar of Co-operative Societies, President of the Board of Examiners, President of the Municipal Corporation of Madras City; and the Board of Revenue, centralized and far more important in Madras than in other provinces (which had Regional Commissioners), was an ICS preserve—all four members were ICS men, three of whom had Secretaries, all ICS.

The agents of provincial governments worked mostly in districts. Collectors, however, were special. Their lines of authority to provincial headquarters in each province ran up to the Chief Secretary in the secretariat (and to the Board of Revenue), not to government departments. Senior heads of government departments at provincial headquarters could not issue orders to a Collector. This meant that in each district the Collector presided over the district administration from without, so to speak. Only the Collector had a direct line to the top, that is to the secretariat. ICS men were therefore set apart to some extent from the rest of the government apparatus in control posts at both district and provincial levels.

The data in Table 1 show that 11 per cent of the ICS worked for the Government of India, each province sending a few men to the centre to help make up the total. ICS men at the centre were on deputation from their home province, and most of them (except for some very senior men) reverted back to their province after some years, to be replaced by others. Filling top administrative posts in central government in this way was called the 'tenure system'—a system unique to India. It required that key posts were reserved in central government for ICS men; and its main purposes, according to a definitive statement, were first, 'to prevent officials becoming stale in their posts', second, 'to ensure an infusion of fresh blood . . . at the centre', and third, 'to give all members of the ICS a fair share of what have always been regarded as prize appointments'.[7] The administrative framework at the centre was similar to the provinces. In 1919, for example, the Viceroy, Lord Chelmsford, was advised by his seven-member Supreme Council (three of whom were ICS). His Private Secretary was ICS. Policy questions which came up were referred to the central secretariat, set apart from the rest of central government. There were eleven Secretaries, ten of whom were ICS. Other ICS men worked as Deputy and Under Secretaries. Outside the secretariat were the main departments of the Government of India. There were thirty of them, of which five were headed by ICS men—President of the Board of Examiners, Comptroller and Auditor General, Director General of Posts and Telegraphs, Director General of Commercial Intelligence, Director of Criminal Intelligence. ICS men also held central government posts outside Delhi; for example, Noyce (ICS, Madras) was Controller of Cotton Cloth, Bombay. By 1938 the central government including the secretariat had grown and some departmental names had changed, reflecting the changing policy orientations of the

[7] NAI Home Dept. File 35/5/35—Ests., 1936, 'Views of the Home Department on the question of the procedures to be followed in filling posts under the Government of India, reserved for members of the ICS. Advantages and disadvantages of the tenure system'.

state, but otherwise the position was similar. Ten of the twelve Secretaries in Delhi, for example, were ICS.

Table 1 also shows that within the all-India pattern there were certain regional variations. In 1938, for example, Punjab and United Provinces (UP) had a more pronounced district location than Madras and Assam. Also, some provincial cadres had a far higher percentage of their men in Delhi than others. In 1919 Central Provinces and Berar (CP) had 23 per cent of its cadre there, whereas Madras had only 7 per cent and Assam only 2 per cent. In 1938 CP had 15 per cent in Delhi, while all the other provinces had 10–12 per cent. These figures, by the way, do not support the widespread belief that the Punjab and UP cadres of the ICS were by far the best jumping-off places for central government posts. The regional variations suggest that individual provinces were unable to adhere in a mechanical way to standard ratios as between different level postings, despite regulations laying down such ratios. Some of the reasons for that are considered shortly.

A final point about Table 1 arises from the fact that the data on ICS location for both 1919 and 1938 can be placed together in a single table. It suggests the basic similarity of ICS location right through this period of British rule, a static picture of ICS location in control posts at central, provincial, and district levels of the raj. In fact the picture masks a situation of surprising fluidity within the overall framework, in the sense that ICS men were constantly moving from one post to another. This aspect of structure has not been analysed previously, yet it was a main ingredient of the ICS tradition.

ICS memoirs are full of postings and transfers. Solomon's memoir, for example, shows that he moved ten times in ten years, including going home to England on leave in his fifth and tenth years of service. To say, however, that Solomon moved to another post once a year is misleading. His career shows that he held four posts (Giridh, Bettiah, Balasore, Bihar Secretariat) for a period of between two and three years each, and other posts for considerably less than a year, sometimes only for several months. By any standard this was extremely rapid movement. However, it was not some new or temporary phenomenon; the *Bengal Administration Report* (1871–2) complained that all but six of the Collectors of Bengal at the time had been in charge of their district for less than two years.[8] Nor was the phenomenon confined to Bihar and Bengal. Young Barlow (ICS, UP)

[8] Cited in Misra, B. B., 'The Evolution of the Office of Collector', *IJPA* xi. 3 (1965), 359.

arrived in India in November 1929 and was posted to Agra District; ten months later, as he was being transferred elsewhere, he wrote to his parents: 'I shall be quite sorry to leave . . . People change so quickly out here that I feel quite like an old inhabitant.'[9] Macleod, (ICS, Bombay) observed that the personnel of a 'station' were forever changing—'you are always travelling . . . packing and unpacking . . .'.[10] Data available on length of time in Collectors' posts in 1936 in eight of the provinces highlight frequency of movement. The data in Table 2 show that two-thirds of the Collectors at this time had held the post for less than a year.[11] When the Home Secretary in Delhi saw these data,

Table 2. *Length of time Collectors had been in Post in Certain Provinces, Summer 1936*

Province	No. of districts	Collector in post for less than 1 year	Collector in post for 1–2 years	Collector in post for more than 2 years
Assam	14	6	6	2
Bengal	27	18	8	1
Bihar	16	13	0	5
Bombay	19	13	5	1
Central Provinces	19	15	1	3
Madras	25	18	5	2
Punjab	29	11	5	13
United Provinces	48	29	9	10
Totals	197	129	39	35

Source: NAI Home Dept. File 278/36—Ests., 1936. The figures are compiled from this file.

Note: Orissa and Sind are excluded from the Table, since these provinces had only just been created and all their Collectors had been in post for less than a year. NWFP is also excluded.

[9] Barlow Papers, Cambridge Archive, letter dated 14.9.1930.

[10] Macleod, R. D., *Impressions of an Indian Civil Servant*, London, 1938, pp. 140–1.

[11] It is possible that the data exaggerate slightly the rapidity of movement in and out of Collectors' posts, because they were obtained by provincial governments for the Home Department in Delhi during the hot weather; this meant that some Collectors were officiating or 'acting' for others who were on leave. Also, some provinces may have been freer than usual in allowing men to go home on leave in 1936, in order to have a strong staff available the following year when elections were due to take place to implement the constitutional reforms under the Government of India Act, 1935. But it is most unlikely that the general picture portrayed here of frequent movement from post to post in the provinces is misleading for the period generally. Various sources confirm it.

he noted on the file: 'the number of officers who have been in a district over two years is regrettably small except in Punjab . . .'.[12]

Why did ICS men move so frequently? Quite apart from meeting the requirements of the tenure system, meant to replenish ICS posts with 'fresh blood', there were a number of other circumstances which quickened the speed with which the ICS hurtled from post to post. One reason was that British ICS men went home on leave every five years or so. Put differently, every year roughly one-fifth of the ICS Europeans left their posts for the reason of home leave alone. This was a problem peculiar to colonial rule in which key posts were held by men who went 'out' to rule the empire and went back 'home' from time to time ('staying on' in India after retirement was very unusual[13]). The knock-on effect of all these leave vacancies every year was considerable. If, say, the post falling vacant was that of Collector of a particularly large and important district, then a 'double transfer' would often be necessary—taking an ICS man from a smaller district and putting him in the large one, and then finding a new man to place in the smaller one. A whole chain of vacancies could develop behind a move like this. In April 1934, recalls Platt (ICS, Madras), 'a chain of postings, which started with a Government of India officer in South Africa going on leave, led to my temporary posting in the Niligiris as Sub-Collector, Coonoor, before I had completed the whole of my training'.[14] If a senior man in the district or secretariat was to be away for only a few months in the hot weather, and would be returning to that post, then a more junior ICS man frequently 'acted' for him, then 'reverted' to a more junior post, often in a different district. One ICS man acting for another was not the only way to supply the missing links in a chain of vacancies. Another way was to appoint senior non-ICS people from the provincial civil service to fill temporary vacancies.

It would be misleading to suggest that British ICS men were anxious to go home on leave as frequently as possible, or that they all did every five years. Most men clearly were attracted to India and found the work, the way of life, and the amenities appealing. Occasionally, they had to be ordered to go on leave. Lines (ICS, Bihar), for example, was enjoying himself immensely as Collector of Bhagalpur in April 1944,

[12] NAI Home Dept. File 278/36—Ests., 1936. M. Hallett (ICS, Bihar and Orissa), Note of 29.7.1936.

[13] The phrase comes from Paul Scott's delightful novel *Staying On*, London, 1977, about one British couple who did.

[14] Platt Papers, IOL MSS Eur. F.180/57, TS p. 9.

up to his ears in work related to dividing the district, when he was 'told to report to Bombay for home leave'. So, he says, 'I had to leave my beautiful Dutch style home, with its four bedrooms . . . six bathrooms, stables and two acres of garden and grounds, with a public and private staff on the premises numbering about a dozen . . . '.[15] Nor was he allowed to return to Bhagalpur after his leave, being posted on his return as Collector of Patna District. Lines, by the way, held fourteen principal appointments in ten years.

Transfers attendant on leave vacancies were a regular factor that could to some extent be anticipated. So was the formation of new provinces, like Sind and Orissa in 1937, creating new secretariat posts which then had to be filled—all of this having knock-on effects in other provinces. There were also wholly unpredictable reasons why transfers had to be made, sometimes in a hurry. A plot was unearthed in January 1942 to kill Orr (ICS, Bihar and Orissa), and he was rapidly transferred from his district to provincial headquarters.[16] Narasimhan (ICS, Madras) was in charge of Devakottai Subdivision in Ramnad District when severe disturbances took place in August 1942. He sent his wife and children away to Madras City and lived for some time in the police station under constant protection; there were 'a number of situations when we had to open fire and I saw with my own eyes people being shot and falling down dead'. Once the worst was over (in September) it seemed wise to transfer him to the Madras Secretariat (as he says, he was 'delighted to leave Devakottai').[17] Transfers were also arranged quickly to head off certain ICS men retiring prematurely. Westlake (ICS, Madras), for example, became very unhappy in Ramnad District in 1940 and a senior member of the Board of Revenue from Madras went out to Ramnad to try to cheer him up; but Westlake still considered giving up and retiring until he was 'suddenly posted' to Madras to act as Director of Agriculture for six months (while the permanent ICS incumbent was on special duty with the Government of India), a posting for Westlake which 'breathed new life' into him.[18]

Another unpredictable reason for removing individuals from certain posts was incompetence. Swann (ICS, Bihar and Orissa) had to be moved in (in the early 1940s) as Private Secretary to the Governor, Sir William Lewis (ICS, Bihar and Orissa), when his 'predecessor, an

[15] Lines Papers, IOL MSS Eur. F.180/19A, TS p. 13.
[16] Orr Papers, IOL MSS Eur. F.180/22, TS p. 13.
[17] Narasimhan Papers, IOL MSS Eur. F.180/56, TS p. 7.
[18] Westlake Papers, Cambridge Archive, TS p. 50.

agreeable man but given to lapses of memory, and his wife—a Canadian lady of shattering tactlessness—failed to please, and the climax was reached when he forgot to bring along the citations for a distribution of honours by the Governor'. The man was 'speedily despatched' to another post.[19] Bonarjee (ICS, UP) reported in a confidential handing over note as Divisional Commissioner in 1946, that his successor Hume (ICS, UP) 'has done much to bring order out of chaos in Benaras [District], which had been completely ruined by Lyde [ICS, UP] and his gang of rapscallions—headed by Bhup Narain Singh, Raza Mohammed etc; all these have been removed, thank God, for the place reeked to heaven of corruption.'[20] There are a number of other examples.

Political interference also caused unexpected transfers, always with knock-on effects for other ICS men. Complaints from politicians demanding the transfer of individual ICS men began to be noticed especially from 1937 onwards. For example, transfers into and out of Larkhana District in Sind had been frequent, according to Raza (ICS, Bombay and Sind) who was Collector there in 1943, and the district was widely perceived as 'one of the most difficult to run as almost half the Provincial Cabinet came from Larkhana'.[21]

Finally, transfers of individuals frequently had to be arranged due to illness, accident, and sudden death. The diaries often refer to such matters, for conditions in parts of the country were not particularly healthy and the work sometimes involved considerable danger. The secretariat file on Scott (ICS, Assam) contained the note 'offer young Scott the job of Under-Secretary [in the Finance Department at provincial headquarters], he might jump at it for family reasons'. Scott did not jump at it, but for family reasons (an ailing wife and a young baby) he took it and hated it.[22] Dharma Vira (ICS, UP) was quickly transferred in 1934, when his wife became ill, from Aligarh to Almora in the hills.[23] Accidents were fairly common. One of the most bizarre was when the Collector of East Godavari was badly injured one night in 1932; he was walking in his sleep and fell off his first-floor verandah. The young Georgeson (ICS, Madras) was rapidly brought in

[19] Swann Papers, IOL MSS Eur. F.180/25, TS p. 6.

[20] Hume Papers, Cambridge Archive. Bonarjee's handing over note (n.d.—probably 1946) is in Box VII.

[21] Raza Papers, IOL MSS Eur. F.180/29, TS p. 113.

[22] Scott Papers, Cambridge Archive, TS p. 54.

[23] Vira, Dharma, *Memoirs of a Civil Servant*, Delhi, 1975, p. 15.

to act until a new Collector could be found.[24] Sudden death also claimed a number of ICS men; Bolton (ICS, Bombay) was drowned with all his children in a car accident while driving up to Kashmir, Sharpe (ICS, Assam) was beheaded by the Japanese during the war, and three successive ICS Collectors at Midnapur (in Bengal) were shot and killed by terrorists—Peddie in a school, Douglas at a district board meeting, Burge on the football field. Bengal lost a number of ICS men killed by terrorists in the early 1930s. The Government there was getting so short-handed that notices were sent around other provinces appealing for volunteers. Johnston (ICS, UP) said he would go to Bengal on a five-year loan if he could first have a year as Collector at Garhwal, a 'plum job' in UP (if you liked mountains). His request was granted. Not surprisingly, there were only two volunteers, Johnston and the man who sent the notice.[25]

Every province had its plum jobs. They were a principal object of striving and individuals could be given such posts as a reward for good service. Mason (ICS, UP) recounts lobbying in the mid-1930s for the plum job in Garwhal.[26] In Punjab, the Commissionership of Rawalpindi was considered 'the best ICS job in North India',[27] while for the more junior men, Kulu Subdivision in Kangra District was a 'prize posting', according to Muhammad Azim Husain (ICS, Punjab).[28] Being Collector of Bombay was a plum job in that province because it was in the city and had excellent amenities (including the huge official residence on Malabar Hill facetiously referred to as 'Buckingham Palace').[29] When Martin (ICS, Bengal) was posted to Darjeeling as Collector in 1930, he considered it 'the best job in the whole province'.[30] Certain posts at provincial headquarters were also viewed in this way. For example, Twynam (ICS, Bengal) was 'pleased with the appointment' in 1927 as Land Acquisition Collector, Calcutta Improvement Trust: 'It was not much in my line which tended rather towards law and order subjects, such as political movements, police, jails and such like; but the job was something of a plum job with allowances which included the responsibility of disbursing some £500,000 per annum on Calcutta

[24] Georgeson Papers, IOL MSS Eur. F.180/52, TS p. 6.
[25] Johnston Papers, Cambridge Archive, TS p. 193.
[26] Mason, P., *A Shaft of Sunlight: Memories of a Varied Life*, London, 1978, p. 124.
[27] Penny Papers, Cambridge Archive, TS p. 50. Penny (ICS, Punjab) was Commissioner there in 1932.
[28] Muhammad Azim Husain Papers, IOL MSS Eur. F.180/68, TS p. 18.
[29] Faruqui Papers IOL MSS Eur. F.180/27, TS pp. 10–11.
[30] Martin Papers, Cambridge Archive, TS p. 171.

Improvement Trust projects, and I regarded my selection as in the nature of a reward for the work I had done in Mymensingh.'[31] Other postings were regarded more as a punishment. Stuart (ICS, Bengal) was dispatched in 1930 to the malarious Krishnagar in the middle of the province and remarked: 'What crime I had committed to be posted there, I cannot imagine (I may have trumped the ace of the wife of the Chief Secretary).'[32]

ICS men moved through transfer; they also moved up through promotion. As an official file pointed out in 1936, 'the ordinary course of promotion, not only from Assistant Collector to Collector . . . [but also beyond] tends to follow the order of seniority in nine cases out of ten, and it is only in one case out of ten that an exceptionally good officer is given accelerated promotion, or an exceptionally bad officer is passed over.'[33] Thus, when a batch of five or six ICS recruits was posted to the same province in the same year, the first man in the batch might get a promotion a year ahead of the others, but essentially the whole batch moved up steadily together into higher and higher posts. Seniority rather than selection by merit normally determined promotion, except in the realm of prize postings at the highest levels, for example, Secretary, Chief Secretary, Governor. Only the 'meritorious' were appointed to these posts, which carried extraordinary responsibilities and amazing pay, pomp, and circumstance. The comparative salary figures for 1935 (computed at rupees per month) shown in Table 3 suggest how lucrative top ICS posts were.[34]

The cost of living in the USA and Britain was, of course, far higher than in India. Poland was far richer than Bihar; and Japan had more than twice the population of Madras. These sorts of salaries, together with the fact that the Viceroy was paid more than the President of the United States of America, led one student of the subject to refer to British rule as a 'Rolls-Royce administration in a bullock-cart country'.[35] Certainly the prize ICS posts at the top that ambitious men sought were glittering indeed.

Not all ICS men wanted such posts. Some senior men preferred to remain as Collectors to the end (their salary at the top of the ICS scale

[31] Twynam Papers, Cambridge Archive, TS p. 96.

[32] Stuart Papers, Cambridge Archive, 'Chaudanga' TS p. 1 Box II.

[33] NAI Home Dept. File 58/36 Ests., 1936.

[34] The Indian salaries were obtained from the *Indian Office and Burma Office List, 1938*. The comparative salaries in rupee equivalents come from Schiff, L. M., *The Present Condition of India: A Study in Social Relationships*, London, 1939, pp. 145–7.

[35] Schiff, *Condition of India*, p. 145.

Table 3. *Comparative Salary Figures, 1935*

Top ICS posts (a few examples)	Pay per month rupees	Comparative posts (a few examples)	Pay per month rupees
Governor of United Provinces	10,000		
Governor of Bihar	8,333	Governor, New York State	5,687
Member, Viceroy's Council	6,666	Cabinet Minister, UK	5,555
Governor of Assam	5,500	Chief Justice, Supreme Court (USA)	4,550
Secretary to Government, Delhi	4,000	Secretary to Treasury (UK)	3,333
Chief Secretary (Madras)	3,750	Cabinet Member, USA	3,412
Commissioner, Bombay	3,500	President of Poland	1,560
Chief Secretary, Bihar	3,000	Governor of South Dakota	682
Secretary, Madras	2,750	Prime Minister, Japan	622

was handsome enough). One such inveterate Collector in UP advised his juniors: 'The Acheron of promotion will gape before you . . . you will fall into a commissionership, still deeper into an officiating seat on the Board of Revenue; *Facilis est descensus*. Enjoy your work as District Officer while you have a chance.'[36] Nevertheless, it is clear that most ICS men had the normal career ambitions. Twynam was unusually candid about it. In early 1939 the Governor of Bengal, Lord Brabourne, died suddenly, Reid (ICS, Bengal) came down quickly from Assam to act in Bengal, and Twynam went to Assam to act for Reid. 'I was thrilled', says Twynam, 'to go there as Governor and occupy the lovely Government House in Shillong, one of the fairest places in the world—it would be the realization of secret hopes . . . a fitting end to my service.'[37]

The overall picture one obtains of the ICS in terms of location and movement is a curious one: a very few young men trusted by the imperial power were recruited to a highly select service and then whirled about by rapid transfer while being pulled by automatic promotion into higher and higher control posts reserved for them at all levels of government. Such rapid movement every year or two, particularly in the district, was not deliberate policy. It is clear that Chief Secretaries and other senior ICS men would have liked to slow it

[36] Note by E. F. Oppenheim (ICS, UP) appended to *Handbook for the Guidance of Junior Collectors*, Allahabad, 1936.

[37] Twynam Papers, TS p. 96. See also Reid, R., *Years of Change in Bengal and Assam*, London, 1966.

down, even though it was considered 'dangerous to stay more than three years in a district because of the risk of "putting down roots" and becoming too personally involved in local issues'.[38] Yet movement could not be slowed for the reasons indicated. Certain broader consequences followed.

For one thing, recruiting a few young men each year to a separate service and then giving them, and only them, a clear run to the top, commanding handsome salaries most of the way, is the height of *élitist* administration. This meant that other administrators who did not, or could not, get into that service were forever denied access to the top positions, however able they might subsequently become. Colonial administration was in consequence highly stratified, with little movement up, and hence there were few rewards or incentives on offer for ambitious civil servants at lower levels. The lack of dynamism amongst subordinate civil servants in the raj, except in moments of emergency, can be traced at least in part to the structure of the colonial state and ICS location within it.

Such a structure also placed *generalists* on top and technical experts on tap. ICS men were the most general of generalist administrators. Baker (ICS, Bengal) wrote in 1932 to his father that 'this service provides its members with more diverse kinds of labour than any other in the world'.[39] There was not only immense variety within a generalist post; the ICS also moved from one type of post to another, while technical experts stayed put in subordinate departments or offices. The whole structure of the raj celebrated generalist control and continuity, not specialist expertise and innovation.

ICS location and movement also set up a distinctive form of administrative fragmentation, involving splits in the secretariats and districts between mobile élite officers and more stationary subordinates. Having such a superior and separate group of generalists moving freely into and out of control posts in government organizations was built into the fabric of Indian administration. One consequence of such fragmentation of government organizations was the difficulty of obtaining committed and speedy action on a regular basis. In the routine administration of the raj, however, speed was of little account.

Even the mountains of files and elaborate records so characteristic of Indian administration were, at least in part, a product of the distinctive pattern of ICS location and movement. Wadsworth (ICS,

[38] Belcher Papers, IOL MSS Eur. F.180/64, TS p. 20.
[39] Baker Papers, Cambridge Archive, reel 1, letter to father, 23.4.1931.

Madras), for example, was struck by this connection when he worked in the Madras Secretariat in 1919; he observed that the 'constant changing of the superior personnel in government offices . . . makes it necessary to keep much more elaborate records not only of decisions, but of the reasons for them, than would otherwise be necessary'.[40] Enlightened ICS officers worked to reduce red tape and streamline complicated procedures. What they failed to see was that the very existence of an ICS—and its pattern of location and movement—was part of the problem.

BEHAVIOUR PATTERNS: POLITICAL WORK

Characteristic behaviour patterns of ICS administrators were clearly political, even if the persons involved rarely labelled them as such. This was true of the work they did in both the district and the secretariat. Certainly they were involved in overseeing and organizing the implementation of decisions made by political leaders. They also, as leaders within the state structure, made authoritative decisions themselves. Most importantly, they were centrally involved in pursuing partisan objectives by mobilizing groups in society to support and work for those objectives, usually in opposition to other groups who had different political orientations.

Collectors in the districts had literally thousands of enumerated powers as administrators at the head of the magistracy, the police, revenue collection, other government departments, and local authorities. Standard works on district administration in British India describe what ICS Collectors did broadly in terms of the administrative aspects of these spheres of activity—organizing, co-ordinating, supervising, controlling, and directing all the component parts of the district administration towards achieving the overall objectives of the colonial state.[41] From 1919 onwards, much of that work was shot through with political considerations. The point can be made swiftly with reference to the maintenance of law and order, the principal responsibility of ICS men in the districts. It is manifestly clear from the numerous accounts by ICS men of their work in this sphere that they took a definite position in administering law and order. It was British law and order that they were bending their energies to maintain, not anyone else's. Haig (ICS,

[40] Wadsworth Papers, Cambridge Archive, TS p. 72.

[41] Hunt, R. and Harrison, J., *The District Officer in India, 1930–1947*, London, 1980, is one of the best of the genre.

UP) expressed this basic political orientation very clearly: 'our main responsibility was the maintenance of 'Pax Britannica' . . . we were against Congress who were trying to chuck the British out of India' and we 'tended to regard with favour those Indians whom we considered "loyal", and with disfavour those whom we consider "disloyal".'[42] Solomon's early career in Bihar provides another example.[43] Wadsworth (ICS, Madras) was Additional District Magistrate in Godavari District in 1920–1 and reports that 'much of the work was in the nature of "showing the flag"—taking every opportunity to demonstrate that the government intended to govern and that those who wanted to help the authorities must come out into the open as loyalists'. Action was required because 'far too many people were sitting on the fence and it was politically desirable to get as many as possible to come down on our side of it'.[44]

Political considerations also affected another major area of responsibility for ICS men in the districts, the collection of revenue. Wadsworth in Godavari District, for example, spent much of his time in spring 1921 making arrangements for the imposition and collection of a new tax—conferring with clerks at district headquarters about precedents, reading and amending draft regulations, and touring in certain parts of the district to talk with subordinate revenue officials about the arrangements for the new tax. Its purpose was to take 'offensive action' against people in those parts of Godavari District who had come out on the Congress side of the fence during the agitations at that time. 'Notifications were issued under the Police Act declaring that special police were necessary for the maintenance of law and order in these areas and that the cost of those special police would be recovered from those people whose misconduct had made them necessary.' Another example: in January 1921 the water level of the Godavari River fell rapidly, and it was necessary to reduce the area of second crop irrigation. The Collector, Bracken (ICS, Madras), and Wadsworth, when making decisions on this, gave preference to those villages that had not joined the non-co-operation movement, 'thereby demonstrating in the most convincing fashion that it paid to be loyal'.[45]

This account is particularly candid. It also could be argued that it is unrepresentative in that it relates to a time when British administration was under particularly intense political pressure. But to a greater or

[42] Haig Papers, IOL MSS Eur. F.180/75, TS p. 6.
[43] Solomon Papers, TS p. 38.
[44] Wadsworth Papers, TS p. 140.
[45] Wadsworth Papers, TS p. 141.

lesser extent, depending on time and place, ICS men in India were under that kind of pressure from 1919 up to 1947. Collectors and SDOs were constantly on the lookout for support from collaborators, and from people with local weight and influence. Arthur (ICS, Punjab) in his Handing Over Note when leaving Murree District in the early 1940s identified collaborators for his successor: one 'has worked extremely well in a quiet and conscientious fashion giving considerable assistance to the Police and Forest Departments'; another is 'an important landowner with character and influence—he may not be absolutely honest but is worth supporting as he can be of good assistance to the administration'; another is 'a rich Army Contractor and a loyal supporter of Government'. Arthur lists the 'rewards for such collaboration—one KCIE, one knighthood, one MBE, two Khan Sahibs', together with various grants of land.[46] When Raza (ICS, Bombay and Sind) was Collector in Larkhana in the early 1940s, he found that the presence of the principal *jagirdar* there 'was worth six police stations' and Raza 'made out a case for the grant of a knighthood to him'. As Raza noted, 'Whenever my police were unable to trace an absconder and reported that he had moved to the Ghaidero Jagir [the *jagirdar*'s estate], all that I had to do was to write a letter to the Nawab and the absconder was handed over to us within 48 hours!' In due course, a knighthood was conferred on him. For *jagirdars* and *zamindars* it was no secret that 'the Honours List was eagerly awaited'.[47] All Collectors in United Provinces were given the following confidential instructions:

> Receiving visitors is one of the most important duties of a Collector. Properly treated, your *mulaqatis* ['visitors who want to see the Collector on business'[48]] can keep you informed of the conditions in the district in a way in which the official reports cannot, and thus be of great assistance to you in the successful administration of your district. Do not, therefore, be led to look upon them as an unavoidable evil; rather learn to cultivate their goodwill . . .
>
> You should make brief notes about each of your important visitors—official or non-official—and have these systematically kept in your confidential almirah. They can be made either in the old *mulaqatis* book or you can start a modern card index . . . In the case of a non-official, your note should indicate

[46] Cited in Hunt and Harrison, *District Officer*, p. 92. It is not in the Arthur memoir.
[47] Raza Papers, TS pp. 113, 123.
[48] The translation is by Wingate, R. E. (ICS, Punjab), *Not in the Limelight*, London, 1959, p. 35.

his position in life, the influence he wields in society, his views, and how far you may count on his help . . .[49]

In Bombay Province, instead of a *Mulaqatis* book there was a '*zamindars*' book—a 'confidential document in which all Assistant Collectors and Collectors recorded their opinions about *zamindars* and others in their area'. Some were more useful than others, but a book 'that had been well maintained over a number of years made interesting and amusing reading, and was invaluable to an officer taking over for the first time'.[50] The value of the book lay not only in identifying those whose support could be relied on, but also prominent people who were not helpful. Collectors could make life difficult for the latter. Raza gives an example of what is reputedly an entry for one *zamindar* who fell foul of successive Collectors in that District, as recorded in the *zamindar*'s book:[51]

1st Collector: 'This *zamindar* is a scoundrel. He needs to be crushed.'
2nd Collector (5 years later): 'I have crushed him.'
3rd Collector (5 years later): 'Found him crushed.'

Collectors could harass opponents in all sorts of ways. Even a small thing like not renewing a firearms licence could hurt because if an individual did not have one it could affect his social status and prestige. Or an ICS SDO could make effective use of a battalion of Gurkhas if they happened to pass through the subdivision, as Hume did in Roorkee in late November 1930. He told his parents in a letter home: 'I whispered the names of one or two ('Congress Dictators') in Captain Billy Gough's ear and hinted that they might advantageously be interviewed by a few Gurkhas' and 'Billy took and acted on the hint to the full . . .'. One, 'a fat and greasy *bania* (moneylender) who had given us endless trouble for six months was found in a canal bathing, and was whitewashed and paraded about nearly nude'. The other received similar treatment. All this had 'an electrifying effect on any other minded to assume the office of (village) dictatorship, more especially that it is known that another battalion of Gurkhas is coming on 2nd December'.[52]

[49] Panna Lal (ICS, UP), *Handbook for the Guidance of Junior Collectors*, Allahabad, 1936 (marked confidential).

[50] Barty Papers, IOL MSS Eur. F.180/26, TS p. 41.

[51] Raza Papers, TS p. 113. I use the word 'reputedly' because variations on this entry also crop up in other sources.

[52] Hume Papers, IOL MSS Eur. D.724/3, vol. 3, letter dated 26.11.1930.

It was not only Collectors who were centrally involved in political work. SDOs and others were similarly engaged. Solomon's early career provides an illustration, including his posting as SDO Darbhanga, where the leading landlord of Bihar resided.[53] Political considerations could also determine where a young Sub-Collector in Madras Province was placed. It was widely known there, for example, that the 'real reason' for placing a young ICS man as 'Sub-Collector in a one-horse place like Gudur was in order to keep in touch with the *Maharaja* of Venkatagira, who owned about half the land in the division and was one of the biggest *zamindars* in South India'.[54]

Given the political context in which ICS Collectors and their subordinates worked with 'instruments' of rule only very thinly spread round the district and with nationalist forces pressing more or less firmly (depending on time and place) for an end to that rule, it is hardly surprising that ICS men, in order to maintain British rule and their own position, took every opportunity to try to get people in the district to come down on 'their side'. As political administrators, ICS men were constantly alert to possible sources of support, moving to meet, or reward, or (if need be) thwart and harass those with power. The sources suggest that *zamindars*, *jagirdars*, and landed classes more generally were on the whole seen as sources of support by ICS men all over India. Raza's assessment that a particular *jagirdar* in Larkhana District was worth six police stations was one rough measurement of one man's power. Similar assessments were continually being made elsewhere. If they were loyal they were rewarded with honours, invitations to official functions, and other favours in the power of the Collector to dispense, such as tax concessions, and jobs for relatives or friends; if they were opponents, there were other powers that could be used to harrass. The ICS connection with the landed classes in the districts recorded in *zamindars* books and Handing Over Notes (needed because of rapid transfers) is unmistakable in the sources for the period, although few ICS men talk about it explicitly at any length.

What the sources *are* full of is the constant work, both at headquarters and on tour, of keeping tabs on that other support structure of British rule, the state apparatus. For every ICS man in a

[53] The Maharajadhiraja of Darbhanga's huge estate sprawled across six Bihar districts. A description of how it was managed in the 1930s is provided by Heningham, S., 'Bureaucracy and Control in India's Great Landed Estates: The Raj Darbhanga of Bihar, 1879–1950', *MAS* 17. 1 (1983), 35–55.

[54] Wadsworth Papers, TS p. 44.

district there normally were (so to speak) a thousand or more subordinate officials. The ICS Collector did not have to supervise all of them directly—many were in specialist departments and were supervised by others—but the army of subordinate revenue officials, generalists in the provincial administrative service, staff at the collectorate, and others were his constant concern. He also had a watching brief over all the rest, spending a lot of his time reading reports about them in his office or in the seclusion of his own study. The stated purpose of all this supervision was to try to ensure that the state apparatus performed its various functions effectively. At the heart of the exercise, also, was the need to be sure that the apparatus remained loyal to British rule.

This was never a problem in the 1920s and 1930s. Although nationalist forces gathered strength during the period, and put subordinate Indian officials under pressure, their support for the raj remained firm. No doubt one reason was the unemployment in the 1930s among educated Indians which, as Haig (ICS, UP) believed, 'helped to create the great loyalty which we received from Indian subordinates and the diligence with which they did their work'.[55] Holland (ICS, Bengal), when Additional District Magistrate in Dacca District in the early 1930s, was struck by the 'astonishingly high standard of loyalty to Government'.[56] Even as late as 1940 that loyalty and support appeared to be very firm. One young ICS SDO in Coimbatore District (Madras) recalls that as the bad news came in from Europe in May–June of 1940, it was 'my *Indian staff* who kept me in good cheer; to them British defeat was literally unthinkable, so solid, so secure seemed the British Empire in India in those days'.[57]

To keep tabs on subordinates ICS men moved incessantly amongst them when 'on tour'. Saumarez Smith (ICS, Bengal) writing home in 1936 shortly after arriving at his first post in Faridpur District, remarked that his life as SDO was 'a succession of days spent on tour, followed by frantic bursts of work at headquarters trying to catch up the accumulation of (paper) work'.[58] Arthur (ICS, Punjab) wrote home in 1939: 'Touring is superb fun',[59] although not all revelled in the

[55] Haig Papers, TS p. 7.

[56] Holland Papers, Cambridge Archive, 'Terrorism in Bengal, 1930–35', (handwritten reminiscence).

[57] Lamarque Papers, IOL MSS Eur. F.180/54, TS p. 26.

[58] Saumarez Smith, W. H., *A Young Man's Country: Letters of a Subdivisional Officer of the Indian Civil Service, 1936–1937*, Salisbury, 1977, p. 15.

[59] Arthur Papers, IOL MSS Eur. F.180/63, TS p. 5.

exercise. 'I did not like touring,' said Faruqui (ICS, Bombay and Sind), but he got used to it.[60] He had to, for it was widely regarded as mandatory for 'good Collectors to get out of the office'. As Edye (ICS, UP) remarked, a Collector's 'value is in inverse ratio to the wear on the seat of his trousers'.[61] The many tour diaries and weekly letters home present a powerful picture of ICS men proceeding relentlessly back and forth across the district—inspecting, encouraging, warning, keeping in touch and informed about the continuing loyalty of the administration. The picture is matched by the available autobiographical accounts by subordinate Indian administrators.[62] The details of how they toured and how much varied—some went in motor launches on rivers (in parts of Bengal); others by camel, or elephant, or horse, others (increasingly from the 1930s onwards) by car; some made frequent short trips into the interior from headquarters, others went out for longer sessions. An extreme instance was the Collector of Nasik in 1934–5 who was out on tour continuously for eighty-one days.[63] Whatever the details, however, the overriding purpose was clear: to act as 'the eyes and ears of government' and on the basis of the knowledge gained to work to ensure the continuing loyalty of the people who worked for the raj.

The account so far has been ahistorical in the sense that evidence has been reported from all over the period. It is important to note, however, the slowly declining authority of the ICS Collector in the eyes of the public, and the possible effect this changing situation had on the Collector's political work. Venkatachar (ICS, UP), for example, observed that by the 1930s in the United Provinces 'the decline in the influence of the Collector's position was visible. . . . Fear of the raj was going; its prestige was dwindling, being undermined by Congress workers, unobtrusively working' in the villages. One of Venkatachar's ICS colleagues reportedly remarked after the results of the 1937 provincial elections that 'it was the beginning of the end of British rule as it was hitherto thought that Congress had some influence in the urban areas

[60] Faruqui Papers, TS p. 5.

[61] Cited in Mason, *The Guardians*, p. 217.

[62] e.g. Noronha, C., *My Life*, (privately published and printed, 1975), pp. 92–3, copy in Stuart Papers, Cambridge Archive; Chak, B. L., *Himalayas to Bay Islands: Recollections of a Bureaucrat*, Lucknow, 1978 (Chak entered the UP provincial service in 1941); Jilani, S. G., *Anatomy of a State Civil Servant*, Ranchi, 1959; Tripathi, P. K., *Reminiscences of a Public Servant*, Cuttack, 1960(?). (Tripathi entered the Bihar and Orissa provincial service in 1929.)

[63] Government of Bombay. *Report of the Reorganization of District Revenue Offices* (1959), p. 103.

and over the urban intelligentsia; now, it had convincingly demonstrated that it held the rural area in its grip.'[64] This development may have been particularly noticeable in United Provinces, but the same general tendency for the peasantry to turn increasingly towards Congress was evident elsewhere.[65] Why they turned is not entirely clear.[66] But their turning did tend to undermine the Collector's authority. So also did changes in technology (for instance, telephones linking Collectors to secretariats and provincial Indian ministries) and the growth of the state. Furthermore, a Public Service Commission had come into being in Madras in 1927 and Appointments Boards in other provinces, and these developments were gradually reducing the number of patronage appointments an ICS Collector could make to reward his supporters. To the extent this happened, the Collector's political support began to turn elsewhere for rewards, and his authority declined.

Although some ICS men appear to have been well aware of the increasingly precarious nature of their political support, the sources which relate well to the period in question (those without the benefit of hindsight) suggest that most of them either were unaware that the Congress was acquiring a mass base or, if they did sense it, did not take it very seriously until the end of the 1930s. The general picture one gets is of most Collectors continuing to rely on *zamindars*, *jagirdars*, and other 'big' landlords, failing perhaps to realize that the power of this rural class was fading as nationalist forces mobilized a successor. Even if ICS men did realize that their rule in the district rested precariously on a dying class, their way was blocked from forging a different alliance. If one views the political changes of the period that way, then one can see that such changes did not fundamentally affect what ICS Collectors continued to *do* as political administrators. Another general point concerns the common notion that political developments in the 1920s and 1930s resulted in increasing 'political interference' in what ICS Collectors did. Such a notion of political interference, however, is otiose, for it implies that there was

[64] Venkatachar Papers, IOL MSS Eur. F.180/85, TS pp. 26, 32.

[65] For Bombay, see Epstein, S., 'District Officers in Decline: The Erosion of British Authority in the Bombay Countryside, 1919 to 1947', *MAS* 16 (1982), 493–518. For the work of the Congress Ministry in Bombay Province, 1937–9, see Ravi Dhavan Shankardass, *The First Congress Raj: Provincial Autonomy in Bombay*, Delhi, 1982. More generally, see the essays in Low, D. A. (ed.), *Congress and the Raj: Facets of the Indian Struggle, 1917–47*, London, 1977.

[66] A critique of conventional explanations is Tomlinson B. R., 'Congress and the Raj: Political Mobilization in Late Colonial India' (Review Article), MAS 16. 2 (1982), 334–49.

interference in an activity which was not previously political, which is nonsense. ICS Collectors had always been political administrators in the districts. Increasingly, as ministers and politicians began to move in on provincial politics, ICS men became political instruments of provincial ministries, whether they liked it or not. This was not political interference; it was rather a new political context within which ICS Collectors had to operate when administering a district.

A final general point: arguing that ICS Collectors and SDOs were political administrators does not necessarily imply that they administered the district in the sense of controlling most of what went on there. To call the ICS 'the men who ruled India' is very misleading. Because the British were so thin on the ground, they had to strike what amounted to political bargains with local collaborators who could normally rule for them. As Seal has aptly remarked, the terms of the bargain were that ICS Collectors 'could depend on the collection of revenue, provided they did not ask too officiously who paid it', and 'they might take public order for granted, provided that they themselves did not play too obtrusive a part in enforcing it'. Hence, beneath the Collector 'lay a ground-floor reality where Indians battled with Indians', sometimes for the Collector's favours, 'sometimes to do each other down without reference to him or his book of rules'.[67] The British in India governed, in the sense of controlling large policy issues bearing on the economy, the army, and the legal framework of the raj; they could bring force to bear on a particular district when things threatened to get out of hand; but in the normal life of a district it was Indians who did most of the ruling. Even most of what subordinate officials in the district did in a detailed way largely escaped the notice of the ICS,[68] which was hardly surprising given the deliberate policy of not allowing an ICS man to remain in a district for very long. The power of ICS Collectors can easily be exaggerated. Whatever one's precise assessment on that score, the important consequence for the argument being made here about behaviour patterns is this: the very fact that ICS Collectors had to rely so extensively on others required them to spend much of their time on political work.

Policy work in the secretariat was very different from political work

[67] Seal, A., 'Imperialism and Nationalism in India', in Gallagher, Johnson, and Seal (eds.), *Locality, Province and Nation*, pp. 8–9.

[68] The classic study here, for an earlier period, is Frykenberg, R., *Guntur District 1788–1848: A History of Local Influence and Central Authority in South India*, Oxford, 1965.

in the district. The bulk of the work for ICS men involved dealing with files prepared by subordinates and either ruling on a matter themselves or sending files 'up' with summarizing notes to a superior. They also attended meetings, occasionally went on tour, and so on. Major policies or schemes involved wide consultation, and frequently required obtaining permission from the Government of India and the Secretary of State in London. Major policy matters were jointly scrutinized from many points of view. How much will it cost? How will it be financed? Is new legislation required? Are new rules necessary, or do old ones need to be modified? What are the views of the various government departments affected by the proposal? What will be the reactions of the legislature? The press? The tax-paying public? Will accepting the proposal create an awkward porecedent? Does it require the sanction of the Government of India, or perhaps the Secretary of State?

Who was 'up' for the secretariat as a whole changed during the period 1919–47. The constitutional reforms embodied in the Government of India Act, 1919, resulted in devolution of legislative and financial powers from the centre to the provinces, along with an extension of parliamentary government at both levels. At the centre, the Viceroy and his Executive Council were 'up' for the secretariat. There was a Legislative Council, with a substantial elected majority, and although due attention was given to its proceedings, neither the Viceroy and his Council nor the secretariat were accountable to it. As for the provinces, the 1919 Act provided for elected majorities in their legislatures, and although some areas of provincial government like law and order and revenue subjects were reserved for the Governor and his Executive Council, others such as public health, education, agriculture were put in charge of Indian ministers drawn from the legislatures and responsible to them. The arrangement was known as 'dyarchy'. ICS men in provincial secretariats under this constitutional arrangement therefore worked for either an Executive Councillor (and the Governor) or an Indian minister, depending on which part of the secretariat he was working in. For example, the Home Secretary would relate to an ICS Executive Councillor and the Governor, whereas the Education Secretary worked under an Indian minister. This framework obtained without major alteration from 1920 to 1937. From 1937 to 1939 the position in the provinces changed quite radically. Under the provisions of the Government of India Act, 1935, public participation in provincial government increased greatly (for example, the size of the electorates increased fivefold), the number of seats in the legislative assemblies doubled, and control of *all* subjects of government at provincial level were given to councils of ministers responsible to the majority party (or parties) in the Assembly (and subject to certain 'safeguards' remaining with the Governor). Secretariats in this context worked with Indian ministries. In 1939 the ministries in most provinces resigned, and executive leadership reverted to the Governor and his ICS Advisers until the mid-1940s. At the centre, throughout the entire period, the basic framework under dyarchy remained unchanged. Policy-making power was, therefore, shared throughout this period between ICS men in the secretariats and executive heads—be they councillors, ministers, Advisers, Governors. The share-out, however, left most of the power and influence over normal decisions with ICS men in the secretariat.

Policy making within the Government of India in early 1945 provides an example. The people involved were the Viceroy (Lord Wavell), his two Secretaries (both ICS men), the Executive Council (of 15 members, including four Europeans for War, War Transport and Railways, Home, Finance), the Council of State (32 elected members, 26 nominated), the Legislative Assembly (102 elected members, 39 nominated), and the secretariat comprising 18 secretariat departments (16 of the 18 Secretaries were ICS men). There were also the Federal Public Service Commission (chaired by a retired ICS man), the Federal Court of India, the Political Department (headed by a former ICS man), and numerous specialist departments and agencies.

Panjabi (ICS, Bombay) worked as a Joint Secretary in the Food Department in early 1945 and was in charge of supplies for the defence forces.[69] Due to the importance of the subject for the war effort, 'red tape was cut to a minimum, and whatever supplies of food and drink the army needed could be made available at short notice'. The Secretary, Hutchings (ICS, Bengal), met other top officials in the Secretariat Department 'every morning to learn the latest developments, and in most cases orders were issued immediately'. The Member of the Viceroy's Executive Council responsible for food, 'rarely interfered in matters of execution, contenting himself with giving general directions'. He delegated authority 'to the Secretary and Joint Secretary, while keeping himself fully informed of what was going on'.

[69] The source for the quotations in this paragraph is Panjabi, K. L., 'My Experiences in the ICS', in Panjabi, K. L. (ed.), *The Civil Servant in India*, Bombay, 1965, pp. 99–100 (hereafter Panjabi, *Civil Servant*).

Even when the Minister did want to make a decision in opposition to the ICS official in the Department, he was not always successful. Panjabi recalls a case when the Food Member, 'on the pressure of his political friends', wanted to make an exception to an agreed line of policy and grant a contract to a particular firm. 'I advised against it', says Panjabi, 'and, being unable to convince him, sought the aid of the Secretary, who had direct access to the Viceroy if necessary.' This standard ploy worked. The Minister 'reluctantly dropped the proposal . . . but he blamed me for being a stickler for rules and in a moment of frankness said "If I cannot occasionally help a friend, what use am I as a Minister?"' Successful ministerial intervention did occur, of course, but only infrequently. As a rule, the ICS 'advice' prevailed.

It was not only ministers or members of the Viceroy's Executive Council who relied on advice from ICS Secretaries. So, obviously, did Viceroys. Lord Wavell, for example, recorded in his diary, on 31 December 1944, that his Personal Secretary, Jenkins (ICS, Punjab), 'has been a great mainstay . . . and I could not have got on without him' this past year.[70] Likewise, Lord Willingdon (Viceroy from 1931 to 1936) relied substantially on Secretaries and ministers whom he trusted. Corfield (ICS, Punjab) worked in the central secretariat at that time and describes how Lord Willingdon disposed of any complicated case put to him. He would ask first *who* in the secretariat (or elsewhere) made the recommendation. 'If it was someone he knew to be sound, he refused to bother himself with the details.' But Corfield insists that the Viceroy was not out of touch, because 'he had regular weekly interviews with ministers and Secretaries, and it was during these personal discussions that he kept himself up to date'.[71]

Most government business dealt with in the secretariat never reached the Viceroy or ministers at all. Much of it was routine and governed strictly by precedent. It was normally disposed of with the minimum of fuss because secretariat clerks in the 'office' were able to collect and collate 'necessary papers', draft letters, consult relevant departments, and eventually reduce such routine business to a straightforward matter requiring only a signature from an ICS officer. Moon (ICS, Punjab) referred to this aspect as 'the work of government running on quietly in the hands of petty clerks'.[72]

Another view of life in the central secretariat at this time is provided

[70] *Wavell, The Viceroy's Journal*, (ed. P. Moon), London, 1973, p. 108.
[71] Corfield, C., *The Princely India I Knew*, Madras, 1975, p. 89.
[72] Moon, P., *Divide and Quit*, London, 1961, p. 153.

by Lamarque (ICS, Madras), who, as a young man, was posted in March 1941 as an Under Secretary, Labour, and who remained in the Government of India until 1947. What struck him first was the imperial splendour of the North Block of Lutyens' vast secretariat building in which the Labour Department was housed, a building 'so vast that notices were needed to remind officers that cycling in the corridors was prohibited (a rule not infrequently broken)'. Lamarque's particular concern, which remained virtually unchanged until 1945, was mines and minerals, particularly coal-mining. On arrival he sized up his superiors; the Secretary Prior (ICS, Bihar and Orissa) was 'an old Etonian, courteous, conscientious and hard working, untidy but good humoured' and Lamarque's immediate superior was Hasan Zaheer (ICS, UP) 'who came from an old Muslim family in Lucknow, able enough if he tried, but easy-going and lazy by nature, and quite happy to leave me to do what I liked . . . '. One of his first policy initiatives with Zaheer led to an error:

Already in 1941 labour was showing signs of drifting away from coal mines to more attractive employment elsewhere, e.g. on military works. One quick way to attract more labour would be to allow women to work underground; something which had been prohibited by law for some years. To British ears this seemed a retrograde step, not to say barbarous step. Women had not been allowed to work underground in British mines for 100 years. But conditions in India were very different. Coal mining was not so arduous physically. Certainly it was hot underground, but seams of coal were thick, pits were not very deep, and coal could be approached and dug out from a standing position, not by crawling along distances on one's stomach. Furthermore, women in India were used to physical labour, and both they and their menfolk liked working together, as a family unit. So we announced that as an emergency measure, and for the duration of the war, women would be permitted to work underground in coal mines. What we had overlooked, but what the other side of the Labour Department could have told us, was that this was in breach of an international ILO convention to which India had been a party some years before. The India Office fortunately came to our rescue, justifying our action in a well-written paper to the authorities in Geneva, as being due to the exigencies of war.[73]

In 1944 coal as a subject was taken out of the portfolio of the Labour Department of the secretariat and transferred to the Supply Department, and Lamarque went with it. He, therefore, served under several

[73] Lamarque Papers, TS p. 31.

different ministers during his time with the Government of India—four in fact, and 'all were men of great distinction'. There was Sir Feroz Khan Noon, 'a member of a wealthy and aristocratic Punjab family, handsome with a fine presence and great charm, but he was intellectually a light-weight, not really up to the administration of a big department'. The other three were of 'outstanding ability'; Sir A. Ramaswami Mudaliar, Mr Rajagopalachari, and Dr Ambedkar. Dr Ambedkar was a member of the 'scheduled' or backward classes and, in addition to his administrative work, one of his main concerns 'was to try to infiltrate other scheduled class members into the Government of India, at any level, but in this he met with little success'.[74] Dr Ambedkar was by no means unusual in wanting to bring his own people into the Government of India. When Narasimhan (ICS, Madras) first went to New Delhi in April 1950, his minister was Jairamdas Daulatram who came from Sind and was so keen on finding jobs for Sindis that the Ministry of Food and Agriculture became known as the 'Sindicate'.[75]

The picture suggested of policy making at the centre in the 1940s is one in which ministers (or members) and ICS Secretaries were both involved; although if a Secretary and a minister disagreed, the Secretary could seek assistance from the Viceroy (or at least threaten to do so), and usually got his way. Most of the detailed work which preformed the decision was done in the secretariat.

A similar picture is obtained from evidence available on the working of the Madras Government during the period 1937–9, when a Congress ministry was in power with Mr Rajagopalachari (or Rajaji as he was called by friends and colleagues) in charge as Chief Minister. ICS descriptions of decision making in Madras at this time are replete with references to ministers.

Masterman (ICS, Madras), for example, was Secretary, Education and Public Health, between 1936 and 1939, and ministers are omnipresent in his account. However, one hardly gets a picture of rule having been transferred wholly from ICS Secretary to Indian minister:

> The position in the Secretariat as a whole was peculiar, almost bizarre. The Ministers were totally inexperienced in administration or the ways of government, even Local Government, whereas the Secretaries . . . had twenty or more years of district or secretariat experience . . . It was said that we ran the government. I do not think that is quite true. No one could run Rajaji. We did

[74] Lamarque Papers, TS p. 29.
[75] Narasimhan Papers, TS p. 9.

of course have a good deal of power inevitably owing to our greater experience . . . In minor matters our views generally prevailed, but in major policy matters the Prime Minister was supreme. In these matters he more often than not agreed with the Secretary as against the Minister concerned. He told me once that he had much greater confidence in the judgement of his British Secretaries than in his Indian colleagues . . .[76]

Ministers differed, of course, some being more 'difficult' from an ICS Secretary's point of view than others. The most difficult was the Revenue Minister, Prakasam, because he frequently disagreed with Uzielli (ICS, Madras), Secretary, Revenue. However, Rajaji usually came down on Uzielli's side when such disagreements were referred to him. These differences are delightfully reflected in Masterman's account of how, when he was once sharing a bungalow with the Uziellis, Uzielli invented a game which they called secretariat cricket—'one run for an initial by the Minister on Secretary's note, two runs for "I agree" initialled, and four runs for "I entirely agree with Secretary" or something of that sort'. Uzielli was at a decided disadvantage, for he had Prakasam while Masterman's two ministers were in the habit of simply initialling whatever he put up to them. Very soon, apparently, the game ended in confusion, Uzielli questioning the rules. The occasion was a file in which Prakasam disagreed with Uzielli, but Rajaji 'intervened and restored Uzielli's view'. Uzielli argued that he had only 'retired hurt', to resume his innings after Rajaji's orders. Masterman maintained that his friend was clearly out.[77]

Secretariat cricket is only one illustration amongst many in the sources of the basic point that ICS men in the secretariat normally got their way with ministers. The word 'normally' is used, however, to convey an important feature of ICS secretariat work: that major provincial issues were always put 'up' to a political leader or Governor during the period, some issues requiring reference to New Delhi or even London. Although the minister or Governor usually agreed with the ICS recommendation, in such important matters the ICS clearly did not rule alone. As Masterman remarks above, the ICS did *not quite* run the provincial government—an able minister like Rajaji might have his way if he disagreed with the ICS.

What secretariat cricket also impies is that any ICS Secretary wanting agreement would make it his business to know where his minister or

[76] Masterman Papers, Cambridge Archive, TS 'Secretariat, 1936–1939' pp. 1–2.
[77] Masterman Papers, TS p. 2.

the Governor tended to stand on major policy issues, and would frame his recommendations as far as possible taking that knowledge into account. Agreement between ICS Secretaries and ministers or Governors 'normally' prevailed in part because the advice they received was normally acceptable. Either the advice ran with the minister's interests anyway or it contained aspects on, say, implementation or 'the facts' of the situation that a minister could not refute. This is the context for the following remark directed by an experienced ICS man at fresh ICS recruits in 1937:

> Where your predecessor of twenty years ago took action, you must ask for orders; where your predecessor gave orders, you must advise. The civilian who used to serve by ruling, must learn to rule by serving.[78]

Attention has been directed so far at the people involved in policy making and their relative influence at provincial level in 1937–9 and at the centre in the 1940s. In turning now to examine policy making during the period of dyarchy, a different aspect is considered. The main concern is not so much with who determined policy (the case reported here took place on the 'reserved' side and therefore the matter was essentially an ICS preserve anyway), but more with method and content when a decision involved all provinces and all secretariats. Important and unusual issues were normally dealt with in this way.

The issue examined here concerns a question that senior ICS men believed to be one of the most difficult to arise in connection with the introduction of provincial autonomy under the Government of India Act, 1935: What do we do with secret secretariat records which, when the Act is implemented, will become accessible to Indian politicians? What follows is a summary of the discussion and decision on the question immediately prior to the implementation of the Act.[79]

On 19 December 1934 the Government of Bombay (more precisely,

[78] Blunt, *The ICS*, pp. 261–2. The first sentence is a slight paraphrase.

[79] The question had been raised in 1932: NAI Home Dept. File 106/III/32—Police (Confidential), 1932, 'Position of the Criminal Investigation Department under the Future Constitution'. The source for the account that follows is NAI Home Dept. File 106/XIII/34—Police (Confidential), 1934, 'Treatment of Confidential Secretariat Records under the new Constitution. Disposal of Records in which the policy of the present Government with political movements of a subversive character, such as civil disobedience movements, have been discussed'. I obtained permission to quote excerpts from this file from The Government of India in their letter to me No. F.5—170/66, 20 Feb. 1967. A longer summary of this file has been published in my article (addressed to a different issue): 'Political Change and Confidential Government Files in India: 1937, 1947, 1967', *Journal of Commonwealth Political Studies*, viii. 2 (1970), 134–46.

the ICS Chief Secretary in that province) wrote a letter to the Government of India (in this case, the ICS Secretary, Home Department) in which, along with other matters related to the intelligence arrangements which would have to be designed under the 1935 Act, the question was raised of what to do with their secret and confidential political records. Bombay suggested transferring such records from the secretariat to the custody of the Governor of the province. Their argument, in part, in support of the proposal ran as follows:

> These proceedings have taken place in a reserved department working under the Governor in Council, and as such they are the property of the British Government. If such records remain in the Secretariat at the time of the introduction of the new constitution they will become the property of the new Government to be dealt with as it likes. Containing, as they do, much highly confidential correspondence between the Secretary of State, the Government of India and the provincial Government, it can hardly be contemplated that they should be left in a position where they might fall into the hands of Indian politicians. Apart from this danger, however, I am to point out that in the past all officers have dealt freely with political questions on the assumption that what they wrote was for the use only of the Governor in Council in a reserved department, and it would be a breach of the confidence of those officers, especially Indians, to place these records at the disposal of the provincial Government which they will in future have to serve.

The Home Department in Delhi wrote back to Bombay on 12 January 1935 saying in effect that they did not know what the procedure should be, and were therefore seeking the views of other provinces. During the next three to four months the other provincial secretariats sent their views. Typically, the efficient Government of Madras sent their reply first. Also typically, since Madras was 'always suspicious of anything emanating from [Delhi]',[80] they dismissed the matter shortly with the remark that they 'entirely agree with the views of the Government of Bombay'.

All the other provincial governments wrote at length disagreeing with Bombay. Assam agreed that 'there is a certain risk if the future Ministers are allowed access to these records but there will be a much greater risk of imperilling the smooth working of the Reforms by creating a feeling of distrust if these records are withheld'. The Central Provinces stressed the importance of such records for

[80] Trevelyan, H., *Public and Private*, London, 1980, p. 7.

administrative continuity and efficiency, whoever the minister might be, and closed with the argument that '. . . the proposal puts a handicap on the proper development of the new constitution compared with which the divulgence to Ministers of a few secrets is of trifling account'. The Government of Bengal were 'not impressed by the arguments' of Bombay, and rebutted them at length.

A spirited reply came from the Government of Punjab on 9 March:

> Time softens asperities, and a future minister who may chance to read a summary related to himself or his friends will view these documents with a juster perspective than if he had known of them at the time they were written. If he is of a vindictive character, the Governor-in-Council feels that the risk of rousing his enmity must be accepted. Law and order are going to be handed over to the minister. He is going to be responsible for preserving it. At the moment when he assumes this responsibility the Bombay Government propose to move out of his reach the files which contain a record of the general policy of government in regard to subversive movements, of the mistakes made by his predecessors, of the ways in which they corrected their mistakes and the methods which in the end they found efficacious in dealing with a particular situation. The suggestion is not, the Governor-in-Council thinks, practical politics. A minister must have access to all records of Government which will help him to discharge his duties properly. If you refuse a minister this essential assistance, you are simply driving him to evade responsibility and to shelter behind the special responsibility of the Governor.

Bihar and Orissa argued that 'making a success of provincial autonomy lies in the creation of responsibility and self-respect in future ministers, and it is probable that a self-respecting Minister would feel bound to resign if he found himself continuously hedged in when he required information about past decisions of Government'. The United Provinces wrote at length showing why they were also 'unable to accept the proposal' of Bombay. The North-West Frontier Province finally replied on 6 April, objecting to the Bombay proposal as impracticable and wrong in principle. Firstly, they pointed out that it would be necessary to apply it equally to subordinate offices in districts, where most of the correspondence was kept. Secondly, 'The mere fact that the "bureaucracy" had gone to the trouble and expense involved in the proposal, with the sole object of secreting papers from the incoming Ministers would from the start be a source of justifiable grievance to the latter and the general public, and would continue so indefinitely; the new building required to house these secret records would be a perpetual monument of distrust.' Their peroration ran as follows: 'Expressions of opinion lose their sting in the course of time, and the papers concerned will (if left undisturbed) rapidly acquire an exclusively historical interest . . . The Governor-in-Council thinks it would be advisable in such matters to trust from the start in the ministers' good sense, aided if necessary by their oath of office and the Official Secrets Act.'

Back in the Home Department, an ICS Joint Secretary then wrote (27 April) a long note summarizing the points made by the various provincial governments; then, using the traditional 'on the one hand . . . on the other' construction, he gave it as his opinion that the Bombay proposal should not be accepted by the Government of India. A letter to Bombay was then drafted by the Home Secretary and put up for approval to the ICS Home Member (Minister) on 1 May. The Home Member noted on 2 May as follows:

> I have no doubt whatever that the line taken by the majority of the local Governments is correct, and that the view of the Bombay Government on the main question is wrong. The draft letter to Bombay is suitable and may issue . . . I think it would be advisable for the draft letter to Bombay to be sent to all other local Governments, unless Secretary* sees any objections. [*Marginal note: 'no objection'.]
>
> Secretary will observe that . . . I have added a sentence calling attention to the urgency of completing the task of weeding out and destroying confidential records relating to individuals. This was, I think, a point stressed* at the recent Police Conference. [*Marginal note: 'yes'.]

The letter, together with copies of the replies from other provinces, was dispatched to Bombay on 9 May, the main message of which was support for the majority of local governments, for example, 'The British Government have agreed to the transfer of responsibility and it would hardly be consistent to refuse to make the records available to those to whom the responsibility is transferred'. The Government of India went part way, however, to meet the fears of Bombay by agreeing that certain classes of records might, under the new constitution, be kept in the office of the provincial Criminal Investigation Department (CID), or of the Governor, or might be destroyed. Particular attention was drawn to dossiers of revolutionaries and Congress workers, which it was thought might most conveniently be kept in the provincial CID. Attention was also directed to the disposal of correspondence written to or by 'very high officials, in particular those dealing with a few prominent politicians or agitators . . . '; the letter said that there 'should not be very many of these files'. It was urged that the work of weeding out or destroying these classes of records should be completed as soon as possible, in advance of the introduction of provincial autonomy.

Bombay replied at length on 6 June, attempting to rebut the points of their critics in other provinces. They went on to insist that, in view of the fact that the Bombay Province 'is particularly the home of the Congress and the civil disobedience movement', they must take into account the possibility of a Congress government encouraging a civil disobedience movement from within the Government (i.e. as the Ministry) in their desire to wreck the new constitution. They proposed (1) leaving in the secretariat such records dealing with civil disobedience that have already become public property (i.e. records dealing with actual decisions which were taken and the results of which were publicly known and seen), (2) destroying records of 'whence information was obtained and the like', and (3) handing over to the Governor's secretariat 'such records as it is necessary to keep for the purpose of formulating plans for action in the event of civil disobedience being started in the future with the help of the Government of the day'. The view was expressed that many civil servants who had served in Gujarat during civil disobedience, and who had been responsible for placing Congress workers in prison, 'have very definite apprehensions of some action being taken against them' by these same persons when they attain power. In a rejoinder to a remark in the letter from the Punjab Government they claimed that ' "time may soften asperities", but on the other hand the opportunity may merely confirm a vindictive individual in a desire to get his own back. Whether or no His Excellency the Governor will in future be *able* to protect officers from victimization remains to be seen. . . '.

On receiving this letter, an Indian ICS Under Secretary in the Home Department retorted angrily (11 June): 'I submit with all deference that the situation envisaged by the Bombay Government will be so rare that no exception may be made to the general policy suggested in . . . Secretary's demi-official letter dated 9th May 1935.' The Home Secretary noted smoothly the same day:

> . . . it is doubtful of course as Under Secretary suggests whether the contingency envisaged by Bombay will arise, but as it may arise, we may agree to the precautions suggested. His excellency Lord Brabourne [Bombay Governor] mentioned this matter when he was here and we are prepared to accept this special procedure for Bombay where probably possible measures against civil disobedience were discussed more freely than in other provinces where the movement was less intense.

The Home Member saw the file the same day and concurred with the decision of the Home Secretary. The reply went to Bombay on 19 June, which read in effect that the Government of India's suggested procedure 'need not be strictly followed'. The file closes with this letter.

The summary of this particular file illustrates more general characteristics of the method and content of policy making in secretariats. As for method, one notices how ICS men even in a single secretariat department, when 'talking' to each other on files, could disagree on what the correct policy line ought to be. Policy making within the raj was rarely a simple and straightforward undertaking. Frequently there was uncertainty in the minds of the ICS men as to how best to serve imperial interests when making policy choices. In the end, within a secretariat department, the Secretary's view normally was decisive. Bombay got its way on the whole, despite most other provinces and the Home Department in Delhi being critical of Bombay's approach to the problem. The actual decision reached in the case here was a bit of a muddled compromise—a not uncommon outcome.

As for content, it is impossible to generalize on the basis of a single example, quite apart from the impossibility of providing a summary statement of all the detailed policy positions taken by ICS men on the myriad issues coming before them. The impossible is not attempted here. What can be done is to indicate two broad features affecting policy content, the results of which are evident in the file summarized above, the various files referred to later in Chapter 2 on recruitment policies throughout the 1920s and 1930s, and in other Government files available in the relevant archives. Firstly, there was the general constraint within which policy was worked out of guide-lines laid down by the imperial power in London. The policy discussions summarized above, for example, suggest that senior ICS men considered themselves bound to ensure the successful working of the new 1935 Constitution once the British Parliament had ruled that this was the direction the raj was to take. The Bombay Government's proposals appeared wrong to most other ICS men involved in the discussions because they would hamper 'responsible' government by popularly elected ministries. The coming of such ministries was hardly regarded with delight by senior ICS men, for they seemed to represent a threat to their own position; but that narrower interest had to give way to the general policy guide-line of the state. If the state ruled that the ICS should commit decorous suicide, then that is what the ICS would do. For they were, above all, civil *servants* working under general direction from above. The existence of this broad constraint on policy making helps to explain why senior ICS men in most provinces had by the mid-1930s a rather more positive attitude towards the impending constitutional changes and increased democratization than one might have expected.

Secondly, within that broad imperial constraint, the contents of policy deliberations were affected by ICS calculations of likely political consequences locally. The content of the policy discussions summarized above makes clear that, even within a 'reserved' subject under dyarchy, the political implications of the problem are apparently to the fore in the minds of the ICS men who dealt with the issue. For example, the Bombay Government was worried about the continuing support of their subordinate officials who feared 'victimization'. The Punjab Government regarded the Bombay Government proposals as not 'practical politics', that is, they were indefensible in the face of probable criticism by ministers and powerful groups in Punjab society behind such ministries, and any attempts on their part to implement them would, amongst other things, weaken their authority. This motiviation in policy discussions to move to defensible ground politically appears regularly in government files; a number of other examples are reported in Chapter 2. Broadly speaking, ICS work in the secretariat—be it advising a minister, passing orders on important policy issues, or even approving routine business governed by precedent—required amongst other things constant use of political antennae. As in the district, so also in the secretariat: ICS men were political administrators.

NORMS AND VALUES: THE SERVICE CLASS

The purpose of this and the following section is to identify the ICS Europeans collectively as gentlemen of the service class. The reason for concentrating on this particular aspect of identity is that it leads straight to central norms and values in the ICS tradition which had important administrative consequences. (A norm is a standard of behaviour to which members of a group are expected to conform; for example, an ICS man believed he should act courageously in the face of danger.) The ICS tradition contained a large and complex set of interrelated norms and values. Three were powerful service-class values; others were essential attributes of that complex character—the

English gentleman. ICS Indians as gentleman of the service class are considered in the next chapter, and take over in subsequent chapters.

The designation 'ICS European' (as distinct from 'ICS Indian') is a curious, old-fashioned category. It is used here because it follows the practice of government files cited below and copes easily with anomalies like Arthur Mario Agricola Collier Galletti Di Cadhilhac (ICS, Madras), Italian by birth but educated at Cheltenham and Trinity, Oxford. Galletti was an exception, for nearly all ICS Europeans were born in Britain. Most of them were English. In saying this, I recognize that there are well-known problems in certifying a man as either English, or Scots, or Irish, or Welsh. To identify place of birth hardly solves the problem for some Scotsmen were born in England, some Englishmen were born in India, and so on. Place of schooling probably gives the nearest approximation to national identity, although it is far from satisfactory. My classification of the schools of 688 ICS Europeans working in India in 1939 shows that 564 were English (and Welsh), 84 Scots and 37 Irish.[81] The figures may understate the number of ICS men who would unreservedly identify themselves as from Scotland—about 12 per cent of the total. A few Scots went south, but then a few people born in England also went north. Certainly there *seemed* to be more than 84 Scots in the ICS—one Governor was able apparently to stock his secretariat entirely with Scotsmen, 'save for one man whose name was Gordon'.[82]

ICS Europeans were in no doubt about their own class location. They identified themselves as 'upper-middle class'. 'It was that class and not the aristocracy', says Moon, 'that was the mainstay of the British Raj and was largely responsible for its character.'[83] 'We brought with us (to India) almost exact replicas of the sort of life that upper middle class people lived in England,' remarked Lady Birdwood; 'it was very homogenous in the sense that nearly everyone in official India sprang precisely from the same educational and cultural background.'[84]

Actually this self-categorization is too neat. Although the dominant element in the ICS was from professional and service families during

[81] The figures are based on the author's classification of individual biographical entries for each of 688 ICS Europeans listed in *The India Office and Burma Office List, 1940*, excluding all those listed who had retired by 1939.

[82] Hubback Papers, Cambridge Archive, TS pp. 67–8.

[83] Moon, P., in *Wavell*, p. 463.

[84] Cited in Allen, C. (ed.), *Plain Tales from the Raj: Images of British India in the Twentieth Century*, London, 1975, p. 72. Lady Birdwood was the daughter of Sir George Ogilvie (Indian Political Service); her ancestors had served in India since 1765.

the period, upwardly mobile people were also steadily entering from a lower class. Evidence on the occupations of the fathers of ICS Europeans supports this point. A reasonable indicator of upper-middle class background includes the upper reaches of the Home Civil Service and Civil Service in India, officers in the Army and Navy, the medical profession, the clergy, the law, university academics, and management levels in the business world (including the world of finance and publishing). Classifying the actual occupations of real people, which do not fall neatly into general categories, always involves some rough judgements, but after studying a number of lists of ICS fathers' occupations, it appears to me that 65–70 per cent of ICS recruits in the period 1919–41 came from that background, the percentage dropping somewhat towards the end. Since no more than 39 ICS Europeans were recruited each year after 1920,[85] the percentages fluctuate wildly from year to year.

Approaching the question of ICS identity by means of social background can be informative, but it has its limitations. It rests on the initial assumption that an adult can be identified, interpreted, and understood in terms of some original sin of family or school background. Certainly social background was important, but an ICS man was also powerfully shaped by living as an adult in India. Anyone who has read autobiographical accounts of careers in the ICS is forced to the conclusion that there was an identity that ICS men in India shared, regardless of whether they came from a wealthy family and public school or a comparatively poor family and a county secondary school. However elevated or humble their social origins, all ICS men moved into the top of the service class.

The designation of 'service class' is used here in preference to 'upper-middle class'. There are a number of reasons why the latter notion is unsatisfactory. The principal one is that it normally forms part of a threefold scheme—upper-middle class, lower-middle class, working class—based on occupational and status differences, which is clear enough but is vague about (or ignores) classes or agencies *above* the 'upper-middle class'. Yet it is precisely in this area, in the higher reaches of the class structure, that clarity is needed in order to perceive the social identity of the ICS in relation to the imperial power. The idea of a service class, first put forward by Renner in 1953, and subsequently developed by Goldthorpe and others, offers a much

[85] See tables in Chapter 2 on ICS recruitment.

more fruitful approach.[86] For Renner, the service class is made up broadly of administrators, managers, and professional employees, in both the public and private sectors of the economy. On this basis ICS men were in the service class in view of their occupation. The crucial point about such service-class people is that they are not part of either the capitalist class or the landed class, for they do not share in the ownership of capital or land; nor are they part of the working class or the peasantry, for their labour is non-productive in the sense that instead of being a source of surplus value their labour is paid for from the surplus value extracted, directly or indirectly, from the working class and the peasantry. In other words, they are salaried employees working *for* other more dominant classes or agents. This way of looking at the ICS, as part of the service class, brings us to the first major trait that all ICS men shared: they were Indian civil *servants*. Their position in the class structure made nonsense of any claim that they ruled India independently. Being a servant was an integral part of their identity.

Renner's major contribution, however, was to specify the relationships between the service class and other classes. Starting with the terms and conditions of working-class employment—having to provide labour in exchange for wages on a relatively short-term basis—and comparing that with the terms and conditions of service-class employment—providing labour in exchange for a salary on a long-term basis, plus career prospects, security of tenure, etc., Renner arrives at the important principle that lies behind these differences: there is an element of *trust* in the latter relationship which is lacking in the former. The employers repose trust in their servants, providing them with distinctive (and distinctively favourable) terms and conditions of employment in the expectation that they will act in ways that are consistent with the interests and values of their organizations. This idea leads to a second major point about ICS collective identity: they were trusted servants of the state, identifying themselves far more closely with the values and interests of those who employed them than with workers or peasants or other classes beneath them. Those who employed them, who stood over the ICS, so to speak, owed their

[86] Renner, K., *Wandlungen der modernen Gesellschaft: Zwei Abhandlugen Uber die Probleme der Nachkreigszeit*, Vienna, 1953, as translated in part, and discussed, in Bottomore, T. and Goode, P. (eds.), *Austro Marxism*, Oxford, 1978, and in Goldthorpe, J., 'On the Service Class, its Formation and Future', in Giddens, A. and Mackenzie, G. (eds.), *Social Class and the Division of Labour*, Cambridge, 1982, pp. 162–85. I rely primarily on Goldthorpe's discussion of Renner's work in subsequent references to Renner.

position to their own power, based on their political success in occupying the commanding heights of the state. The ICS, in contrast, had no independent base of power; they owed their position to appointment by the British state as trusted servants of that state. This was also integral to who the ICS were. It would not have occurred to them to stand forth as independent rulers. They could not because they had no independent base of power. Nor could they break faith, snap the trust reposed in them.

The reason why those who occupy the commanding heights of the state need trusted servants, according to Renner, is because the state and other organizations in modern society are too large to be controlled directly in a detailed way from the top. Control of any large organization must, therefore, be delegated, diffused. The important consequence is that those administrators, managers, and professionals to whom control is delegated acquire an area of relative *autonomy* and discretion within the organization. They must have that in order to make the decisions and professional judgements required of them. They can have it because they can be trusted to choose and judge in ways that are consistent with the interests and values of the organization. These conditions lead to the third main point about ICS European identity. Consistent with their location in the service class, they expected considerable independence and freedom of manœuvre within the state structure to choose and act as they thought best. They expected it as a right, because the bond of trust had been conferred upon them. There was thus a tendency to resent invasions of their autonomy and freedom, as somehow calling into question the bond of trust. An ICS man took it for granted that he could step to some extent outside the rules that bound other civil servants so tightly. Considerable independence, even eccentricity, was allowed; it was part of being a trusted servant. This independent cum servant combination is illustrated in the story,[87] probably apocryphal, of the ICS Collector in the Central Provinces who replied to distasteful orders from his superior in the secretariat with the splendid retort:

> Your letter of the . . . instant, which is before me, will shortly be behind me in another capacity. I am, Sir, your most obedient servant.

Having some autonomy, or area of discretion, within an organization is a general characteristic of service-class life. In the case of the ICS

[87] Noronha, R. P. (ICS, CP), *A Tale Told by an Idiot*, New Delhi, 1976, p. 63.

however, the relative autonomy concerned was very pronounced. It had to be. The leadership of the state was far away in London. They knew little of the details of Indian life and the working of the raj and normally relied on the expertise of their trusted servants to rule the country on their behalf. Because, in the circumstances of imperial rule, the autonomy granted was so extensive, the amount of trust that went with it was large indeed. For this responsibility, quite exceptional rewards were provided. The salary and career opportunities, the security of tenure, and provision for retirement (even on proportionate pension) were extraordinarily advantageous as compared to those for other civil servants. These characteristics combined to place the ICS at the very top of the service class. Any young man, shaped to the ICS, came in course of time to take for granted his very elevated position as a servant of the imperial state *par excellence* in India.

Given their elevated position, it would seem to follow that ICS men would be powerfully motivated to use their considerable authority and knowledge to preserve their advantaged position and the special privileges that went with it, inclining them to a conservative disposition with a substantial stake in the status quo. As a general statement of class interest, this is undeniable. But it must never be forgotten that the specific locus of this conservatism was the service relationship. If the state shifted direction, then the trusted servants (even if they advised against it) ultimately went with it. Their conservatism did not imply necessarily any intrinsic commitment beyond that to capitalism or even to the continuation of British rule in India. Most ICS were able to make the adjustments to changing constitutional arrangements imposed in India by the British Parliament during the twentieth century. Sir William Marris (ICS, UP), for example, is reported to have told the Secretary of State for India (E. S. Montagu) as early as 1917 that 'The Indian Civil Servants were very sorry that their day was done; recognized that it was inevitable and were willing to go ahead'[88]—a wholly appropriate remark from a trusted servant of the state.

The relationship of trust and the conservative orientation within it was basic. But it did not mean that ICS men had no political views, nor that they always agreed with government policy. There is extensive evidence to show that a wide range of views on the constitutional reforms emanating from London were held by ICS men, and that these

[88] Mason, *The Guardians*, p. 220.

views changed over time. In the course of thirty-eight years (1909–47) a series of decisions from London rained down on India, resulting in the Viceroy's powers under Parliament gradually being made over entirely. One gets the impression from the sources that before the First World War few in the ICS thought much about the political future of India. Yet this was not entirely so. Skrine (ICS, UP) vividly recalls arriving as a fresh ICS recruit in 1911 and being vetted by senior colleagues at the club bar in Allahabad. 'Do you mean to say your father was in the ICS and let you come out here? How extraordinary! We'll have handed over power to the Indians long before you reach the top.'[89]

There is no doubt, however, that the first big jolt came with the Montagu–Chelmsford reforms embodied in the Government of India Act, 1919. There was considerable hostility. Lothian (ICS, Bengal) claims that the reforms were forced through 'against the all but unanimous opposition of those on whom would fall the burden of putting them into operation';[90] and Kincaid (ICS, Bombay) spoke for a number of people who had long family associations with India when he said that he believed at the time, and continued to believe afterwards, that the reforms 'would ruin the Indian Empire which my ancestors had helped to create', adding that 'had the ICS been united, it could possibly have saved the situation, but nothing shocked me more than the way in which the senior members rushed to sell themselves in the hope of obtaining high office'.[91] On the other hand, Maconochie (ICS, Bombay) claims that 'from the first the Service accepted the Reforms . . .'.[92] Both Maconochie and Lothian claimed to speak for the Service as a whole, but of course they did not. Some were very negative, some very positive, and many others held a variety of other cautious positions in the middle. Hubback (ICS, Bihar and Orissa) remembers in 1918 opening the Montagu–Chelmsford Reform document 'one morning at

[89] Skrine was impressed with this gloomy cynicism, contrary to his own expectations when going out to India, 'otherwise I would not remember the conversation as vividly as I do'. Skrine, C., *World War in Iran*, London, 1962, pp. xvi–xvii.

[90] Lothian, A. C., *Kingdoms of Yesterday*, London, 1951, p. 197.

[91] Kincaid, C. A., *Forty-Four Years a Public Servant*, Edinburgh, 1934, pp. 208–9. His father was a General at the time of the mutiny, his son and father-in-law were both ICS; his mother's family were also connected with India, including her uncle who was killed during the mutiny, along with his three daughters who were butchered and flung down the Cawnpore well. For similar views of the Reforms, see the critique by a number of ICS men from Central Provinces in Barker, E., *The Future Government of India and the Indian Civil Service*, London, 1919.

[92] Maconochie, E., *Life in the Indian Civil Service*, London, 1926, p. 4.

breakfast, and finding the word "Ministers" which seemed to me rather alarming at first sight'.[93] And Mansfield (ICS, Bihar and Orissa) reacted to the reports of the Reforms in the *Statesman*, when writing home to his parents in 1920, with this remark: 'the more I read the more I feel interested in the future of India . . . I only hope crusted officials in Simla and elsewhere won't do their best to make the reforms a fallacy and a farce . . .'.[94] Whatever their particular view of the Reforms, most ICS Europeans probably shared the general belief expressed by Pullan (ICS, UP) that 'in the early 1920s no one dreamed of an independent India'.[95]

Almost immediately, however, came the next big jolt—the Lee Commission report of 1924. This made clear that Indianization of the services would be pursued in earnest. 'Most officials then sensed', reports Masterman (ICS, Madras), 'that the British raj would eventually end . . . but in a remote future beyond our lifetime.' Then came the new constitution embodied in the Government of India Act 1935, when 'everyone realized that Indian independence was inevitable, and only a matter of years ahead. There were many shades of opinion as to whether this was a good thing or a bad thing but generally speaking I do not think we resented it, certainly not the younger officials.'[96] Wingate (ICS, Punjab) says that ICS men in the 1930s 'almost without exception were in favour of self-government for India',[97] as does Symington (ICS, Bombay and Sind): in 1930 'the great majority in the Service . . . were not at all opposed to the idea of Indian independence', and 'even thought it was intrinsically desirable'.[98] Hume, on the other hand, told his parents in a letter home in 1932 of an ICS dinner in Lucknow at which Sir Malcolm Hailey (ICS, UP) made a speech commenting on the forthcoming reforms: 'Old Malcolm was a bit wind-baggy and poured forth fine oratory to the effect that we should pass away with honour and in the best traditions of the Service; to which I, and I think many others felt like saying, "It's all very fine for you old codgers who have flung your fling and are doomed to 'die' in any case in a year or two, but you seem to forget that there are others of us who are not at all prepared to 'die' nobly or otherwise just yet."'[99]

[93] Hubback Papers, TS p. 143.

[94] Mansfield Papers, Cambridge Archive, letter of 4.1.1920.

[95] Pullan Papers, Cambridge Archive, TS (written in 1947) p. 20.

[96] Masterman Papers, paper 8f: answers to questions put to him by Dr C. Bayly, p. 11.

[97] Wingate, R., *Lord Ismay: A Biography*, London, 1970, p. 131.

[98] Symington, D. (pseud. James Halliday), *A Special India*, London, 1968, p. 53.

[99] Hume Papers, IOL MSS Eur. D.724/4, vol. 4, letter dated 7.2.1932.

Indian constitutional reforms emanating from London were obviously important to ICS men; they read about such developments in their newspapers or elsewhere with interest, and held views about what was taking place 'above them', so to speak. But the essentials of their class position *vis-à-vis* those 'above them' was that, as trusted servants, they dutifully carried on even if they held critical views about the direction of state policy in London. For they had entered into a covenant. They were under a bond of trust to their rulers.

Summing up the ICS class position in relation to those above them, it has been suggested that three attributes were important—indeed, were so central to the ICS collective identity that they were taken largely for granted. Firstly, ICS men were *servants* of the imperial power in London; secondly, they had a special relationship of *trust* with that power; and thirdly, within that relationship, they were given considerable *autonomy* and discretion to act appropriately in Indian circumstances. These attributes derived from their position at the very top of the service class. However humble his social origins, an ICS man eventually went to the very top *in India*. This distinctive feature of colonial rule, which was not true of the service class in Britain, was noticed by a very wealthy and superior man from England one evening in the 1930s at Government House, Ootacamund, when he remarked: 'I cannot help thinking that these (ICS) people who go into dinner ahead of me are the wretched people who put up little bungalows round my place in Hampshire.'[100]

From that elevated vantage point in India, the ICS view in the other direction—down, in relation to subordinate groups and classes—was rather different. There was a standard formulation of that downward view held by ICS men in all the provinces of British India. Symington provides a succinct summary. 'It is true that, broadly speaking, we [the ICS] were not fond of the middle classes, especially the shopkeepers, money lenders, produce brokers, most of the pleaders (a grotesquely overgrown profession), many landlords, and the parasites who hung about the village in the guise of political workers; we objected to their ruthless and unceasing exploitation of the poor and the ignorant, the small holders, the landless labourers, the industrial workers.' He also quotes with approval K. M. Panikkar: 'They [the ICS] developed a common tradition . . . and a general attitude towards India . . . True, it was not the India of the Indians, but a special India of their own

[100] Trevelyan, H., *The India We Left*, London, 1972, p. 112.

conception. They visualized it as a country whose millions of inhabitants were entrusted to their care.'[101] 'Not fond' of the middle classes, a concern for the teeming millions of poor and ignorant peasants and workers, and a conception of all of India as being 'entrusted to their care' encapsulates the general ICS Europeans' view of groups and classes beneath them in Indian society.

It is an unusual view for people in the service class to hold. For the theory of the service class advanced by Renner and others suggests that the main line of conflict runs between these trusted servants of the state and the thrusting demands of labouring classes produced by the structural contradictions of capitalism, which threaten the position of the service class and the dominant classes they serve. Such a theory may well be appropriate to the characteristic situation of a more fully developed capitalist society; indeed, Renner's interest lay essentially in that direction. In India, however, in the period which concerns us (at least up to the 1930s), the industrial workers were slowly gaining in importance in the Indian economy, but were not yet the thrusting and mobilized class of major consequence suggested by Renner; nor was India's massive but largely inert peasantry mobilized at this time (although Gandhi's influence began moves in that direction between the wars). The main line of cleavage ran, instead, between the colonial state (containing service-class groups) allied generally with indigenous landed classes, and the indigenous 'middle strata', those engaged in trade, commerce, and industry and in the legal and other professions, who were mobilized to some extent in the Indian National Congress. Therefore, when Symington and other ICS Europeans said that 'we were not fond of the middle classes', this important identifying trait can be explained in terms of their service-class positions in the class structure of colonial rule. Indigenous business and trading classes, and other middle strata posed far more of an immediate threat to the interests of the ICS than did workers or peasants. Expressive of these particular class alignments in India, was the 'up front' political struggle between the raj and the Congress or other nationalist political forces in Bengal and elsewhere.

If class position and political interest combined to help to sort out for an ICS gentleman who was friend and who was foe, the same combination of forces offered no guide to ICS relations with other groupings *within the colonial state*. How, then, did they identify

[101] Symington, *A Special India*, pp. 97–8.

themselves in relation to other service-class sections of the state in India? Within-class distinctions of this kind have always been difficult to make. Renner suggests that such distinctions within the service class, although difficult, are in principle possible on the dimension of more or less trust reposed in a section. Those who have secure and well-rewarded career structures within the service class may have a distinct identity as compared to those who are less secure and less well rewarded. On this dimension, as it happens, ICS identity within the state was very distinct: they were members of one of the Secretary of State's services, exceptionally secure and well rewarded. There were only four other such services between the wars.[102] None of the others had this special identity. This arrangement, peculiar to imperial rule, tended to set up a conflict of interest between the ICS, who wanted to retain their special identity, and other services within the state.

Finally, a word about ICS identity in relation to those whom Symington referred to above as 'the poor and the ignorant, the small holders, the landless labourers, the industrial workers'. This formed part of what Panikkar called that 'special India' in the minds of ICS Europeans, which included those millions 'entrusted to their care'. Once again, that conception of India in the minds of ICS men came from a combination of class position and political interest. As long as peasants (and industrial workers) were not effectively mobilized, they posed less of an immediate threat to the interests of the ICS than the other indigenous classes. The notion of a 'special India' of the 'poor and ignorant' entrusted to their care flowed easily from the gentlemanly mode of thought and valuation. That many ICS Europeans unselfishly devoted their lives to serving this 'special India' is certainly true; it is no less true that such a conception of service operated within a larger framework of class and interest.

NORMS AND VALUES: THE GENTLEMANLY MODE

Who was, or is, a gentleman? The last person to ask, I'm told, is a gentleman, for no gentleman would think of asking the question, let alone answering it. So ICS memoirs cannot help me and I must seek help from others.[103] It seems that one of the best ways to begin to get to

[102] More precisely, from 1924: the Indian Police Service, the civil branch of the Indian Medical Service, the irrigation branch of the Indian Service of Engineers, and the Indian Forest Service (except in the provinces of Bombay and Burma).

[103] When I realized that the gentlemanly mode was central to the tradition of

the heart of the gentlemanly mode is to examine the culture of the English public school—those 'factories for gentlemen'.[104] The best identifier of an English gentleman was someone who had been to a public school, and having been to Oxford or Cambridge also helped. So one needs first to establish the ICS—public school connection, then identify certain cultural characteristics of the schools that helped to shape the young men who attended them, and then indicate the extent to which this gentlemanly mode was modified by the circumstances of life at the top of the service class in India.

The first problem in establishing a connection between ICS Europeans and a public school education is that there is no generally accepted definition of a public school in the extensive literature on the subject. The one used here is the least provocative: a public school is one that belongs to the Headmasters' Conference and consequently is listed in the *Public Schools Yearbook*. In 1914 there were 113 such schools, in 1939 there were 188.[105] Virtually all of these schools were in England. Scotland, Ireland, and Wales had rather different (and more progressive) state school systems. Since the majority of ICS Europeans in India up until the mid-1930s had been to school prior to 1914, the data in Table 4 have been extended to cover all ICS Europeans working in India from 1914 to 1942, including 217 who retired between 1930 and 1939 (but excluding those who retired before 1930).

The main point that comes from Table 4 is that if you met an ICS European in India between the wars who did not have a Scots or Irish accent, you could be nearly certain that he had attended a public school (especially if he was an older man). A note on the Scots and the Irish: of the 136 Scots altogether, 36 attended three (of the five in 1939) Scottish public schools: George Watsons', Edinburgh Academy, Fettes; the others came from 37 of the best grammar schools, high schools, and academies in the land. As for the 55 Irish, 19 came from

administration the British brought out to India, it took me a long time trying to understand it. In the end this account in the next few paragraphs owes most to the following: Williams, R., *Culture and Society, 1780–1950*, Harmondsworth, 1958; Wilkinson, R., *Gentlemanly Power*, London, 1964; Mason, P., *The English Gentleman*, London, 1982; Letwin, S., 'The Morality of the Gentleman', *Cambridge Review*, xcviii (7 May 1976), 141–5, (4 June 1976), 168–73; Raven, S., *The English Gentleman*, 1961; Mannheim, K., *An Introduction to the Sociology of Education*, London, 1962, pp. 40–3; Hampden-Turner, C., *Gentlemen and Tradesmen: The Values of Economic Catastrophe*, London, 1983.

[104] Mason, *English Gentleman*, p. 161.

[105] *Public Schools Yearbook, 1914* (London), and *Public and Preparatory Schools 1939* (London). I have used these two sources in the classifications that follow.

Table 4. *ICS Europeans: Schools Background*

Schools attended	Number and per cent of ICS Europeans			
	Those who entered ICS in 1914 and before		Those who entered ICS after 1914	
	No. of ICS	Per cent	No. of ICS	Per cent
English public schools	354	68	333	64
Other schools (England and Wales)	38	7	81	16
Scots and Irish schools	110	21	71	14
No information	19	4	31	6
Totals	521	100	516	100

Sources: The data are based on the author's classification of individual biographical entries for each of 1,037 ICS Europeans listed in *The India Office and Burma Office List, 1940* (excluding those listed who retired before 1930) together with the 1940 and 1941 ICS Europeans data in NAI Home Dept. File 35/38/41—Ests., 1941 'Appointments to the ICS on Probation in 1940', and Home Dept. File 32/41—Ests., 1941 'Results of the ICS Selection in England in 1941'.

just three schools—Campbell College (Belfast), Clongories Wood College, and Dublin High School; the other 36 came from 21 other schools and academies up and down Ireland.[106] Table 4 shows a decline in Scottish and Irish representation in the ICS during the period. As for those in the 'no information' category, they were spread fairly evenly between the other categories.

Turning now to the bulk of ICS Europeans from public and other schools in England (and Wales and elsewhere), we find that 795 came from 225 different schools. For those 414 who entered the ICS after 1914, the 30 most popular schools are listed in Table 5 in rank order; together they produced 222 ICS men—that is, more than half the total.

Several points emerge from the list of what one might call the top half of the draw. Firstly, all are public schools. Secondly, many of the leading public schools are there; in fact, all but eight are what one authority for the 1930s referred to as 'Great Public Schools'.[107] Thirdly, only seven schools produced more than ten ICS men during

[106] In 1914 only Campbell College, Belfast, was a Public School; by 1939 there were three. As for Scotland, in 1914 there were three Public Schools; in 1939 only two more had been added.

[107] Webster, F. A. M., *Our Great Public Schools*, London, 1937. The work consists of histories of 36 schools.

Table 5. *ICS Europeans: Most Popular Schools*

Rugby	20	Bradfield	6
Winchester	15	Radley	6
Wellington	13	St Olave's Grammar School	6
Charterhouse	10	Epsom	5
Cheltenham	10	Malvern	5
Haileybury	10	Merchant Taylors	5
Marlborough	10	Rossall	5
Christs Hospital	9	Shrewsbury	5
Dulwich	9	Westminster	5
Clifton	8	City of London	4
Uppingham	8	Kingswood (Bath)	4
Bradford Grammar School	7	Manchester Grammar School	4
Eton	7	Oundle	4
St Paul's	7	Sedburgh	4
Bedford	6	Tonbridge	4
		Number of ICS (1915–41)	222

Source: Same as for Table 4 above.

the entire period; in other words, most of these schools in any decade were producing ICS men in ones or twos, not in bunches.

The third point swells to major proportions upon turning to consider the other half of the draw, those who came after 1914. The scatter of schools is even more marked: 182 men came from as many as 141 schools. Of these 66 were public schools producing 71 ICS; the other 75 schools, which produced 111 ICS, were a mixed bag of private, grammar, modern, and post-primary schools or their equivalents run by Local Education Authorities. Some of these 'other' schools were in Wales. State secondary education was only very slowly being established during this period in England. When the Hadow Plan came out in 1926, for example, only about ten per cent of children over the age of eleven were receiving any form of secondary school education; by 1938 the figure had risen to 65 per cent.[108] Thus, in the 1920s most of the 'other' schools were private or grammar school emulators of the public schools; in the 1930s the state schools began to figure somewhat more prominently in ICS recruitment.

Turning now to those 392 ICS men in Table 4 who entered before the First World War, the public school dominance is extremely pronounced. Indeed, only 15 'Great Public Schools' produced more

[108] Bernard, H. C., *The History of English Higher Education*, London, 1947, pp. 235–7. See also, for slightly different figures which none the less suggest the same picture, Mowat, C., *Britain between the Wars 1918–1940* London, 1956, pp. 206–7.

than half (201)—St Paul's (26), Clifton (18), Winchester (18), Charterhouse (16), Marlborough (15), Rugby (14), Cheltenham (12), Dulwich (12), Eton (12), Harrow (11), Malvern (11), Merchant Taylors (11), Westminster (10), Bradfield (8), Haileybury (7). All the rest come from other public schools, except 38 (from 37 'other' schools).

Table 6. *ICS Europeans (England and Wales): Schools Background Classified by Years of Recruitment*

	Per cent of ICS men who attended		
Period of recruitment to ICS (and number of ICS)	'Great' public schools	Other public schools	'Other' schools
up to 1914 (n = 392)	66	24	10
1915–24 (n = 102)	55	34	11
1925–35 (n = 196)	43	37	20
1936–41 (n = 106)	50	30	20

Source: Same as for Table 4 above.

All the data çan now be brought together and the changing proportions shown across the entire period, as in Table 6. Clearly there was some change in school background during the period. The data in Table 6 show that the proportion from 'Great Public Schools' faded somewhat, while those coming from 'other' schools increased. But the main point is that, if you exclude the Scots and the Irish, well over *80 per cent* of the ICS Europeans in India between the wars had attended a public school. Experience of public school life is thus a major identifying feature of ICS men from England and Wales. The data also show that there were always more Englishmen from 'Great Public Schools' than from the other public schools.

It was shown in Table 4 that roughly one-fifth of the ICS Europeans were probably Scots or Irish, although their representation declined somewhat during the period. I want now to join all the ICS Europeans together again, and note one further point about them: the number and spread of schools involved was very large. It was extremely rare for more than one ICS European to have attended the same school at the same time—the most pronounced instance of bunching appears to have been the case of St Olave's Grammar School, London, from which six ICS men came in five years in the latter part of the 1920s.

Furthermore, the 'spread' of schools became more pronounced as the importance of 'Great Public Schools' declined.

Before relating these findings forward to gentlemanly culture, the analysis of educational background needs to be rounded off by looking briefly at the data on universities, set out in Table 7. There are no surprises here. Roughly 76 per cent of ICS Europeans attended either Oxford or Cambridge; no change is evident during the period (except as between the two universities). The Scots and Irish representation declines, consistent with their declining schools representation, the difference being picked up mainly by London and the 'Redbrick' Universities.

Table 7. *ICS Europeans: University Background*

University	Number & per cent of ICS Europeans			
	Those who entered ICS in 1914 and before		Those who entered ICS after 1914	
	Number	Per cent	Number	Per cent
Oxford	244	47	214	41
Cambridge	150	29	180	35
Scots University	68	13	40	8
Irish University	35	7	19	4
Other	20	4	46	9
None mentioned	4	1	17	3
Totals	521	100	516	100

Source: Same as for Table 4 above.

As regards Oxford and Cambridge colleges, there is no significant bunching at either university. At Oxford, Christ Church and Balliol produced the most, Lincoln and St Edmund Hall the least; at Cambridge, Corpus, King's and St John's produced the most, Clare and Fitzwilliam the least. All colleges produced at least one during the entire period, and recruitment was spread widely around the colleges in different years. The only bunching I could find was at Oxford, seven ICS Europeans coming from Balliol in the six-year period 1919–24, and another seven from Christ Church; and, at Cambridge, seven coming from King's in the five-year period 1925–9.

Trawling the data for other possible bunching, I found none. Did men from certain colleges later bunch in certain Indian provinces? No. Did ICS men from certain schools later bunch in certain provinces?

The only instances I could find were Rugby and Wellington, from which nearly half went on to the Punjab. In both cases, however, the take from these schools was spread fairly evenly across the period.

These negative findings actually serve to underline again a major fact about the school and university background of ICS Europeans: they came from a large number of schools, primarily in ones and twos in any decade. Even within the dominant ICS educational pattern of public school followed by Oxford or Cambridge, the spread of schools and colleges was extensive. The data, therefore, render dubious any claim that significant networks within the ICS had already been formed on the basis of a shared experience at a particular school or college. Many ICS Europeans entered the service essentially as loners. Their networks, friendships, and enmities were formed later.

Although many entered as loners from different schools and colleges which had different traditions and practices (even public schools differed from each other more than is commonly supposed; for example, some gave prefects far more autonomy than others), they all, or nearly all, entered knowing the gentlemanly mode to be a standard of right conduct. For the gentlemanly mode was utterly dominant at public school. And although many public school boys were never gentlemen, those that entered gentlemanly occupations run by gentlemen made that mode they knew so well their own. Even then, not all boys accepted it without reservation, but they did accept it as a standard. The position was roughly similar for those few ICS Europeans who had been to an 'other' school, primarily after the First World War. Many of these were grammar schools which 'tended more than ever to model themselves on the public schools, and to seek admission to the Headmasters' Conference'.[109] Scots and Irish schools hardly produced English gentlemen, but they did produce men who subscribed to what can be identified broadly as a gentlemanly mode of thought and valuation. And it is this mode which concerns us here.

Simon Raven sums up the main features of the gentlemanly mode.[110] A gentleman was 'an agent of justice and effective action, having the fairness and the thoroughness to examine facts and the integrity to act on his findings'. He had 'much regard for the old loyalties—to country, to kinsmen, to Church—and as a guardian of such institutions, and no less to assist him in his other duties, he saw fit to adopt a grave and somewhat aloof attitude of mind which was

[109] Ogilvie, V., *The English Public School*, London, 1957, p. 198.
[110] Raven, S., *English Gentleman*, pp. 58–9.

matched by dignified demeanour and a superior, though not ostentatious, style of maintenance'. Rule and administration 'were among the many obligations on which his honour was based'. 'According to this notion of honour, he was bound, not only by such commonplace rules of decency as chivalry to women and charity to the poor, but by direct and imperative. necessity to pay for his privileges by rendering service—service to his Sovereign and his superiors in office, service to his dependents, service to his Church.' He also, however, 'set store by his freedom; if he met his obligations it was because honour bade him do so, not because any absolute authority compelled him'. And, 'as his position required, he had pleasing manners intended to reassure his inferiors and to show the proper respect, free of any hint of servility, to those above him'.

One major feature of the gentlemanly mode which stands out in Raven's account is of special interest here—the identification of *public service* as *morally virtuous*. A gentleman was bound to render service both to his superiors and to his dependents—a norm which justifies perfectly the work of administators as *trusted servants* in a *service class*. At the same time, one notices a powerful sense of hierarchy built into this conception of public service. Raymond Williams points out that public service 'has been the charter of many thousands of devoted lives', but 'the real personal unselfishness', which ratified the idea of service, can be said to have existed 'within a larger selfishness' of existing unequal distributions of wealth, power, and prestige.[111] Since the charter existed within this 'larger selfishness', the people who came to live by the charter were not only virtuous, they also considered themselves to be morally *superior*—hence the gentleman's traditional assumption that his private privileges naturally went with his performance of public service for the community.

Public or community service and superior status were linked together in the culture of the public schools. When a rugger player won his 'colours', he was honoured for his contribution to the 'House' or 'School', less for his individual or private ability. Team-work was rewarded with praise, reverence for the tradition of the school community was emphasized in church or chapel and other ceremonies, and individual eccentricity was sat upon (at least in the traditional Victorian public schools). A gentleman who had been to public school and then gone into the civil service knew deep down that he was

[111] Williams, *Culture and Society*, p. 315.

engaged in virtuous work, and this helped to give him a sense of confidence and superiority.

This leads to a second main feature of the gentlemanly mode evident in Raven's account—the high valuation placed on *confidence* in one's own judgement and, allied to that, the low valuation placed on servility to one's superior and hence the powerful gentlemanly norm of *courageous self-discipline*. Such gentlemanly norms and values served to strengthen the value noticed earlier of trusted servants in the service class, believing it to be right and proper that they be given considerable *autonomy* and *freedom* in performance of their duties. Confident, self-disciplined (because relatively independent), and courageous gentlemen were thought to possess 'an aura of command'. They had 'character'. Those who went off to battle at Ypres or the Somme were officers and gentlemen. Another popular image of the period is of that 'very gallant gentleman', Captain Oates, who in 1912 willingly sacrificed his life in a fearful blizzard at the South Pole trying to save his comrades. All this was part of the gentlemanly ideal.

Certainly the public schools tried to emphasize these qualities, for it has frequently been pointed out that these schools were as much concerned to 'build character' as they were to teach academic subjects. The unheated dormitories, cold baths, cross-country runs, rugby, and tough discipline were meant to build courage and endurance. It was hoped also that the discipline 'would somehow enter the individual and become self-discipline', as Wilkinson suggests.[112] Such Spartan hardships, did, of course, enable many public school gentlemen to move easily into military life as officers. Mason (ICS, UP) draws a connection between this aspect of Victorian public school life and producing gentlemanly rulers for the Empire:

> Hardness, self-composure, coolness in the face of pain and danger, confidence in one's own decisions—these were qualities required by the imperial class which a growing empire demanded. But the public schools claimed to teach more . . . A boy learned to do as he was told without question; later, he learned to take it for granted that he would be obeyed. He learned to punish and to encourage. He learned in short to rule.[113]

A third broad aspect of the gentlemanly ideal was the celebration of the *amateur*. A nice illustration of this was the annual cricket match at Lord's between Gentlemen and Players; the Gentlemen were amateurs

[112] Wilkinson, *Gentlemanly Power*, pp. 16–17.
[113] Mason, *English Gentleman*, p. 170.

and came out to play from the centre of the pavilion, while the Players, who were professionals, came out from a side door. (It is perhaps significant that the match was discontinued after the Second World War.) The amateur ideal was linked to the older idea of the man of leisure, with the time and ability to engage in a wide variety of pursuits that were unremunerative. The professional, by contrast, was a narrow specialist paid for his technical skills. Gentleman amateurs were *generalists*. And a whole hierarchy of careers and occupations existed reflecting the ideal. Wilkinson has pointed out that, for public school boys, narrowly technical professions had inferior prestige, whereas 'the barrister and bishop had high occupational status because their doings made a *general* impact on the *public* mind'.[114]

The amateur ideal reigned in the public schools. Young men who were 'glorious' at school got their 'colours' in several different sports, engaged in voluntary community service, were leaders or prefects, and were also intelligent enough to get in to Oxford or Cambridge to read classics (its justification being it broadened the mind without leading in any very evident remunerative direction). A boy who was only brilliant at maths was less glorious, and might even be a 'swot'.

A public school gentleman appears in the preceding sketch as a confident, courageous, and self-disciplined amateur for whom public service for the community was valued over individual achievement. Put that way in summary fashion it is an idealized characterization bordering on caricature. But it would be wrong to concretize the sketch in terms of persons. Only certain aspects of a dominant mode of thought and valuation in the public schools have been indicated. Not all boys accepted that mode without reservation, but they carried it to a greater or lesser extent into gentlemanly occupations. In this sense it can be safely assumed that the gentlemanly mode was an essential idea in the collective identity of the ICS European.

It should be noted that the gentlemanly mode had its heyday in the Victorian (and Edwardian) era, that is, in the period up to the First World War. A majority of all ICS Europeans in India until the 1930s had attended public school in that era. But was this Victorian gentlemanly mode modified after the war? To what extent were public school boys recruited to the ICS *after* the war different from their predecessors?

There was no doubt that public schools came in for attack during and after the war. Bertrand Russell led the way:

[114] Wilkinson, *Gentlemanly Power*, p. 20.

'Good form' as taught at the public schools 'is as destructive to life and thought as the medieval church'. 'Its essence is the assumption that what is most important is a certain kind of behaviour, a behaviour which minimizes friction between equals and delicately impresses inferiors with a conviction of their own crudity.' It's evils arise from two sources: 'its perfect assurance of its own rightness, and its belief that correct manners are more to be desired than intellect, or artistic creation, or vital energy'.[115]

Pekin lashed the public schools for producing boys 'stamped with the deadly uniform stamp of the English Gentleman'.[116] In response to such criticisms and for other reasons the public schools did change in certain ways; some of the Spartan hardships began to be eased, more respect was given to the intellectual, the individual, the eccentric. But how far these changes went is difficult to say. Mack, in his authoritative history, is very cautious: the scepticism of the early 1920s, 'even by those who attended or taught at public school, gave place in large measure by the late twenties to a renewed faith in the public schools, either as they were or as they would be'. And, more forthrightly, he concludes that 'change was more in external arrangements than in the spirit of the school, in the regulations than in the minds and hearts of boys; the key ideals and key practices of the Victorian schools remained virtually intact;' public schools were 'still a class institution, devoted to making leaders and statesmen out of privileged British youth'.[117] An Etonian, when asked in 1930, 'Has Eton changed?' replied with delight, 'It is our belief that she has not, and never will.'[118] Cheltenham's advertisement in the 1930s still proudly identified the school as 'the training place beyond compare for defenders of the Empire'.[119] It seems safe to conclude that the young men from Cheltenham and Eton and other public schools who entered the ICS after the First World War still subscribed to gentlemanly norms and values.

Working in India did not wipe out gentlemanly norms and values,

[115] Mack, E., *Public Schools and British Opinion since 1860: The Relationship between Contemporary Ideas and the Evolution of an English Institution*, London, 1941, p. 353, paraphrasing and quoting an essay written by Russell during the war and published later in Russell, B., *Selected Papers*, New York, 1927, pp. 108–9.

[116] Pekin, L. B., *Public Schools*, London, 1932, p. 124, cited in Mack, p. 439.

[117] Mack, *Public Schools*, pp. 368, 372, 272. See also Worlsey, T. C., *Barbarians and Philistines: Democracy and the Public Schools*, London, 1940.

[118] *Change: A Review of Eton in the Last Hundred Years* (1932), p. 1, cited in Mack, *Public Schools*, p. 372.

[119] Cited in Mack, *Public Schools*, p. 371.

for this mode of thought and valuation ran deep. Yet there were noticeable differences. Kiernan suggests, for example, that 'the gentleman (in India) was a rough diamond compared to his metropolitan self, less tainted by the vices that public schools were often accused of spreading from the upper to the middle classes, but toughened by life in outposts, coarsened by too much power'.[120] Nevertheless, such noticeable differences did not alter the high valuation that ICS Europeans continued to place on public service, the amateur ideal, and courageous self-discipline.

As for courage, self-confidence, and self-discipline, these qualities figure largely in the popular image of the ICS man in India. The fit between these aspects of the gentlemanly ideal and the post of Collector was perfect. Moving self-confidently, unarmed, and virtually alone in the midst of a communal riot—an experience most ICS men went through at least once—did take courage. One learns from ICS memoirs that there was usually, and understandably, a private fear behind the mask of public courage and confidence, but these gentleman had learned years ago at school to hide that fear. To express fear was ungentlemanly, emotional, bad form. If the popular image of the courageous and self-confident English gentleman doing his duty in a remote rural district was real enough, so was his self-discipline and capacity for hard work. ICS Europeans 'slaved away' in India, regardless of any private reservations about the point of it all.[121] It was part of the tradition that ICS men worked hard, harder than other administrators, in fulfilment of their manifold duties and responsibilities. 'We worked ceaselessly—it was the tradition in the Punjab that two men did three men's work,' Wingate claims.[122] This was the case despite exceptions to the contrary. Mangat Rai (ICS, Punjab) recounts entering his Chief Secretary's room one afternoon to find him reading Dickens. The Chief Secretary, a senior ICS European, put the book aside without embarrassment and explained that he made it a practice to read only good literature during office hours.[123]

[120] Kiernan, V., *The Lords of Human Kind*, London, 1969, p. 33.

[121] e.g. Swann Papers, TS p. 2: 'The great mass of the people [remained] on the borderline of starvation and oppression, at the mercy of the money-lender and other leeches. Looking back, it now seems remarkable that this realization did not produce disillusioned inactivity: quite the contrary, one slaved away regardless . . .'

[122] Wingate, *Not in the Limelight*, p. 36.

[123] Mangat Rai, E. N. *Commitment my Style*, Delhi, 1973, p. 92. Another Chief Secretary, (Roughton, (ICS, CP)) in the 1930s 'usually had a chess problem on the table at the side of his desk'; Paterson Papers, IOL MSS Eur. F.180/46, TS p. 15.

Reading Dickens while ruling an empire actually fits well into the ideal of the amateur. Again, it seems almost as if both district and secretariat posts in India were designed precisely for public school boys. Being transferred frequently from post to post, without ever questioning the 'rightness' of being put in charge of the thing, whatever it was, was the very essence of life in the ICS, and wholly suitable for amateur generalists. Gentlemen in secretariats advised on general policy; professional experts and others who implemented policies were elsewhere, in 'subordinate' or 'attached' offices. As for the post of Collector, it is no exaggeration to call it the apotheosis of the generalist, and thus a wholly satisfying charter for a gentleman.

As for public service, the high valuation put upon that led many public school boys to dedicated lives in the army, the clergy, the civil service, the law, and so on in England. Taken to India by ICS Europeans, the sense of dedication to a life of service could also be very pronounced: 'service, service, service . . . the word runs like a response through the litanies of Anglo-India'.[124] But the valuation placed on service also tended to accentuate a feature less noticeable at home: racial superiority. Its breeding ground was the very superior position that ICS Europeans did in fact have in India, as contrasted with their private position in England when home on leave. Kathleen Griffiths (wife of Percival Griffiths, ICS, Bengal) remembers going home on leave in the early 1930s with her two children and getting into a train at Plymouth, bound for Cornwall, whereupon the younger one, aged five, piped up in front of a carriage full of people:

> 'Mummy, why hasn't the guard come along and asked your permission to start the train?'
>
> 'Darling,' she replied, 'we are not in daddy's district now. They do not come along and ask me if they may start the train here. This is England, you must get used to English customs now.'[125]

'There's no doubt that you did feel you were the ruling class,' her husband remarked in a separate interview; 'British rule in India was jolly good for India, but it wasn't always good for the British, because we did, no doubt, tend to get aloof and perhaps a little bit conceited.'[126] 'We realized that we were members of a very successful race,' says Symington; 'we realized that we were working in a country which was

[124] Allen, *Plain Tales*, p. 182.

[125] Allen, *Plain Tales*, p. 32.

[126] Interview broadcast on BBC Radio 4, 15 Dec. 1975, in the series 'Plain Tales from the Raj'.

as pre-eminently unsuccessful as we were successful . . . and I suppose that that produced a frame of mind in which we tacitly—not explicitly—felt ourselves to be rather superior people.'[127] A boy nurtured in the cloistered setting of public school and then an Oxford or Cambridge college, imbued with the idea of public service as morally virtuous, and then placed on top of the world in India, could easily be misled into thinking that 'the only seamy side to life was in India',[128] and that 'we' British were not just marvellously successful as a nation but also morally superior, and that those who did not belong to 'us' were inferior. In an Indian setting such beliefs were translated into a sense of racial superiority.

Although a gentleman tried not to show this in public, for he had 'pleasing manners', it was widespread. There are some references to it in the sources. Orr, for example, remembers overhearing Justice Meridith (ICS, Bihar and Orissa) in the locker room of the Bankipor Club, Patna, in the early 1940s give vent to his racialist feelings in relation to two Indians whom Orr had proposed for the club (and who later got in). 'They were the same racialist feelings which had sustained the empire-builders and administrators for generations . . .' says Orr, yet the event shocked him. It 'made me look objectively at the political scene, which in essence was a rejection by India, or at least by all self-respecting Indians, of British rule because of its implicit assertion of racial superiority. It strengthened my sympathy for the Indian cause and my belief in its rightness; but in those days this was a feeling which one kept to one's self . . .'[129] There are other remarks in the sources referring to racial feelings amongst ICS Europeans. Hume, for example, told his parents in a letter in 1929 about his Collector (Cooke, ICS, UP), who was 'not a bad fellow' but 'rather one of the "big stick" type, with a deep rooted contempt for the "nigger" whom he abuses in language not always very choice', and Hume himself believed, as a young man, that 'the Indian is at heart a funk, i.e. the Hindu' and that 'it is indeed a consideration whether one would care to work a life time subject to "popular wog" control'.[130] Carritt (ICS, Bengal) reports that in Midnapur in 1930 Jameson (ICS, Bengal) had 'an almost pathological contempt for Indians in general and a desire to

[127] Allen, *Plain Tales*, p. 182.

[128] Holt Papers, IOL MSS Eur. F.180/30, TS p. 2, makes this point effectively.

[129] Orr Papers, TS p. 23.

[130] Hume Papers, IOL MSS Eur. D.724, vols. 2 and 3, letters of 11.8.1929, 24.5.1930, 31.5.1930.

make them suffer. His judicial sentencing was notoriously severe.'[131]

A clear distinction must be made, however, between a *generalized* sense of racial superiority and relations between *individuals*. Individual ICS Europeans frequently had a high regard for ICS Indians, and vice versa (a point developed in Chapter 2). Maher (ICS, Madras) usefully draws attention to this distinction. He says that when he first arrived in India he did feel a contempt for Indians generally and this 'was due partly to youthful arrogance, but mainly to youthful ignorance . . .' but he also remarks that his relations with individual Indian officials from the outset were happy and life in India eventually changed his feelings and he came to realize 'that there was often more merit in the Hindu madness than in the English method'.[132] How widespread the sense of racial superiority was within the ranks of ICS Europeans is hard to say, although one suspects that it was more common than is implied in the ICS literature, which virtually ignores the subject. Probably a majority of ICS men held more or less strong feelings of racial superiority *vis-à-vis* the rest of Indian society and culture. This was perceived by many intelligent Indian nationalists as racial arrogance, and that perception fuelled their drive for independence from British rule.

SUMMARY

The content of the ICS tradition consisted of a particular structure of rule and ICS location within it (section 1), characteristic behaviour patterns in these locations (section 2), and appropriate norms and values (sections 3 and 4). ICS location within the state was typified by rapid movement between control posts set apart in secretariats and districts from main line departments at each level of government. Behaviour patterns formed part of the political process: ICS Collectors allocated scarce resources with an eye to their political support, and ICS Secretaries were centrally involved in the formulation of policy both at the centre and in the provinces. ICS men placed a high valuation, as members of the service class, on being loyal servants of the imperial government, on utmost trust being reposed in them by the political leadership, and on considerable autonomy and discretion being allowed to them to act appropriately on behalf of those they served. As gentlemen, they believed fundamentally in the virtue of public service, the amateur ideal, and the norms of courage, confidence, and self-

[131] Carritt, M., *A Mole in the Crown*, Hove (published privately), 1985, p. 26.

[132] Maher Papers, IOL MSS Eur. F.180/55, TS p. 1.

discipline. Gentlemanly norms and values were not accepted by each ICS administrator *in toto* or in the same way; there were many differences of individual behaviour, and idiosyncracies, in the Service. But the analysis has not been about persons. It has been about a collective identity. Persons who shared that collective identity shared a particular location in society and a particular mode of thought and valuation attached to that location. It was that location and that mode that carried on as the ICS tradition, not the persons who came and went.

Structures, behaviour patterns, norms and values were related to each other. It is that which gave the tradition overall coherence and strength. The ICS learned to perceive the state, and their special place in it, through these concepts and valuations embodied in their tradition. The particular administrative framework of rule and the appropriate ways of behaving in district and secretariat made sense to them, were perceived as 'right' in the circumstances, because the principles on which the framework and behaviour rested conformed to the gentlemanly mode. For example, the framework of the raj had as a central feature the location of a small élite of generalist political administrators moving frequently between control posts reserved for them at the top of each level of government. For young gentlemen entering the ICS such a framework appeared as utterly appropriate. Not only were 'rule and administration . . . the special provinces of the gentleman',[133] but also the very high place given to the mobile generalist was perceived as right and proper by gentlemen who placed a high valuation on the amateur ideal. Gentlemen prided themselves on having no specialist expertise, and being always confident and willing to hold any administrative post. Symington, for example, received a telegram, when he was posted in Sind in 1941, ordering him to take up duties immediately as ARP Controller, Bombay. He had no idea what ARP meant, but he remarked characteristically that 'it did not occur to me to question the rightness of putting me in charge of the thing, whatever it was'.[134]

Gentlemanly norms and values not only legitimized ICS location within the framework of the raj; they also provided normative support for what ICS men were asked to *do* in districts and secretariats. Political work in the district, for example, called for men who, amongst other things, were adept at moving for political advantage in the

[133] Raven, *English Gentleman*, p. 178.

[134] Symington, *A Special India*, p. 204. (ARP = Air Raid Precaution.)

absence of close control from above, while at the same time acting in a manner that was consistent with the interests and requirements of distant overlords. ICS men had no difficulty in behaving as 'autonomous servants', for duty and public service, allied to self-discipline and independent courage, were basic to their collective identity as gentlemen of the service class.

Norms and values, however, do 'not descend from heaven', as Barrington Moore remarks, but have to be 'recreated anew in each generation' by a 'complicated process of transmitting culture from one generation to the next'—a process which serves 'concrete interests and privileges'.[135] In short, the content of a tradition must be actively and continuously reproduced through time, or it quickly breaks down. Chapter 2 is about this essential process.

[135] Moore, *Social Origins*, p. 486.

2

Finding and shaping ICS successors

Reproducing the ICS tradition was quite impossible without a steady supply of fresh recruits. Yet obtaining them during the last decades of the raj posed surprising problems for the imperial power in London. Indeed, deliberate political initiatives were required from time to time to avoid complete breakdown of the recruitment process. The first section of this chapter shows these interconnections between recruitment and political support. It was not enough, however, just to obtain a regular supply of recruits; it was also necessary to shape them—both Europeans and Indians—to the norms and values of the ICS tradition. The working of this deliberate shaping process is considered in a second section of the chapter. A final short section comments on the ease with which the Indians who entered the ICS were able to make gentlemanly norms and values their own.

POLITICAL SUPPORT FOR THE RECRUITMENT PROCESS[1]

1914–1924

Prior to 1914, recruitment to the ICS took place on the basis of an annual competitive examination held each year in London. Any Indian seeking entry to the Service was obliged to travel to London to sit the examination. Only a few succeeded. During the ten years (1904–13) before the Great War, of the 538 men recruited to the ICS, 501 or 95 per cent were European.[2] 1914 destroyed all that. The ICS examination of that year was in progress when war was declared in August. Men moved so swiftly at that time that when the results of the examination were announced, it was found that, out of 47 successful candidates, 11 had already entered military service. Six more candidates were immediately selected from the examination list to make up the

[1] Evidence for portions of this section appeared previously in the writer's 'Manpower Shortage and the End of Colonialism', *MAS* 7. 1 (1973), 47–73. The article was actually addressed to a different issue.

[2] Figures compiled from each *India Office List* for the years 1905–14. The annual breakdown is as follows:

See table p. 84.

deficiency, but even before these additions could be announced, three more candidates had joined up. The net result was that 39 successful candidates entered on probation at once. Of the 14 who chose military service, nine were posted to India with territorial units, and all but one of them were ultimately appointed to the ICS after the war (the other one resigned); the remaining five fought in Europe and all of them died there.[3] 1914 broke for ever the measured regularity of previous ICS recruitment. In contrast, ICS recruitment from 1915 to 1924 presents a comparatively irregular and complicated picture. The complete recruitment figures, classified in terms of avenues of recruitment for each of the ten years involved, are produced in Table 8.

It is clear from these data that the London examination ceases suddenly to be the main avenue of recruitment. The disappearance of European candidates during the war is understandable, but their failure to reappear after it is striking. As the table shows, 80 per cent of all European recruits during this period were not secured by examination but by appointment of persons who had served in (and survived) the war.[4] For Indian candidates an additional avenue of recruitment was provided in 1922 when an annual competitive examination was introduced at Allahabad. A second innovation

Year	European	Indian
1904	52	1
1905	47	3
1906	58	3
1907	54	4
1908	49	3
1909	50	1
1910	59	1
1911	50	3
1912	40	7
1913	42	1
Totals:	501	27

[3] NAI Home Dept., Establishments Division (hereinafter Ests.), Part 1, File No. 591, serial 26, 1922, 'Indian Civil Service: Note on Recruitment during the war period'. All the Home Dept. Files cited in this section of the chapter are in the National Archives of India.

[4] Details of these recruitments under the Indian Civil Service (Temporary Provisions) Act, 1915, are found in Home Dept., Ests., Part 1, File No. 591, serials 1–28, 1922. Also Home Dept., Ests., A, Proceeding 234, May 1921, 'India Office Memorandum, December 1920'.

Table 8. *ICS recruitment: 1915–1924*

Year	European Recruitment			Indian Recruitment			
	London Exam.	Nomination	Total	Total	London Exam.	Indian Exam.	Nom.
(1)	(2)	(3)	(4)	(5)	(6)	(7)	(8)
1915	11	0	11	1	1	0	0
1916	4	0	4	5	2	0	3
1917	2	0	2	4	3	0	1
1918	0	0	0	9	9	0	0
1919	0	62	62	39	5	0	34
1920	0	44	44	6	6	0	0
1921	3	21	24	25	13	0	12
1922	6	3	9	24	10	9	5
1923	7	14	21	15	4	9	2
1924	3	0	3	15	8	5	2
Totals	36	144	180	143	61	23	59
Percentages	20%	80%	100%	100%	43%	16%	41%

Sources: Data compiled by the author from the annual India Office and Burma Office lists for those years, the *Report of the Royal Commission on the Superior Civil Services in India, 1924*, p. 135, *Report of the Government of India Secretariat Committee, 1937*, p. 67, and unpublished government files relating to recruitments during those years, e.g. Home Dept. Files 44—Ests., 1931; 13—Ests., 1923; 163—Ests., 1923; 547/31—Ests., 1931. The files are on deposit in the National Archives of India, New Delhi.

Note: In cases where figures are inconsistent between different sources, I have taken the government files as authoritative.

introduced in 1922 was the practice of nominating Indians from minority communities who were unsuccessful at the examinations. As a result of these changes, despite the resort to appointment of European candidates without examination, Indians accounted for 44 per cent of all ICS recruits during the period. This proportion exceeded considerably the percentage of Indian recruitment officially laid down in existing orders. The proportion was high not so much because Indian recruitment was excessive, but rather because European recruitment was severely short. Between 1915 and 1923 there was a deficiency of 125 in the number of Europeans who should, in accordance with existing orders, have been recruited, while, in the same period, 12 Indians were recruited above the number laid down.[5]

[5] East India (Civil Services in India), *Report of the Royal Commission on the Superior Civil Services in India*, 27 Mar. 1924, p. 17. (Hereinafter referred to as *Lee Commission Report*.)

Indianization of the ICS had begun in earnest even before the Lee Commission made recommendations on the matter.

The deficiency in European recruitment during this period occurred in part because there were fewer war service officers available for nomination after the war than had been anticipated; more importantly, there simply were very few Europeans who were interested in taking the ICS examination. For example, at the London examination in 1922, four years after the war had ended, out of 80 candidates who appeared, only 19 were Europeans (6 were successful).[6] This lack of interest in the ICS as a career on the part of the new generation of young college men first became known to the India Office in 1920–1 from confidential letters received from Cambridge and Oxford. The Board of Indian Civil Service Studies at Cambridge wrote to the India Office on 7 December 1920: 'So far as we can see at present we think the number of Cambridge European candidates for the Open Competition for the Indian Civil Service in August 1921 will be in all probability a mere fraction of those who competed in pre-war days.' Extracts from notes from Oxford colleges convey the same message, for example:

> . . . we have no candidates from this college, and I do not think it likely that there will be any in the immediate future;
>
> . . . there appears to be a widespread disinclination among men of the sort which used to gain most places in the Indian Civil Service to compete at all . . .;
>
> . . . Balliol will have only one European candidate likely to sit for Competitive Examination for the Indian Civil Service in August 1921.[7]

This information led the Secretary of State to invite a Committee to advice him privately '(1) as to the steps to be taken to remove any impediments to recruitment that they might find to exist, or, if those impediments should be considered too serious for any remedies, (2) as to how he should set about a more formal enquiry'.[8]

Not only was the British Government failing to secure new European recruits to the ICS, but a number of more senior ICS men

[6] Home Dept., File 497—Ests., 1922, 'Recruitment to the Indian Civil Service in 1922'.

[7] Supplementary Memorandum, Jan. 1921, attached to Home Dept., Ests., Part 1, File No. 591, 1922. The notes from Oxford colleges were included in a letter to the India Office from the Indian Civil Service Delegacy, Oxford, 21 Dec. 1920.

[8] Home Dept., Ests., Part 1, File No. 965, serials 1–4, 1922, 'Report of the Committee (MacDonnell's) appointed by the Secretary of State for India to enquire into the impediments to European recruitment for the Indian services' (hereinafter called MacDonnell Committee Report).

were taking the opportunity to retire prematurely on proportionate pension.[9] In India a serious challenge to British rule was taking place, reflected most visibly in serious disturbances in the Punjab in 1919 (including the massacre at Amritsar) and the first great non-co-operation movement of the Indian National Congress in 1920–2 which brought the raj almost to its knees.[10] It was hardly a happy time for ICS Europeans in India. They made their unhappiness clear to both the Government of India and the British Government in London, receiving a more sympathetic response from the latter.[11] Nor did an Indian career look promising to the young men graduating from Oxford and Cambridge. This was so, despite the fact that the British economy was depressed and jobs were hard to come by. 1921, for example, was 'one of the worst years of depression since the industrial revolution'.[12] In the early 1920s the failure to attract new recruits to the ICS 'irritated and excited both the Right and the Left' in Britain, recalls a Conservative politician who later became Secretary of State for India; 'it looked, indeed, as if the machine of Government in India would break down for want of the political support to direct it and the manpower to work it'. 'The Services upon which the whole system depended were running down at an alarming rate.'[13]

In 1922, however, the Government of India moved to re-establish their supremacy under direct orders from the Cabinet in London,[14] and in Parliament the Prime Minister made a lengthy speech designed

[9] The scheme commenced in 1922, and by the end of 1923, 69 men had taken advantage of it. For a regional breakdown of the figure, see Home Dept. File 96/2/24—Ests., 1924. For discussions of types of men who retired prematurely see Home Dept. File 47/27—Ests., 1927. By 1938, 181 had retired prematurely; details in Home Dept. File 12/37—Ests., 1937: 'Particulars of ICS officers permitted to retire on proportionate pension up to the quarter ending 31 March 1938'.

[10] Low, D. A., 'The Government of India and the First Non-co-operation Movement—1920–22', *Journal of Asian Studies*, xxv (1966), 241–59. More generally, Brown, J., 'Imperial Facade: Some Constraints upon and Contradictions in the British Position in India, 1919–1935', *Transactions of the Royal Historical Society*, Vol. 26, Fifth Series, 35–52.

[11] Problems of recruitment during the period and the different responses to it in London and Delhi are discussed in detail in Ewing, A., 'The Indian Civil Service 1919–1924: Service Discontent and the Response in London and in Delhi', *MAS* 18. 1 (1984), 33–53. See also correspondence dealing with the memorials written by 150 ICS men from CP, Madras, and Punjab on their prospects under the Montagu–Chelmsford Reforms, and the need to keep this from becoming public knowledge, in Home Dept. Ests. Proceedings A, File No. 10–14, Jan. 1921.

[12] Taylor, A. J. P., *English History, 1914–1945*, New York, 1965, p. 145.

[13] Templewood (Samuel Hoare), *Nine Troubled Years*, London, 1954, pp. 42–3.

[14] For details of these, and the history of this period more generally, see Rumbold, A., *Watershed in India 1914–1922*, London, 1979.

to dispel feelings of insecurity amongst ICS Europeans in India and to encourage potential candidates in the public schools and universities. In a remarkable speech Lloyd George said:

I can see no period when they [the Indians] can dispense with the guidance and the assistance of this small nucleus of the British Civil Service, of British officials in India . . . they are the steel frame of the whole structure. I do not care what you build on it—if you take the steel frame out, the fabric will collapse. . . .

We cannot keep a continuous eye upon what happens in India . . . It depends upon the kind of Government that you have there. It is essential that they should be strengthened, but whatever you do in the way of strengthening it, there is one institution we will not interfere with, there is one institution we will not cripple, there is one institution we will not deprive of its functions or of its privileges, and that is that institution which built up the British Raj—the British Civil Service in India.[15]

This speech was criticized in Parliament as going back on the declaration of 1917 for responsible government and the aims of the Government of India Act, 1919. It created a furore in Delhi. But the speech 'delighted the diehards' in Britain and the Prime Minister's 'bold words undoubtedly helped recruitment',[16] although not immediately. In the spring of 1923 many Cambridge undergraduates were still informing the Secretary of the Cambridge University Appointments Board that 'wild horses would not drag them into the ICS'.[17]

More important in fact for ICS recruitment were the results of the Royal (Lee) Commission on the Superior Civil Services in India published in 1924. The Lee Commission was appointed in part to pursue the questions raised in the earlier MacDonnell Committee Report. The major finding of this report, which was never made public, was that it was not so much the constitutional changes introduced by the Government of India Act of 1919 which deterred Europeans from going to India, but uncertainty regarding amenities, job security, ordered promotion, and financial prospects.[18] The careerist emphasis in the report was striking. With this in mind, the major recommendations of the Lee Commission regarding the ICS (apart from Indianization discussed below) concerned conditions of

[15] Great Britain. *Parliamentary Debates*, HC, 157 (1922), columns 1513, 1517.

[16] Templewood, *Nine Troubled Years*, p. 43.

[17] Letter from Elliott to Erch, 6 Mar. 1925, cited in Ewing, 'Indian Civil Service 1919–1924', 35.

[18] MacDonnell Committee Report, para. 10.

service. Financial concessions included an increase in the overseas allowance fixed in 1920 and its conversion into sterling; passage allowances for return trips to Britain for all European officers, their wives, and children (single passage); and improvements in provident fund and pension arrangements. It was also stipulated that 'medical officers of their own race would be available to members of the Services and their families'.[19] The recommendations were estimated to cost nearly 125 million rupees a year and were subsequently criticized by Indians as 'Lee loot'.[20] They had the desired effect in Britain. The number of Europeans entering the ICS immediately leaped from three in 1924 to 20 in 1925, 29 in 1926, and 37 in 1927. Thus, the shortage of European recruits to the ICS was temporarily checked by political initiatives from the British Government.

1925–1935

Between 1925 and 1935 a regularized system of recruitment to the ICS operated in accordance with Lee Commission recommendations and previous existing practices. As Table 9 shows, under this system recruitment rose significantly during the later 1920s, then fell away again in the early 1930s.

The system of recruitment to the ICS in any one year had normally to satisfy four conditions. In the first place it was necessary to recruit a sufficient number of persons in Britain and India to keep up the strength of the Service. The precise number of persons to be recruited each year was calculated on the basis of actuarial figures worked out by Mr H. G. W. Meikle in 1919.[21] The figure varied from year to year, for example, in 1925–6 it was 56, in 1926–7 it was 64. The figure served two functions. Recruitment up to that figure was guaranteed to maintain the strength of the Service on a continuing basis. Any recruitment beyond that figure would have the undesirable effect of creating a block in promotion later for persons appointed that year.

[19] *Lee Commission Report*, p. 75.

[20] Sinha, V. M., 'The Problem of Reorganization of the Superior Civil Services in India', unpublished Ph.D. dissertation, Saugar University, 1957, p. 24.

[21] Home Dept. File 675—Ests., 1922, 'Recruitment Rate for the Indian Civil Service'. Mr Meikle's Note of 16 June 1919 is contained in this file. In order to ascertain the number of recruits required for a particular province, the calculation was to multiply the number of senior posts in the provinces by 7.7/100. For instance, if the number of senior posts in a province was 130, then the recruitment figures would be $130 \times 7.7/100 = 10.1 = 10$ recruits per annum. The total of annual recruitment figures for the ICS as a whole was arrived at by totalling all the provincial figures, plus making certain other adjustments.

Table 9. *ICS recruitment: 1925–1935*

Year	European Recruitment			Indian Recruitment			
	London Exam.	Nomination	Total	Total	London Exam.	Indian Exam.	Nom.
(1)	(2)	(3)	(4)	(5)	(6)	(7)	(8)
1925	20	0	20	22	15	5	2
1926	29	0	29	18	11	3	4
1927	37	0	37	37	21	9	7
1928	36	0	36	31	16	6	9
1929	35	0	35	37	17	9	11
1930	25	0	25	38	24	8	6
1931	24	0	24	29	10	11	8
1932	14	0	14	28	16	5	7
1933	17	0	17	25	18	5	2
1934	13	0	13	23	14	5	4
1935	5	0	5	23	15	6	2
Totals	255	0	255	311	177	72	62
%	100%	0%	100%	100%	57%	23%	20%

Sources: Data compiled from the India Office and Burma Office lists for these years, *Report of the Government of India Secretariat Committee, 1937*, p. 67, and unpublished government files, e.g. Home Dept. Files 86/30—Ests., 1930, 44/35—Ests., 1935.

Secondly, it was necessary to meet the recommendations of the Lee Commission on Indianization.[22] These required that direct recruitment on the results of annual competitive examinations and nominations be 40 per cent European and 40 per cent Indian in composition, the remaining 20 per cent to be filled by promotion of Indians from Provincial Civil Services.[23] Thus, the second condition required that an equal number of Europeans and Indians be secured each year from the examination in London and the examination and nominations in India (referred to as 'the 50:50 ratio' in documents cited below).

Thirdly, in the event that Indian candidates from minority communities were under-represented in the list of successful candidates at the examinations, it was necessary to nominate persons from such communities to redress these inequalities, in accordance with an undertaking given by Sir Alexander Muddiman in the Council of State on 2 March 1925. This undertaking, subsequently referred to as 'the Muddiman pledge', served in effect to reserve some places mainly for

[22] *Lee Commission Report*, p. 19.

[23] A regular check was made by the Home Department on the position of individual provinces in meeting this 20 per cent promotion quota, e.g. Home Dept. File 9/35/27—Ests., 1927.

Muslims and Burmans who failed to get their due proportion of places as a result of the competitive examination. Of the 87 Muslims who entered the ICS during the period 1922–43, 11 were successful at the London examination, 18 were sucessful at the examination in India, and the remaining 58 (68 per cent of the total) were not successful at the examinations but were nominated to the ICS in order to redress communal inequalities.[24] Nomination of Europeans had ceased.

Fourthly, it was necessary to ensure that a reasonable number of vacancies were available for Indians who took the examination in India. Previous to 1922, ICS examinations were held only in London. In that year, and henceforth, the ICS examination was also held in India, first in Allahabad, then in Delhi in 1928. Indian candidates could take the examination either in London or in Allahabad (later Delhi), although the intention was that the Indian examination would be the main avenue of Indian recruitment. European candidates could only take the examination in London. For purposes of calculation, the London examination in August of one year and the Indian examination and nomination in January of the *next* year were taken together as forming one recruitment year. This fourth condition had the important consequence of requiring that the London examination in August yield a considerable excess of successful European candidates over Indian candidates, in order to leave a number of vacancies for the Indian examination the following January.

The selection by examination in London involved six major steps. Firstly, formal applications were received by the Secretary of State for India establishing to his satisfaction that the candidates were between the ages of twenty-one and twenty-four, physically fit, and of 'good character' (this involved a security clearance). Secondly, in late summer an examination was held, in which a number of papers were written during a period lasting up to two weeks. Thirdly, examination papers were graded, vivas conducted, and a list of candidates drawn up in order of merit. Fourthly, the Secretary of State, in consultation with the Government of India, made a provisional decision regarding the number of candidates to be selected from the examination list. Fifthly, since the ICS examination was part of the Combined Civil Service examination and British candidates could enter for the Home Civil Service and the ICS and other services (and most of them did), the Secretary of State had to wait for those British candidates who were

[24] Source: author's head count of recruitment lists for the period. The figure may, therefore, not be exact, although the broad percentages probably are.

initially successful at the examination to decide to which service they wished to accept appointment. Finally, the Secretary of State, after obtaining definite commitments from British candidates and, if need be, going further down the order of merit in order to obtain candidates to make up the deficiency, announced the names of the successful candidates, who then entered upon probationary training in England before proceeding to India.

The evidence regarding ICS recruitment during 1925–35 illustrates clearly the working of the system and the alterations which were made to it in order to meet political and other considerations, especially the difficulty of obtaining enough European recruits.

The Secretary of State found the results of the London examination of 1926 'exceedingly satisfactory'. He wired immediately to Delhi.[25]

> Civil Service Commission have now confidentially informed me of results of Indian Civil Service Open Competition which will be published toward the end of next week and which you will I think agree are exceedingly satisfactory. Of first 55 candidates successful for ICS, 44 are Europeans . . . and after deducting 7 of these who may go for other services, we shall thus be able to fill all European vacancies, while reserving in January substantial number of Indian vacancies for Allahabad . . . In view of extremely satisfactory result of examination and desirability of removing as rapidly as possible unfortunate results under recruitments in previous years, I would urge that we should this year recruit up to 36 or 37 Europeans instead of 33 . . .

The Secretary of State obviously wanted to obtain a large excess of Europeans over Indians made possible by the results of the 1926 London examination, and to obtain them while the taking was good. He ultimately obtained only 29 Europeans, not 36 as planned, owing to an unanticipated number of candidates accepting appointment in other services or otherwise declining to accept appointment to the ICS. But the entire correspondence relating to the 1926 examination may be seen as the British response to the general difficulty experienced in previous years of obtaining a suitable number of European recruits.

The system of recruitment to the ICS worked fairly well from 1926 to 1930. Parity of Europeans and Indians was maintained, and an acceptable number of vacancies was available at the Allahabad/Delhi examination and nomination. The detailed correspondence for each of these recruitment years in the late 1920s resembles the correspondence

[25] Telegram from Secretary of State to Home Department, 25 Sept. 1926, in Home Dept. File 38/26—Ests., 1926.

in 1926. In 1928, for example, the Secretary of State (to Viceroy, 13 September 1928) wired 'Confidential information from Civil Service Commission shows results of Indian Civil Service examination are unusually satisfactory . . .'. An office note in the Home Department (15 September 1928) records the nature of the response to this telegram in the Home Department:

> The Secretary of State, however, is strongly in favour of going down to No. 63 on the [examination] list, which is likely to give us 48 Europeans (of whom 10 will be lost [to other services]) and 15 Indians from the London examination, leaving 23 appointments to be filled in India. The ground for this proposal is his anxiety to secure all the good Europeans he can while they are still available, and this again raises a question of policy, viz. whether it is proper at this stage to go out of our way to push extra European candidates into the Service . . .[26]

The decision was to maintain parity, not to push extra Europeans into the ICS.

A dramatic break from the pattern of the previous four years occurred in 1930. The London examination that year yielded 25 Europeans and 24 Indians. The Secretary of State wired to Delhi:[27] 'You will see that the position is even worse than I anticipated.' To hold to the 50:50 ratio would mean that only one Indian could be taken in India, and there was discussion of not holding the Delhi examination and nominations for that year. The Government of India rejected that solution for essentially political reasons:[28]

> So far as minority communities are concerned, we consider it extremely undesirable to depart from the Muddiman pledge, especially having regard to the fact that minority communities, and especially the Muhammadans, have given Government their support against civil disobedience movement. While realizing the objections to departure from the 50:50 ratio, we consider that the objections to adhere to it this year are far more serious, and that we could not defend a system of recruitment which has the result of giving 21 Hindus, 2 Parsis and only one Muhammadan. While accepting the view that the maintenance of the 50:50 ratio is a matter of first rate importance, we believe that the interests of the principals will be better served by a temporary deviation from it than by attempting to defend rigid adherence to it against the

[26] Home Dept. File 168/28—Ests., 1928.

[27] Telegram from Secretary of State to Home Department, 9 Oct. 1930. Home Dept. File 86/30—Ests., 1930, 'Recruitment for the ICS, 1930–31'.

[28] Telegram from Home Department to Secretary of State, 22 Oct. 1930, in ibid.

strong public criticism which the anomalous consequences are certain to evoke.

They go on to argue that to abandon the Delhi examination would (1) be unfair to candidates who had been working for the examination, and (2) discourage candidates from working for the examination in the future. 'Further encouragement', they say, 'would thereby be given to (Indian) candidates to appear at London, a result which we particularly desire to avoid.' The result was that the Delhi examination was held, and the theoretical recruitment figure for 1930–1 of 68 was filled with 25 Europeans and 43 Indians.

The results of the 1931 London examination appeared to the Secretary of State to offer an opportunity to correct at least partially the under-recruitment of Europeans in 1930. He wired to Delhi:[29]

Out of 75 candidates following Indian: 22, 25, 28, 32, 37, 45, 48, 51, 54, 56, 57, 58, 60, 63, 65, 68, 70, 71, 72, 75. . . . There are at present 16 Home Civil Service vacancies and first 10 on Home List have not entered for India. We are therefore certain to lose 6 and I anticipate that we shall lose at least 15. If so, intake of Europeans, if we stop at No. 67, will be 37 and Indians 15 . . . in this way, under-recruitment of 13 Europeans last year would be reduced by 8, do you agree?

The Government of India did not agree. They wired back as follows:[30]

. . . any attempt to justify filling more than 34 vacancies on the results of the London examination on the ground of making up last year's deficiency in Europeans would inevitably meet with much justifiable criticism. We consider that present situation ('grave deterioration in central and provincial finances') offers ample justification for departing from actuarial standards of recruitment and also for not attempting to repair deficiency in Europeans last year.

The Secretary of State immediately telegraphed to Delhi reiterating his desire to correct last year's deficiency of Europeans. The Government of India immediately replied even more forcefully:[31]

. . . Indian opinion has hardened very much during the past year owing mainly to financial conditions and partly to political causes. There is in particular very strong feeling with regard to the heavy cost of European officers . . . We have difficult and dangerous months in front of us and when this can be avoided, it is most unwise to offend Indian opinion. We have no doubt whatever that a

[29] Telegram from Secretary of State to Home Department, 18 Sept. 1931, in Home Dept. File 135/31—Ests., 1931, 'Recruitment for the Indian Civil Service in 1931–32'.

[30] Telegram from Home Department to Secretary of State, 26 Sept. 1931, in ibid.

[31] Telegram from Home Department to Secretary of State, 2 Oct. 1931, in ibid.

large excess of Europeans over Indians would be very keenly resented and would be regarded as further evidence of intention of not relaxing control over India. In fact, we would, in spite of financial considerations, prefer to increase total intake rather than have a large excess of Europeans.

The force of this argument for the Government of India was of less moment for the Secretary of State, who was responsible to a different constituency. He wired to Delhi in due course:[32]

. . . I do not now expect to get more than 25 Europeans and nine or ten Indians. It is therefore impossible to repair last year's under-recruitment of Europeans to the extent that I hoped, but although I recognise the difficulties with which you have to contend, I still think that some repairment ought to be made to reassure opinion in this country which attaches great importance to maintenance of European element . . .

In the end, the view of the imperial power in London prevailed. Despite a theoretical recruitment figure of 66, only 24 Europeans from the London examination and 22 Indians from the London and Delhi examinations were ultimately appointed. The consequence, however, was that 20 places in the theoretical recruitment figure for 1931 were not filled; to have filled them might have resulted in 24 Europeans and 42 Indians.

In 1931 the Secretary of the Home Department in Delhi informed the Chief Secretaries in the provinces that 'the difficulty of securing European recruits is increasing'.[33] This difficulty increased so sharply during the next four years that the position regarding an adequate supply of European recruits quickly reached crisis proportions. In 1932 the Government of India required 31 Europeans but secured only 14; in 1933 they required 32 and secured only 17.[34]

Only 13 Europeans were successful at the 1934 London examination. To get them, the Secretary of State had to take 14 Indians. In the final order of merit Europeans were placed as follows: 5, 8, 9, 10, 13, 15, 16, 17, 19, 20, 23, 24, 26.[35] In the original order of merit, 18 of the first 20 candidates were Europeans. Of these, however, only four actually joined the ICS, ten joining the Home and Consular Services and four

[32] Telegram from Secretary of State to Home Department, 15 Oct. 1931, in ibid.

[33] Letters from Home Department to Chief Secretaries, in Home Dept. File 547/31—Ests., 1931.

[34] Data obtained from Government of India, *Report of the Government of India Secretariat Committee*, New Delhi (1937), Appendix VI.

[35] Home Dept. File 44/35—Ests., 1935, 'Note by Sir David Petrie, Chairman, Public Service Commission, on the results of the ICS examination in London in 1934'.

refusing to go to India in spite of there being no other appointment available to them.[36]

In the 1935 London examination, only five Europeans could be secured for the ICS, at a cost, from the Secretary of State's point of view, of 15 Indians. In the final order of merit for the 20 successful candidates, Europeans ranked 4th, 12th, 15th, 19th and 20th, a very poor record indeed.[37] These disastrous results provoked a retired ICS officer in England to fire off a letter to *The Times* (10 January 1936); the figures are accurate and the inference drawn doubtless reflects the judgement of the ICS at that time on the part of conservative opinion in Britain:

> . . . this year the vacancies for the ICS were 20 and for the Home Service 33. The first 20 places on the joint list went to British candidates of whom not one would accept the ICS. . . . In fact, no candidate who could secure any home appointment elected for the ICS. More than that, of the 12 British candidates who were not high enough for the Home Service, but high enough for the Indian, 10 refused the latter Service . . . Only five British candidates were secured—against 23 Indians here and in India—and these were all low on the list. What a contrast to the period before the War when the ICS was generally selected in preference to the Home Service . . . a pathetic illustration of the disrepute into which that once great Service has now fallen.

What happened during the early 1930s can be summarized as follows: (1) there was a severe shortage of European entrants to the ICS; (2) the number of Indian entrants was consequently reduced so that the Service would not be swamped by Indians; therefore (3) control posts in the colonial structure meant for ICS officers were gradually being abandoned. A combination of reasons was responsible for this inability to obtain a suitable number of successors for the ICS. The economic depression had consequences for the Europeans in particular. ICS pay was cut by 10 per cent in 1932 (reduced to 5 per cent in 1933–5); the rates of Indian income tax were raised and a surtax of 25 per cent was also imposed; customs duties (particularly important for Europeans in India) were also greatly increased; ICS Europeans 'were thus hit very hard'.[38] There was also uncertainty within the ICS as to what their position and privileges would be in the

[36] *Hindustan Times*, 9 May 1935. Figures recorded by Mr H. St B. Philby, a retired ICS officer.

[37] Home Dept. File 35/4/36—Ests., 1936, 'Note by Sir David Petrie, Chairman, Public Service Commission, on the results of the ICS examination in London in 1935'.

[38] Blunt, *The ICS*, p. 58.

forthcoming new constitution, embodied in the Government of India Act, 1935. Once again, a political initiative was necessary to shore up the ICS. It came swiftly in 1936.

1936–1943

The figures for the final period of ICS recruitment are produced in Table 10. The data show clearly the improvement in European ICS recruitment in the late 1930s until the war rapidly wiped out those gains and all ICS recruitment stopped. The results were a direct consequence of a political initiative by the British Government.

Table 10. *ICS recruitment: 1936–1943*

Year	European Recruitment			Indian Recruitment			
	London Exam.	Nomination	Total	Total	London Exam.	Indian Exam.	Nom.
(1)	(2)	(3)	(4)	(5)	(6)	(7)	(8)
1936	15	24	39	31	22	4	5
1937	18	15	33	25	13	5	7
1938	16	11	27	21	11	5	5
1939	12	11	23	17	8	5	4
1940	0	12	12	17	0	8	9(6)
1941	0	4	4	19	0	8	11(4)
1942	0	0	0	8	0	5	3(2)
1943	0	0	0	9	0	7	2(0)
Totals	61	77	138	147	54	47	46
Percentages:	44%	56%	100%	100%	37%	32%	31%

Sources: Compiled from India Office and Burma Office lists, 1937–40, and data in unpublished government files related to ICS recruitments for the years 1940–3, e.g. Home Dept. Files 35/38/41—Ests., 1941; 32/42—Ests., 1941; 35/49/42—Ests., 1942; 35/41/42—Ests., 1942.

Note: The figures in parentheses in column 8 designate those Indians nominated to the ICS from London.

In the first place, the British Government decided to limit the number of ICS places available to Indian candidates at the London examination (12 in 1937, 10 in 1938, 8 in 1939, 6 in 1940 and subsequent years), in order to force Indians to enter mainly by way of the Delhi examination.[39] In addition, it was decided to raise the age limit for candidates recruited in India from 21–3 to 21–4, so that they

[39] Home Dept. File 35/33/37—Ests., 1937, 'Note regarding the nomination of Indians to the ICS by selection in the UK'.

would be on a par with the limits which obtained in London. The effect of this decision was to abolish direct competition between European and Indian candidates at the London examination from 1937 onwards.

The second feature of this aggressive programme meant to increase European recruitment was announced in May 1936:

> . . . in order to remedy the under-recruitment of Europeans for the Indian Civil Service which has occurred in recent years, the Secretary of State for India proposes to begin selecting this year a certain number of candidates for admission to the Service otherwise than by written examination . . .[40]

Europeans were to be admitted after an interview and without examination.

There was, of course, a public outcry in India on the part of Indian politicians. On an adjournment motion in the Legislative Assembly regarding the revised system of ICS recruitment,[41] Mr Satyamurti (Congress) exploded:

> Our boys are willing to go to London, spend their money, compete with you on your own soil, pass your examination and defeat you. . . . We go and beat you, and you turn around and say 'Because you are cleverer than we, we shall appoint men who are dullards in our homes and who cannot compete at the open examination'.

Eventually, Sir Henry Craik (ICS), Home Member in the Government of India, replied in a lengthy speech. Two points are of direct relevance here. Firstly, he declared flatly that the recruitment system had broken down. One of several supporting arguments for this statement was the revelation that in the past five years, of the 175 Europeans and 175 Indians who should have been appointed, there was a shortage of 96 Europeans and 13 Indians. This was a serious state of affairs, he said, and 'the shortage must be made good (by selecting more Europeans) to avoid serious administrative breakdown'. Secondly, in an attempt to refute the argument of Mr Satyamurti and others that better brains from India were beating European brains, he divulged that the Secretary of State had recently made an enquiry into the question of why European recruits were not forthcoming in

[40] Press communiqué of 11 May 1936 found in ibid. Details of the procedures worked out to implement this decision are contained in Home Dept. File 38/2/36—Ests., 1936, 'Appointment of (*a*) a preliminary Interviewing Committee, and (*b*) a Final Selection Board, in England, for recruitment to the Indian Civil Service by Selection'.

[41] India. *Legislative Assembly Debates*, 6 (1936), 140–60 (31 Aug.).

sufficient numbers, and found that the following, essentially careerist, reasons obtained: (1) uncertainty as to the future of the Service, (2) counter attraction of other services, and the very much larger number of appointments offered for the Home Civil Service in recent years, (3) appointments to other services generally made and filled earlier in the year than was the case for the ICS, (4) disinclination of a boy who had just passed a stiff Honours Examination to sit another examination shortly afterwards, and (5) results of the London examination not announced until very late in the year. Pandit Pant had the last word in the debate, ending with the following, brilliant peroration:

> . . . the simple question is this: whether Indians desire that incompetent Britishers who cannot compete with Indians in a common examination, in their own country, conducted in their own language, in the midst of alien and uninviting surroundings, should be allowed to oust Indians. Our men, however, know how to beard the lion in his own den and will continue to do so in spite of all subterfuges.

As Pandit Pant spoke in Delhi, Indians were once again in the process of bearding the lion in the examination halls of London. The Secretary of State wired shortly afterwards to Delhi: '. . . to go to 54 on the (order of merit) list might give 18 Europeans and 20 Indians; to stop at No. 49 might give 15 Europeans and 18 Indians'; and the Home Secretary in Delhi, on receiving this telegram, noted in the file: 'the large number of Indians securing high places makes the position difficult'.[42] He was also shortly to receive figures, 'sufficiently striking', to send on to the Secretary of State, which showed that during the past five years 91 Europeans had been appointed to the ICS and as many as 150 had retired, while during the same period 150 Indians were appointed and only 11 retired.[43] On top of this, the Home Department was receiving strong pleas from provincial governments not to post so many Indian ICS recruits there because they claimed to be acutely short of Europeans.[44] Attempts were immediately started to find 'suitable'

[42] Telegram from Secretary of State to Viceroy, 18 Sept. 1936, in Home Dept. File 30/36—Ests., 1936. The Home Secretary's note is dated 20 Sept. 1936.

[43] Home Dept. File 29/9/36—Ests., 1936, 'Question in the Council of States regarding the number of officers who have retired from, and the number of officers recruited to, the Indian Civil Service during the last five years'.

[44] Home Dept. File 31/36—Ests., 1936, 'Results of Indian Civil Service Examination held in India in 1936, Nominations to the Indian Civil Service in 1936'.

ICS officers home on leave in Britain to talk to schools and colleges about the advantages of the ICS as a career.[45]

The subterfuges, from Pandit Pant's point of view, had also begun to operate. In addition to the 15 Europeans secured from the London examination, 24 more were appointed that year by a Selection Board under the new recruitment policy.[46] The following year (1937) the full effect of the new regulations came into force: 13 Indian candidates at the London examination were allowed to be successful;[47] 18 Europeans entered by examination and 15 more by selection. In 1938 11 Indians were allowed to enter from London.[48]

On the outbreak of war in 1939 discussion ensued between the Secretary of State and the Home Department as to the possible consequences of a cessation of ICS recruitment similar to that which occurred during the First World War. The position of the Home Department was made unmistakably clear. Any stoppage of ICS recruitment 'might easily prove disastrous for India . . .' and in support of their position they reviewed at length the unfortunate consequences of under-recruitment during the First World War. However, they pointed out,

. . . we do not suggest that present conditions are a complete parallel to those

[45] Home Dept. File 35/18/36—Ests., 1936, 'Propaganda work to stimulate European Recruitment for the Indian Civil Service'.

[46] Home Dept. File 38/2/36—Ests., 1936.

[47] The regulations called for 12. It is clear from the notes and tables in Home Dept. File 32/2/37—Ests., 1937, 'Results of the ICS examination held in London in 1937', that the intention was to stop at no. 12 on the list, T. C. Puri, but that they moved down the list to no. 13, D. G. Bhore, because (1) 'Bhore who is the son of Sir Joseph Bhore is an Anglo-Indian Christian but is not likely to be appointed by nomination in view of the fact that three Indian Christians were successful at the examination', (2) Puri and Bhore actually had identical marks in the examination (494) and in the viva voce (300), although Civil Service Commissioners placed Puri above Bhore, (3) the next two places on the list were Europeans, and hence were taken into the ICS. Office note on 27.9.37: 'I am strongly in favour of taking him [Bhore] because (1) he was as far as marks are concerned, bracketed with Puri; (2) he is probably a good type; (3) his father deserves well of Government.' Bhore had lived in England since an early age.

[48] The regulations called for 10. The Civil Service Commissioners announced the name of no. 11, Y. K. Puri, by mistake having overlooked the second Indian on the examination list, F. K. Sheldon, under the impression that he was a European. 'All sorts of difficulties may arise by now rejecting the 11th Indian . . . The mistake is, however, most unfortunate, especially at this juncture when we are faced with the problem of finding accommodation for the 14 extra Europeans that we have decided to recruit by 'selection' in the United Kingdom over and above the theoretical recruitment of 18 Europeans, which are expected to be taken by open competition in London . . .' office note, 9.9.38, in Home Dept. File 32/38—Ests., 1938, 'Results of the Indian Civil Service examination held in London in 1938'.

of 1915. On the conrary, while conditions in India are more difficult and unsettled, the number of European officers in both the ICS and IP is less than during the last war, and the necessity of keeping up recruitment of the services both in number and quality in respect of Europans and Indians is, in the circumstances, all the greater.

Therefore:

The Government of India are of the view that His Majesty's Government should declare openly that service in the ICS or in the Indian Police is in the national interest. A peaceful India is an asset to the Empire while a disturbed India is a grave liability; and to ensure that India shall be internally peaceful, it is necessary to maintain a steady flow of both Indian and European recruits to these services during the period of the war.[49]

1939 was still the period of lull before the storm. The following spring Hitler's troops began their march on Paris, Churchill replaced Chamberlain, and the situation was transformed. The 1940 ICS examination was never held, and European recruitment then dried up completely despite the efforts of the Secretary of State to find suitable candidates.[50] All ICS recruitment was, accordingly, stopped in 1943. Political support was not enough when there were no men available.

THE SHAPING PROCESS IN THE DISTRICT[51]

As each wave of new recruits arrived each year in India, attempts were immediately begun to shape them to the norms and values of the ICS tradition. The importance of shaping was frequently remarked on by ICS men, both European and Indian. Mehta (ICS, CP), as Collector, Saugor, recorded confidentially in July 1941 that the young recruit Willan (ICS, CP) 'is shaping well'; and Layard (ICS, CP) wrote in his

[49] Letter from Home Department to Secretary of State, 28 Dec. 1939, in Home Dept. File 35/56/39—Ests., 1939, 'Question of the recruitment of Indians by examination for the ICS in England during the period of the war'.

[50] Telegram from Secretary of State to Home Department, 27 Sept. 1941, in Home Dept. File 35/27/41—Ests., 1941, 'Recruitment of Europeans to the ICS and the IP during the war'. '. . . field this year was extremely poor and only 4 recruits have been obtained for ICS . . . supply of qualified European candidates is now practically exhausted and as there is little chance of securing further releases from armed forces I fear that recruitment may have to be suspended probably for duration of war. No announcement to this effect need be made however for if opportunity occurs to secure one or two good candidates from time to time I will take it.'

[51] The following section contains some evidence reported previously in the writer's 'The Shaping of Young Recruits in the Indian Civil Service', *IJPA* xxiii. 4 (1977), 575–89.

confidential report on young Mainprice (ICS, CP) that 'Mr Mainprice is in my opinion shaping very well, and should shortly be fit to hold a district charge'.[52] The necessity of shaping is inferred by Zinkin (ICS, Bombay), who asserted on the basis of his own experience that a young man 'knows nothing' when he first gets into the Civil Service. 'If the recruitment is properly done,' he continues, an ICS recruit 'should have the capacity to become a good bureaucrat . . . but what constitutes being a good bureaucrat is something he has still to learn, and it can only be learnt by experience, for it is a lot of things which never get into books.'[53]

If ICS Europeans 'knew nothing' about the work when they first arrived, most also knew little about India. Those recruited between the wars whose parents had served in India or who, for other reasons, were knowledgeable about the country, were a small minority. Lines (ICS, Bihar), when deciding whether or not to accept the ICS offer in 1937, asked 'what did I know about India, or the ICS—virtually nothing really'.[54] Moon joined in 1929: 'I was the victim of propaganda when I was a schoolboy at Winchester', for 'someone came down to speak to the two top forms on India, and painted a very idealistic picture of the sort of work to be done.'[55] Matthews (ICS, CP) 'examined the prospects of a career in India' in 1930; 'I was greatly attracted to it—especially, to be frank, by the high rate of emoluments and security offered.'[56] These and numerous other such confessional remarks in the sources suggest generally that the main reasons why most ICS Europeans went into the Service were because they had heard or read vaguely about work in India at school or college, the pay was good, and the work suited their generalist qualifications.

Furthermore, most ICS Europeans between the wars had rather ordinary academic achievements to their credit. Admission to Oxford or Cambridge as a commoner at that time 'was not difficult if you had the money, and had passed the requirements for Matriculation which had become almost trivial';[57] and most ICS recruits went on to obtain

[52] Home Dept. File 35/47/39—Ests, 1939, Appendix: 'Views of Provincial Governments on Examination and Selection Recruits, 1936–39', dated 26.4.1942.

[53] Zinkin, M., *Development for Free Asia*, London, 1963, p. 89.

[54] Lines Papers, IOL MSS Eur. F.180/19a, TS p. 1.

[55] Moon, P., in an interview broadcast on BBC Radio 4, 17 Nov. 1974, in the series 'Plain Tales from the Raj'.

[56] Matthews Papers, IOL MSS Eur. F.180/44, TS p. 1.

[57] Rose, J. and Ziman, J., *Camford Observed*, London, 1964, pp. 27–8. 'Since the war, all that has changed . . .'

only a second class degree (in the final stage), contrary to the widely held belief that 'nobody without a first class degree stood a chance'.[58] In 1928 only 33 per cent got firsts, in 1931 24 per cent, in 1936 21 per cent.[59] Certainly the Civil Service examination was arduous and difficult, but many were successful in part because their parents were able to buy the services of efficient crammers, whose success rate was fairly impressive.[60] Vernon Davies in London was one of the most popular; in 1931 more than half of the successful ICS recruits had been crammed there.[61]

ICS Indians were also crammed. And many had to take the examination several times before finally managing to pass it. Of the eighteen successful Indian candidates at the 1933 London examination, only six passed on their first attempt, seven on their second attempt, five on their third.[62] Fourteen Indians were successful at London in 1934, of whom only five succeeded at their first attempt, six on their second, one on his third; the remaining two set some sort of record by succeeding on their fourth attempt—one of them first tried his luck in Delhi in January 1933, then travelled to London to try again in August of that year, then returned to Delhi to sit the next examination in January 1934, and then (in a great show of perseverence) removed himself once again to London, where he was finally (barely) successful.[63] Such scrambling and cramming by many successful Indian candidates was a recurrent feature.[64] And it cost a good deal of money, underlining the fact that ICS Indians came from comfortable professional and service-class family backgrounds.[65]

[58] Allen, *Plain Tales*, p. 38.

[59] Source for 1928: Beaglehole, 'From Rulers to Servants', pp. 246–7. For 1931 and 1936: figures compiled by the author from data in NAI Home Dept. File 405/31—Ests., 1931, and NAI Home Dept. File 32/36—Ests., 1936.

[60] Wingate (ICS, Punjab) was surprised when he passed into the ICS 'quite well, scoring badly on the subjects I knew and excellently on the subjects which I had crammed'. His father paid for his cramming at Wrens. Wingate, *Not in the Limelight*, p. 26.

[61] Platt Papers, IOL MSS Eur. F.180/57, TS p. 3. 'Of 55 successful candidates in my year, 30 had been to Davies.'

[62] NAI Home Dept. File 126/34—Ests., 1934.

[63] NAI Home Dept. File 44/35—Ests., 1935. The other Indian who succeeded on his fourth attempt had a similar exam career.

[64] e.g. NAI Home Dept. File 35/4/36—Est., 1936; Federal Public Service Commission (India), *Pamphlet for the Competition for the Indian Civil Service held in India in January/February 1941* (Delhi, 1941), p. 131. The Chairman of the Public Service Commission (London) drew attention to the fact that repeated appearances at ICS exams by Indian candidates had been a 'recurrent' feature in NAI Home Dept. File 126/34—Ests., 1934.

[65] This point is developed in the next section of this chapter.

In consequence, as Pandit (ICS, UP) pointed out, 'most Indian ICS had an urban background and had probably not seen a village before they entered service'.[66] Moreover, many were total strangers to the part of India to which they were posted. Downing (ICS, Madras) recalls that the four ICS Indians posted to Madras Province with him in 1941 'were all Northern Indians or Mahrattas for whom Dravidian India was almost as new as for me'.[67] And Faruqui (ICS, Bombay and Sind) remarked: 'When I landed in Bombay [in 1933] . . . I was no stranger to India but an utter stranger to that area which I had never visited before.'[68] Indian recruits, like their European colleagues, needed to be shaped to the ICS tradition.

Shaping began immediately on arrival in India. For some the initial rite of passage was rough. When Khosla (ICS, Punjab) reported to the Chief Secretary in 1926, he was greeted with a hostile glance and the remark: 'So, you are the son of the man who doesn't want to serve the satanic Government.' Khosla was able to keep his temper and reply, 'Well, I hope I shall be able to discharge the duties entrusted to me honestly and competently.' His father, who was a member of the judicial service and about to be promoted to the Punjab High Court, had only a few weeks before resigned, saying he could no longer serve 'such a monstrous Government'.[69] Another apprehensive new recruit on arriving in Madras was asked by a crusty old Chief Secretary, 'How did you occupy your spare time in London?' 'I was keenly interested in the stage.' 'Ah! At the stage door, I presume?'[70] Other Chief Secretaries, however, were much more affable. Rustomji (ICS, Assam) and Wynne (ICS, Assam) were invited on arrival in 1942 to stay as guests of the two most senior ICS officers in Shillong. 'This gave us at once a sense of being part of a team, almost of a family.'[71] Baker (ICS, Bengal) described to his parents in his first letter home in 1927 how he and Martyn (ICS, Bengal) reported to the Chief Secretary, 'who proved very affable' and 'took us to Government House, and presented us to "HE" or "the Gov", as they call Sir Stanley Jackson. The state kept up there is most regal, and most amusing . . . I drove back here from Government House, alone in the Chief Secretary's car, to the

[66] Pandit, A. D., 'Little Gandhis for IAS', *Public Administration* (India), 12. 2 (1974), 57.

[67] Downing Papers, IOL MSS Eur. F.180/50, TS p. 6.

[68] Faruqui Papers, IOL MSS Eur. F.180/27, TS p. 4.

[69] Khosla, G. D., 'My Work in the ICS', in Panjabi, *Civil Servant*, pp. 110–11.

[70] Chettur, S. K., *The Steel Frame and I*, Bombay, 1962, p. 1.

[71] Rustomji, N., *Enchanted Frontiers*, Bombay, 1971, pp. 32–3.

accompaniment of salutes from the mounted guards at the gate.'[72] Symington reported in 1926 to the Revenue Secretary, Smyth (ICS, Bombay), who invited Symington to dinner that same evening. Exaggerated hopes and fears that Symington had brought to India were laid to rest when 'it was gently made clear to me . . . between the soup and dessert . . . [that] practical and well-defined tasks lay ahead', and he 'discovered with warmth and gratitude, that although my fellow cadets and I were among the lowest of God's creatures, we were nevertheless being received as members of a fraternity'.[73]

Most ICS men have a vivid recollection of their first encounters with their first Collector, and a number of quite detailed descriptions are available. What stands out is the varied nature of these encounters, despite later claims that they were always pleasant and useful. P. A. Menon (ICS, Madras), for example, has claimed that in the Madras Presidency the new ICS recruit 'was entrusted to a selected Collector' who provided training that was 'comprehensive and thorough'. Menon's own experience in Salem District in 1929–30 with Todd (ICS, Madras) was certainly a happy one.[74] At the same time, over in Tanjore District, Chettur (ICS, Madras) was having a similar experience with Thorne (ICS, Madras) who 'was extremely kind and good to me' and 'took me out touring with him for nearly a fortnight, Mrs Thorne being away at the time in England. I had the opportunity of watching a senior Collector's life at close quarters and of trying to model myself on his fine example.'[75] In sharp contrast, however, Trevelyan (ICS, Madras) in 1929 was totally ignored by his first Collector, 'an unpleasant brute' although a 'worthy brute, dead honest and doing his work competently'.[76] Kaiwar (ICS, Madras) had an unfortunate encounter in his first district in 1934 with his Collector, who reported on him adversely to his superiors, and from whom Kaiwar learned nothing.[77] Carritt (ICS, Bengal) reports that in 1930–2 in his first district he learned much from Peddie, but from the two ICS Collectors who followed Peddie 'I learned nothing because they did nothing. Douglas was too far gone on gin; French was too far gone on fat and laziness.'[78]

[72] Baker Papers, Cambridge Archive, letter of 7 Dec. 1927.

[73] Symington, *A Special India*, pp. 18–20.

[74] Menon, P. A., 'My Years in the Public Service', *IJPA* xxi. 1 (1975), 55.

[75] Chettur, *The Steel Frame and I*, pp. 1–2.

[76] Trevelyan, *Public and Private*, p. 5.

[77] Kaiwar, S. R., to the author in an interview at the offices of the Board of Revenue, Madras City, 23 Jan. 1967.

[78] Carritt, *Mole in the Crown*, p. 37.

K. P. S. Menon (ICS, Madras) also claims to have learnt almost nothing about district administration in 1922 from his first Collector, MacQueen (ICS, Madras), in Trichinopoly District. MacQueen 'was not one of those masterful bureaucrats who were out to mould the young lives entrusted to their care after their own pattern', for he 'had a healthy doubt whether his own pattern was worth holding up as an example' and 'was as nervous of having to train me as I was to be trained by him'. The MacQueens were extremely kind to Menon, 'with no trace of condescension or patronage about it' ('I am afraid that I cannot say this of the rest of the British community in Trichinopoly'), and 'their house was always a home to me', but MacQueen had little interest in training, more in his main hobby which was 'to translate Malabar folksongs into English'.[79] 'Whatever I learned in Trichinopoly I learned from an experienced "camp clerk" Valdamanikka Nadar, who was attached to me and who knew a great deal about revenue and judicial work.'[80] Reid (ICS, UP), Collector of Hardoi in 1925, to whom Bonarjee (ICS, UP) was initially sent, was similarly diffident:

> Considerably embarrassed at the idea of having anyone inflicted on him for training, Reid wrote to the Chief Secretary with the suggestion that, since he himself was ignorant of the work, and was hardly in a position to instruct anyone else in it, I should be sent to a more suitable person. The Chief Secretary, a humorist by the name of Lambert [ICS, UP], merely replied that such being the case, Reid and I could not do better than learn the work together. And so we did . . .[81]

Other Collectors were considerably more strict. When Shukla (ICS, UP) first arrived at Bareilly in 1939, the Collector, Acton (ICS, UP), invited him to accompany him on his inspection of the jail early next morning. As Acton proceeded on his rounds, he saw Shukla with his hands in his pockets ('it was a cold winter day in Bareilly'), and asked him in the presence of warders and others to take them out. 'You do not look smart that way,' he said. Shukla comments that this 'lesson went home' along with others that morning. Nor was there any hostility; Acton was transferred shortly afterwards, and later, when Shukla passed his departmental examinations with distinction, Acton wrote congratulating him on his achievement.[82] C. C. Desai still vividly

[79] Menon, K. P. S., *Many Worlds: An Autobiography*, London, 1965, pp. 68–70.
[80] Menon, K. P. S., 'My Life and Work in the ICS', in Panjabi, *Civil Servant*, p. 32.
[81] Bonarjee, N. B., *Under Two Masters*, London, 1970, p. 129.
[82] Shukla, J. D., *Indianization of All-India Services*, New Delhi, 1982, p. 437.

remembers the day in 1923 when he met his first Collector, Crofton (ICS, CP), at Buldana:

> He asked me several questions and I gave the required information; but apparently I did not say 'sir' or show signs of rigid discipline. Immediate was the reaction . . . 'Look, this is a matter of discipline. You are a junior officer and it is your duty to say "sir" to me until I tell you not to say "sir" and you should exact the same discipline from your subordinates in your own time.' Thus began not only a life of service but also a life of discipline and a life of straight talking . . .

He also recalls his first dinner with the Croftons. He did not know the custom of gentlemen staying behind after dinner when the ladies retired to the drawing-room. When the ladies stood and went, he failed to see what the gentlemen were doing and walked out with the ladies, to their dismay and to Crofton's annoyance. 'I was called back and was told what the correct custom was. I was a raw graduate from Cambridge, and was not used to those high-brow social customs which were current in the British ruling circles of the day.'[83] That same year, Panjabi (ICS, Bombay) was sent to Irwin (ICS, Bombay) in Shikarpur District in Sind. 'His war service had made him a strict disciplinarian, so much so that the very first evening, while relaxing after dinner at a cosy fireside, he handed me a copy of the Bombay Land Revenue Code, saying: 'Not a day to be lost; begin with it now. Tomorrow morning we start on our tour to the villages. I have arranged for you tents and a camel until you can get a horse.'[84]

All the evidence available on these early encounters suggests that district training and first postings were perceived by new recruits, both British and Indian, as taking place in strange and uncertain environments. To ease the tensions set up, the new recruit immediately sought to connect (unless he was very independent) with a person or persons who could provide some security, some support, and understanding about this strange new world. In the first instance, and ideally placed to provide that security, there were other members of the ICS. In some cases it would be the Collector. In other cases it would be a younger ICS man, holding, say, the post of SDO or Assistant Collector. But it would invariably be other ICS men. When Watson (ICS, CP) arrived in 1932 he was invited immediately by two other ICS men a few years senior to him to share their house.[85] Hunt (ICS, Madras) remarked that

[83] Desai, C. C., 'My Work in the ICS', in Panjabi, Civil Servant, pp. 72–3.
[84] Panjabi, K. L., 'My Experiences in the ICS', in Panjabi, *Civil Servant*, pp. 86–7.
[85] Watson Papers, IOL MSS Eur. F.180/48, TS p. 3.

'one of the most attractive things about service in India was the instantaneous freemasonry among those who served there . . .'[86] ICS recruits sought out other ICS, but even more surely ICS already settled sought out and assisted ICS recruits. It was a tradition of the service.

The letters of Barlow (ICS, UP) illustrate this sequence well.[87] The first letters home in 1929 remark on the strangeness of India, the sights, the smells. On arrival at Agra District, however, the letters suddenly become preoccupied with people. Other ICS figure most prominently. The Collector 'hasn't been a success here, he got into the ICS with the crowd directly after the war'. The Commissioner is 'rather a difficult man to deal with', but 'decent'. The Assistant Commissioner, Hafazat Hussain (ICS, UP) 'is a pleasant fellow, been to Cambridge, etc., and has helped me a lot'. A 'second class of persons here are the military . . . some I know vaguely—only a few stay for long'. There are also the police, such as 'one police officer named Bolan whom I like particularly'. Then there are what Barlow calls 'the business and odd people'; 'there is one young fellow living in the club whom I like—Lockyer, he works in the bank.' Finally, there are 'the teaching and missionary folk'—several are friendly people who know former connections of Barlow's at Marlborough and Oxford (his school and university). Two weeks later he writes that there is a new Collector, Williamson (ICS, UP). 'I liked him at once . . . the young Englishman who was in my position last year likes him, and Hussain likes him.' Christmas three weeks later finds him staying at the home of James Dunnett (ICS, Punjab) and family in New Delhi. Barlow had been with Dunnett's son at the same Oxford college. The Home Secretary, Harry Haig (ICS, UP), and Mrs Haig and others joined them for dinner, and 'we drank "absent friends" at dinner most feelingly because everyone had some part of their family in England'.[88] The relevant people for Barlow initially were ICS (including Indians) and other Europeans. It is a familiar pattern: Martin (ICS, Bengal) 'did not see much of Indian society' in his first district in 1913–14, apart from another ICS Indian, educated at Cambridge. He saw much of 'the District Judge, the Joint Magistrate, the Steamer Agent, the Superintendent of Police, and their respective wives'; also some missionaries, 'excellent company'.[89]

86 Hunt Papers, Cambridge Archive, TS p. 8.

87 Barlow Papers, Cambridge Archive, Box 1, letters of 17.11.1929 and 24.11.1929.

88 Barlow Papers, letter of 8.12.1929. This particular statement about absent friends actually appears in Barlow's Christmas letter from the Dunnett's a year later.

89 Martin Papers, Cambridge Archive, TS p. 8.

Indian ICS, also, were immediately taken in hand by other ICS during district training and early postings. Pimputkar (ICS, Bombay) in 1941 saw little of his Collector, but lived with three other ICS officers several years his senior, from whom he learned much.[90] Rustomji was told bluntly by Mohammed Khurshid (ICS, Assam) shortly after arriving in Sylhet District in 1941 that 'we would spend Christmas slaying tigers. My idea of Christmas was plum pudding, crackers, and carols, but he was determined to make a man of me.'[91]

New ICS recruits began almost immediately to identify very strongly with the ICS as a separate institution. They were also being pushed up 'high' by relevant others in Indian society. Dunlop (ICS, Madras) noticed immediately in 1937 how 'everything was done for me, I was still not used to this, didn't like it and at first tried to do things for myself but it was not long before I gave that up.' When he arrived at a railway station, he was met by the Collector's camp clerk who presented him with two limes; and two *peons* in official sashes salaamed and a policeman saluted 'and I felt embarrassed'; but 'I was also beginning to appreciate what a special aura surrounded the ICS.'[92] Iengar (ICS, Bombay) on arrival at Ahmedabad in 1926, immediately 'was made aware, on my very first day in the service, that I was a member of a new caste which had its own rigid rules and regulations and lived a life far removed from that of the common people.'[93] Wakefield (ICS, Punjab) also found almost immediately, to his consternation, that in meetings with local councillors in Lyallpur in 1927 nobody would express a view until he had given a lead. 'This deference annoyed and embarrassed me,' he recalls; 'I had come to India to serve . . . but I was not permitted to serve. I was permitted only to lead.'[94] These and many other such examples involving councillors, landlords, members of the bar, subordinate officials, and so on, serve to indicate how the new ICS recruit was gently, but fairly quickly, assigned a high position and leadership role by both the colonial bureaucracy and other prominent people in Indian society. Later, of course, such experiences went unnoticed, because the ICS man had been shaped to this high position and took it for granted.

Despite being pushed up 'high' to rule and becoming immediately

[90] Pimputkar, M. G., to the author in an interview at the National Academy of Administration, Mussoorie, 23 June 1967.

[91] Rustomji, *Enchanted Frontiers*, p. 39.

[92] Dunlop Papers, IOL MSS Eur. F.180/51, TS p. 45.

[93] Iengar, H. V. R., 'My Life in the ICS', in Panjabi, *Civil Servant*, pp. 119–20.

[94] Wakefield, E., *Past Imperative: My Life in India 1927–1947*, London, 1966, pp. 5–6.

part of a rather exclusive 'fraternity', they still 'knew nothing' about the work, as Zinkin put it. 'For several months at first', recalls Mansfield (ICS, Bihar and Orissa) in 1915, 'I found myself almost unable to take part in the general conversation at all, because two-thirds of it was about matters of which at that stage I knew nothing; another quarter was about people whom I have never seen.' Nevertheless, his Collector kept urging him to go down to the treasury office, the courts, and so on, to 'try to pick up how things are done'. One day after lunch Mansfield's Collector went to inspect the treasury, and Mansfield went along. 'On the way, I asked him something about the honorary magistrates, whether they did their jobs merely for honour's sake . . .' and the matter was patiently explained to him. 'We passed the jail, which he says he always inspects at the end of his visit, because the prisoners are generally better treated when the Collector is about, so he gives them as long as he can.'[95] A new recruit, by observing and questioning an experienced officer at work, is beginning to learn 'how things are done' that 'never get into books'. 'We were ill-equipped,' Pullan (ICS, UP) remarks, 'but apart from mere deficiencies in the necessary elements of our future work, we were ourselves in need of much shaping and paring in order that we might conform to the pattern of our service.'[96] That 'shaping and paring' to the specific requirements of the ICS role in the districts began in earnest almost immediately and continued for a number of years.

A young man was handed various written materials relating to his district training on arrival at provincial headquarters or his first district. These included relevant Acts, rules, codes, etc., on which he would be examined within the first year, and also written instructions regarding the training programme itself. The details of the district training programme for ICS recruits varied from province to province, but the main features were common to all. Each trainee was supposed to be 'attached' for short periods to certain officers in the revenue and other departments in that district; this meant basically that he was to watch experienced officers at work and learn from their example. He was also given minor responsibilities, such as work in court as a third class magistrate. He was expected to work very hard on learning the language of the province. He had to prepare for departmental examinations. Most of the time was spent on attachments. One gets

[95] Mansfield Papers, Cambridge Archive, Vol. 1 (Intro.), and letters of 15 Dec. 1915 and 8 Feb. 1916.

[96] Pullan Papers, Cambridge Archive, TS p. 42.

the clear impression from the evidence that the young recruits took these attachments fairly light-heartedly, that not a great deal was learned about the work of these subordinate officers. After watching for a while, the young recruit would be given a chance briefly to do the work himself. Most young recruits found the work boring; Mangat Rai records that in 1938 the 'only thing I learnt during Treasury training was to greatly abbreviate my initials'.[97] Wakefield at one point was sent to an agricultural college at Lyallpur for a three-week course of instruction in 1928 and 'the lectures on wheat cultivation vividly recalled to my mind the advice given to farmers by Virgil in his first Georgic', so 'I amused myself by writing up my notes in flowing Virgilian hexameters'.[98]

Yet gradually the recruits were beginning to learn things about the official routine of the colonial bureaucracy and life in a rural district. Noronha (ICS, CP) 'learned much that was to be useful' in his future career, when attached to a Subdivisional Officer in 1940, by watching what he did rather than what he said. This man 'had all the tricks of the lazy officer which must be detected during inspection'. For example:

> Periodically he cleared his files by marking them to the *tehsildar* for enquiry and report. He was also an expert at dismissing cases in default, taking pains to call a case as soon as he saw that the applicant had gone to the urinal. His field inspections were made without ever visiting a field, with the help of the village map and the *patwari*. And yet, he got on reasonably well with the raj; if he was not promoted, neither was he dismissed.[99]

'Gradually (towards the end of my district training in 1917) I began to feel at home in this strange new world with its placid and official routine . . .' writes Fitze (ICS, CP).[100] Hunt (ICS, Madras) recalls his period of attachment in 1939 with the *karnam*; 'after a week or two of plodding and questioning I began to feel more familiar with the problems of Krishnapuram', including the nature of the local hierarchy and the location of the Government's political support.[101] Barlow learned a similar lesson about political support in the United Provinces. In February 1930 he went to his first 'civil service week' at Lucknow, and wrote home about the 'most marvellous fete given by

97 Mangat Rai, *Commitment my Style*, p. 57.
98 Wakefield, *Past Imperative*, p. 6.
99 Noronha, *A Tale Told by an Idiot*, p. 8.
100 Fitze, K., *Twilight of the Maharajas*, London, 1956, p. 13.
101 Hunt Papers, TS pp. 23–4.

the *taluqdars*, all done regardless of expense'. In April he is writing home about political conditions in his district being 'very difficult at present for those responsible' and riots in Calcutta, 'the inevitable result of Mr Gandhi's "non-violent" campaign'. In May, 'what a farce all this salt making is!' and 'I am thankful I am not a policeman in these troubled times', for 'they are bearing the brunt of all that is going on' and 'get cursed by magistrates and slandered by newspapermen and jeered at by fellow countrymen, yet remain loyal'. In October the landowners of the district gave the departing Collector a farewell garden party and 'everyone of importance was there'. He goes on: 'Congress are now embarked on the very dangerous policy of encouraging the peasants not to pay their rents . . . the only possible gain is that the Congress will finally alienate all the landowners.' Some months later in 1931, in his first post, he writes: 'I have summoned a meeting of all the biggest landowners in my subdivision . . . (who are the titled classes in this country) to discuss the political situation with them.' Later, 'they actually decided much to my surprise to organize a little counter-propaganda' against the Congress.[102] Barlow was beginning to learn about the location of his political support in the district. The lesson was important, because to be able to locate and work with such support was an essential behaviour pattern in the ICS tradition.

The transmission to young ICS recruits of behaviour patterns, norms, and values during district training and in early postings was not enough. There were also continuing controls on recruitment meant to ensure as far as possible that those entering into that process were likely to be receptive to the specific norms and values being transmitted. The deliberate attempts by the Secretary of State to get young gentlemen from public schools into the ICS throughout this period is an example. European recruitment in 1936 provides an effective indicator. In that year, for the first time in the 1930s, some recruits were obtained simply on the basis of an interview by a Selection Board. It is clear that the new procedure was designed at least in part to get more of the 'right sort' of person into the Service which the examination was increasingly failing to do. The examination in 1936 produced 15 Europeans, of whom only seven had been to public school; however, the Selection Board were freer to get the sort of person wanted, and selected 24 Europeans of whom 20 had been to

[102] Barlow Papers, letters from 7 Feb. 1930 to 12 Apr. 1931.

public school.[103] One Selection Board member remarked: 'the type sought is endowed with qualities which are fostered and brought to the surface more by the public school cum Oxford (or Cambridge) kind of education than by . . . secondary (day) school and non-residential University system.'[104]

Even more care was taken with Indian candidates. The entrance examination, being in the English language and tied to English language school curricula, clearly influenced the intake. As important was the screening of each Indian candidate by the relevant provincial government. Considerable care was exercised in this secret operation, which involved both a security clearance and a character reference. In 1923–4, when the criteria employed in this process were again discussed in the Home Department (particularly the question of whether or not ICS candidates whose near relatives were 'undesirable' should be refused permission to sit the entrance examination), it appears that the security clearance was chiefly concerned with assessing whether or not the candidate could be trusted politically.[105] The character reference assessed whether or not the candidate was 'up to the ICS standard socially . . .'. For example, the Bihar and Orissa Government in 1931 regarded a candidate as 'not suitable' because 'his father is a retired bank clerk who has no property and is reported to visit courts occasionally as a tout', and 'his elder brother is a *swarajist* who used to work in a Gandhi Ashram as a master tailor'; another from the same province is unsuitable because of 'his poor physique, lack of personality, and humble social status'; a candidate from Mysore in 1934 was judged by the Resident there as 'a suitable candidate for the ICS' because 'he comes of a very respectable . . . family who are well represented in the Mysore State Service', and he 'bears a good character and has not been concerned in political movements;' the United Provinces Government reported to Delhi and the Secretary of State in 1936 that 'enquiries regarding the character of the following 16 candidates were made by the Superintendent of Police, Allahabad, who reports that their characters are good and that they have not taken part in any movement subversive of law and order.'[106]

[103] Data compiled from biographical information in NAI Home Dept. File 32/36—Ests., 1936: 'Results of the ICS Examination held in London in 1936'.

[104] Report by E. H. Jones, 7 June 1938, in L/S G/6/181, S. G/3751/34(I), cited in Ewing, A., 'The Indian Civil Service, 1919–1942', Cambridge University Ph.D. dissertation, 1980, p. 178.

[105] NAI Home Dept. File 492/23—Ests., 1923.

[106] NAI Home Dept. Files 63/31—Ests., 1931; 285/34—Ests., 1934; 31/37—Ests., 1937.

The other set of controls on the process was the regular assessments made of young ICS by their more senior colleagues informally and in confidential reports. Some of these reports which indicate the criteria employed are available; a few examples must suffice from assessments made of young ICS recruits from Central Provinces in the late 1930s by their seniors (both European and Indian ICS):[107] 'I have seen a great deal of [*A*]—both officially and socially—and he certaily has got the ICS calibre and stamp'; *B* 'is an extremely nice boy, with good manners and popular with all—a good tennis player and "mixer" '; *C* 'has plenty of ability and self-confidence, and is at the same time quiet and reserved'; *D* 'proved himself a most competent officer, got into close contact with the people by carrying out most thorough and detailed tours'; *E*, however, was considered 'either thoughtless or definitely irresponsible in some ways—many cases have been pending 6 to 10 or 12 months . . .' and it is 'doubtful' that he will 'settle down' and become 'more steady and reliable'; *F* 'has good manners', is 'a nice boy, and keen', although 'he gives one the impression of being just a little "pansy", but this may be wrong—I have told him that he should get a horse, and ride if an opportunity occurs'.

It is not part of the argument here that younger ICS recruits were shaped to share all the attitudes of their seniors. Clearly there were generational differences within the ICS, reflecting changing views at universities amongst other things, and the shaping process did not remove these differences. There is a widespread belief, for example, that younger ICS Europeans were more liberal politically than their seniors, neatly summed up by Griffiths (ICS, Bengal):

> The first World War was the watershed. Those of us who came out after the War had been imbued with liberalism (good or bad as one may regard that) and our attitudes were very different from our superiors. We had a great deal more to do with Indians, for instance. I had many Indian friends in my early districts and spent most of my time with them. I don't think this would have been approved by my superiors in the Secretariat—rather letting down the Raj.[108]

But this is misleading as an overall judgement. There are many instances of liberal views expressed by ICS Indians and ICS Europeans both senior and junior, some of them reported earlier in this chapter.

107 NAI Home Dept. File 35/47/39—Ests., 1939, Appendix: 'Views of provincial governments on exam and selection recruits, 1936–39', dated 20.4.1942.

108 P. Griffiths to J. Broomfield, in Calcutta, 1961, and reported to me in a personal communication, 30 Sept. 1966. I am grateful to Professor Broomfield for this reference.

Nor will the evidence support any claims about social relations between ICS Europeans and ICS Indians being always friendly. There is too much evidence to the contrary. Take Griffiths' province, Bengal. Baker's letters home in April–June 1940 from the Hotel Windermere in Darjeeling speak of it as 'a hive of the Service', and it is clear from all the gossip about the comings and goings of 'the Windermere crowd' that they are all European ICS and their wives; earlier, his letters record his experiences when posted in 1938 to 'an excellent station' with 'rather a good crowd', but 'the crowd' was entirely European; 'one saw little of Gupta the S.P. [Superintendent of Police] and not more than one could of Swarup . . .' and in August of that year he made over charge to 'the incomprehensible Iyengar'.[109] There are similar examples from other provinces suggesting that such social distance between Europeans and Indians was common.

Official relations at the work place, however, were close during the 1920s and 1930s. Europeans and Indians were shaped together by Indians and Europeans, as has been made clear, and they continued to work closely together at this official level. Jenkins (ICS, Punjab) assumed he was explaining the obvious when he told Mosley that 'all civil officials were quite accustomed to serving under Indians' and 'the idea that any of us would object if our boss was an Indian was ridiculous, or that we would refuse to obey one of his orders.'[110]

INDIAN GENTLEMEN

I have argued that Indians and Europeans were shaped together to norms, values, and behaviour patterns in the ICS tradition. To strengthen the argument, some attention needs to be given to the apparent implausibility of ICS Indians really making this British administrative tradition their own. To put the issue most bluntly: since the gentlemanly mode (from which ICS norms and values flow) is essentially a product of Western (Protestant) society, can Indians really be gentlemen?

The first main point is that ICS Indians came from comfortable, professional, and service-class family backgrounds. Indeed, they had an even more solid service-class background than their European

[109] Baker Papers, letters, Apr.–Aug. 1938, and letters from Darjeeling, 14 Apr.–20 June 1940.

[110] Sir Evan Jenkins to Leonard Mosley in a personal communication, as reported in Mosley, L., *The Last Days of the British Raj*, London, 1961, p. 252.

colleagues. The Home Department noted in 1919 that 'practically all the [Indian] candidates came from the professional middle class'; in 1928, 19 Indian recruits came from the following family backgrounds: government service—8, teaching—4, medicine—2, law—2, landowner—2, business—1; in 1941, three of the four Indians selected in London for the ICS were sons of government officials, the other was the son of a barrister.[111] ICS Indians were not only overwhelmingly from the professional middle class, they also had been educated in English language schools and universities. Data on all ICS Indians recruited between 1919 and 1939 show that 22 per cent were graduates of Madras University; Allahabad, Bombay, and Punjab Universities each supplied 14 per cent; 12 per cent came from Calcutta University; 12 per cent attended one of several other Indian universities; and the remaining 12 per cent had worked for a degree at a British university.[112] The content of the educational curriculum was essentially Western.[113]

Gentlemanly norms and values were hardly unknown to young men coming from such occupational and educational backgrounds. Furthermore, Indian recruits spent a year on probation at a British university (Oxford, Cambridge, or London), two years if they entered via the examination (and nomination) in India. 'The chief object in sending the [Indian] probationers home', it was privately noted in the India Office in 1920, 'is that they may be, to put it crudely, to some extent Europeanised.'[114]

Bearing these considerations in mind can lead one to accept uncritically the fashionable view that an ICS Indian was merely a 'Brown Sahib', as one of them confessed, 'who entered service not out of patriotic motives but with an eye to the emoluments, security and enormous power that were attached to the job', and for whom 'early promotions and titles came' if he could 'act the sedulous ape to his white bosses and carry out their policy faithfully'.[115] The standard work

[111] For 1919, NAI Home Dept. Ests.—A, Proceedings, Sept. 1919, No. 294; for 1928, Beaglehole 'From Rulers to Servants', p. 246; for 1941, NAI Home Dept. File 32/41—Ests., 1941.

[112] Compiled by the author classifying each of 450 Indian recruits in the *India Office and Burma Office List, 1940*. The figures do not include Indian recruits of 1939–43, 38 Burmans from the University of Rangoon, and 11 for whom no university is mentioned.

[113] The standard work on this background is Misra, B. B., *The Indian Middle Classes: Their Growth in Modern Times*, London, 1961.

[114] NAI Home Dept. Ests—A, Proceedings, 29 Aug. 1920, No. 509, letter dated 26 Mar. 1920.

[115] Pandit, 'Little Gandhis for IAS', 7–8.

on the 'Brown Sahib' identifies them as Asian administators who 'speak English at home, dream in it, scold their children in it, make love in it'; such an administrator has 'tastes that are carefully cultivated, his values conform to the British public school tradition and his manners are, generally, as good or as bad as those of the average educated Briton'; 'the Brown Sahib has been schooled to think British, feel British, talk British, act British, and buy British.'[116] Perhaps a few Indians would fit the label of 'Brown Sahib', but as a general description it is seriously misleading. ICS Indians were Indians and proud of it. Moreover, nearly all were Hindus or Muslims with distinctly Indian religious practices and beliefs reflecting values and life-styles very different from those of their European colleagues.

The data in Table 11 show that 90 per cent of ICS Indians were Hindus or Muslims or Sikhs. They also show the gradual increase in the proportion of Muslims during the period, a consequence of efforts by the Secretary of State to improve their position by way of nomination. For example, in 1928 21 Hindus, two Muslims, and one Sikh were successful at the examinations in London and Delhi, so five Muslims and one Indian Christian were nominated to the ICS; in 1941 11 Hindus and one Parsee entered by exam, so six Muslims and one Anglo-Indian were nominated.[117] Even so, Muslims remained a relatively small contingent. Table 11 shows that most ICS Indians were Hindus. High-caste *Brahmans* were predominant, although that

Table 11. *ICS Indians: Composition by Community, 1933 and 1941*

Community	1933		1941	
	No.	Per cent	No.	Per cent
Hindus	271	72	352	69
Muslims	61	16	99	20
Indian Christians	23	6	29	6
Parsis	8	2	10	2
Sikhs	6	2	10	2
Others (mostly Anglo-Indians)	6	2	8	1
Totals:	375	100	508	100

Sources: Compiled by the author from data in the following: for 1933, NAI Home Dept. File 50/36—Ests., 1936; for 1941, NAI Home Dept. File 42/42—Ests., 1942.

[116] Vittachi, T., *The Brown Sahib*, London, 1962, pp. 52–4.

[117] For 1928, Beaglehole, 'From Rulers to Servants', p. 246; for 1941, NAI Home Dept. File 32/41—Ests., 1941.

dominance began to fade somewhat in the latter part of the 1930s. For example, in 1928, of 18 Hindus who entered, 14 were *Brahmans*, one was a *Kshatriya*, and three were *Kayasths*—from Kayasth kin groups (it is misleading to identify them as a caste)[118] which have traditionally been much involved in administrative service occupations; in 1937 however, of the eight Hindus who were successful at the London examination, only four were *Brahmans*; and in 1941, of the eight successful candidates at the Delhi examination, three were *Brahmans*, four *Kayasths*, and one a *Vaishya*.[119] Only one member of the scheduled castes (or 'depressed classes' as they were referred to at the time) entered the ICS—he was nominated in 1940.[120]

That *Brahmans* and *Kayasths* from well-to-do professional and service-class families predominated in the ICS is understandable, given the nature of the entrance examination and the weeding-out operation as a result of obtaining character references. *Brahmans*, *Kayasths*, and other high castes have received some attention from scholars, and what can be gleaned from such studies about those in 'public service' bears little relation to the 'Brown Sahib' picture.[121] Instead, performing in a modern administrative setting according to an initially European tradition was consistent with maintaining also much of the traditional Hindu way of life. Put simply, 'when I put on my shirt to go to the office, I take off my caste, and when I come home and take off my shirt, I put on my caste.'[122] Khare, for example, has described very fully the ways that an ICS *Brahman* handled these role changes between the office and the home.[123] *Kayasths*, Muslims, and Sikhs were also able to operate effectively with other administrators in an all-India, secular realm while still considering themselves as members of their particular community.

[118] The authoritative study is Leonard, K., *Social History of an Indian Caste: The Kayasths of Hyderabad*, Berkeley, 1978.

[119] For 1928: Beaglehole, 'From Rulers to Servants', 246; for 1937: NAI Home Dept. File 32/41—Ests., 1941.

[120] NAI Home Dept. File 31/40—Ests., 1940.

[121] e.g. Khare, R. S., *The Changing Brahmans*, Chicago, 1970; Conlon, F., *A Caste in a Changing World: The Chitrapur Saraswat Brahmans 1700–1935*, Berkeley, 1977; Nair, B. N., *The Dynamic Brahmin*, Bombay, 1959; Leonard, *Kayasths*. More generally, Singer, M., *Traditional India: Structure and Change*, Jaipur, 1975; Srinivas, M. N., *Social Change in Modern India*, Berkeley, 1966; Bottomore, T. B., 'Modern Elites in India', in Unnithan, T. K. N. *et al.* (eds.), *Towards a Sociology of Culture in India*, New Delhi, 1965, pp. 180–8.

[122] Kathleen Gough to M. N. Srinivas in a personal communication, reported in Srinivas, *Social Change*, p. 123.

[123] Khare, *Changing Brahmans*, pp. 134–6.

Furthermore, the content of *Brahman* and *Kayasth* culture actually made it easy to move each day between family life and ICS work where gentlemanly norms and values prevailed. This is unmistakably clear from Khare's study of the *Kanya-Kubja Brahmans* of North India, Leonard's of the *Kayasths* of Hyderabad, and Singer's of Madras *Brahmans*. The importance of *dharma* for Hindus placed a high valuation on duty and excellence in one's social location; this was allied with the fact that administrative work had high prestige for 'modern' *Brahmans* and *Kayasths* in 'public service'.[124] Indeed, 'public service' was highly valued. Bayly, for example, shows how certain *Brahman* and *Kayasth* families in Allahabad were regarded by others as 'service families'.[125] Similar connections can be made between *Brahman* and *Kayasth* culture and self-confidence and courageous self-discipline. The *Kanya-Kubjas*, for example, prided themselves on being brave in the face of danger.[126] ICS Indians, in short, were very different socially from their European colleagues, but at the same time in their official capacity Indians had no difficulty (indeed it seemed right and proper) in accepting the gentlemanly norms and values of duty and public service, allied to self-discipline and independent courage.

Indians and Europeans could work together within the shared ICS administrative tradition, and then retire at the end of the day into separate social settings. There were also friendships formed within that official setting. For the Europeans, if Indians had not been gentlemen, this would have been difficult. But Indians could be gentlemen; an ICS Collector during the Second World War had no difficulty at all in entering into a gentleman's agreement with Jawaharlal Nehru.[127] That Indians and Europeans from different cultural backgrounds did share as gentlemen a common administrative tradition is captured poignantly by Martin (ICS, Bihar) who, long after he left the ICS in 1947, returned to Delhi on business in the late 1960s and called on 'an old friend', H. C. Sarin (ICS, Bihar), who had been Martin's contemporary in the late 1930s and early 1940s. Sarin had

[124] On public service and Hindu values, see also Mayer, A. C., 'Public Service and Individual Merit in a Town in Central India', in Mayer, A. C. (ed.), *Culture and Morality*, London, 1981, pp. 153–73.

[125] Bayly, C. A., *The Local Roots of Indian Politics, Allahabad, 1880–1920*, Oxford, 1975, esp. pp. 57–68. More generally on origins and general significance of service groups, Bayly, C., *Rulers, Townsmen and Bazaars: North Indian Society in the Age of British Expansion 1770–1870*, Cambridge, 1983.

[126] Khare, *Changing Brahmans*, p. 45.

[127] Mason, *English Gentleman*, pp. 210–11.

been a 'charming and intelligent Punjabi' and he was 'as charming as ever' when they met again in Sarin's office in the New Delhi Secretariat, 'but looked tired and desperately overworked'. 'Pride of achievement and exasperation over what had been left undone or bungled were evident in equal proportions in what he told me,' Martin records, and as he left Sarin said, 'Goodbye, Hugh, it's a pity you weren't born thirty years earlier, or an Indian.'[128]

In sum, Indians and Europeans were shaped together to the gentlemanly norms and values that prevailed in the work context, even though their cultural milieu may have been very different at home. It was in such a setting that the content of the ICS tradition was passed on to ICS Indians between the wars.

[128] Martin Papers, IOL MSS Eur. F.180/21, TS p. 56.

3

Political support in the 1940s

POLITICAL administrators do not last very long if they become isolated from the political leadership of the state and dominant social classes in society.[1] In India in the 1940s the transfer of power resulted in one set of political leaders being replaced by another. The ICS survived this political transformation while being badly mauled in the process. A majority of the members either retired, quit, left for Pakistan, or were sacked. Yet, by the end of the 1940s, the ICS and its fledgling successor, the IAS, had been guaranteed an extraordinarily secure position in the new Indian constitution. The larger drama of partition and *swaraj*, which has received so much attention in the literature,[2] provides only a backdrop here to the particular story of how and why the ICS survived during those years.

CHANGING SUPPORT STRUCTURES

When war came in 1939, the ICS, and the colonial bureaucracy more generally, were still basically loyal to the British Government. The main opposition to the raj and to the ICS as its agent came from the Indian National Congress. Nehru had repeatedly made his position clear as to what he thought of the ICS, and many in the Congress agreed with him. Certainly there was no place in Gandhian ideology for a highly paid administrative élite. Yet only ten years later Indian ICS men had leaped into the top administrative posts in the land, an ICS successor had been created, and nearly all the roughly three million colonial officials who were working for the British at the time of independence had been asked to stay at their posts. Why did the Congress change its position during the 1940s and opt for retaining an ICS framework and the tradition of administration it represented? There were, clearly, various factors involved.

[1] Bottomore, T. B., 'The Administrative Elite', in Horowitz, I. L. (ed.). *The New Sociology: Essays in Honour of C. Wright Mills*, New York, 1965, pp. 357–69.

[2] For a guide to the enormous literature on this subject, see Majumdar, A. K., 'Writings on the Transfer of Power', in Nanda, B. R. (ed.), *Essays in Modern Indian History*, New Delhi, 1980, pp. 182–222.

Of major importance was the changing character of the Congress organization.[3] Under Gandhi's influence from 1919 to 1931 the Congress was as much concerned with social uplift as with political mobilization. During the 1930s, however, the right wing became increasingly alarmed at the strength of socialists and communists within the organization and gradually took control, suspending civil disobedience, forming Congress Parliamentary Boards during 1934–6 (most of the work was initially done by Provincial Boards), and gradually converting the Congress into a political party contesting elections and taking office within existing institutions. The conversion of the Congress into a party driving for power alarmed many Muslims, and the Muslim League was able later to capitalize on these feelings. By the 1940s the Congress certainly had no commitment to destroy or transform the state structure. One can be misled by concentrating on Nehru's radical outbursts. Even the Left was deceived by them. As late as 1946–7, for example, the socialist parties still looked to Nehru for guidance and expected him to resign from the Interim Government at 'the right moment' to lead 'the revolution'. Nehru, of course, never resigned. In 1947 the more conservative Congress and Muslim League parties divided the spoils; the Left, which might have abolished the ICS and transformed the bureaucracy (and much else), got nothing.

This changing, more conservative orientation of Congress was a consequence in part of changes in the broader structure of classes within which the political struggle between Congress and the raj was conducted. Summarily,[4] the support of two classes was seen as important for the maintenance of the raj. One was the landed class (including the princes) in India, the other was the capitalist class in Britain. This latter alignment had been openly acknowledged in the nineteenth century: the Viceroy stated publicly in Calcutta in 1888 that he considered the prime duty of his Government to be to watch 'over the enormous commercial interests of the mother country', and that 'it would be criminal to ignore the responsibility of the Government

[3] The sketch in this paragraph follows the account of Misra, B. B., *The Indian Political Parties: An Historical Analysis of Political Behaviour up to 1947*, Delhi, 1976.

[4] The following summary leans on: Misra, *Political Parties*: Moore, *Social Origins*, esp. ch. 6; Bagchi, A. K., *Private Investment in India, 1900–1939*, Cambridge, 1972; Frankel, F. R., *India's Political Economy, 1947–1977*, Princeton, 1978; Tomlinson, B. R., *The Indian National Congress and the Raj, 1929–1942: The Penultimate Phase*, London, 1976; Markovitz, C., *Indian Business and Nationalist Politics, 1931–39: The Indigenous Capitalist Class and the Rise of the Congress Party*, Cambridge, 1985.

towards those who have sunk large sums of money in the development of Indian resources on the faith of official guarantees, or who have invested their capital in the Indian funds . . ;' 'the same considerations apply with almost equal force to that further amount of capital which is employed by private British enterprise in manufactures . . . on the assumption that English rule and English justice will remain dominant in India.'[5] It became less fashionable in later years to acknowledge this connection openly, but it was still there at the close: Linlithgow (Viceroy, 1936–43), for example, reminded Wavell (Viceroy, 1943–7) privately in 1945 of the importance 'of the interests of big business [in Britain] in maintaining something like the status quo in India'.[6] For a number of reasons, however, the political leadership of the British state was already beginning to come around to the view that abandoning colonial rule in India was probably inevitable.[7] Churchill amazed King George VI at one of their Tuesday luncheons as early as July 1942 when he gloomily disclosed that 'all three parties in Parliament were quite prepared to give up India to the Indians after the war.'[8]

The main opposition to British rule came from a nationalist movement loosely co-ordinated under the capacious umbrella of the Indian National Congress. The Congress represented a curious amalgam of interests, classes, and groups, and there were considerable differences from province to province. Nevertheless, it is perhaps fair to say that in the 1920s and 1930s it began to gain some support from sections of the urban working class and from the peasantry (especially in the late 1930s), and also from certain professional groups in the towns, including the few radical intellectuals who were there. It also represented, although less solidly, India's small (but increasingly important) indigenous capitalist class, whose interests to some extent were in conflict with the maintenance of British rule because of restrictions placed on their activities for the benefit of British capital. Bigger Indian capitalists were divided and uncertain as to whether they should align with the Indian National Congress or with the raj,

[5] IOL MSS. Eur E.243(25), p. 201A, 3 Dec. 1888. Cited in Misra, *Political Parties*, p. 90.

[6] *Wavell* entry for 24 Mar. 1945 (at p. 118).

[7] For what is perhaps the most definitive general analysis of the causes of the end of British rule in India (and elsewhere) in the 20th century, see Gallagher, J., *The Decline, Revival and Fall of the British Empire*, ed. A. Seal, Cambridge, 1982, pp. 73–153.

[8] Wheeler-Bennett, J. W., *King George VI: His Life and Reign*, London, 1958, from the King's Diary, 28 July 1942, cited at p. 703.

although by the late 1930s they were moving more certainly towards the former. They tended, however, to keep aloof from provincial politics. At lower levels of the Congress organization, merchants and traders appear to have increased their influence, mainly through their control of the financial resources the Congress increasingly required to contest elections. These relationships affected ideological struggles within the Congress, particularly in the 1930s, and steps were taken from time to time by those representing capitalist interests to try to counter or at least contain the economic radicalism within the Congress of Nehru and others.[9]

By the end of the Second World War, these efforts had had a measure of success. More conservative elements in the Congress were in the ascendancy and increasingly in a position to control the state. Unity, strength, order, and a political posture not unfriendly to capitalist enterprise became the main orientations, and were indeed paramount considerations in the decisions taken by the new political leadership. Retaining the ICS framework and the colonial bureaucracy within the new Indian state reassured Indian capitalists, and that decision appears to have had an important influence on the increasingly favourable attitude of Indian businessmen towards the political leadership.[10] Industrial policy resolutions were also generally acceptable to the indigenous capitalist class, and Indian capitalists went on to do well in initially uneasy, and then increasingly confident, alliance with international capital.[11] The traditional landed class—princes, *zamindars*, and other big landlords—were hurt (although not decisively) by the integration of the princely states and land reform legislation, and then gradually replaced by a new landed class made up of prosperous peasant proprietors and capitalist farmers (notably in Punjab). Very broadly speaking one can say that after the end of colonial rule the political leadership of the Indian state took a position generally responsive to international capital while benefiting, and being supported by, Indian capital and newer landed groups (for example, progressive peasant proprietors), both of whom did particularly well out of the

[9] Sharnkar, G., 'Socialist ideas of Jawaharlal Nehru', *Journal of Indian History*, lvii (Aug.–Dec. 1979), 441–9.

[10] Markovitz, *Indian Business*, p. 187.

[11] e.g. Weiskopf, T., 'Dependence and Imperialism in India', in Selden, M. (ed.), *Remaking Asia*, New York, 1974, pp. 200–46; Posgate, W. D., 'Fertilizers for India's Green Revolution: The Shaping of Government Policy', *Asian Survey*, xiv (Aug. 1974), 733–50.

policies and practices of the political leadership after independence.[12]

The general orientation of political thinking in the 1940s within the Congress leadership in the Interim Government and the Constituent Assembly was framed by this broader structure of classes and class interests. It has been summarized by Rothermund as one in which 'the necessity of maintaining the *status quo* overruled all revolutionary or quasi-revolutionary claims'.[13] Such thinking saved the ICS. Even Jawaharlal Nehru remarked in the Constituent Assembly in November 1947: 'First things must come first and the first thing is the security and stability of India',[14] including coping with the slaughter and its aftermath in Punjab, crushing opposition in Hyderabad, and containing it in Kashmir. It was no time to start tampering with the bureaucracy.

Another factor was the sheer size of the problem of radical restructuring of the bureaucracy. There were other models to choose from, but Congress leaders had no experience of them. Once in power, why not use the known instruments at hand in a time of political uncertainty rather than experiment with the unknown? Even the very traditional within Congress could rationalize keeping the westernized bureaucracy on the ground that it had its counterpart in earlier state forms. For example, there were instances of cadres of professionally trained civil servants in the Mughal Empire and before that in the Gupta Empire; a Persian manuscript of the Bangash Pathans of Farrukhabad suggests that Mughal provincial governors were expected to recruit about 100 boys each year who were then trained, posted initially to a province, and later transferred from province to province and to the imperial court; and in some cases bureaucratic cadres were controlled by imperial secretariats.[15]

Perhaps of decisive importance was the great status within the Congress in the 1940s of Sardar Vallabhbhai Patel, who became Home Member in the Interim Government. At a conference of provincial premiers on 21 and 22 October 1946, he came down heavily in favour of keeping the ICS and the Indian Police and in creating two successor all-India services—the IAS and IPS (Indian Police Service).

[12] Bettelheim, C., *India Independent*, New York, 1968.

[13] Rothermund, D., 'Constitutional Reforms versus National Agitation in India, 1900–1950', *Journal of Asian Studies*, xxi (1962), 520. More generally, see Austin, G., *The Indian Constitution: Cornerstone of a Nation*, Oxford, 1966.

[14] India. *Constituent Assembly (Legislature) Debates*, 1947, Vol. 1, pp. 793–5.

[15] For elaboration, see Gupta, B. K., 'Some Aspects of Indian Bureaucracy in the Gupta, Mughal and British Empires', *Journal of the National Academy of Administration* 6.3 (July 1961).

The provincial premiers who attended the conference were not wildly enthusiastic about retaining all-India services within their provinces. They acquiesced, however, because of the other factors already mentioned, because Patel leaned heavily on them, and because many Congress leaders in the provinces by this time had worked with some ICS Indians and knew them to be able and loyal. Between 1946 and 1949 Patel worked tirelessly to save the ICS and its steel frame. His efforts reached a climax in 1949 in the Constituent Assembly debate on the ICS, when he rose to defend the ICS against its critics: 'I have worked with them during this difficult period . . .' (he had indeed); they are 'patriotic, loyal, sincere, able . . .' (no doubt they were); 'remove them,' Patel thundered, 'and I see nothing but a picture of chaos all over the country.'[16] Patel and the Congress leadership did not want that. Nor did the interests they represented.

The ICS tradition of administration survived the 1940s because there was continuing political support for it from first the British Government and then the Congress Government. Also, its continuation did not pose any threat to dominant classes at the time. Although this broad *structure* of support is important in explaining why the ICS tradition survived, so also is the *agency* of Indian ICS initiatives in actively cultivating the support of leading politicians during the 1940s.

THE THREE-WAY SPLIT

By 1939–40 an unmistakable political divide was opening between European and Indian members of the ICS. Such divisions may have been particularly noticeable in Punjab and the United Provinces but they were appearing everywhere. Mangat Rai (ICS, Punjab), being a Christian, was perhaps better placed than most to perceive them.[17] What struck him about the Indian officials he met during district training in 1939 was 'the extent of disloyalty to the British government'. He did not meet a single Indian 'who advocated the continuation of the regime' and he 'met several who were impatient for its abdication'. At the same time, there were surface expressions of loyalty on public occasions from some, silence from others, and no open sign of indiscipline from any. European ICS were generally respected as hard-working, friendly, honest, and just. Indeed, the Europeans seemed particularly anxious to be friendly after war broke out in Europe, but 'it

[16] India. *Constituent Assembly Debates*, x (Oct. 1949), 48–52.

[17] The following comes from Mangat Rai, *Commitment My Style*, p. 51.

was now the Indians who hung back, and the essential guts of the situation of genuine loyalty for British rule did not exist' despite public discretion or silence on the matter. Muslim attitudes were more equivocal: they 'were not consumed with love for the British', but they 'had a deep distrust of the Hindu'.

Mangat Rai has also given one of the fullest statements of the insoluble contradiction faced by Indian college graduates in the 1930s contemplating a career in the civil service and their continuing ambivalence within that contradiction. He went through St Stephen's College, Delhi University, and 'the national movement was the very air that every student breathed'. The 1930s 'was the era of Gandhi, Nehru, and the group of distinguished men and women who surrounded them'. Most students were placed in an ambivalent atmosphere when considering the question of work after college because there were few jobs in industry (because of the economic slump), the legal profession was 'a bottomless pit', and therefore the civil service was 'an inescapable consideration'; yet entering the civil service necessarily 'involved a duality of purpose, and a contradiction between the independence we all desired for India and the need for work with a foreign-controlled government'. Each individual had to work out his own way of coping with this contradiction. As for Mangat Rai:

> I do not think many of us resolved this contradiction or integrated the duality of motive and emphasis which this situation thrust on us to a logical or final answer. Most of us took whatever opportunity offered and hoped for the best. That was certainly my position . . .[18]

There are many similar references by ICS Indians to the problem of coping with this contradiction. Dharma Vira (ICS, UP) recalls that when he joined the ICS in 1930, he was 'in a bit of a fix' because he was bound 'to maintain the prestige of the Crown', yet he 'could not be totally oblivious of the legitimate desire of the country to be free and for the British to depart'. So, he says, 'We had to balance our existence between these two extremes'.[19] Nationalists they certainly were during the 1930s, yet there was not any clear institutional focus for these feelings. When Zinkin (ICS, Bombay) arrived in 1938, he found ICS Indians in that province 'nationalist almost to a man, though

[18] Ibid., pp. 19–30.

[19] Interview broadcast on BBC Radio 4, 17 Nov. 1974, 'The Heavenborn' in the radio series 'Plain Tales from the Raj'.

profoundly ambivalent about the Congress', because 'they wanted an India which they could run, not a Gandhian India'. Muslim ICS, 'even in 1938 and even in low-temperature Bombay, were on the whole anti-Congress' although not yet pro-Muslim League. Muslims 'saw the Congress as a Hindu organization which did not consider their special interests' and they objected to Gandhi's 'Hindu religious symbolism and to the use of 'Bande Mataram' as a national song'.[20] Narasimhan (ICS, Madras) in 1940 was under surveillance by the CID, being suspected of having affiliations with Congress. 'It is quite true' he remarks, 'that at home I wore *khadi*' and 'of course I was as patriotic, I suppose, as the next Indian, and I longed to see the day when India would be free; but I actually had no political affiliations because I strongly believed in an apolitical civil service.'[21]

Some European recruits at this time were keenly aware of the contradictory position of their Indian colleagues. Downing (ICS, Madras) was at the ICS training camp in Dehra Dun in 1941 with all other probationers of that year.[22] 'We were a happy party,' he says, 'though occasionally the arguments could become sharp.' He noticed immediately that 'all the Indian probationers were keen nationalists, some with family connections in the Congress Party'. The Europeans 'found this rather surprising' at first. They were 'not unsympathetic', however, because most 'had the mildly left-wing views which were prevalent in the British universities in the thirties' and 'we accepted that India would become self-governing in some form or other after the war, but at first sight it seemed odd that men whose object was the end of foreign rule saw nothing strange in entering government service while that rule was still in being.' In attempting to account for this duality, Downing concluded that, in practice, the Indians 'made a sub-conscious distinction between the government as the instrument of a foreign power and, in its purely administrative capacity, as the established government of the country, which in all non-political matters they expected to operate impartially in the public interest and

[20] Zinkin, M., 'Impressions, 1938–47' in Phillips, C. H. and Wainwright, M., (eds.), *The Partition of India*, London, 1970, pp. 546–7.

[21] Narasimhan Papers, IOL MSS Eur. F.180/56, TS p. 8.

[22] The training camp was instituted as a wartime measure, to compensate in part for the termination of probationary years at British universities during the war. The camps were considered so successful in official circles that there were suggestions to continue them after the war. See NAI Home Dept. File 35/44/41—Ests., dated 1941 and 35/58/41—Ests., dated 1941.

hence had no inhibitions about taking part in it'.[23] Not all Indians were keen nationalists; Rustomji (ICS, Assam) was at the Dehra Dun camp in 1942 and records that political issues 'were argued heatedly in the mess, but for myself, I felt no emotional stir'.[24]

Some were more than keen nationalists. They were friendly with, or even related to, Indian politicians. Some of the twenty ICS Indians who write of their experiences in *The Civil Servant in India* make explicit reference to friends in the Congress; Deshmukh (ICS, Bombay) recounts how, in his first post, he avoided the club and 'mixed with the city gentry', and later 'had many friends in the Congress'.[25] When Narasimhan (ICS, Madras) arrived in his province in 1937, the leading Congressman and Premier in the Government was Rajaji, 'whom I knew well personally'.[26] Govind Narain (ICS, UP) arrived in 1939 and was soon in touch with Congress leaders; his father-in-law was friendly with Jawaharlal Nehru and the Congress Premier in the UP Government, Govind Ballabh Pant.[27] Nehru actually had three close relatives in the ICS (and many others in lesser services). Mrs Sucheta Kripalani, while on the run from the British in 1942, often stayed with her cousin—an ICS officer posted in Patna (Bihar); and when she wanted to see Gandhi during his fast in February 1943, she got in touch with Iengar (ICS, Bombay), who was Additional Secretary in the Home Department, Bombay, at the time, and Iengar both made the necessary arrangements and made sure she was not arrested.[28]

The British Government and senior ICS Europeans were not unaware of what was going on. Hallett (ICS, Bihar), when Governor of the United Provinces in 1941, reported secretly to the Viceroy that ICS Indians were waiting and/or ready for a Congress return after the war, and hence were becoming less reliable for the raj; 'we must never lose sight of the fact', he said, 'that at the back of the minds in particular of every Hindu officer is the anticipation, and possibly the hope, that a Congress Ministry will return to power.'[29] Nothing that Hallett or

[23] Downing Papers, IOL MSS Eur. F.180/50, TS pp. 7–8.

[24] Rustomji, *Enchanted Frontiers*, p. 22.

[25] Deshmukh, C. D., 'Looking Back on my Service Days', in Panjabi, *Civil Servant*, pp. 3–4.

[26] Narasimhan Papers, TS p. 4.

[27] Narain, Govind, 'Bureaucrats Frown upon Authority and Direction', *Sunday*, 14–20 Aug. 1983, 29–30.

[28] Hutchins, F. G., *Spontaneous Revolution: The Quit India Movement*, Delhi, 1971, pp., 297, 309.

[29] NAI Home File 3/31/40 Poll. (I), 'Secret Report from H.E. The Governor of U.P. to H.E. The Viceroy', No. UP 92, 23 Apr. 1941, cited in Hutchins, pp. 195–6.

other ICS Europeans did could stop the gradual drift of non-Muslims towards the Congress during the war. Indeed, the split between ICS Europeans and non-Muslim ICS Indians had appreciably widened during, and as a consequence of, the 1942 Quit India revolt. This was particularly so in Bihar and the United Provinces, where the movement was most intense. Ewing suggests that the 1942 revolt in these two provinces 'helped to prise open a gaping fissure within the ICS along racial lines'.[30] Raman (ICS, Bihar) refers to 'the great divide of 1942', when 'some of us were torn with a sense of conflict', and one major consequence was 'a complete social separation of the Indian and the British officers in the Civil Service'.[31] Even in Bombay and Madras Provinces, the 1942 revolt 'alienated many British officials totally' from Congress and from those non-Muslim ICS Indians sympathetic to Congress.[32] After all, in 1942 the British were at war with the Axis, including the Japanese in Burma, and it was hard for them to relate closely to people who did not support the war effort.

The movement of Muslim ICS towards alignment with the Muslim League and the demand for Pakistan was not so gradual. Muslim ICS, on the whole, had never been pro-Congress, as has been noted, but neither were they pro-Muslim League in large numbers, until almost the end. Indian politcs polarized sharply in 1946, and this rapidly split Muslims and non-Muslims. This was noticeable even in the South. Downing (ICS, Madras) vividly remembers a surprising conversation in the summer of 1946 between his Collector and another ICS in the district, both North Indian Muslims, and 'as I listened to the bitterness with which these two highly intelligent and well educated men spoke of the Congress Party and Hindus in general, I realized the intensity of communal feeling . . .'[33] By the autumn of 1946 all Indians in central government 'were either Congress, more or less, or League, more or less'.[34] When the Muslim League entered the Constituent Assembly-cum-Interim Government on 26 October 1946, they did so not to co-operate with Congress but to prevent Congress from tightening its hold on the whole government machinery. The government almost immediately became a dual government. Moon (ICS, Punjab) reports that each block 'began to attract to itself its own supporters from

30 Ewing, A., 'Administering India: The Indian Civil Service', *History Today*, 32 (June 1982) 48.

31 Raman, K. S. V., 'Reminiscences of a Government Officer', *Searchlight* (Patna), 8 Dec. 1966, 4.

32 Zinkin, 'Impressions', p. 548.

33 Downing Papers, TS pp. 24–5.

34 Zinkin, 'Impressions', p. 548.

among the civil servants and to build up its own separate and exclusive empire'.[35] The divide was not total. In the Punjab cadre, for example, two Muslim ICS (Tyabji and Muhammad Azim Husain) actually opted for India, and two non-Muslims (Cornelius and Burke, both Indian Christians) opted for Pakistan.

To complete the three-way split, Europeans by the beginning of 1946 had distanced themselves from both Congress and League, but most still had made no preparation for early termination of their career. Only twelve months later nearly everyone knew the end was near and many were scrambling for jobs elsewhere. This change in fortunes was remarkably swift.

THE EUROPEANS MOVE (ARE MOVED) OUT

A classification of relevant civil lists suggests that in December 1946 there were still 608 ICS Europeans working in India.[36] Only about thirty were left one year later, and only three by 1952—Bowman (Bombay), Orr (Bihar), and Gwynn (Madras), the last to go.[37] ICS Europeans did not gradually hand over; they suddenly vanished in 1947. Why? A generally accepted explanation supported by some ICS implies that they were invited to stay but opted to go for various personal reasons, including reluctance to serve under an Indian Government. Wakefield (ICS, Punjab) records having been invited by the new Indian Government to stay as a Joint Secretary in Delhi and the Government of Pakistan pressed him to accept appointment as their first Governor of Baluchistan, but 'I had spent my life in the service of the Crown and did not feel disposed to serve a different master. Moreover, I was weary from over-work and yearned to be at home again . . .'[38] Trevelyan (ICS, Madras) claims that 'we could have

[35] Moon, *Divide and Quit*, p. 60.

[36] The figure 608 comes from Braibanti's classification of the *Combined Civil List for India and Burma, Jan.–Mar. 1947*, No. 156 (Lahore, 1947), as reported in Braibanti, *Asian Bureaucratic Systems* p. 645. My own classification of the contents of the *India Office and Burma Office List 1947*, London, 1947, shows 429 Europeans still on active service (summer, 1947). Mosley, *The Last Days of the British Raj*, claims, however, that only 300 Europeans remained in the ICS by mid-1947 (p. 152).

[37] Braibanti reports 33 in *Asian Bureaucratic Systems*, p. 646 for both Aug. 1947 and Dec. 1948. He also reports that 50 stayed on in Pakistan. Orr (in Orr Papers, IOL MSS Eur. F180/22, TS pp. 138–9) says there were only 12 left in India in Dec. 1947, but his is a fairly offhand remark. A few retired ICS returned to India to do other work. Penderel Moon, for example, retired voluntarily in 1944 after his correspondence with Rajkumari Amrit Kaur was intercepted, but he later returned first as Resident, Manipur State, later as Adviser to the Planning Commission in New Delhi—he was still there in 1960.

[38] Wakefield, *Past Imperative*, pp. 218–9.

stayed until we had earned a full pension, but were given no special encouragement to do so'. In his particular case, Nehru asked him to stay on for a few months after independence, but he was already lining up a new career. Nehru wrote on his file: 'I will not stand in his way, but I am sorry to see him go.'[39] Symington (ICS, Bombay) asserts that 'much larger numbers of us would have stayed on and served under Indian governments if it hadn't been for three things'. One was that 'everybody was very tired' after the war and 'pretty browned off . . . by all the political failure'. Another was the British Government's handsome offer of compensation for loss of career which 'made it easy for us to go'. Most important, 'you had to serve a Hindu Government or a Mohammedan Government, and now had either to be pro-Mohammedan or pro-Hindu accordingly, and that was contrary to everything that we thought right or possible'.[40] The problem with these standard explanations is that they lump together several factors of importance without examining their sequence and timing. A closer analysis suggests an explanation for the wholesale departure of the ICS Europeans with a rather different emphasis.

During the first half of the 1940s the raj was still firmly in control. The Quit India movement of 1942, during which there was considerable unrest across North India (with portions of Bihar and the United Provinces particularly disturbed), was put down forcefully by the army and the police working with civilian authorities. At the same time many saw that important political changes would have to take place once the war was won. De Montmorency (ICS, Punjab), who retired in 1935, remarked in 1941 that 'the question is no longer whether India is to govern herself at the centre but by what machinery she can do so'.[41] Indeed the Cripps offer made in 1942 actually promised independence within the empire after the war in exchange for Indian support for the war effort and that offer remained open even though Congress rejected it at the time. Even so, there is no evidence that ICS Europeans believed these developments necessitated their own sudden departure. And it therefore seemed quite appropriate that, near the end of the war, ICS recruitment was resumed.

This little-known activity underlines the assumption, that the British Government and the Government of India continued to make throughout the war, that ICS Europeans would be needed after the war.

[39] Trevelyan, *The India we Left*, p. 244.

[40] Allen, *Plain Tales*, p. 214.

[41] De Montmorency, J., *The Indian States and Indian Federation*, Cambridge, 1942, p. 156.

ICS recruitment had been stopped in 1943; but in late 1944 the Viceroy ordered that the administration be reinforced and officers in the Indian Army were invited to apply. Hugh Tinker applied and was selected with about forty others.[42] Seven were then posted to the United Provinces as 'Civil Administrative Officers'. Four were European, three Indian; significantly, the Europeans were placed in law and order posts in districts, the Indians were shunted into technical posts. At the end of 1945 applications were invited for the post-war ICS. It was envisaged that these recruits might not work out their full service so a compensation scheme was offered guaranteeing generous payment in that event. Compensation rose steeply after 9/10 years. A number applied (including Tinker), some were brought back to London and put through the 'Country House' assessment used for the Foreign Service; they were informed in March/April 1946 that they had been selected and told they would shortly be returning to India. Then there was a long silence. As will become clear, a critical juncture in Indian affairs had been reached. Finally, in August 1946 the new recruits received letters conveying the regrets of the Secretary of State that ICS recruitment had been terminated.

The turning-point came during the spring of 1946. Why? Relying on conventional explanations about the fading 'will to empire' on the part of the British people, the pressure of 'world public opinion', or the war-weariness of Europeans in India who had had no home leave for a long time will not do. The British people did not bring Attlee and the Labour Party to power at Westminster in 1945 because they wanted Britain out of India; and Gallagher has shown convincingly that the Labour Government was not initially in any hurry about India until decisions were forced upon them.[43] The pressure of world public opinion—more particularly the Government of the USA—on the British Government was not an irrelevant consideration, but it has been overrated and in any case is too general to explain the precise timing of developments in India. As for war-weary Europeans, there is no doubt that a negative reaction set in after the jubilation of victory in Asia in August 1945 and that many were in need of home leave; but many ICS Europeans did in fact go on home leave in 1945 and 1946, and then returned to India before independence. Again, this factor

[42] Tinker, H., to the author in a personal communication. I am grateful to Professor Tinker for assistance with this point.

[43] Gallagher, *Decline, Revival and Fall.* For details, see Moore, R. J., *Escape from Empire: The Attlee Government and the Indian Problem*, Oxford, 1983.

does not explain why the decision to quit came in the spring of 1946. What does explain it are political developments in the provinces of British India and their effects on the power of provincial administrations.

The raj held firm in 1945, but only barely. There is no doubt that morale was low in the ICS. 'One of my preoccupations', says Lord Casey about his time as Governor of Bengal in 1945, 'was sustaining the morale of the Services, which I endeavoured to do by all the means available to me.'[44] Dow (ICS, Bombay), when Governor of Sind in 1945, spoke to the Viceroy on 21 March 'of the general weariness of the European side of the administration, and the general subservience of the provincial administrators to the ministers'.[45] Sind had a ministry, but most provinces where Congress was dominant had been without a ministry since 1939, when they had resigned. Many Congress leaders had also spent at least part of the war in prison. By 1945, however, they were out and active again, and talking of possibly launching another Quit India rebellion. Gandhi was in favour of moderation, but his influence within Congress was on the decline. Congress were also preparing for elections in the winter of 1945 for forming new ministries in these provinces. Their hostility to the ICS was plain. The Viceroy reported to London on 24 October: 'Depressing reports continue to come in from Provinces of the intemperate attitude of Congress, their attempts to intimidate the Services by threats of revenge when they come to power, and so on. Nehru in particular seems quite unable to restrain himself, and perhaps imprisonment has quite upset his balance which was never his strong point.' Two weeks later, Wavell warned: 'ICS and IP are dispirited and discontented; the Indian members of these services are uneasy about the future and under strong political and social pressure; while the Indian subordinates on whom the administration so largely depends are naturally reluctant to make enemies of the future masters of India.' Again, 'Service morale is now bad in many districts and is being steadily undermined.'[46]

The violence of Congress speeches continued in November, excited by the first trials of members of the Indian National Army in the Red Fort at Delhi. (The INA had fought with the Japanese against the British and Indian armies on the Burma front.) Some Congressmen openly talked of employing INA officers and men to lead a rebellion, remarks which Europeans found both offensive and alarming. At the

[44] Casey, Lord, *Personal Experiences, 1939–46*, London, 1962, p. 199.
[45] *Wavell*, entry of 21 Mar. 1945, p. 117.
[46] *Wavell*, entries for 24 Oct. and 6 Nov. 1945, pp. 178, 184.

same time, people like G. D. Birla (a major industrialist) and other important Indian capitalists providing support for Congress were expressing alarm at the violence of Congress speeches. Such expressions of course began to have an effect. By the end of the year, Vallabhbhai Patel had started to 'come around to the view that Independence could be gained quite soon by peaceful means and it would be foolish to stir up trouble and create disorder in the country', so he began 'to throw the weight of his great influence in favour of keeping the peace'.[47]

As Congress turned towards order and keeping the peace, the ICS and the rest of the bureaucracy gradually turned to meet them. Early in 1946 at the centre, for example, a Cabinet secretariat was organized for the first time modelled on the cabinet office in Whitehall. Coates (ICS, Bengal) was appointed the first Cabinet Secretary. Several other ICS officers were also posted to it, including H. M. Patel (ICS, Bombay). As Patel remarks, it had become apparent by early 1946 'that a responsible Government, if not independence, in some form or other was almost certain to come within a very short period and it would help the successor Government if they could find in existence a secretariat trained in cabinet procedure and practices, ready at hand to assist it'.[48] In the provinces similar moves were made to prepare for incoming ministries which would be formed in March/April following the elections in the winter of 1945–6. A few ICS Indians also openly moved to assist Congress politicians. Narain (ICS, UP), for example, was Collector of Farukhabad when Pandit Pant campaigned there on an election tour. 'I knew the local leaders', concedes Narain, 'and had a quiet understanding with them according to which my duty did not stand in the way of Pant's getting full facilities for his campaigning in my district.'[49] (This is actually an extraordinary admission for a civil servant to make publicly.) Pant soon after became Chief Minister of the United Provinces.

For ICS Europeans the resumption of provincial politics posed a different test of power. As the election results became known and the Congress move back into provincial government was imminent, ICS Europeans felt unmistakably their power slipping away. In the United Provinces, for example, Johnston (ICS, UP) was Commissioner at Agra

[47] Moon, P. in *Wavell*, p. 173.

[48] Patel, H. M., 'Cabinet Government in India', in Aiyar, S. and Srinivasan, R. (eds.), *Studies in Indian Democracy*, Bombay, 1965, p. 197.

[49] Narain, Govind, 'Some Stray Thoughts', *Administrator*, xxi 2 (1976), 597.

and records that Evans (ICS, UP) as Collector, Agra, and other Europeans in the division were faced with increasing difficulties in the spring of 1946. 'Maintenance of law and order depended on Indian personnel', he asserts, and although in earlier days their support was assured, now it could not be relied on and 'conditions become steadily more frustrating'. And then in an unusual fashion in ICS memoirs he states the position faced by Collectors in relation to the exercise of power:

> theorists might talk of a gradual transfer of power, but it was not like that in fact. If you are to be held responsible for law and order, you simply must have power to enforce your authority. The fact that you have this power and are prepared to use it will mean that it will seldom be used. If you do not have the power, this will quickly become known and you may expect widespread disorder with which you will be unable to cope. There is no easy half-way house.[50]

A similar sense of power draining away was felt by ICS Europeans in the secretariat at Lucknow. For example, one of the main activities embarked on by the Provincial Government early in the spring of 1946 before the Congress Ministry took office was dealing with a food shortage. It was decided that a grain levy had to be organized to obtain enough grain from the cultivators in 'surplus districts' in the province in order to meet the food requirements of the towns. A number of meetings involving senior administrators took place; one of the most important occurred on 7 February 1946, involving senior administrators and all the thirty-five Collectors from the 'surplus' districts.[51] The minutes of this meeting and the work of the administration in relation to it before and after the Congress Ministry took power in the United Provinces make clear that ICS administrators now saw themselves as 'powerless' (their word) to deal with the food problem without the political support of the dominant political organization in the province. In 1942 the ICS had been in control, able to crush the Quit India movement in eastern districts of the province; by early 1946 they realized they no longer had that power, and had accepted that they were quite unable to make their writ run there in the face of Congress opposition.

This provincial perspective on powerlessness, evident amongst ICS

[50] Johnston Papers, Cambridge Archive, TS p. 296.

[51] A summary of the meeting, written on 15 Feb. 1946, is in Haig Papers, Cambridge Archive, Box 1.

Secretaries and Collectors in the United Provinces, was made known to the Viceroy and the Secretary of State in London. Reports were also coming in from other provinces that the support of subordinate Indian personnel for the British raj was finally beginning to crack, or at least Indians were 'inclined to delay difficult and controversial decisions, to keep their ears to the ground for political portents, to avoid offence rather than wield authority without fear or favour'.[52] Reports from Madras Province in the spring of 1946 made clear that disaffection in the Madras Police had 'contributed to the overall British awareness that they could no longer command the strength to rule a hostile India'.[53] A revolt of a section of the Royal Indian Navy on 18 February 1946 in Bombay was perceived by the British Government as even more grave in its implications. The next day it was announced that a Cabinet Mission would be coming to India to discuss the transfer of power with the Indian parties. British power in India, which depended utterly on the support of subordinate Indian personnel, both civil and military, was perceived to be fading fast. The recognition in New Delhi and London that this was so perhaps found its fullest expression about a year later in Sir Stafford Cripps's important statement on the political reasons for the British departure from India—a statement he delivered in Parliament when introducing the Indian Independence Bill.[54] We quit, he said in essence, because, quite apart from the moral question as to the rightness of our rule, the essential instruments of our rule (especially the ICS and the Indian Police) no longer have the power to carry out their responsibilities within the provinces of British India.

Nevertheless, even though there was much disquiet amongst ICS Europeans in 1946, there was still no recognition that they would all be out a year later. The Cabinet Mission came to discuss arrangements for an eventual transfer of power, but at the same time ICS recruitment was apparently starting up again in earnest. As many as seventy-three European candidates for the ICS had been offered appointments and fifty-four had accepted the offer by the early summer of 1946 and were waiting to proceed to India; a still larger number of European candidates had been through the selection process, had been found suitable, and had been informed that they would be considered for

[52] Hodson, H. V., *The Great Divide: Britain, India, Pakistan*, London, 1969, p. 185.

[53] Arnold, D., 'The Armed Police and Colonial Rule in South India, 1914–1947', *MAS* 11. 1 (1977), 124.

[54] Great Britain. *Parliamentary Debates*, HC, 434 (1946–47), col. 497–508.

appointment in due course.[55] At the last minute, however, this vein of 'fresh blood' was cut off. At the end of May the question whether European recruitment should be abandoned in the event of the Cabinet Mission's plan being accepted had been referred to Provincial Governors who were asked to consult their Ministries. The Provincial Governments had replied 'almost unanimously' against European recruitment and 'at least three' were also opposed to the recruitment of Indians.[56]

However, the response was not as cut and dried as might appear. In Orissa the Premier and his colleagues in the Ministry met and discussed the question, and then sent a draft of their written reply to the Governor for his views. The Governor was Sir Chandulal Trivedi (ICS, CP). The Secretary to the Governor was Orr (ICS, Bihar). Orr was not supposed to see such correspondence but 'I was the post-box through which it passed and unofficially I sneaked a look.' The Ministry proposed resuming ICS recruitment of both Europeans and Indians on a 50:50 basis. There were flattering references in the draft to ICS Europeans who frequently 'made better Indian civil servants than the Indians themselves'. Trivedi's response (which Orr also saw) was not surprising. He stated categorically that there was nothing inherently superior in European officers, refuted each of the Ministry's arguments, asserted that no more British officers should be recruited, and suggested to Harikrishna Mahtab (the Premier) that he rewrite his memorandum for the Secretary of State accordingly. The Premier did so.[57]

On 14 August 1946 the Cabinet in London made the decision to cease recruiting both Europeans and Indians to the ICS and the Indian Police, and to cancel the offers of appointment already made earlier in the year. In recommending the proposal to the Cabinet, the Secretary of State said that appointment of further Europeans to the ICS and the Indian Police would provoke resentment in India and that he had learned that Provincial Governments would be unwilling to employ them.[58] This left the position of the ICS as a whole very uncertain. The Governor of the United Provinces (Wylie, ICS) reported secretly to the

[55] India Office, Cabinet memorandum IB (46) 26 L/S G/7/263, dated 25 July 1946, in Mansergh, N. *et al.* (eds.), *Constitutional Relations between Britain and India: The Transfer of Power, 1942–7*, viii (HMSO, 1979), 119. (Cited hereafter as *Transfer of Power Documents*.)

[56] Ibid.

[57] Orr Papers, TS p. 117.

[58] British Cabinet. CM (46) 78th conclusions, minute 4, L/S G/7/263, 14 Aug. 1946, in *Transfer of Power Documents*, viii 234–5.

Viceroy that ICS Europeans 'do not know where they are' and most ICS Indians are in much the same position. 'They require', he said, 'a lead or positive move of some kind making clear their position in the uncertain political context and an indication of their future prospects' (or lack of them).[59] No such lead came either from London or from the leadership of the Congress Party.

At the same time there was a belief amongst ICS Europeans that ICS Indians were beginning to be given more attractive postings where possible. Twynam (ICS, Bengal), when Governor of Central Provinces, reported in his diary on 20 July 1946: 'I doubt whether there are six European couples left in Nagpur . . .' because the Prime Minister, Pandit Shukla, 'has transferred all European officers he could to out-stations.'[60] When Downing (ICS, Madras) returned from home leave in November 1946, the Chief Secretary of Madras told him that he had hoped to bring him into the secretariat but 'that it was the policy of the new Congress Ministry to post the European officers to districts'.[61] Downing would have preferred 'a more central situation more in touch with colleagues'. In fact the relevant Civil List does not provide confirmation of these exaggerated claims, although it shows that ICS Indians were moved into a dominant position in some secretariats—notably Orissa, Madras, Central Provinces, and United Provinces.[62] Nevertheless, Europeans saw these tendencies and drew their own conclusions. They would be at a disadvantage in the new India. A few were 'beginning to slip away' in 1946 to find jobs elsewhere, although 'most of us decided to stick it out to see what would happen'.[63]

Increasing numbers of Indian ICS were beginning to make connections with Provincial Ministries in 1946. Eventually similar moves began to take place even in central government in September 1946. The Interim Government was sworn in on 2 September, and a few days later Bewoor (ICS, CP) approached N. V. Gadgil (a minister in the Interim Government) and said some senior ICS Hindus would like him to arrange an informal meeting with Nehru. They wanted to give Nehru 'some vital information' (about ICS Muslims passing inside information to the Muslim League) and 'they wanted to disabuse Nehru of his prejudices against them—they too were Indians and

[59] Wylie to Wavell, 7 Aug. 1946, in *Transfer of Power Documents*, viii. 200–3.
[60] Twynam Papers, Cambridge Archive, TS p. 314, diary entry for 20 July 1946.
[61] Downing Papers, TS p. 26.
[62] *Combined Civil List for India and Burma, October–December, 1946.*
[63] Hunt Papers, Cambridge Archive, TS p. 90.

welcomed the advent of freedom and would like to convince Nehru of it'. Gadgil spoke to Nehru, who 'flew into a temper and said that nothing prevented them from seeing him in his office'. Gadgil reported this to Vallabhbhai Patel, the new Home Member, who 'saw a few of them at his residence and won them over, allaying their fears with his usual statesmanship'.[64] From this point onward ICS Hindus began to look to Patel as the man at the centre who would satisfy their interests. They were not disappointed.

Patel's support was apparent when, as Chairman of the Provincial Premiers' Conference on 21 and 22 October, he urged retention of all-India services and creation of new successor institutions. At that time he certainly was in favour of retaining the services of as many ICS as possible, both Indian *and European*. When he first learned on 19 October of plans being discussed in London to offer compensation to ICS officers for loss of career, which he construed as offering an incentive for them to leave, he angrily remarked to the Viceroy that such a scheme 'would have some bearing on the personnel that would be available to us to start an All India Service if and when formed'.[65]

The British Government's position regarding the Secretary of State's Services after a transfer of power remained unclear until the following spring. Wavell noted in his diary on 31 December that 'the British ICS is disheartened and looking over its shoulder' and 'the delay in settling terms of compensation, date for winding up and future prospects has had an adverse effect'.[66] Meanwhile, trends within the ICS set in motion earlier in terms of a three-way split deepened as Patel's prediliction for appointing non-Muslim ICS Indians to key posts gathered speed. Wavell records a typical example: on 17 March 1947 Patel came to see him to discuss the appointment of a new Director of Intelligence and said he wanted 'to put in an Indian ICS man on the grounds that there is no Indian policeman good enough' (actually there was a good Muslim available but 'Patel will not have him and he will not serve under Patel'). Wavell said that it would be bad for police morale if the plum appointment in the Indian Police went to an outsider, but Patel persisted with his choice of the ICS Indian.[67]

On 22 March Mountbatten arrived to take over as Viceroy. One

[64] Gadgil, N. V., *Government from Inside*, Meerut, 1968, pp. 16–17.
[65] Minute No. R/3/1/181 by Sardar Patel, 19 Oct. 1946, in *Transfer of Power Documents*, viii. 751.
[66] *Wavell*, entry for 31 Dec. 1946, at p. 402.
[67] *Wavell*, entry for 17 Mar. 1947, at p. 429.

thing he had finally secured from the Cabinet before coming was a decision on generous compensation for the Secretary of State's Services.[68] The Indian leaders reacted heatedly to the proposals. The issue was raised at the first meeting between Nehru and Mountbatten. It was madness, Nehru remarked, to want to compensate civil servants to whom the offer of remaining on in their jobs was open, under the same conditions of contract as they had previously enjoyed. And why compensate them so generously? This would only encourage them to leave their posts. Nehru implied throughout his remarks that of course the new Government wanted the ICS, both Indians and Europeans, to stay on.[69] Patel spoke in similar vein to the Viceroy, and was also adamant that ICS Indians would not be kept on if they accepted compensation.[70] After all, their prospects would actually improve under the new Government. In the end, when the compensation scheme was announced publicly, a compromise had been reached. ICS Europeans would get compensation in full; as for ICS Indians, it was announced that 'the Government of India feel that sentiments of patriotism will naturally impel Indian officers to continue to serve their country and that, in the light of the undertaking that they have given and the consideration that, in fact, Indian members of these Services will have improved prospects, there is no ground, save in . . . special cases, for the payment of compensation to Indian officers on account of the transfer of power.'[71]

The compensation scheme was announced on 30 April 1947 both in New Delhi and in London. Even at this late date it appeared that ICS Europeans contemplated staying on, at least for a while, and that the new Indian Government wished them to do so. There was a difference, however, between words and deeds regarding Congress treatment of ICS Europeans. Wavell was aware of it and Mountbatten wrote privately to the Secretary of State about it shortly after his arrival: 'Patel . . . has always been one of the Congress leaders who have stated publicly that he is anxious to keep British officials after the transfer of power.' But he has 'never shown any practical signs to support these statements'. A particularly clear case was that of the appointment of someone to act for Porter (ICS, Bengal), Secretary of

[68] Great Britain. *India. Compensation for the Services* (London), (Cmd. 7116), Apr. 1947.

[69] Campbell-Johnson, A., *Mission with Mountbatten*, London, 1951, p. 45.

[70] Mountbatten Papers, Minutes of Viceroy's Second Staff Meeting 26 Mar. 1947, Item 6, in *Transfer of Power Documents* x (1981), 24–5.

[71] India. *Compensation for the Services* (1947), p. 5.

the Home Department, who was going home on leave for seven months. Mountbatten records:

> The obvious person to succeed Mr Porter is Mr Williams [ICS, Madras], the Joint Secretary of the Home Department, who is a competent official with Home Department experience and 24 years service in the ICS. Patel however proposed that Mr Banerji [ICS, CP], who is now Secretary of the Commonwealth Relations Department, should be appointed in Mr Porter's vacancy, and this can hardly be resisted as Mr Banerji is senior to Mr Williams.
>
> Mr Banerji is not however a particularly competent official, and Mr Williams having heard of the recommendation has asked to be allowed to go home on leave. Mr Williams, as Joint Secretary of the Home Department, is concerned with Service questions, compensation, proportionate pension, terms of repatriation, and so on. He is thus a key man at the present time, and with the greatest regret I have had to turn down his application for leave; though in the circumstances it would be too much to expect that we can get the best out of him. I feel very sorry for him.[72]

There was a string of other cases of a similar nature. For example, it was an 'open secret' in the spring of 1947 that Patel wanted to replace Christie (ICS, UP) as Chief Commissioner of Delhi with an ICS Indian, but Wavell had refused, and in May 'Patel had trumped up two charges against the Chief Commissioner' which came to Mountbatten with recommendations that Christie should be called upon to resign. In the end Mountbatten agreed to Patel's wishes and Christie was replaced by an ICS Indian.[73]

No doubt there were two sides to such cases, and in many of them it could as easily be shown that Patel acted correctly in the circumstances as he saw them. That is not the point. The point is that Europeans perceived them as partial and that perception fuelled a growing belief that, despite public statements to the contrary, Europeans would not be treated on a par with Indians. Europeans accepted that there was nothing personal in this, only that it was bound to be a fact of life.

That perception explains the response of a number of ICS Europeans to the Government of India circular letter sent to each ICS officer on 18 June 1947, asking him if he was willing to stay on.[74] A number replied 'yes' on certain conditions meant to safeguard their

[72] Mountbatten Papers, Letter to the Secretary of State, 24 Apr. 1947, in *Transfer of Power Documents*, x. 399–402. Mountbatten's Mr Banerji was actually R. N. Banerjee (ICS, CP).

[73] Mountbatten Papers, Letter to the Secretary of State, 8 May 1947, in *Transfer of Power Documents*, x. 679–80.

[74] GOI Home Dept. Letter No. 160/47—RR, 17 June 1947.

positions. But Patel took the view that any ICS European who attached conditions to his option to serve in India showed thereby a lack of trust in his new masters, and ruled that he must go.[75] One of these was Holland (ICS, Bengal), who replied to the circular letter saying he was willing to stay if he could keep his present post. As 15 August approached, he sought an interview with the Chief Minister designate. He said: 'No, Mr Holland, you can make no stipulation and we will give you no guarantees. Either sign on and agree to go where we order and to do whatever ordered, or GO.'[76] He went.

Other Europeans made no stipulation, but were ordered out anyway because they had offended local political leaders in the past. An almost total veil of silence has subsequently been drawn over the fact that many ICS Europeans were bitter and unhappy at being dismissed.[77] Ray (ICS, Bihar) was one, 'abruptly dismissed by a brief telegram' on 14 August.[78] Hope (ICS, Madras) was another: 'shorter notice than a housemaid!' he remarked in disgust.[79] Georgeson (ICS, Madras), however, applied to be kept on in service and was permitted to do so, leaving in 1950 'for reasons that had nothing to do with my relations with the Government'.[80] But as has been indicated, very few Europeans stayed with him. The trickle of departing Europeans had by the end of July and early August become a flood, and 'no one had expected an exodus on such a large scale'. One Indian Medical Service Officer in Bombay, looking around the lounge of a ship about to depart at that time, remarked that he had never seen so many ICS people in one place before. 'These people', he said, 'were once described as India's steel frame but now they are more like a cargo of scrap-iron.'[81]

Why the mass exodus from India at the end (although not from Pakistan)? To say, as most ICS Europeans did later, that 'very few of us visualized staying on in an independent India'[82] is too simple as an exaplanation. The evidence suggests that many would have been willing to stay but decided at the last minute to opt out. Younger officers in particular might well have served on until the mid-1950s when the compensation scheme would have paid maximum benefits; Orr did just that, as did many ICS Europeans who served in Pakistan.

75 Orr Papers, TS p. 135.
76 Holland Papers, Cambridge Archive, TS p. 59.
77 Orr Papers, TS p. 8.
78 Ray Papers, IOL MSS Eur. F.180/23, TS p. 8.
79 Dunlop Papers, IOL MSS Eur. F.180/51, TS 'Independence', p. 1.
80 Georgeson Papers, IOL MSS Eur. F.180/52, TS p. 24.
81 Orr Papers, TS p. 137.
82 Hunt Papers, TS p. 91.

The principal reason why they did not stay in India is that political support from the Congress was lacking. The Congress both at the centre and in the provinces gave no special encouragement to ICS Europeans to stay, that is, the Congress did not bar ICS Europeans in principle but neither did they encourage them, and in individual cases they simply got rid of them. Furthermore, with Patel's deeds not words during 1946–7, they perceived the reward structure as not very promising. Hence, when ICS Europeans say they opted to go, it is important to notice that this was no 'free' choice. In the end, 'deciding' to go seemed the only sensible thing to do because of the political context in which the decision had to be made.

Although the political support was lacking for certain ICS personnel, it came in time to save the service itself within the structure of the state. Admittedly, it came late. It was not until the autumn of 1946 that Patel went to work in earnest to create the IAS as a successor. The support came as a consequence of broader structural forces combined with the agency of ICS Indian initiatives. Without that support, the ICS tradition could not have survived.

THE INDIANS MOVE IN

As Europeans and Muslims departed, a whole array of plum postings in the ICS frame opened up for those who remained. Indians had been aware of this possibility since the beginning of the 1940s. The lopsided nature of the age structure of the ICS accentuated the position (see Table 12.)

Table 12. *Age Structure in the Provinces, 1939*

	ICS Indians		ICS Europeans	
	Number	Per cent	Number	Per cent
Less than 10 years' service	248	52	206	37
10–20 years' service	187	39	182	32
Over 20 years' service	44	9	178	31
Total	479	100	566	100

Source: Figures compiled from NAI, Home Dept. File 35/26/41—Ests., 1941.
Note: The data do not include those holding Listed Posts, nor those posted to the centre.

The comparative youth of the Indian side was a consequence of Indian recruitment only starting in earnest in 1919. If one then wiped out the

European side, Indians were bound to move a long way up, fast. This is indeed what began to happen in 1946–7. H. M. Patel (ICS, Bombay) entered as a young man in 1927; by 1947 he had made a monumental leap to the top, becoming both Cabinet Secretary and Secretary to the Prime Minister. Similar leaps were being made elsewhere. Many Congress politicians were not happy about it. Mahavir Tyagi complained in the Constituent Assembly in 1949: 'In India today persons of the civil service having only seven, eight or nine years service are acting in the secretariat as secretaries and joint secretaries and getting much higher pay, a pay which if India were not independent, they would get after serving for 18 or 19 years'; Ayyangar observed that under the previous regime Europeans became Secretaries after 25 years of service and become Joint Secretaries after 20 years, but 'now, on account of Europeans having gone away, persons who were in the lower range of the ladder, deputy secretaries with 10 or 12 years service, have immediately become joint secretaries . . .'.[83]

There were also knock-on effects for other civil servants immediately after independence. The ICS was so depleted that rapid promotion of non-ICS people from lower services was necessary to fill middling and even some more senior postings. Civil servants 'who had never any reasonable expectations for higher jobs found themselves rapidly moving up the hierarchy'.[84]

Special efforts were also made to find suitable recruits for the new IAS which was locked on to the ICS frame. First, the 'war service' people were added to the group. Since this recruitment netted only 87 IAS candidates altogether, there was an 'emergency recruitment' from which an additional 146 were selected for the IAS (and 135 for the new Indian Police Service).[85] The integration of the princely states opened up additional posts for the ICS/IAS after a Conference of Premiers of those states agreed in July 1948 to accept all-India services, the ICS frame, and the rest.[86] There was another emergency recruitment in 1949–50 in response (in part) to these additional posts opening up. It netted a further 85 appointees to the IAS.[87] Regular

[83] India. *Constituent Assembly Debates* x (10 Oct. 1949), 37, 44.

[84] Hejmadi, V. S. (ICS, Madras) and Panandiker, V. A., 'The Public Services: Recruitment and Selection', *IJPA* ix. 3 (1963), 356. See also Gorwala, A., *Role of Administrator: Past, Present and Future*, Bombay, 1957, p. 23.

[85] Government of India. Ministry of Home Affairs, Special Recruitment Board, *Report*, 1955, pp. 3–7.

[86] Government of India, Ministry of States, *White Paper on Indian States*, 1950, para. 181.

[87] Hejmadi and Pai Panandiker, 'The Public Services', pp. 356–7.

annual competitive examinations also began in 1948. These brought 30–40 IAS recruits each year until 1954, after which the numbers increased.

This rapid move to build up the IAS to strengthen the ICS was not accomplished easily. There was considerable hostility from Indian politicians, particularly from those who had suffered at the hands of the raj only a few years previously. Even Nehru and many of his colleagues in the Cabinet were not enthusiastic. What made the difference was the resolute support of the Home Member—Sardar Patel. With his commanding influence in the Congress Party during the years 1946–9, he was able to overcome that opposition at three crucial junctures.

The first was the occasion when provincial premiers were called to the conference on 21 October 1946 to consider the question of replacing the ICS and the Indian Police.[88] ICS recruitment had been cancelled several months previously by the British Government and many felt the disappearance of the ICS was imminent. Patel, in the chair, argued for a new 'all-India administrative service' on the grounds that it was obviously important (1) to maintain the highest possible standard of efficiency, (2) to give the civil service 'experience . . . at the Centre leading to efficiency, and administrative experience of the district', (3) to serve as 'a liaison between the provinces and the (central) government', and (4) to introduce both in the provinces and in the centre 'a progressive and wide outlook and freshness and vigour of administration'. He received rough treatment. The Premier of the United Provinces, Pandit Pant, is reported to have opposed the proposal with unusual force. Sir Khizar Hayat Khan, Premier of Punjab and leader of the Unionist Party there, publicly repudiated the arrangement, declaring 'Punjab is one of those provinces which would prefer to have a superior service of their own instead of an all-India administrative service under contemplation for this purpose'.[89] Punjab was joined by Bengal and Sind, all of whom as Muslim majority provinces saw danger in an all-India service controlled by the central government dominated by Hindus. The timing of the Conference was fortunate for Patel, for the Muslim League had not yet joined the Interim Government. After debate, the participants at the Conference,

[88] A summary is given in Maheshwari, S., *Indian Administration*, 2nd edn., New Delhi, 1974, pp. 210–12, from which this paragraph draws. See also Thakur, R. N., *The All India Services: A Study of their Origin and Growth*, Patna, 1969, pp. 231–2.

[89] *Hindu*, 25 Oct. 1946, 4.

most of whom were from Congress provinces, reached a 'consensus' in favour of an all-India administrative service.

The second crucial moment came at a Cabinet meeting on 30 April 1948 at which the question of special protection for the all-India services in the constitution was on the agenda. The draft constitution at this time made no reference to an all-India service. Again Patel was the main proponent and the proposal went through. It helped that Nehru was muted. Patel had written to Nehru several days before the Cabinet meeting, setting out at length the reasons why special protection was important.[90] To leave the regulation of these services to central or provincial legislation would be a 'grave mistake', said Patel, for if we leave matters like that, 'the chances of interfering with the services and seriously prejudicing their efficiency on account of the interaction of Central and Provincial politics are closer'. He also cleverly (and correctly) implicated Nehru in undertakings made by Nehru and himself during negotiations over the transfer of the Secretary of State's Services to Indian control, in which there was 'an understanding' that 'we would see that the rights and conditions of service of the existing members of the Secretary of State's Services are . . . fully safeguarded'. Therefore, 'we are in honour bound to carry out that undertaking and the only way that undertaking can be fully and satisfactorily discharged is to make provision in the Constitution itself.'

The third and final step was when the Constituent Assembly debated the proposed Articles related to the services—later numbered Articles 308–14 in the Constitution. All but one were considered by the Assembly on 7 and 8 September 1949 and after considerable discussion were approved. They provided (1) that central and all-India services would hold office during the pleasure of the President of India and those in the states during the pleasure of the Governor—this was intended to make clear that civil servants were not the employees of a particular minister and also that they had no right to hold office; (2) that a civil servant could not be dismissed, removed, or reduced in rank without being given a reasonable opportunity to defend himself, except in a few specified cases; (3) that a civil servant could not be dismissed or removed by an authority subordinate to the one which appointed him—this was meant to provide protection against victimization by a minister and also central government protection for all-India civil

[90] Patel to Nehru, letter 27 Apr. 1948. Extracts in *The Framing of India's Constitution: Select Documents* ed. B. Shiva Rao, iv (New Delhi, 1968), 332–3.

servants serving in states, since members of these services were appointed by the President; (4) that Parliament be authorized to create additional all-India Services and expressly specified that the new IAS and Indian Police Services were already deemed to be services created by Parliament.

The one remaining Article not moved on 7 and 8 September went back to the Drafting Committee, was eventually amended on 9 October, and was finally moved in the Assembly on 10 October.[91] This later became Article 314, providing guarantees for those civil servants who were recruited in the past by the Secretary of State—that is, the ICS and the Indian Police. It was provided that these services would be entitled to the same pay, leave, and pension rights and other conditions of service as they had enjoyed previously. Few actually opposed the Article, but they did take the opportunity to ventilate their grievances at the privileged position of the ICS. Ayyangar, for example, characterized the guarantee as extraordinary: it 'means that they were the rulers under the old regime and that they will continue to be so in this regime'; it 'asks us to forget that these persons who are still in service—400 of them—committed excesses thinking that this was not their country'.[92] Saksena said that since the beginning the Congress had regarded the ICS as 'the steel frame which enslaved us'. Others said the ICS was 'heaven-born' and excessively 'pampered'—why tie Parliament's hands for the future regarding this particular Service?

Sardar Patel then rose and, in an extraordinary statement, both defended the ICS against its critics and praised their actions since the transfer of power. The following are excerpts:

> In point of patriotism, in point of loyalty, in point of sincerity and in point of ability, you cannot have a substitute. They are as good as ourselves, and to speak of them in disparaging terms in this House, in public, and to criticize them in this manner, is doing dis-service to yourselves and to the country.
>
> I wish to place it on record in this House that if, during the last two or three years, most of the members of the services had not behaved patriotically and with loyalty, the Union would have collapsed . . . you ask the Premiers of all Provinces. Is there any Premier in any province who is prepared to work without the Services? He will immediately resign. He cannot manage. We had a small nucleus of a broken Service. With that bit of Service we have carried on a very difficult task.
>
> As a man of experience I tell you, do not quarrel with the instruments with

[91] India. *Constituent Assembly Debates*, ix (1949), 1082–1119.

[92] *Constituent Assembly Debates*, x (1949), 33–53.

which you want to work. It is a bad workman who quarrels with his instruments. Take work from them. Every man wants some sort of encouragement. Nobody wants to put in work when everyday he is criticized and ridiculed in public . . . So, once and for all decide whether you want this Service or not. If you have done with it and decide not to have this Service at all . . . I will take the Services with me and go.

The Union will go—you will not have a united India, if you have not a good all-India service which has the independence of mind to speak out its mind, which has a sense of security . . . If you do not adopt this course, then do not follow the present Constitution. Substitute something else. Put in a Congress Constitution or some other Constitution—whatever you like—but not this Constitution. This Constitution is meant to be worked by a ring of Service which will keep the country intact.

There was no reply. The extraordinary guarantee was adopted and placed in the constitution. The ICS was finally safe.

ICS Indians knew it. The Chairman of the ICS (Central) Association, Sukthankar (ICS, CP), wrote to Patel on 13 October expressing his most grateful thanks for all that Patel had done for the ICS. He arranged to have the full text of Patel's speech in the Constituent Assembly sent to all the ICS Associations in the provinces with the instructions that a copy be sent to every member of the ICS. He closed by saying 'your speech will . . . be a source of great encouragement to the members of the ICS'.[93]

Patel's Secretary, Shankar (ICS, Bombay), noted on a report about a proposed salary cut for top civil servants being considered at this time that 'in view of the *present hostility against the Services in the rank and file of the Congress Party* and the *terrible burden we have been imposing on (Patel) in regard to the defence of the Service*, it would be a good gesture if we left the matter' of salary cuts entirely in his hands.[94] More broadly, V. P. Menon, one of the most distinguished civil servants in Delhi, wrote to Patel: 'Your speech in the Constituent Assembly has heartened the Services and had a tonic effect on their morale.' 'We are most deeply indebted to you,' he went on, for 'the Services have always regarded you as the guardian of their legitimate interests.'[95]

[93] Sukthankar to Patel, 13 Oct. 1949, in *Sardar Patel's Correspondence, 1945–50*, ed. Durga Das, ix (Ahmedabad, 1973), 351.

[94] Note to V. Shankar, 10 Oct. 1949, in *Patel's Correspondence*, ix, 351–2.

[95] Menon to Patel, 12 Oct. 1949, in *Patel's Correspondence*, ix, 348–9.

4

Political support and administrative reform: 1950–1983

THE survival of the ICS and the creation of an IAS successor required initially in the late 1940s an act of political will from the centre. Once secured, however, the ICS/IAS then required continuing political support in order to survive mounting opposition to it. Reproducing the ICS tradition between 1950 and 1983 did not just happen in a fit of absent-mindedness. The whole subject is a very large one, touching on the entire history of the modern Indian state and its political economy. Inevitably, therefore, this chapter must concentrate on certain aspects of the process to the exclusion of others. The early part of the chapter looks at three main features of the new constitution and argues that the old ICS tradition did not sit comfortably in any of them. One was the formal provision for a parliamentary system of democratic government and the consequent spread of democratic politics, with politicians increasingly involved in administration at central, state, and district levels. The second feature related to the Directive Principles of State Policy and all the steps taken subsequently in the Five Year Plans to pursue in an active manner the economic and social developments the Principles called for. The third feature was the federal structure of government, which was hardly new, but in combination with the democratic feature did set in motion forces opposed to an all-India administrative service. In the face of such opposition, how and why did the ICS/IAS manage to survive? The latter part of the chapter develops an explanation for the reproduction of this particular state form by concentrating on two aspects of the process in relation mainly to the periodic attempts at administrative reform. One aspect was the existence of broad political support from the ruling Congress party at the centre, a structure of support which blocked any move for radical administrative reform that might have undermined the position of the ICS/IAS from without. (The Janata Government in 1977–9 did not have the time or inclination to change the position.) The other aspect was the agency of power exercised by members of the ICS/IAS from within.

PARLIAMENTARY DEMOCRACY

India's constitution provided a form of government and politics that was almost wholly consistent with the liberal democratic conception of democracy popular in Western Europe and North America—equality of citizens before the law, government responsible to majority vote, and an obligation on the part of both government and citizens to obey laws expressing the will of the majority, provided that there is 'universal' suffrage by free secret ballot, regular elections involving more than one political party, and freedom of speech, the press, and religion as well as other civil liberties. The working of this constitution brought about a spread of democratic politics far beyond that which existed, say, during provincial automony in 1937–9. Political leaders coming into these new democratic institutions of government ran into entrenched political administrators in the districts and secretariats attempting with difficulty to adjust to the new politics. Relationships between these new democratic politicans and political administrators representing an older tradition were bound to be uneasy. As a leading representative of central government administrators remarked: 'emergent India was compelled, for various historical reasons, to accept the entire colonial administrative machinery and even the high ranking personnel who had so loyally served the British'; this colonial administration, on the one hand, and democratic governments 'elected by the people claiming to represent the will of the people and working in the interests of the people', on the other, 'became the principal contradiction in the Indian situation'.[1]

As democratic politicians swarmed in, many political administrators defined the new situation as political interference. Panikkar put it delicately when he remarked that ICS men in the early 1950s were not clear in their minds 'where their authority ended and that of the ministers began'; they expected that 'ministers would be satisfied with the functions that Members of the Executive Council used to exercise in the past'.[2] A Chief Minister put it more bluntly when he informed an ICS Secretary where the ultimate authority now lay: 'You may think you are doing your duty, but if I think you are going beyond it,

[1] Gupta, N. P., 'Administrative Reforms: How?', *Link* (15 Aug. 1970), 85. Mr Gupta was President, All India Confederation of Central Government Officers Associations, at the time.

[2] Panikkar, K. M., 'India's Administrative Problems', *Eastern Economist*, 26 (9 Mar. 1956), 408–9.

remember I am the judge.'[3] Collectors were even more exposed. An anthropologist who worked in Orissa in the 1950s reported that electors in villages demanded two things of their MLA (Member, Legislative Assembly). The first was his reliability in saying 'my constituency right or wrong'. The second was that the MLA 'should be effective, and by this they do not mean that he should make a mark in the legislature, but that he should be able to stand up to local officials in the interests of his constituents'. For a successful MLA is a 'fixer' in the eyes of many people, someone who can get a man a job, divert development monies into the constituency, help secure a contract, find a place in a school or a hospital.[4] When the pressure intensified, there was now no recourse for the IAS man to the Governor or Viceroy or other undemocratic outsider.

Many Collectors and secretariat officers were able to cope with this new form of pressure. Some revelled in it. One such struggle in Madhya Pradesh in 1954 between the Minister of Development and the Secretary (Development Commissioner) ended in the Minister resigning; the Secretary was able to get the support of the Chief Minister in the dispute.[5] Others did not get their way, and they resigned. In West Bengal in 1952, after an examination had been held for recruitment of some Inspectors for the Co-operative Department, Noronha (IAS, West Bengal) submitted a list of names in order of merit. The minister 'was aghast'. He was being pestered by various ministers and others to appoint their own people who were not on the lists. 'I was not prepared to send up a fresh list,' says Noronha, 'but I suggested that the minister could appoint whomever he chose and this was eventually done and deserving candidates were not appointed.' Noronha then left the Service, 'unwept, unhonoured and unsung'.[6] Bonarjee (ICS, UP) also found in the early 1950s that he could not abide 'the conversion of the Administration into a playground for political parties' nor the apparent ease with which so many of his service colleagues fitted 'snugly into the altered administrative ethic'.[7]

[3] Bhatia, L. M., 'Public Service Ethics', *Journal of the Lal Bahadur Shastri National Academy of Administration*, xix. 3 (1974), 441, citing A. D. Gorwala's 'An Independence Day Tale'.

[4] Bailey, F. G., 'Parliamentary Government in Orissa, 1947–1959', *Journal of Commonwealth Political Studies*, 1 (May 1962), 120.

[5] Reported in Dwarkadas, R., *Role of Higher Civil Service in India*, Bombay, 1958, pp. 177–82.

[6] Noronha, C., *My Life* (privately printed), 1975, p. 82. Copy in Stuart papers, Cambridge Archive.

[7] Bonarjee, *Under Two Masters*, pp. 254–5.

Others left for similar reasons.[8] To survive the rough and tumble required political skill. 'From the first day of independence the administration was indeed in politics,' observed Mangat Rai (ICS, Punjab), for 'politics influenced the administration and administrators learnt to be sensitive to politics.'[9] Lall (ICS, Bihar and Orissa) found that, while in theory he was supposed to be politically neutral when advising ministers, 'in reality the political and practical considerations are often inseparable'.[10]

There was a continuing preoccupation in the 1960s on the part of ICS/IAS people with 'political interference' and relations generally between administrators and politicians. It would be difficult to make the case that the political aspect of administrative life became more prominent. At the same time it certainly did not diminish in importance. At the district level IAS men from every state except Punjab who were, or had been, Collector wrote about their experiences in a special issue of the *Indian Journal of Public Administration* published in 1965, and in doing so gave considerable attention to the political dimension of district administration.[11] As for the Punjab, the working group for the Committee on Punjab District Administration reporting to the Punjab Government's Administrative Reforms Commission drew particular attention in 1967 to the standard problem in the district: the prestige of the Collector, they claimed, 'has declined due to day-to-day interference by politicians with his authority'.[12] These relationships, however, were by no means always fractious. It was reported in Madras State (as it was then called) that 'it did not take long for Government to realize that a strong Collector who can withstand local political pressures and decide things in a dispassionate way, far from being a hindrance, would actually save Government considerable embarrassment'.[13] A similarly relaxed view appeared to prevail also in the Madras secretariat at this time. The political set up in this state is 'quite good', one young IAS man there cheerfully informed me in 1967; 'if we tell a minister that a particular course of action will lead to certain difficulties he is quite amenable to reason

[8] e.g. Baksi, N., 'In Bihar: The State of My Adoption', in Panjabi, *Civil Servant*, pp. 141–213.

[9] Mangat Rai, E. N., *Patterns of Administrative Development in Independent India*, London, 1976, Commonwealth Paper 19, p. 52.

[10] Lall, S., 'Civil Service Neutrality', *IJPA* iv, 1 (1958), 2.

[11] *IJPA* xi,. 3 (1965).

[12] Reported in *Statesman*, 18 May 1967, 7.

[13] Ramachandran, G. (IAS, Tamil Nadu), 'The Collector in Madras', *IJPA* xi. 3 (1965), 510.

and many times alters his views.'[14] He added that a batch mate of his from Bihar, who had recently visited, said the position was 'much worse there'. The Governor of Bihar during 1962–7 would have agreed. In an extraordinarily candid statement of his experience there he said that he 'never felt that either the ministers or the officers seriously addressed themselves to economic and social problems' in Bihar, so preoccupied were they in their political struggle with each other.[15] Such relationships at the centre were also 'uneasy' in 1966, according to the new Prime Minister, Mrs Indira Gandhi; the problem had come to a head in the latter part of 1966 when several ministers had 'asked for the transfer of their Secretaries and the appointment of new ones of their choice, but Mrs Gandhi has been resisting these pressures'.[16] Even more striking was the occasion when the Home Minister resigned on 9 November 1966, alleging in his letter of resignation that the ICS Home Secretary had been insubordinate and uncooperative.[17] Other ministers complained publicly from time to time about the system whereby, as the Minister for Food and Agriculture remarked in 1966, they could 'choose their advisers only from the top ranks of the IAS', and were not allowed 'to secure the services of top level advisers from outside'.[18]

One consequence of this preoccupation with the political dimension of administrative life was that comparatively little attention was paid to other matters such as improvement of the administration itself, including its organization and techniques. L. P. Singh (ICS, Bihar), widely regarded as one of India's outstanding administrators in the post-independence period, drew attention to this with great candour on the eve of his retirement as Home Secretary in the Government of India when talking privately and informally in 1970 with some civil servants on an in-service training course in New Delhi. He said (and I

[14] T. 584, to the author in a personal interview at Fort St George, Madras, 19 Jan. 1967.

[15] Ayyangar, M. Ananthasayanam, 'Administration of a State as seen by a Governor', *Management Perspective* (Delhi), vii (Apr.–June 1969), 37–43, 71. The particular quotation is at p. 38.

[16] Reported in *Times of India*, 14 Nov. 1966, 1, 7.

[17] For details of this case and others involving political relations between senior administrators and ministers, see Bhambhri, C. P., *Bureaucracy and Politics in India*, Delhi, 1971, Chs. 4–8.

[18] Mr Subramaniam dwelt on this aspect in a talk in Ahmedabad, reported in *Hindu*, 12 Dec. 1966, 1.

paraphrase):[19] I think that we civil servants are too concerned with the political element in administration. I know that thousands of civil servants spend a lot of time bemoaning political interference, complaining of unjust orders passed, and so on. I personally think that these preoccupations have done a great deal of harm to the civil service and to the administration of this country. For they have tended to deflect the civil service away from going more deeply into what I would describe broadly as its professional problems. Now I have worked under many different ministers in the states and at the centre, and I have yet to know one who disapproved of quick disposal of work, of using modern methods, of being inquiring and critical and so on. If we have not modernized the administration, if we have not started using modern tools and techniques, if we haven't had a sufficiently inquiring mind, if we haven't been sufficiently critical and analytical, and if we have taken far too many things for granted, if we have never tried to calculate the cost of various operations and think of doing things more economically or more speedily, let's be honest, we have to blame ourselves, not ministers, not politicians, not legislators. To my mind this preoccupation with the political and comparative neglect of professional problems of administration has been the greatest single failure of the civil service in independent India. Let me add that when I say this I am really pointing the accusing finger at people like myself and not at you because those of us who were in positions of some responsibility when India became independent ought to have given the lead in this matter, and we did not.

Senior ICS/IAS officers did not heed L. P. Singh's advice to cease being preoccupied with political interference. They were, if anything, even more preoccupied with it in the 1970s. Congress Party leaders set the tone in 1969 with calls for a civil service more 'committed' to their programme. Jagjivan Ram, in his Presidential address to the Bombay session of the All India Congress Committee declared that 'the so-called neutral administrative machinery is a hindrance, not a help' . . . and 'is hardly relevant to Indian conditions'. Mrs Gandhi also called for more commitment, and Chandra Shekhar, Mohan Dharia, and others, in an important note to the Party (later published) said:

the present bureaucracy under the orthodox and conservative leadership of the

[19] Singh, L. P., 'Talk to some Officers on an In-service Training Course, New Delhi, 7 Mar. 1970', IIPA 1970, mimeo., 3–4.

ICS with its upper-class prejudices can hardly be expected to meet the requirements of social and economic change along socialist lines. The creation of an administrative cadre *committed* to national objectives and responsive to our social needs is an urgent necessity.[20]

Those remarks were hotly debated by ICS/IAS men during the next few years.[21] Mrs Gandhi was even forced to try to clarify what she had meant by commitment (for example, in the *Lok Sabha* on 9 March 1970). But it was clear to IAS men whom I interviewed in 1983 both in Delhi and in the states, that in the early 1970s it seemed that loyalty to the party in power became part of their reward structure which had not been true before. Those who were 'loyal' were now much more likely to get promotion and desirable postings.

Subsequent political events in the 1970s drove home these tendencies. First, there was the Emergency imposed by the Prime Minister Mrs Gandhi on 25 June 1975 which remained in force until early 1977; the constitutional right of citizens to move courts regarding civil liberties was suspended, as were all restrictions on executive action: and the Maintenance of Internal Security Act (MISA) was amended so that anyone, including the Prime Minister's political opponents, could be 'detained' in prison with no disclosure of the reasons necessary. Evidence which appeared in the Shah Commission of Inquiry Reports after the Emergency suggests that most IAS officers in secretariats and districts, who were responsible for advising on, and implementing, MISA, accepted orders they believed to be improper and politically motivated. 'Even the cream of the talent of the country in the administrative field often collapse at the slightest pressure,' the Shah Commission found.[22] Many Collectors 'obediently carried out the instructions emanating from politicians and administrative heads issued on personal or political considerations'; these men said to the Shah Commission that in the circumstances they had no choice—they were 'helpless' for fear of the consequences of not obeying.[23] In the

[20] All three of these references and others from Congress leaders are cited and discussed in Aiyar, S. P., 'Political Context of Indian Administration,' *IJPA* xvii. 3 (1971), 337–54.

[21] e.g. Dubhashi, P. R., 'Committed Bureaucracy', *IJPA* xvii. 1 (1971), 33–9, and Chaturvedi, M. K., 'Commitment in Civil Service', *IJPA* xvii. 1 (1971), 40–6; 'Committed Civil Service: A Symposium', *Seminar*, 168 (Aug. 1973), with articles by six ICS men; Chaturvedi, T. N., 'Commitment in Public Service', *Journal of Constitutional and Parliamentary Studies*, 11 (Jan–Mar. 1977), 17–29.

[22] Shah Commission of Inquiry, *Interim Report II*, Government of India Press, 1978, p. 142.

[23] Shah Commission, *Third and Final Report*, 1978, p. 229.

secretariat the Shah Commission found instances of ICS and IAS officers engaged in 'forging of records, fabrication of ground of detention, ante-dating of detention orders, and callous disregard of the rights of detainees as regards revocation, parole, etc.'[24] There were many cases where officers 'curried favour' with politicians 'by doing what they thought the people in authority desired', for 'many excesses did not originate at the political level'.[25] In short, the Emergency represented (as one journalist remarked) 'the high water mark of the politicians' victory in the long drawn out struggle against the service'.[26]

The 'long drawn out struggle' continued during the remainder of the 1970s in unique political circumstances. The elections of 1977 swept the Congress out both at the centre and, later, in most states. Some IAS administrators were rewarded at that time for the rapidity with which they moved to assist the new government. Then in January 1980 Mrs Gandhi swept back to power at the centre and in May the Congress was back in most states. IAS administrators formerly loyal to Congress were reinstated, whereas others who had done well under Janata were shunted aside. That experience was still being talked about in 1983 as having marked the IAS by making political loyalty an even more important value than before as one of the norms for advancement to plum jobs.[27]

L. K. Jha, formerly of the ICS and still prominent in government, wrote a paper in 1983 analysing the factors contributing to the 'declining standards of administrative performance'.[28] Four factors were singled out as important. The most important, he said, is 'the deterioration in working relations between ministers and civil servants'. Newly elected ministers usually want to do certain things—'possibly in fulfilment of electoral promises given generously rather than wisely'; the civil servant, in advising the minister, often has to point out obstacles and pitfalls in pursuing that course of action, even though in the end they must carry out the minister's orders. Experienced and

[24] Shah Commission, *Interim Report II*, 1978, p. 142.

[25] Shah Commission, *Third and Final Report*, 1978, p. 230.

[26] Vohra, B., 'Anatomy of Mal-administration', *Seminar*, 230 (Oct. 1978), 14. For a more general assessment written at the time, see Heginbotham, S. J., 'The Civil Service and the Emergency', in Hart, H. C. (ed.), *Indira Gandhi's India: A Political System Reappraised*, Boulder, Colorado, 1976, pp. 67–91.

[27] Two very senior IAS Secretaries made this point: R501 to the author in an interview, North Block, New Delhi, 29 Nov. 1983; U531 to the author in an interview, Shastri Bhavan, New Delhi, 27 Sept. 1983.

[28] Jha, L. K., 'The Role of Bureaucracy in a Developing Democracy', Training Abstract No. 2, Training Division, PAR, GOI 1983, mimeo.

confident ministers welcome such advice. Less experienced ministers interpret such advice as obstruction. As the proportion of less experienced ministers increases, the more there is a ministerial preference for administrators who support their line of action without raising uncomfortable questions or doubts. There then begin to emerge within the civil service persons who 'curry favour' with ministers, anticipate their views, and make recommendations to please them. They get the promotions and increasingly fill coveted posts, while others who give correct and factual advice are pushed aside or penalized by being transferred from post to post. All this has a deleterious effect on the morale of the whole administration. It also can result in programmes that have not been carefully thought through as regards their administrative implications, and are thus poorly implemented. Such studied comment by respected administrators was matched by a barrage of more sensational comment in the press along similar lines at the time—for example, 'Bureaucrats and their bosses' (in Maharashtra), 'Alarming tussle among UP politicians and officials', 'Bureaucrats versus politicians in Bihar'.[29] The whole experience showed generally that the relationship between elected democratic politicians and political administrators representing an older tradition remained a difficult one, produced in part by having retained an ICS tradition of administration in a changed political context.

PLANNED DEVELOPMENT

The second main feature of the new constitution set up a challenge to the ICS tradition from a different direction, although unlike the political change this second one took some time to come to the fore. The constitution in its Directive Principles of State Policy gave general guide-lines for legislation and administrative action for promoting 'the welfare of the people by securing and protecting as effectively as it may a social order in which justice—social, economic, and political—shall inform all the institutions of the national life'. They called for action across a broad front, including efforts to ensure that in the domestic field wealth and its sources of production are evenly distributed so as to subserve the common good and are not concentrated in the hands of a few persons; that adequate means of livelihood are ensured for all

[29] *Indian Express*, 10 Mar. 1982; *Statesman*, 28 Mar. 1982; *Indian Express*, 14 May 1982.

and no exploitation of labour takes place nor is labour forced to operate in inhumane conditions; that the standard of living is raised and all possible steps are taken to improve public health; that the sick are afforded public assistance; that free and compulsory primary education is provided for all; that agriculture and animal husbandry are improved; and that village government receives encouragement. One can in fact point to legislation and official pronouncements in all these areas, particularly in the Five Year Plans.

Implementing the Directive Principles through the preparation of national plans for economic and social development affected the whole posture of the state, shifting it from an essentially *laissez-faire* holding operation towards a much more interventionist role. This obviously began to affect the administration. The pace and volume of work increased. Public sector employment more than doubled during the period of the first three Five Year Plans. It had nearly doubled again by 1983, as Table 13 suggests.

Table 13. *Growth of Public Sector Employment: 1953–1983* (figures in millions, rounded)

	1953 (estimate)	1963	1973	1983 (estimate)
Central government	1.5	2.3	2.9	3.7
State government	2.2	3.2	4.6	6.0
Quasi-government	0.1	1.0	2.5	4.4
Local bodies	0.3	1.4	1.9	2.1
Totals (in millions)	4.1	7.9	11.9	16.2

Sources: For 1953: from GOI Directorate General of Employment and Training, 'Census of Central Government Employees', 1961, mimeo., which uses 1953 as base year; for 1963; Gupta, D. and Premi, M., *Sources and Nature of the Official Statistics of the Indian Union*, Delhi, 1970, p. 281; for 1973: GOI Ministry of Finance, Economic Division, *Economic Survey, 1973–74* (1974), p. 28; the 1983 figures are based on evidence reported in *India Today*, 15 May 1983, p. 6 together with certain projections made by the author based on data in GOI Directorate of Labour and Rehabilitation, 'Census of Central Government Employees (as of 31 Mar. 1980)', 1983, mimeo., pp. 50–4 (where data for states are also given), and GOI PAR, *Annual Report, 1982–83*, (1983), pp. 11–12.

New ministries and departments in development fields emerged in the 1950s, each with their own separate hierarchies reaching down into the districts. Many of them were set up to implement specialist programmes, each having their own technical requirements. They tended to resent having to go through an ICS or IAS political administrator in the secretariat in order to get ministerial approval for schemes. At the district level they were unhappy about being subject to the supervision and control of a generalist Collector, the principal representative of the state government there. As the technical specialists moved in to help implement the developmental plans, they came up against an older tradition of administration with generalist administrators in charge.

These developments led to increasing dissatisfaction with ICS/IAS generalists being 'on top', and technical experts only 'on tap'. This aspect of the ICS tradition came under increasing pressure during the 1960s. Professor Paranjape's attack was an example. He said that the ICS had contained some outstanding individuals, but it 'is a symbol of inequality, casteism and amateurish dilettantism in our administration', and went on: 'The tradition may have been appropriate to a colonial regime when the functions of government were limited and comparatively simple;' but 'with the increasing complexity of functions and the technical nature of many of the problems faced, the continuance of this tradition is bound to affect the successful conduct of our attempts at planned development.'[30] No critique like that had appeared in the 1950s.

There is no doubt that the ICS tradition was open to such charges. 'Symbols of inequality'? Of course they were. ICS men were not only on top, they were 'heaven-born'. There was an extraordinary 'distance' between such men and their subordinates. In 1963–4, a top ICS Secretary in New Delhi received Rs 3,500 per month; a *peon* (messenger) got Rs 55 per month. The pay differential here was 63.64/1, one of the highest in the world. By contrast, the comparable differential for Pakistan was 38.96/1, for the USA 7.24/1.[31] The high and the low were somewhat less far apart in the early 1980s, but the differences were still very marked. Nearly 60 per cent of all central government employees were earning less than Rs 300 per month, nearly 90 per cent less than Rs 500 per month; nearly all IAS officers were earning more than RS 1,000 per month, and top Secretaries got Rs 3,500 per month.[32] Senior IAS officers also occupied sumptuous government bungalows, were driven by chauffeurs, and saluted by armed guards as they entered secretariat buildings.

[30] Paranjape, H. K., 'A Trojan Inheritance', *Seminar* (New Delhi), 84 (Aug. 1966), 32–3.

[31] For details, see Braibanti, *Asian Bureaucratic Systems*, p. 656.

[32] 'Census of Central Government Employees', 1983.

'Symbol of casteism'? Paranjape's charge here was perhaps a bit hard, but if castes are, in part, mutually exclusive social groups ranked on a purity–pollution dimension loosely within four *varnas*, then the ICS/IAS represented casteism to the extent that it was one of hundreds of exclusive different services into which India's administrative structure was divided all located within one or another of four classes—Class I, or II, or III, or IV. Endogamy and ascription did not apply, however, although there had been some intermarriage between ICS families.

'Symbols of amateurish dilettantism'? Perhaps they were dilettantes, certainly they were generalists. There was probably no other single group of civil servants in the world holding such an incredible array of administrative posts. Young IAS direct recruits were moving all over the place after only a few years in the Service. By the end of 1965, for example, young men and women recruited to the IAS in the years 1957–61 had already held (or were holding) such diverse posts as Secretary of an electricity board, Deputy Secretary of a finance department, Deputy Commissioner in a municipal corporation of a large city, Collector in a remote rural district, Joint Director of a training institution, public administration expert advising an African government, Under Secretary in a specialist central government ministry like the Ministry of Petroleum and Chemicals, or Manager of the Pine Wood Hotel in Shillong.[33] This was generalism gone beserk. By the late 1970s the central government was beginning to press for 'career planning' for the IAS, conceding that 'it is neither desirable nor easy for [the IAS] to flit from one kind of job to another without being specialized in any'.[34] Detailed guide-lines were sent to Chief Secretaries asking that each IAS officer be posted in one broad area of specialism until his or her eighteenth year of service, but few states took this up seriously.

Inequality, casteism, and amateurish dilettantism were only three of many charges levelled increasingly from the 1960s against the ICS tradition of generalist administrators on top. Such criticisms were taken up even more powerfully by the Administrative Reforms Commission in the late 1960s and later in other government reports and academic writings; and technical specialists in the civil service

[33] Source: *IAS Civil List, 1966*, pp. 2–315.

[34] Lal Bahadur Shastri National Academy of Administration, 'National Training Conference on Training of Civil Servants in India, 21–23 September, 1982, Recommendation', mimeo., pp. 20–21.

began to organize and demand parity with the IAS as regards pay and position. Here, again, one can see the origins of these conflicts in the contradictions between the need for specialist expertise in implementing development plans and an older tradition of administration reserving top positions at all levels for gentlemanly amateurs.

FEDERALISM

The other main feature of the constitution, the federal structure of government, was hardly new, but it was profoundly important for the position of the IAS in the new democratic polity. A constitution is federal, according to a well-known definition, if three conditions are satisfied: '(1) two levels of government rule the same land and people; (2) each level has at least one area of action in which it is autonomous; and (3) there is some guarantee (even though merely a statement in the constitution) of the autonomy of each government in its own sphere'.[35] The Indian Constitution met these tests. Two levels of government were established, and Article 245 of the Constitution provided that both Parliament and state legislatures could make laws for the same area. The seventh Schedule of the Constitution gave three detailed lists which apportioned legislative responsibility between the centre and the states. Parliament had jurisdiction over 96 subjects in the 'Union list' such as defence, atomic energy, foreign affairs, railways, ports, posts and telegraphs, interstate trade and commerce, banking, insurance, and a number of specified avenues of taxation. The 'State list' included 66 subjects which were within the exclusive jurisdiction of a state legislature such as public order, prisons, local government, public health, education (with certain exceptions), land tenures, forests, mines, and some specified avenues of taxation including land revenue. There was also a 'Concurrent list' of 47 subjects on which both levels of government could legislate. Any matter not on the lists—the residual power—lay with the central government. Disputes between the central and state governments were referred to the Supreme Court. The actual working of India's federalism corresponded generally with the formal constitutional guarantees. For example, a study in the early 1960s of union–state relations with special reference to Rajasthan found that, although the powers of the central government were very wide indeed, co-operative federalism best characterized

[35] Riker, W. H., *Federalism*, Boston, 1964, p. 11.

union–state relations, in which 'the personality of the states and their operative freedom may at times be compromised but it is certainly not crushed and denied altogether'.[36] The study cited, for example, the fact that the central government had no device to ensure that its general directives in the Five Year Plan would be complied with. It instanced the Third Five Year Plan directive that people who benefited from irrigation projects were required to dig field channels, a directive that remained inoperative in Rajasthan because the Rajasthan Legislature failed to make the necessary state law. This experience was possible only in a federal structure of government. Similar examples were reported in a detailed study in the early 1960s of relations between the centre and the State of West Bengal.[37]

The question arises: since virtually all of India was divided into states (with the exception of Union Territories), how did the central government exercise its power and carry out its responsibilities in the country? The answer, briefly, is that it relied on its own administrative personnel in the states for some purposes, for example, defending the country, delivering the post, collecting its revenue, running the railways; and it relied on state governments' personnel for others, for example, regulating and controlling scarce commodities and implementing various programmes contained in the Five Year Plans. It also had the IAS, which straddled the federal structure without fundamentally violating it. The existence of such a service in a federal system of democratic government was a remarkable feature.

Like its predecessor, the IAS as a whole was made up of state cadres. There was no central government cadre. What made the IAS all-India was that during the course of a member's career, he might work from time to time for the central government; and, if so, he was placed on deputation to it for a period of years and, except in unusual circumstances (or if he was a very senior man), he reverted at the end of his deputation period to the state of his cadre. While serving under a state government, an IAS officer was formally under its control. However, he was governed by service rules made by the central government,[38] and these could not be altered or interpreted to his disadvantage except by, or with the approval of, that government; and

[36] Narain, I. and Mathur, P. C., 'Union–State Relations in India: A Case Study of Rajasthan', *Journal of Commonwealth Political Studies*, 2 (May 1964), 138.

[37] Franda, M., *Bengal and the Federalizing Process in India*, Princeton, 1968.

[38] GOI Ministry of Home Affairs, *All-India Services Manual*, 2nd edn., corrected up to 1.8.1969, bound under one cover; the rules ran to 790 pages.

he could appeal to the central government when he considered that his service rights had been infringed by an order of the state government.

Such an all-India administrative arrangement, appropriate for a colonial regime, was hardly likely to delight political leaders in the state governments. In effect, what the central government was doing was to recruit a group of administrators and send them into the states to hold the key administrative posts there. State ministers, in consequence, were severely restricted in their choice of whom they could appoint to be responsible for the implementation of their policies. When, for example, a new Chief Minister took office and found that he could not work well with the existing Chief Secretary, his range of choice for a successor was limited to only a few individuals—the men who happened at that time to be at the very top of the IAS cadre in that state. If he liked none of these individuals, he was stuck. For the post of Chief Secretary, and other senior posts borne on the IAS cadre, had to be filled by IAS men under rules made by the central government 'in consultation' with the states.[39] It was not a rigid system of earmarking certain key posts for the IAS.[40] Individual state governments were consulted from time to time and they did have some say over which posts were placed on the IAS cadre. But in the end, if there was dispute about the matter, the central government's decision was final.

As federal politics developed during the 1950s and 1960s, this arrangement began to rankle. There was hardly any overt expression of hostility during the 1950s because of the close association of the Congress Party and government at all levels of political activity. Conflicts between states and the centre were handled to a large extent within the framework of the Congress umbrella. From the end of the 1950s, however, regional parties began to come more to the fore demanding greater independence from the centre in administrative areas for which states are responsible under the constitution. One aspect of this was unhappiness with IAS officers sent in by the central government controlled by Congress. For example, when the DMK Government came to power in Madras State in 1967, it promptly told the centre it did not require any more IAS officers.[41] But they had no control over the situation, and IAS men and women continued to arrive

[39] This rendering is in *The All India Services Act, 1951*, section 3, and repeated in many of the IAS Rules made subsequently to implement the Act.

[40] Mehta, B. (IAS, Rajasthan), who was Chief Secretary in Rajasthan 1958–66, draws attention to this lack of rigidity in *IJPA* xvii. (1971), 156.

[41] 'Madras Wants Fewer IAS Officers', *Statesman*, 4 June 1967.

there. In Kerala, E. M. S. Namboodiripad, former Chief Minister and member of the Communist Party of India (Marxist), openly complained in 1969 that the IAS 'are recruited and trained by the Congress Party government at the Centre and posted to states in many of which there are non-Congress governments', adding, 'suddenly one morning I find young boys and one or two girls before me saying they have been posted to Kerala. What shall I do with them? What do I know of them?'[42] Similar remarks were made by the former Chief Minister of West Bengal.[43]

It did not help that ICS/IAS officers were frequently perceived by politicians as confident and rather arrogant agents from Delhi. Nor were such perceptions entirely misplaced. A. N. Jha (ICS, UP), when Secretary, Ministry of Information and Broadcasting in 1965, admitted that Secretaries like him 'have tended to think out problems on their own on an all-India scale and have tended to assume that deviations from their way of thinking are acts of sacrilege'. Furthermore, 'in practice . . . we Secretaries and our advisers insist on laying down the policy even for subjects that concern the states alone'.[44] Not surprisingly, one highly respected political leader in the 1960s on the Agra Municipal Corporation remarked in exasperation that 'the bureaucracy in India is united in doing wrong, and no one can actually bring a successful action against an IAS officer. It is like a dictatorship.'[45] Such arguments against the IAS continued to be heard in the 1980s.[46] Such an all-India service, controlled from the centre, restricted the states' right, as they saw it, to recruit and control their own civil servants needed to implement the tasks allocated to them under the federal constitution.

The argument so far has been that the all-India administrative frame, and the ICS tradition of administration it represented, did not fit well into the three main principles of India's new constitution—federalism, democracy, and the development-oriented posture of the state. This is not to deny that many ICS and IAS officers as individuals identified closely with the state in which they worked, were keen

[42] *Statesman*, 23 Feb. 1969, p. 7. [43] *Statesman*, 14 Sep. 1970, p. 7.

[44] Jha, A. N., 'Planning, the Federal Principle and Parliamentary Democracy' *IJPA* xi. 2 (1965), 165.

[45] Rosenthal, D., *The Limited Elite: Politics and Government in Two Indian Cities*, Chicago, 1970, p. 189.

[46] e.g. *EPW* xvii. 22 (29 May 1982), 887, reporting efforts by the Prime Minister and her colleagues to get 'the top echelons of the state bureaucracy' in West Bengal 'to non-co-operate with and conspire against the Left Front government'.

democrats, and believed absolutely in the importance of development. The point is that the *institutional* fit was poor when viewed more broadly. As has been suggested, the ICS/IAS as an institution within a democratic federal constitution committed to development set up contradictions that had unfortunate administrative consequences more generally—preoccupation with the political, demoralization amongst technical specialists in the civil service denied access to the top posts, and so on. Despite these tensions the IAS was still firmly in position in 1983.

THE POLITICS OF ADMINISTRATIVE REFORM

The reason why the ICS/IAS survived, indeed prospered, despite increasing hostility needs explanation. Why did that institutional form persist despite opposition? Two aspects of an answer to the question are explored here: first, IAS people had a major say in all attempts at administrative reform during the period, and second, there was never sufficient political clout from the political leadership at the centre for radical reform of the existing administrative framework.

Politicians are prone to 'blame the bureaucrats', and India's politicians are no exception. Yet there was never during the period 1950–83 any serious proposal from the political leadership of the Indian state to end the IAS and its pre-eminent position in the administration. Even Prime Minister Nehru during the 1950s and early 1960s, a man who had formerly been such a critic of the ICS, offered only mild criticism of their 'colonial mentality', while stressing their value in the maintenance of national unity.[47] The Estimates Committee of Parliament, normally a trenchant critic of all it surveyed, was strangely muted when it brought the IAS within its sights; it contented itself with recommending various measures to improve its efficiency.[48] The Planning Commission took a similar line; each of the three Five Year Plans during the 1950s and early 1960s paid attention to problems of implementing the Plans and the need for reform, but the IAS framework largely escaped their criticisms.[49] Reports on

[47] e.g. Nehru, J., 'A Word to the Services', *IJPA* 1. 4 (1955) 289–302: the text of a speech Nehru made to an audience of public servants in Kurnool, Andhra Pradesh, on 9 Dec. 1955.

[48] Lok Sabha Secretariat, Estimates Committee (1965–6), *Ninety-Third Report (Third Lok Sabha)*, 1966, ch. 3. See also Lok Sabha, Estimates Committee, *Ninth Report, 1953–54, Administrative, Financial and Other Reforms*.

[49] Planning Commission, *First Five Year Plan*, (1951), pp. 111–51; *Second Five Year*

aspects of central administration by Gorwala in 1951,[50] Appleby in 1953 and 1956,[51] Chanda in 1958,[52] and Krishnamachari in 1962[53] each contained a number of proposals for reform, but altering the IAS institutional form was not one of them. The Das Commission of Inquiry (1957–9) made a searching study of administration at the centre, but the IAS was declared outside the Commission's terms of reference.[54] When a high-powered Committee on Administration was set up within the Government of India in 1961 to consider administrative reform, its chairman was Vishnu Sahay (ICS, UP) and the six members were all ICS men.[55]

ICS/IAS men were as energetic in working to preserve their position within existing structures in the states. For one thing, they had a major say in the form and procedures of administration. Many of the bureaucratic codes and manuals from the raj, which tied most other administrators to largely routine tasks, were not altered in any fundamental way; ICS men merely updated, amended, expanded them. How did clerks in the Government of Bihar handle files in the 1950s and 1960s? They followed procedures established when the Province of Bihar and Orissa was created in 1912, procedures written down by an ICS officer in 1914 and merely 'revised' by Mr Agarwal of the ICS in 1952.[56] How did Assistant District Commissioners in Maharashtra do their work in the 1950s and 1960s? They followed for the most part the Manual of Procedures for Assistant District Commissioners in the Province of Bombay initially written by Sir Frederick Lely of the ICS in 1905, revised by another ICS man in 1938, and updated by another in

Plan (1956), pp. 26–47; *Third Five Year Plan*, (1961), pp. 276–90. There were occasional vague references to the need for reform of administrative structure, e.g. 'the introduction of *panchayati raj* raises the wider question of the reorganization of district administration' (*Third Plan*, p. 341).

[50] GOI Planning Commission, *Report on Public Administration*, by A. D. Gorwala, 1951.

[51] GOI Cabinet Secretariat, *Public Administration in India: Report of a Survey* by Paul Appleby, 1953; Cabinet Secretariat, *Re-examination of India's Administrative System with Special Reference to Administration of Government's Industrial and Commercial Enterprises*, by Paul Appleby, 1956.

[52] Chanda, A., *Indian Administration* London, 1958.

[53] GOI Planning Commission, *Report on Indian and State Administrative Services and Problems of District Administration*, by V. T. Krishnamachari, 1962.

[54] GOI Ministry of Finance, *Commission of Enquiry on Emoluments and Conditions of Service of Central Government Employees, 1957–59*, 1959.

[55] Office Memorandum No. 2/28/61—O & M, 5 Aug. 1961, constituting the Committee on Administration, in Cabinet Secretariat, Organization and Methods Division, *Paper on Measures for Strengthening of Administration*, 1961.

[56] Government of Bihar. Cabinet Secretariat, *Rules of Executive Business* (Patna), 1965.

Bombay State after independence.[57] ICS men authored the reports on reorganization of district administration in Punjab and UP.[58] ICS/IAS men not only serviced Administrative Reforms Committees but also served as committee members in Andhra Pradesh,[59] Kerala,[60] Rajasthan,[61] and elsewhere; in Andhra in 1960 their dominance was particularly striking—the Chairman and Vice-Chairman were ICS, and four of the five members were IAS.[62] Some of the proposals for reform and reorganization were quite important, but one thing that never surfaced was any proposal that would have diminished the power and position of the IAS in state governments. As for political leaders in the states, they might complain about IAS invasion of states rights, but they were in no position to propose its abolition, given the constitutional guarantee and central government responsibility.

Any threat to the pre-eminent position of the IAS in the framework of India's administration would have had to come as the result of a comprehensive examination of the administration as a whole with central government impetus behind it. Such a potential threat came only once during the entire period. It came with the decision in November 1965 by the central government to set up an Administrative Reforms Commission (ARC).[63] This time the IAS was not declared out of bounds. And the work of the ARC in the late 1960s did in fact pose a most serious challenge to the IAS.

The ARC's terms of reference were very wide, and a vast number of studies of public administration in India were prepared under its auspices. In the end, when it was wound up in 1970, the ARC had

[57] Government of Bombay. *Assistant Collector's Manual* (Bombay), 1951. For striking examples from UP, see Masaldan, P. N., *Planning in Uttar Pradesh* (Bombay), 1962, p. 25.

[58] Government of Punjab. *Report on the Reorganization of District Administration in Punjab* (Chandigarh), 1954. Fletcher (ICS, Punjab) and two other ICS men wrote the report. Government of Uttar Pradesh, *Reorganization of Collectorates* (Lucknow), 1956. Das (ICS, UP) did this one.

[59] Government of Andhra Pradesh. *Report of the Administrative Reforms Committee, 1964–65* (Hyderabad), 1965.

[60] Government of Kerala. *Report of the Administrative Reforms Committee* (Trivandrum), 1958.

[61] Government of Rajasthan. *Report of the Administrative Reforms Committee* (Jaipur), 1963.

[62] Government of Andhra Pradesh. *Report of the Administrative Reforms Committee* (Hyderabad), 1960.

[63] The definitive study is Maheshwari, S., *The Administrative Reforms Commission*, Agra, 1972; most of this book is a summary of the reports. Also excellent is Narula, B. S., 'Administrative Reforms Commission: Perspective and Findings', *IJPA* xvii. 4 (1971), 634–60.

submitted nineteen formal reports containing a total of 581 recommendations. Of these reports the one on Personnel Administration[64] attracted the most comment; and the recommendation in that Report that stood out most strikingly cut at the very foundations of the IAS. The line of thinking in this Report was set by a Conference on Personnel Administration at the Indian Institute of Public Administration in 1968, which in turn was influenced by the Fulton Committee recommendations in Britain which appeared at that time and which were viewed with great interest in India. In brief, the ARC recommended that the pre-eminent position of IAS generalists in the central secretariat be ended. All competent Class I officers from all services should have access to middle and senior management posts in the secretariat. Where specialist services already existed to attend to specialist subjects, top posts in that subject area in the secretariat would normally be held by people from that specialist service. In non-specialist areas, all middle level posts like Deputy Secretary in the secretariat would be demarcated into eight broad areas of specialization, and selection to the posts thus made would be on the basis of a mid-career competitive examination, from all Class I officers. The eight broad areas of specialized administration into which middle and top level management personnel would be placed were economic, industrial, agricultural and rural development, social and educational, personnel, financial, defence and internal security, and planning. These radical proposals were meant to pursue the ARC's aim of reorienting the administration increasingly towards specialization and the belief that 'the doors of senior management should be open to all sectors of the civil service'.[65] The Commission believed the IAS could be accommodated within one of the broad areas of specialization. They made no mention of the fact that by opening up a road to the top to all comers, and thereby putting an end to IAS generalists coming on deputation from states to command automatically all (or most) of the top posts, they were in fact sounding the death-knell of the IAS and the tradition of administration it represented.

IAS men were well aware of the implications. One said quite bluntly that the 'élitist concept is the very substance of the IAS, and any arrangement that disturbs this concept also demolishes the service,' and added that the 'more honest course for the Commission would

[64] GOI Administrative Reforms Commission, *Report: Personnel Administration* (New Delhi), 1969.

[65] ARC, *Report: Personnel Administration*, p. 14.

have been to suggest the abolition of the IAS'.[66] Others developed powerful arguments showing that the ARC's Report rested on a fallacious distinction between functional and non-functional areas, and other wrong premises and assumptions.[67] Spirited support in favour of the ARC's proposals also appeared, written by civil servants not in the IAS.[68] They argued that ending the élitist arrangements would have a beneficial impact on the morale and effectiveness of the civil service as a whole. These arguments pro and con were no doubt rehearsed by the advisers to the Prime Minister and her political colleagues responsible for implementing the reforms.

Reform proposals were one thing, implementing them quite another. The Chairman of the ARC had no illusions on this score. He poignantly remarked in his covering letter to the Prime Minister, Indira Gandhi, when submitting the Report on Personnel Administration to her:[69]

> the reforms we have recommeded are bound to raise resistance from those who are adversely affected. Resistance from within the service is a very difficult problem for the Government to deal with. The declarations made from time to time by the Prime Minister and other Cabinet Ministers have emphasised that reforms of a fundamental character are needed. Resistance based on sectional or personal interests should not be allowed to come in the way of putting them into effect.

Resistance there certainly was from groups like the IAS whom the ARC Chairman recognized would be 'adversely affected'. Responsibility for the detailed work involved in implementing the 581 recommendations of the ARC was delegated by the Cabinet to the small Department of Administrative Reforms in the Home Ministry (an IAS preserve) and a new Department of Personnel created in 1970 on the recommendation of the ARC and located in the Cabinet Secretariat.[70] (These two

[66] Mohanty, N. (IAS, Orissa), 'ARC on Personnel Administration: A Study in Bias', *IJPA* xv. 4 (1969), 643–4.

[67] e.g. Dubhashi, P. R. (IAS, Mysore), 'ARC's Report on Personnel Administration: Faulty Superstructure on False Premises', *IJPA* xv. 4 (1969), 623–34; Chaturvedi, M. K. (IAS, UP), 'Personnel Administration: The Need for Realism', *IJPA* xv. 1 (1969), 32–73.

[68] e.g. Butani, K. N., 'Personnel Administration: A Muffled Cry for Change by the Administrative Reforms Commission', *IJPA*, xv. 1 (1969), 11–31; Chandra, B., 'Personnel Administration: Time for Action', *IJPA* xv. 2 (1969), 277–87.

[69] Letter from K. Hanumanthaiya (Chairman ARC) to Indira Gandhi (Prime Minister), 18 Apr. 1969, para. 12, in ARC, *Report: Personnel Administration*, 1969, p. iv.

[70] The new departments had a number of functions, one of which was the 'formulation of personnel policies on all matters common to the Central and All-India

departments were amalgamated a few years later and placed in the Home Ministry.) Characteristically, the IAS poured into the new Personnel Department. As many as twenty had arrived in this one Department by the end of 1971, and the Secretary and the seven Additional or Joint Secretaries were all IAS officers.[71] They were kept very busy. By 1975 the Department of Personnel and Administrative Reforms claimed that decisions had been taken on 506 of the ARC's recommendations.[72] But no action was taken on the ARC's proposals undermining the pre-eminent position of the IAS. The power of the IAS within the bureaucracy to control the process of administrative reform is certainly an important part of the explanation of how and why they managed to beat off the challenge of the ARC's major recommendations in the Report on Personnel Administration.

The agency of IAS initiative in blocking such reforms succeeded because there was not the political will to force them through against such powerful resistance. In the absence of that, the IAS was safe. Two particular considerations help to account for this lack of political will. One was political timing. The government under the prime ministership of Lal Bahadur Shastri announced its intention of setting up an ARC in November 1965, and the plan was that the Commission would have finished its work before the general elections due in 1967. But the ARC did not actually start work until April 1966 and then rambled on for four years until Mrs Gandhi's Congress (I) Government finally wound it up in 1970. The creature of one government, its proposals had to be powerfully pushed by another. Much had happened in the interim. For one thing, Morarji Desai, the first Chairman of the ARC, left to become Deputy Prime Minister and Minister of Finance in March 1967, and then was propelled out of government altogether when the Congress Party split in 1969. Thus, the political coloration of the Commission was not wholly to the liking of Mrs Gandhi and her supporters when it was time to implement the ARC proposals.

More importantly, the general elections of 1967 brought a number of non-Congress governments to power in the states and reduced the strength of the Congress government at the centre. The ARC's

Services, and inspection and review of their implementation'. Mattoo, P. K. (IAS, Union Territories), 'The Civil Service System in India', in Raksasataya, A. and Siedentopf, H. (eds.), *Asian Civil Services*, Kuala Lumpur, 1980, p. 78. Mr Mattoo was Joint Secretary in the Department of Personnel in the mid-1970s.

[71] Source: the writer's analysis of the *IAS Civil List*, 1972, pp. 2–167.

[72] GOI PAR, *Report, 1975–76*, (1976), p. 133.

authority, initially established in a more propitious time for its creator, proceeded to shrink somewhat after 1967.

The other consideration related to the lack of political determination on the ARC recommendations is the fact that administrative reform was not a current political issue of any importance. Opposition political parties barely mentioned the subject in the general election of 1967.[73] It was not a vote getter. And anyway, why should the Congress Party push for radical change as long as it continued to win power within the existing structure of the state? A. H. Hanson remarked years ago: 'there is a strong vested interest in retaining the familiar and employment-creating complexities of the [Administrative] system', along with 'reluctance to tamper with the going concern—even though it may be going far too slowly—for fear that the results may be a complete breakdown'.[74] For Congress to have taken on such vested interests at that time would not have been politically sensible.

That Congress Party support for the system was vital to the survival of the IAS in the early 1970s was pointed up starkly by what was happening simultaneously next door in Pakistan. On 20 August 1973 Prime Minister Bhutto announced precisely the sort of radical new public personnel system the ARC in India had pointed towards. The old system, he said, 'has created a class of "brahmins" or mandarins, unrivalled in its snobbery and arrogance, insulated from the life of the people and incapable of identifying itself with them . . .' Hence, said Bhutto, there was to be a new system: (1) all services and cadres—including the remaining ICS men and their successors in the CSP—were to be merged into one service with equality of opportunity for all; (2) there would be a unified grading structure, from the *peon* at the bottom to the Secretary at the top, on a simple 22-grade pay scale; (3) each post would be graded by job evaluation; (4) vertical and horizontal movement would be possible for all civil servants. In consequence, the dominance of the generalists was over, and specialists were to move into the mainstream of higher management and contribute to policy making. These proposals spelt the end of the ICS tradition in Pakistan (even though there was not time to implement them in full before conservative forces once again asserted themselves).

[73] The Jana Sangh Party promised to tone up the civil service by stopping political interference in administration, and the Samyukta Socialist Party promised to abolish the post of Collector. But both these were only very minor items in their programmes. *Why Jana Sangh?* by Balraj Madhok, Delhi, Popular Prakashan, 1967, p. 31; *Why Samyukta Socialist?* by Madhu Limmaye, Delhi, Popular Prakashan, 1967, p. 26.

[74] Hanson, *The Process of Planning*, p. 290.

By contrast, as Maheshwari remarked at the time, India's efforts at reform 'pale into insignificance . . .' amounting only to 'correction slips to the inherited administrative system'.[75]

There was no dearth of critics of India's system in the 1970s, but they had no political power to make any difference. Some of the most trenchant were retired civil servants. Mullick, for example, who had been Director, Intelligence Bureau, under Nehru for many years, lamented in 1971 that the all-India services' 'vested interest in the colonial system of administration' dies hard, and asserted that the 'system . . . has to be completely changed before any marked improvement in the implementation of Government policies can be expected'.[76] And Dass (ICS, Madras) in 1975 complained that 'the present ruling élite for all its tears over the plight of the common man does not have the muscle, still less the inclination, to bring about the revolutionary changes that our situation demands'.[77] It seemed that it was business as usual during the 1970s as regards administrative reform, IAS control of it, and lack of political will. The Department of Personnel and Administrative Reforms continued to be dominated by the IAS, and continued to do useful work, without changing the basic structure. Mrs Gandhi had no cause to tamper significantly with the structure of administration during the Emergency. After all, she relied heavily on civil servants at the time.[78] During the Janata period of government, 1977–9, the Shah Commission said vaguely that the whole administrative system must be overhauled, for there is a 'long standing problem of relations between politics and administration in India . . . yet nothing is done'.[79] But no concrete proposals were forthcoming. Indeed, as of 1983, the government had not accepted any recommendation which undermined the IAS and the ICS tradition it represented.

Throughout the 1970s, however, the ICS tradition came under increasing pressure from a different direction. It came from below, from within the ranks of civil servants in other services. A report in

[75] Maheshwari, S., 'United Civil Services in Pakistan', *Public Administration* (Kanpur), 12 (Nov. 1974), 12. The quotation from Bhutto earlier in this paragraph is from this article, p. 16. The standard early works on the ICS successor in Pakistan are Goodnow, H., *The Civil Service of Pakistan: Bureaucracy in a New Nation*, New Haven, 1964; and Braibanti, R., 'The Higher Bureaucracy in Pakistan', in Braibanti, R. and Associates, *Asian Bureaucratic Systems*, pp. 209–353.

[76] Mullick, B. N. *My Years with Nehru*, Bombay, 1971, pp. 593–4.

[77] Dass, K. K., 'Rules', *Seminar*, 192 (Aug. 1975), 19.

[78] e.g. 'Back to the Days of the Raj', *Guardian* (London), 9 May 1976, 4.

[79] Shah Commission, *Third and Final Report*, 1978, p. 231.

1970 that certain technical services in Dehli were in an angry and sullen mood, instanced by a demonstration of 250 engineers at a minister's residence, protesting against the appointment of an IAS officer to a top post in the ministry,[80] was an indicator of things to come. There had always been some dissatisfaction of this sort,[81] but increasingly it became more public and vociferous. Central government civil servants not in the IAS set an example on the occasion of the work done by the Third Central Pay Commission. They formed an All-India Confederation of Central Government Officers' Associations, made up of all service associations except the IAS Association. The Confederation demanded an end to the IAS special position, parity of pay, emoluments, and status, and that policy making in specialist areas by entrusted to specialists. They got none of it. The Pay Commission reported in 1973 and recommended increased minimum pay, a reduction in the number of pay scales, improved pension rates and retirement benefits, along with an increase in working hours, but they did not recommend a unified grading structure or meet other non-IAS demands, and gave their reasons for not doing so.[82] The Report was widely regarded as 'pro-IAS' and virtually all groups of central government employees were unhappy with it.[83]

By the time the Fourth Central Pay Commission was appointed in July 1983, the pressure from below was more intense. When, in 1982, the IAS went through a trying time over the Appu affair (summarized in Chapter 5), it was reported that 'predictably, the IAS has not many sympathizers among the vast majority of Government servants'—one said that 'IAS stands for Incompetent and Arrogant *Sahebs*'.[84] At the same time there were indications that the IAS was attempting to strengthen its own organization; the IAS (Central) Association was reviewing its convention not to lobby, and there was talk of the 'need for organized administrative resistance'.[85] The fact that in 1982–3 as

[80] Reported in *Link*, 15 Aug. 1970, 87.

[81] Taub *Bureaucrats under Stress*, reports instances of this in Orissa in the 1960s.

[82] GOI Ministry of Finance, *Third Central Pay Commission*, 4 Vols., 1973. The Commission had a chairman and three members. The Member-Secretary was H. N. Ray (ICS, West Bengal).

[83] Jain, R. B., 'Classification of Services and Pay Structure: Absence of a Rationale', in Jain, R. B., *Contemporary Issues in Indian Administration*, Delhi, 1976, pp. 72–104.

[84] Rajan, K., 'Decline of the Civil Service', *Tribune*, 15 Mar. 1982. See also 'Slipping IAS', *Business Standard* (Calcutta), 13 Apr. 1982.

[85] 'Ranks of IAS Rebels Swelling', *Statesman*, 2 Apr. 1982. Chatterjee, A. K. (IAS, Bihar), 'Tinkering with the Rule of Law', in Jain, R. (ed.), *Public Services in a Democratic Context*, New Delhi, 1983, p. 34.

many as twenty-seven IAS officers had retired after only twenty years service in order to take advantage of the pay and perquisites private corporations offered[86] was used by the IAS to press the Fourth Pay Commission for much better IAS pay scales.

Each state also appoints a Pay Commission from time to time. State pay commissions are influenced by what Central Pay Commissions do, and also influence each other. These relationships are explicitly recognized in each Pay Commission report—for example, Maharashtra 1975–77, Karnataka 1976, Punjab 1977–9, Kerala 1978, Tamil Nadu 1978, Rajasthan 1979–81. Two points about these state commissions are relevant here. First, close study of their contents indicates that pressure on them from government employees' associations is intense and appears to be increasing. This is certainly the impression one gains from comparing, say, the contents of the Rajasthan Pay Commission Report of 1979–81 with its predecessor in 1968.[87] Demands from service associations were a prominent feature in both reports, but in 1979–81 there were far more associations representing a much better organized civil service.[88] The demands centred, of course, on better pay scales and reduction in pay differentials between different cadres, but in the later report one notices more vociferous demands from the Rajasthan Administrative Service and other top state services for parity with IAS pay scales. The Commission's award for top state civil servants was indeed very close to IAS scales. The other point is simply that the state commissions cannot touch the IAS, dearly as state employees' associations would like them to. As the Rajasthan Commission stated; 'The IAS is outside the rule-making power of the State Government.'[89] The overall picture in 1983 was one in which increasing pressure was being put on the IAS from within the ranks of the civil service, both at the centre and in the states, but the central government had not yet made any move to remove the IAS from its pre-eminent position within the administration at both levels.

One further example of such pressure from below in the states, and the structure of support that continued in 1983 to resist such pressure

[86] Nayar, K., 'How Bureaucrats Make and Break Rules', *Sunday*, 28 Aug.–3 Sept. 1983, 11.

[87] *Report of the Rajasthan Pay Commission 1979–81* by B. P. Beri (Jaipur), 1981. The 1968 Report was by J. S. Ranawat. Both men were retired Chief Justices of the Rajasthan High Court.

[88] 179 persons representing public employees' associations appeared before the 1979–81 Commission. See *The Pay Report*, pp. 942–9.

[89] *The Pay Report*, p. 58.

for reform, is found in the Report of the Administrative Reforms Committee of the Government of West Bengal.[90] The Report is considered here in some detail. The Committee, which reported in 1983, had the standard make-up: the Chairman (Dr Ashok Mitra, Minister of Finance) and the one member were politicians; the Secretary-Member was an IAS man (R. N. Sengupta) and the Secretary and Deputy Secretary of the Committee were respectively S. Goswami (IAS) and T. K. Dasgupta (IAS). Proposals aimed at undermining the position of the IAS were unlikely to emerge from there. The result, nevertheless, was quite a radical critique of existing structures and procedures of public administration in West Bengal, and a set of 91 recommendations across a very broad field—including reorganization of departments and public enterprises, revival of the system of inspections at all levels to make sure that orders and rules as set out by a minister and Secretary 'are conformed with' (p. 17), and a broadening of the 'extremely narrow scope' for promotion 'up' from level to level within the bureaucracy as a whole.

The Committee's terms of reference included making recommendations 'for speedier disposal of work' and for 'improving the pace of implementation of Government decisions consonant with public accountability'. They gave considerable attention to these aspects in their Report. There was a large measure of agreement on the part of all the people who discussed these matters with the Committee as to what the problems were: poor co-ordination between a secretariat department and its directorates (attached offices) and the inordinate length of time it takes for proposals initiated in a directorate to be finally disposed of in the secretariat. 'Any such proposal', the Committee learned, 'usually goes through several rounds of laundering'; a two-day vertical sojourn within a directorate is, as a procedure, simply repeated when proposals are forwarded to the secretariat. To learn more, the Committee arranged for a number of sample studies on the movement of files in the Departments of Health, of Education and of Land and Land Reforms 'with a view to forming a judgement on the extent and nature of delay in inter- and intra-departmental transactions'.

The results of one such study pertaining to the Department of Land and Land Reforms was appended to their Report. It is perhaps a particularly grotesque case but, nevertheless, serves to draw pointed

[90] Government of West Bengal. *Report of the Administrative Reform Committee*, Home (Personnel and Administrative Reforms) Department, Apr. 1983.

attention to general problems found by the Committee. The case concerns a complaint of defalcation of funds against an employee of the department. The complaint was made in 1973, the file then went around as many as 104 different desks both inside and outside the department during the next *ten years*, and when the Reforms Committee finally found the file in 1983 a decision had still not been reached (the employee had long since retired).

Careful examination of this case illustrates clearly the way files move in West Bengal (and elsewhere in India). As the file moves from office to office, from Board of Revenue to secretariat department and back, it is handled in each place by the old 'dealing and reference clerk system'. Assistants and clerks initiate action, the file is put up with background papers to officers who endorse and approve, and then back down it goes. The file is 'laundered' in this way each time; and behind this particular case is the reality of thousands of such files moving constantly from desk to desk when they are not waiting on some clerk's desk in the office. The office prepares, the officer disposes—the case shows the centralization of power in the 'officer' (the old ICS men) in each case. This case also illustrates one of the main snags in the system. Officers get transferred, even if clerks do not. Some of the principal delays in this case came at times when officers were transferred. The overall impression one gets from reading this file and other evidence in the Commitee's Report is one of an administration that can move quickly but is generally marked by cautious and (in some cases) rather aimless shuffle.

Such a state of affairs 'cries out to be mended', said the Committee. They recommended, therefore (amongst other things), merger of departments and directorates in some instances, placing the 'memory' (history of precedents, rules, etc.) of how similar proposals were dealt with in the past not only in secretariats but also in directorates, doing away with the old dealing and reference clerk system (they proposed another system, in which an officer deals with incoming business in the first instance), laying down strict time-limits for disposal of files, and imposing disciplinary proceedings on those who deviate from the time-limits. Some of these recommendations were in conflict with certain main principles of Indian administration, and were therefore unlikely to be implemented. For example, in recommending the merger of some secretariat departments and directorates, the Committee was attempting to abolish the traditional split that has divided administrative organizations in India since colonial times. They were right to see the split as a major reason for slow movement of files and inefficient dispatch of government business. But the tradition of Indian administration centres on providing for roving political administrators who require a separate secretariat where they can freely come and go, who require secretariat 'memories' (because officers are never there for long), who require that files of consequence be put up to them (centralization of power). The West Bengal reform proposals ran up against this all-India administrative frame. The Committee was well aware of these wider constraints. An 'interlocking system of administrative, legislative and judicial arrangements binds the Centre and the states to one another', they remarked, and this 'present constitutional framework' places limits on us beyond which we cannot go. In making our recommendations, we 'had to take cognizance of this reality' (p. 28). Ashok Mitra, as a member of the Communist Party of India (Marxist) Government in West Bengal, was no doubt keenly aware of the existence of the broader structural reality.

The West Bengal experience serves to illustrate three major points. First, there is an indication that the ICS tradition was still very much alive in West Bengal in 1983. Second, the case provides an illustration of the considerable pressure from below (in states) at this time to move beyond an administrative tradition now seen as unsuitable for changed circumstances. Third, one sees clearly in this case how such pressure from below was held in check by an all-India state structure in which the West Bengal Government was entangled.

More generally, several points are worth making about the reasons why the IAS framework remained untouched by the various attempts at administrative reform from 1950 to 1983. First, a tremendous prop at the outset and lending the framework legitimacy at all levels, was the specific guarantee in the constitution setting out the whole structure of the state at the centre and in the states. The guarantee in such a document made the IAS a powerful 'given' in the minds of persons considering any administrative reforms. It should be remembered also that this was a constitution made for both the central and state governments in India's federalism; the states did not have their own separate constitutions, as the states do, for example, in the United States. Second, there was broad political support from the ruling Congress Party at the centre for the continued existence of the IAS right through the period. If the IAS had become a political issue, and the Congress had come to believe that radical restructuring of the administration was necessary, then sufficient political will might have been found, despite the opposition of powerful vested interests, to alter or even wind up the IAS and the ICS tradition of administration. But administrative reform did not become such an issue, and support for the IAS, or at least acquiescence in existing arrangements, from Mr Nehru, Mr Shastri, Mrs Gandhi, and other Congress leaders continued. Third, ICS/IAS men did not simply rely passively on this continuing structure of political support; they worked actively to preserve existing administrative arrangements from their own powerfully entrenched position within the state.

5

Shaping IAS successors

THE institutional pattern of the ICS survived into the 1980s because continuing political support enabled the ICS/IAS to beat off any threats to it from administrative reform. Political support alone, however, could not ensure the survival of the ICS tradition. Administrative traditions are not only made up of institutional frameworks. They also include norms and values which do not pass on automatically from generation to generation even if the framework remains unchanged. Attempts were in fact made deliberately to plant them on fresh recruits. For it was widely assumed within the ranks of the ICS/IAS that, as Jha (ICS, Bihar) put it, 'administrators unlike poets are not born but made'.[1] They were made by the shaping process. For some recruits the norms and values that this shaping process carried did not 'take', so to speak, and they went their own way. Most recruits, however, embraced them more or less, and later attempted to plant them on their successors. The working of this process since independence is the subject of this chapter.

The literature on this subject is very unbalanced. There were excellent works in the 1950s and 1960s on the recruitment and training of the IAS and on their social background. Two outstanding studies were by Subramaniam[2] and Marz.[3] But almost nothing was known about what happened to the young IAS men and women after they left the National Academy of Administration and were posted to the states for district training. The unstated assumption in the literature was that studying social background and initial institutional training provided the most fruitful approach to understanding IAS behaviour and attitudes. I shared this general assumption when I

[1] Jha, L. K. 'Time for New Norms', *Seminar*, 230 (1978), 33.

[2] Subramaniam, V., *Social Background of India's Administrators*, New Delhi, 1971.

[3] Marz, T., 'The National Academy of Administration: Normative Vocabularies and Organizational Reality', in Schaffer, B. (ed.), *Administrative Training and Development: A Comparative Study of East Africa, Zambia, Pakistan, and India*, New York, 1974, pp. 315–82. There were other studies from this general standpoint, e.g. Prasad, B. *The Indian Administrative Service*, Delhi, 1968.

undertook in 1966–7 a study for the ARC of IAS training in the states.[4] But doing the study shattered the assumption. Young IAS men and women who had finished the training a few years before said they had been affected by it; but they also volunteered the information that experience in their first posts had had a more pronounced influence on their subsequent behaviour in administrative life than prior training.

In attempting to explain how and why the ICS tradition was reproduced in the post-independence period, it is not sufficient, therefore, simply to describe the IAS training programme. The shaping process was far more complex than that. Although a thorough examination of it cannot be attempted here, attention is directed at three main features. First, the IAS shaping process involved both initial training and experience in early career postings. Second, the content passed on during the process included the ICS norms and values discussed earlier. Third, this process was in fact necessary, that is, IAS men and women were influenced to adopt a particular tradition with which they were previously unfamiliar; they did not simply enter the IAS with the norms and values of their original class background and then retain them unchanged.

All three features came through powerfully in my study for the ARC, based on interviews from the recruitment batches 1958–64 who had completed their training between 1960 and 1966 (see Table 14).

At the time they were interviewed (November 1966 to March 1967), four of these young IAS officers were on deputation to the Government of India; 15 were holding posts in districts; the other 46 were holding secretariat or public enterprise posts in either Patna, Madras City, Bombay, or Jaipur.

Most of the 65 interviews took about one hour to complete; a few took about 30 minutes, one lasted six hours. With only three exceptions I felt that these men and women spoke very frankly about their experience in the IAS. The interviews were fairly informal in nature, although I did have an interview schedule with me (which they expected); each interview was structured loosely around an identical set of questions. I took notes as we went along which I wrote up immediately after the interview ended. The 65 interviewees are named

[4] Permission to undertake the study was obtained from the Ministry of Home Affairs. The Ministry also secured the approval of the four state governments involved. A full report of the findings was submitted privately to the Ministry and the ARC. Some of the findings on district training were later published in the writer's 'The Relevance of Training for the Indian Administrative Service', *Political Science Review* (Jaipur), 8 (1969), 325–46.

Table 14. *Interviews with IAS Officers Who Completed Training 1960–1966*

Cadre	Number interviewed (by batch)							Total interviewed	Total of direct recruits in cadre (batches 1958–64)	% to total
	1958	1959	1960	1961	1962	1963	1964			
Bihar	5		4		6		2	17	49	36
Tamil Nadu (Madras)	5		6		2		1	14	39	36
Maharashtra	1		4	7	3	1	2	18	49	39
Rajasthan	2	1	3	4	1	1	4	16	32	50
Total	13	1	17	11	12	2	9	65	169	40

in the bibliography, but particular comments reported in this chapter are referred to by code (e.g. B581, M622) so that comments cannot be traced to individuals. I am still obliged to preserve the anonymity of my respondents' remarks because they were still, in 1983, active in government service.

THE NATIONAL ACADEMY

An IAS training school had been set up in 1947 in Delhi at Metcalfe House to train war service emergency recruits. The first batch of regular recruits (having passed the new competitive examinations) were trained there in 1949. A new batch arrived each year. An IAS Staff College at Simla also functioned for a while in the 1950s, partly because of cramped quarters at Metcalfe House. The College and the school were merged in 1959 into the National Academy of Administration; and the old Charleville Hotel in Mussoorie (a hill-station in UP) was acquired to house it. Built in 1880 with a majestic view of the Himalayas, the Charleville had been preserved intact from the days of the raj. Anyone who spent time there could not help but be reminded powerfully of an age gone by. King George V and Queen Mary had stayed there. The Queen had even planted a sapling in the hotel premises; it is now full-grown. The Academy was still at the Charleville in 1983, although it had been renamed the Lal Bahadur Shastri Academy of Administration in 1972 and had expanded far beyond the original hotel buildings (they still serve as a central focus).

The formal training schedule in the early 1960s for each batch of IAS probationers in their first year was as follows:

(*a*) Foundation Course at the National Academy	5 months
(*b*) Army attachment	1 month
(*c*) *Bharat Darshan*	1½ months
(*d*) Visits to Delhi and the Central Police Training College	15 days
(*e*) Further study for the IAS at the National Academy	4 months

The content of this training and methods of instruction used are described in detail in the Academy's publications at the time and in standard sources.[5] Briefly, IAS probationers first attended a Foundation

[5] The Academy's library has all the manuals and instructions issued to each set of probationers. Marz also gives a very full summary of the Academy's programme and methods.

Course together with probationers of the Indian Police Service, the Indian Foreign Service, and Class I Central Services. The main idea behind the course, as the Krishnamachari Report put it, was:

> that officers of the higher services should acquire an understanding of the constitutional, economic and social framework within which they have to function, as these largely determine the policies and programmes towards the framing and execution of which they will have to make their contribution. They should further acquaint themselves with the machinery of Government and the broad principles of public administration . . . [they] should also have a clear appreciation of the role of the civil service in a parliamentary democracy. The foundational course is also intended to cover such matters as aims and obligations of the civil service, and the ethics of the profession—objectivity, integrity, thoroughness, impartiality, etc.[6]

After the Foundation Course the probationers from the other services dispersed to separate training. IAS probationers were first sent to army units in Kashmir for a short course of military training. Then they went on a cultural-cum-study tour of India, better known as *Bharat Darshan*, which included visits to important public enterprises as well as to famous places of historic and cultural significance. Next there was a brief visit to New Delhi to meet the Prime Minister, Home Minister, and other national leaders and to spend time studying the working of Parliament. They also visited briefly the Central Police Training College at Mt. Abu in Rajasthan. They then returned to Mussoorie for further IAS training in criminal law and procedure, administrative history of India, district administration (including planning and development work, emergencies, local government, and land revenue systems), and other practical work including physical training, horse-riding, weapon training, and a basic course in first aid. At the end of the year the IAS batch split, each group going to the particular state to which it had been allotted for training in a district.

Embedded in the formal content of the training was a complex 'normative vocabulary' identified in 1969 by Marz, who studied it at some length. This informal vocabulary was part of a whole language of administration. The training process at the Academy was designed to secure the adoption by probationers of this language as a code of professional conduct.[7] Key ideas in this language were the importance of the IAS retaining the 'administrative leadership' of the state; that IAS

[6] GOI Planning Commission, *Report on Indian and State Administrative Services*, by V. T. Krishnamachari, 1962, p. 14.

[7] Marz, 'National Academy', pp. 320–1.

officers should behave with justice and fairness, 'without fear or favour'; that 'society is conflict-ridden, irrational', and the task of government is to contain such conflicts; that there is a marked incongruity between the values of administration (for example, impartiality, rule of law) and the reality of the surrounding society; that IAS officers as administrative leaders have a special responsibility to 'protect the weak' and 'fight vested interests'. One of the most powerful images in what Marz called the 'inherited vocabulary' was that of a 'steel frame' of administrators linking villages to subdivisions and districts, with lines converging on state capitals and ultimately gathered together in New Delhi. This was seen as of great value in the context of the assumed divisive nature of Indian society. Such a vocabulary provided continuing justification for the retention of an institutional framework with an all-India service given the lead role at different levels of the state. Behaviour patterns and norms and values in the ICS tradition were also embedded in the vocabulary, making this framework seem 'normal' and 'right'.

Gentlemanly behaviour and manners were insisted upon at the Academy. Indian recruits unfamiliar with the correct form speedily began to acquire it. Gentlemanly norms relating to social calls, formal invitations, table manners, dress, civic manners, and ceremonial functions were actually printed privately for probationers in a 'Handbook on Etiquette and Manners' called 'Shishtachar'. The introduction states: 'Good manners and etiquette lend confidence and charm to an officer's personality, often help smooth the sharp edge of authority and ease the course of personal relations; the idea underlying the patterns of form and behaviour suggested in the following pages are courtesy, politeness and consideration for others.' Under the section on 'drawing-room manners' (pp. 2–4), there are instructions such as:

> Gentleman officers will rise when they are introduced. Shaking hands on being introduced is quite normal but not with ladies unless they make the first move. Otherwise, a *Namaste* or an equivalent word in any other Indian language is in order.
>
> Do not sit aloof but conduct a conversation with your neighbours. As far as possible, avoid talking 'shop'. As educated young officers you should have sufficiently wide interests to start and sustain a conversation on many subjects.
>
> Do not be condescending. Do not monopolise the conversation or express your views too vehemently. Speak softly but clearly . . .

Avoid effusiveness, gossip or over complimentary or disparaging talk about others. Do not boast of either your attainments or your connections. Avoid personal queries about family and income.

There is a long section on correct table manners and the use of cutlery. They are utterly British in origin. For example:

Sit on your chair from the right and leave it from the left. Place your napkin half-folded on your lap.

Curry and rice may be eaten with spoon and fork or fork alone in right hand. Use the back of the fork to push the rice into the spoon.

The larger knife and fork are intended for the meat dish or its vegetarian equivalent. With the help of the knife in the right hand, build up the food on the back of the fork.

Forks are used for sweet dishes where these are solid. Liquids or semi-liquids are taken with a small spoon. On completion of the course, put the spoon down on the plate below the ice-cream cup and not in the cup itself.

There are miscellaneous injunctions regarding correct behaviour in public settings. They are precisely the form insisted upon by senior ICS Europeans when shaping ICS Indians in the 1920s and 1930s. For example: 'arrive on time—punctuality is politeness and should be cultivated as a habit', 'never speak to your seniors with your hands in your pockets', 'never stare, especially at a lady', 'natural functions like belching, yawning, sneezing and coughing, clearing of throats, noses etc. should be done as silently as possible with an 'excuse me' if in company—if possible, use a handkerchief to sneeze or cough into'. Furthermore, 'as a junior officer, be observant, try to catch the eye of your senior officer and greet him; never be seen avoiding a greeting and never permit this with your juniors or subordinates'.

These are only a very small number of a host of detailed injunctions laid down in the 'Shishtachar'. The manners and etiquette are not just 'western', they come straight out of behaviour patterns common amongst ICS gentlemen in the days of the raj. For many probationers these norms called for a pattern of behaviour different from that which they had known previously. Much was made of them. So much so that Indian visitors to the Academy in Mussoorie have never had much difficulty in recognizing the general ambience: 'typical public school with a distinct western bias'.[8]

The sixty-five IAS men and women I interviewed in 1966–7 had

[8] Prashar, A. S., 'Spotlight on Mussoorie Academy', *Tribune*, 21 Mar. 1982.

been through the Academy in the early 1960s. Their view of it, after working in government for several years, was an ambivalent one—sharply critical of the syllabus and quality of instruction on the one hand, yet aware of certain intangible benefits they acquired by having gone through it, on the other. A few dismissed the Academy as 'absolutely useless' (B624) or a 'complete waste of time' (B641); as one said 'it is ICS training—all dinner-jackets, horse-riding, social niceties', and 'totally useless' as preparation for work in Bihar (B585).

Most were more favourable, however, while being critical of the teaching programme. The most common criticisms were that the training was too general and academic and did not relate very clearly to the posts they had subsequently held. One IAS man from Tamil Nadu (Madras State at the time) dismissed the lectures on public administration as 'irrelevant platitudes' (T641). Others said that the contents of the Five Year Plans were merely described with no critical analysis offered or any attention give to practical problems of plan implementation. Some claimed there was too much emphasis on law and order (a few believed this was because the Director and staff were mostly from Uttar Pradesh where the law and order problem was more acute than elsewhere), and thought the syllabus should be adjusted to give greater emphasis to such subjects as labour relations, industrial management, public enterprises, commercial taxes, employee insurance, and factory acts. Another common criticism was that the quality of instruction at the Academy did not compare favourably with the quality of instruction in the colleges from which the probationers came. An exception to this general indictment was made invariably in the case of law, which the officers, including those who had read law at college, believed to have been quite well taught. A number drew attention to the prevalence of old-fashioned and pedestrian teaching techniques, and suggested that lectures and large syndicate group discussions should be replaced by more imaginative techniques to impart training, such as mock courts using case-studies of actual revenue and other disputes directly relevant to decisions IAS officers have to confront in districts.

Another common criticism was that discipline was not very strict. One remarked at the outset of the interview that the whole orientation at Mussoorie was wrong—the main preoccupation was either displaying or quickly acquiring 'the right English accent and the proper fork-and-spoon technique' (T641). Another, from Rajasthan, said: 'I enjoyed Mussoorie tremendously and had a lot of fun', but 'there should be more concentration on the actual work to be done' (R602). Another said the year's training was a 'paid holiday'; the main thing is 'learning how to drink and socialize' (R641). 'The atmosphere is not conducive to hard work', said another (R621). Virtually all who voiced this criticism about lack of seriousness said, however, that with the arrival of a new Director (Pimputkar, ICS, Bombay), they understood there had been a sharp improvement in discipline, of which they approved.

There is no doubt that the Director in the early 1960s, A. N. Jha (ICS, UP), was very popular with probationers, and also very broadminded and relaxed about discipline at the Academy. 'Jha was wonderful', said one (R612); he would stroll out on to the lawn, have four or five chairs brought, sit down and call passing probationers over to sit and chat about a wide variety of subjects in an informal way; he 'had a fine sense of humour and was very cultured'. When two probationers got drunk and fought in Kulri market with bottles and chairs and tables causing Rs 12,000 damages, a shopkeeper called on Jha demanding reparation; to his surprise, Jha said 'there was no question of any action being taken against the boys as they were like children to him'; as for money, Jha claimed that only dogs and probationers were in Mussoorie at that time of the year (winter), so whatever profit the shopkeepers were making was only from his probationers—hence there was 'no question of payment'.[9] Drink was prohibited on campus, but probationers could guzzle all they wanted in restaurants outside. The important thing was to be able to hold your drink like a gentleman. One probationer at that time remembers that 'there was a deeply ingrained belief that civil servants must take a peg or two; non-drinkers were generally looked down upon.'[10]

Together with such criticisms as pedestrian teaching methods and lack of discipline, most respondents during the interviews also drew attention to certain intangible benefits that they thought they had begun to acquire at the Academy. These can be summed up as (*a*) broadening one's outlook, (*b*) building confidence, (*c*) building IAS *esprit de corps*. Regarding (*a*), 24 of the 65 IAS officers had read for a science degree at college and found that the Academy curriculum did broaden their knowledge in a general way. One interpreted this as a 'bias to culture and the arts' at the Academy (B583). It was also very clear that many IAS recruits were initially quite parochial. Mussoorie, said one, 'cures regional prejudices' (B601). Others said: 'I didn't

[9] Sinha, N., 'The IAS Academy', *Amrita Bazar Patrika*, 28 Mar. 1982.

[10] Bhandari, G., 'The Budding Bureaucrat', *Hindustan Times*, 27 June 1982.

know any Bengali or Madrassi people until I went to Mussoorie'—they were 'aliens', to be distrusted (R643); 'I remained in Poona all my life until I went to Mussoorie' (M361); 'I am definitely a different man after Mussoorie' because of the broadening influence (B642); 'I met people from all over India' (B582). Many opened their remarks about the Academy by saying that it gave them an 'all-India identity'. Virtually all 65 thought the *Bharat Darshan* useful in this connection. One said that on the *Bharat Darshan* you 'see big things, it makes you think big' (T581). Two IAS officers from Maharashtra summarized the dominant feeling: the Academy 'broadens your vision, equips you to converse on subjects outside revenue administration' (M641); it was 'not immediately useful—you only got a general view of things' (M615).

The second 'intangible', building confidence, was referred to by a majority of interviewees. The Academy 'gives you confidence' (T606), 'develops character' (B623), 'makes an officer out of a man' (T584). Instruction in law 'gave me confidence' (M616); physical exercise and trekking were part of the process of trying to make the trainee 'a perfect man', and 'getting rid of any complex that he cannot do any thing' (R582); horse-riding and exercises 'give confidence' (T601); Mussoorie 'didn't teach me much, but it gave me confidence'—it also 'inflates the ego' (T581). Several mentioned this last problem: building up confidence served them well later when they had to take tough decisions in unfamiliar circumstances, but there was a tendency for the Academy to puff up too high their sense of confidence and status, which hindered effective communication later with other civil servants in the district with whom they had to work. One said: 'exaggerated importance of IAS is taught at the Academy' by 'ICS tyrants', making us 'demigods' when we come to a division (in Tamil Nadu); 'we are sadly disappointed—we are not that important' (T602).

The Academy also began to create that sense of separate identity or *esprit de corps*; it 'brought us together—gave us a fellow feeling' (M616), gave a 'feeling of belonging to a Service' (M604), created 'fraternity' (M641). Separateness was underlined by what was not said; only one out of the 65 interviewees mentioned the Foundation Course as being helpful by bringing him or her into contact with probationers from *other services* with whom he would be working closely later (M603). Separate identity on an all-India scale was the rule, for example, 'I keep in touch with a number of my batchmates' (T582); 'other services may not need certain things that IAS needs' (T601). I was asked by IAS officers in Maharashtra if I had interviewed their batchmates in Tamil Nadu, whom they proceeded to name; officers in Tamil Nadu asked about batchmates in Bihar and Rajasthan, and so forth. A few said, however, that *esprit de corps* was just a phrase with no factual basis. A batch at the Academy, one said, 'was no more than a batch of cliques'—Madrassis mix only with Madrassis, public school boys who went on to St Stephen's College mix only with their counterparts (B642). Nor is *esprit de corps* built up later, claimed another: 'the IAS is not an all-India service, it is a collection of state services'; yet this same person also said: 'we are in *the best Service*, and this is important to have confirmed before starting work in Rajasthan' (R641).

The Academy was seen by most of these IAS officers with hindsight as only the *beginning* of their preparation for the work they would be doing. We came 'straight from university, with no experience', said one: Mussoorie marks 'the start of the change from student life to life as an administrator', forcing you 'into a new mood' (T621). It was only a start, however, for clearly they were unprepared for what came next—training in a district: 'I had very crazy ideas about the district' (M581); 'I was really raw when I came to the district' (M616); 'I was unprepared for the district' (R603); district training was 'a real knock, like moving from boiled water to ice cold' (T641); 'you don't know from nothing' (B583).

DISTRICT TRAINING AND FIRST POSTS

After finishing at the Academy, IAS recruits in the early 1960s were sent to the particular state of their cadre for a period of one year or more of additional training before taking up their first responsible post, normally as SDO. The details of the training varied from state to state. The main feature was 'attachments' for short periods to a succession of officers in the revenue and other departments in a district; recruits were also given independent charge of certain district posts for short periods at various points. In short, the general pattern was similar to that which ICS recruits went through in the 1920s and 1930s. In this section of the chapter I shall consider the experience of, and thoughts about, district training and first posts as reported during the interviews. Each of the four states involved in the study is considered separately.

Bihar

Bihar differed from the other states in that the formal description of the district training bore little relation to what actually happened. Trainees were supposed to spend sixteen and a half months on district training before going on to their first post as SDO. The first nine and a half months were to be spent attached to various officers in the district, for example, treasury officials, police officers, subordinate revenue staff, SDOs, and a number of different officers involved in development work. They also were to try several criminal cases. Finally, the trainees were supposed to be sent for six months of settlement and survey work in the district(s) where this operation was currently taking place. In fact, not one of the seventeen officers interviewed completed the nine and a half months of district training; the time actually spent varied from four to six months. Ten of the seventeen officers had no training in a development block, four had only one week of it, and the remaining three had two weeks. Twelve officers spent no time with an SDO, the Additional Collector, or the District Development Officer. Not one officer spent time with the agricultural, co-operation, educational, or *zila parishad* officers in the district. Generally speaking, these officers spent most of their time reading files in the district office, talking with treasury officials, preparing case records, and watching court work. In the case of the six months of settlement and survey work, the deviation was in excess of requirements; ten officers spent more than six months on it.

Only three of the IAS officers interviewed in Bihar looked upon any aspect of their district training as useful, apart from settlement and survey work. The principal complaint was that attachment to a district officer for a few days, during which time you glanced at some of his routine files and chatted with him over a cup of tea, gave one little or no understanding either of the details of that officer's job or of the nature of the problems with which he was concerned. Most of the officers interviewed expressed the view strongly that one learns to be an administrator only by actually doing the work. Other than preparation of case records, this experience was denied to them. With regard, however, to settlement and survey work as part of their training, almost all found this experience 'valuable' or 'useful'. The general explanation given for this positive response was that settlement and survey comes as a sharp and pleasant tonic after a year and a half of general lectures and talks, first for a year at the Academy, then for a few weeks at the Bihar secretariat, and then for four to six months of district training. They felt they now possessed some responsibility, if only for mapping and numbering of plots, and were involved in government work. Many officers also stressed the point that settlement and survey gave them an opportunity for the first time to become intimately acquainted with village life.

A majority of the officers interviewed judged the Collector to whom they were attached during the district training as both friendly and competent. Only a few, however, said that the Collector was able to devote much time to their training. Also, about half the officers held the view that the Collector was not particularly interested in the training. One Collector said to a new arrival, 'enjoy yourself now—soon you'll have to go to work' (B602). One consequence was that a few officers took initiative and arranged most of the training for themselves (e.g. B621).

Most of those interviewed said they did not feel well prepared for their first post as SDO. One said with great candour: 'I was completely unprepared for what I had to do in the SDO post, socially and politically; I recall being terrified the first day I approached my court; I didn't know what a village was' (B585). Another said: during district training you are 'very unsure of yourself', yet you want to learn because 'you are facing the SDO post next year' (B583).

When the Bihar officers were interviewed, most of them were holding a post either in the secretariat at Patna or in a public enterprise after having held several other posts previously, including SDO. When asked about the relevance of Academy and district training to their work as administrators, nearly all said there was none. Some examples: 'district training did not prepare me for my present post' on the Electricity Board, 'I had to learn on the job' (B604); it is 'a long way from the idealized picture portrayed at Mussoorie to the realities of Bihar administration' (he gave specific examples of corrupt practices and political manoeuvres) (B621); 'only successive postings build up official outlook' (of which this very smooth young man approved) (B581). A few others said, however, that the experience in the district (and the Academy) was of value more generally. One man was the only generalist in a department of specialists (engineers); his main claim to his generalist position was that he had had 'mixed field experience—which is terribly important in being able to locate the heart of a problem and move to solve it' (B583). Another said: 'broad training singles us out as generalist; in my work for technical specialists, my contribution is to know the general background for which the Academy training is useful, but as for secretariat procedure I was not prepared for this (but I learned it in about one month)' (B584). The main overall point is that IAS generalist training had not prepared Bihar officers for the posts they had subsequently held, but it may have helped to justify their separate existence in a world increasingly made up of specialists.

Tamil Nadu (Madras)

In Tamil Nadu each trainee was sent for twelve months of district training. During the first ten months the trainee was attached for one, two, or four weeks each to various officers in the district, in this order: the Collector, a *Karnam*, a Revenue Inspector, a *Tahsildar*, a *Panchayat* Union Commissioner, an Assistant Engineer, a Revenue Divisional Officer, a Division *Panchayat* Officer, the District Magistrate (Judicial), the Superintendent of Police, the District Forest Officer, the District Agricultural Officer, and the Deputy Registrar of Co-operative Societies. During two attachments (*Karnam* and Revenue Inspector), the trainee spent half the time holding actual charge of the post, with the relevant officer as his assistant. The trainee was also required to prepare and submit a detailed economic report of one village using an elaborate questionnaire for the purpose appended to the Madras IAS Manual. Finally, the trainee held full charge for a month each as *Panchayat* Union Commissioner and Revenue Divisional Officer. Trainees were also required, concurrently with this training, to try a specified number of contested cases as Third, Second, and First Class Magistrate respectively. All officers completed this training.

Without exception all officers said the success of the district training relied heavily on the interest and amount of time the Collector devoted to it. Eleven of the fourteen interviewed asserted that their Collector had taken a lot of interest. They also said that the district training had prepared them 'quite well' (seven of them) or 'fairly well' (four of them) for their first post as an officer in charge of a division. In this respect the training in Tamil Nadu was more successful than in other states.

The role of the Collector was crucial. Some comments on successful Collectors were as follows: 'we got on famously . . . when he handled problems, I saw him take decisions on the spot . . . *very good*' (T605); 'I landed up in the district with only seventeen rupees; my Collector was good enough to loan me immediately a lump sum; I lived in his house for the first month' (T621); 'extremely fine chap—every few days he summoned me to his bungalow and put a lot of inconvenient questions' about my training based on my daily diary submitted to him (T602). This interest on the part of the Collector had the effect of encouraging district officers to take seriously the attachment to them for short periods of IAS trainees. As one officer put it, 'word quickly gets about a district as to whether the Collector is interested in the trainee' (T601).

A majority of officers were of the view that trainees should be assigned to districts where the Collector is a regular recruit to the IAS and not a promotee from the state cadre. They thought that since a regular recruit Collector would have been through the training himself, he would be able more effectively to supervise the trainee and appreciate his or her problems. They admitted, when questioned, that there were a number of instances, either personally experienced or about which they had heard, where a regular recruit Collector had been a bad trainer and a promotee Collector a good one. Still, they felt that the general principle was reliable.

Most officers made a point of stressing the influence of their Collector during district training on their subsequent behaviour in the IAS. One 1958 batch officer said: 'If I am a good officer today, then the credit is mainly due to my Collector' (T583). Another officer said 'he is the man who shapes us' (T585), while another said 'you try to mould yourself to what he does—he gives you confidence' (T586). One officer went so far as to claim 'I can tell you who is a cynical officer by knowing under what officer he was trained; if he does not have a good experience, is not given responsibility or a sense of accomplishment, then he will come out of the training into his first post as a cynical officer' (T583).

What did they learn from their Collectors? General political education and public posture figure importantly in the responses: for example, 'first Collector teaches you how to deal with the public' (T583); 'a Collector must look like a Collector, there must be some show' (T605). Important as such general shaping was, they made clear that their first post came as a surprise: for example, 'there is quite a lot to learn when you actually take charge' (T622); 'I was not prepared for the local intrigue' (T603); 'being able to solve practical problems in IAS posts depends on how good a politician you are' (T621); divisional life 'is the foundation on which our career is built' (T602). One more example from an IAS officer who was an Assistant Collector at the time of interview: Mussoorie gives 'a bird's eye view' he said; when we come for district training 'we start off too high—we need to know what the common man thinks' but we do not; 'we don't know the tricks of the trade of clerks'; everyone to whom we are attached is 'on their guard—treats us as a boss, as always right'; when we get to our first post we are badly in need of a 'worm's eye view'; later, we look back and realise that in our first post 'we are the biggest suckers in the administration—we are fooled all the time' (T641). Training and early postings together form parts of an overall shaping process that gradually enables them not to be fooled so much.

Maharashtra

The main feature of district training in Maharashtra was attachment for short periods to different officers, for instance, Collector, *Mamlatdar*, SDO, Superintendent of Police, Treasury officer, Survey and Settlement officer, altogether for about six months. The trainee was then posted as a Block Development Officer for sixteen weeks; attached to various clerks in the Collectorate (three weeks); posted as PA to the Collector during which he wrote nine essays on subjects related to district administration; attached to the Divisional Commissioner's office (two weeks); and then appointed as Assistant Collector in charge of one *taluka* until first posting. All IAS officers completed this training, although there were adjustments in the order and some attachments were rather perfunctory.

Attachments as a training method did not work well. Of the eighteen officers interviewed, fifteen expressed dissatisfaction with them. Explanations given were that district officers to whom IAS trainees were attached were 'indifferent, incompetent, or too busy' (M622), or 'insufficient interest was taken by the district officers' (M612), or 'SDO didn't know what to do and I didn't know what I wanted to know' (M581). The three officers who considered attachment an effective training device remarked that as long as the trainee took real interest in the training, the attachments worked well.

One of the reasons for the problem of attachment was that most officers interviewed had initial difficulty with the language during their first few months in the district, that is, during the period of their attachments. Fourteen officers were from out of state and said they experienced this difficulty. It was explained that one is able quite quickly to carry on a simple conversation in Marathi, but that it takes longer to follow legal arguments in the language, and much longer to acquire the ability to draft succinct letters in the language. Several officer's holding junior posts had still not passed their language examination. For these fourteen 'outsiders' the difficulty they had with the language may be an important factor in understanding why their attachments did not work well.

As previously noted, quite a lot of the Maharashtra district training included holding charge briefly of certain posts. Most officers interviewed were quick to point out that although attachments did not work well, holding charge did. Typical comments were: 'I learned more during the short time I held *Taluka* charge than during all the attachments put together' (M601), and 'you really begin to learn when you begin to hold charge' (M612). Also, fourteen of the eighteen officers interviewed asserted that the Collector responsible for their training did not take enough interest in it. The reasons given were (*a*) he was overworked, (*b*) he did not think training very important, and (*c*) there was a personality conflict.

Despite such weaknesses in the training, fifteen of the eighteen officers said they felt they were reasonably well prepared for their first post in the subdivision. Probing on this point brought out the main reason: trainees appear to have bypassed unsuccessful attachments and unsympathetic Collectors and acquired the necessary knowledge required to hold the SDO post from other officers, frequently other IAS, for example, 'my father was IAS in the next district and he helped' (M611), 'I learned more about how to deal with the public from the IAS Executive Officer in the *Zila Parishad* than from the Collector' (M614). In short, they trained themselves for the most part. However, district training quickly became irrelevant to subsequent posts; eleven of those interviewed saw no connection between district training and their present post. But that also was no problem, since there is 'nothing an IAS cannot do—he can learn quickly' what he does not already know, and he already knows quite a lot from the experience of the whole shaping process, for example, 'Nagpur was where I learned man management—the Collector there (during district training) was superb in meetings, dealing with politicians' (M581).

Rajasthan

District training in Rajasthan was arranged as follows, with attachments in this order: one week of meeting the Collector and other senior district officers, three weeks watching court proceedings of senior officers, fifteen days of treasury training, a month and a half of training as Magistrate III Class, a month and a half of institutional training at the Officers Training School in Jaipur (at the end of which they took their departmental examinations), one month of *tehsil* training, one month of survey and settlement training, one month training in a community development block, and six and a half months of training as Magistrate II and I class (during which time a number of cases were transferred to them and they were attached to various district level officers, for example, Superintendent of Police, District Agricultural Officer). A few officers said they were sent to their first post one or two months before finishing their training as Magistrate I Class; otherwise all officers said they completed each aspect of the training.

Many officers mentioned the importance of assignment to the right district. It should be a district where there are a wide variety of problems being faced. It should also be a district where a regular recruit Collector is located; this was stated as a useful general principle by most officers interviewed, and the same reasons were given as by officers in Tamil Nadu. The district also, as one officer put it, 'should not be a dead district politically, that is, it should be a district where Congress MLA are prominent' (R614). The general point he was making here was that the trainee must learn how to deal with political pressures, and must not be shielded from them until he is suddenly confronted with them in a responsible post.

All officers, with one exception, said that the success of the training relied heavily on the interest and amount of time the Collector devoted to it. Ten of the fourteen officers interviewed stated that the Collector, in their view, took little or no interest in the training. The reasons given were that (*a*) he was too busy with his other duties, and (*b*) he did not think training very important. In retrospect, they conceded that they should have taken more initiative during the training than they did. As for the other four, one said: 'I was fortunate—Baraya was my Collector' (R603):[11] 'the Collector's behaviour leaves a lasting impression' (R581); 'public relations work is the heart of district administration—this can only be learned by watching a Collector do it' (R591). At the same time, most officers interviewed expressed the general view that trainees should be given more responsibility, that 'one learns by doing'. Those officers who were assigned specific responsibilities by the Collector during their training were precisely those officers who were most favourably disposed to the training.

One man said: 'I was not well prepared for my first post' (R603).

[11] Baraya was an able IAS officer and for some years Head of the Officers' Training School.

But he was unusual. Most officers in Rajasthan thought the training there was well designed and prepared them fairly well for the SDO post. However, they also felt that the training quickly lost its relevance as soon as they moved on to other postings. Officers stationed in Jaipur asserted that the district training was irrelevant to their present post or, at best, as one officer put it, 'the relationship is thin' (R581). 'I was not prepared for the secretariat,' said another; 'I was sat down and given files; if I made a mistake, then the (IAS) Secretary would correct them, since they were all sent to him anyway' (R612). Nor did the training seem very relevant to IAS officers who went on to become Collectors: for example, 'you cannot, even as a Professor of Criminal Law at Mussoorie, know how to apply Section 145 unless you have had experience of this as SDO' (R613).

Most officers eventually steered the interview around to the political aspects of their work. Clearly political 'pressure' or 'interference' was a central preoccupation and something the training did not prepare them for. 'Political pressures on administrators are more severe here than in other countries,' one IAS officer informed me; local politicians do not like young IAS officers from out of state in field posts because they are less amenable to political pressure than promotees to the IAS from state services; this man thought all IAS should be from out of state (like him): 'if I was working in UP (his home), I might not be quite correct in my impartiality and independence from political pressures' (R613). Another in a remote district, who had recently arrived there and who was currently being transferred again for 'political reasons' (he said), showed me a wooden trunk he had had made, and announced with some heat that he was prepared to be moved every three months, for years but 'I am not going to tolerate any politician bossing over me' (R644).

One further example shows how one interviewee learned about the political aspect of IAS work. It illustrates well the fact that the shaping of IAS officers to IAS behaviour patterns is a process spread over both training and early postings, with experience in early postings of crucial importance. I shall paraphrase what this young IAS officer told me (R611). I was probably excessively hard, he said, in my dealings with local politicians and businessmen in my first post as SDO and City Magistrate. I did not know how to treat these people, assumed they were not correct in their dealings with the administration, and frankly distrusted them. In one case, I recall I passed an order not allowing an assembly relating to a dispute, in a particular place. One representative on one side of the dispute came and requested an interview; but I refused to see him unless a representative of the other group met me also at the same time. I think now I was wrong, and that I might have learned much from him alone. The IAS Collector in the district said to me at the time that he would not have done what I did, but he stood by me. It is only this year in the secretariat that I have learned how to deal with people less harshly. Working here on committees and with politicians has led me now to see that some politicians are sensible and honest men and that some industrialists are not out only for their own gain.

Summary

Generalist administrators in many countries, if asked, would doubtless respond to their initial training experience in much the same critical fashion as those interviewed here. This is because of the known difficulty of designing a training programme for generalists which has more than a marginal effect on post-training performance. General orientations are planted during initial training; but whether or not they 'take' appears to depend primarily on the way the shaping process works immediately after training—in early postings. It is clear from the research report here that the IAS shaping process did involve both initial training and experience in the first posts. 'Looking back,' said one, 'I believe that in the civil service habits are set in the first few years' (R603).

Secondly, it is clear from the response given that this shaping process was necessary, that is, men and women entering the IAS were changed by the process. By their own admission, parochial backgrounds were broadened, uncertainty was converted into confidence, expertise required for posts in subdivisions and secretariats was acquired, political savvy was gradually built up.

Thirdly, the content of the process is important. Attention has already been drawn to gentlemanly norms of behaviour within a complex 'language' of administration at the Academy—a language that gave prominence to the value of public service for the community, the value of the generalist administrator (based on the earlier amateur ideal), and the importance of confidence, courage (for example, in stating your position 'without fear or favour'), and self-discipline. This can be explained in part by the fact that the people involved in directing the shaping process were senior ICS or IAS officers. They ran the Academy in the early 1960s. When the trainees reached the states they were clearly influenced by many administrators and politicians there, but IAS Collectors or other IAS officers in districts stand out from the interviews as especially influential.

The research reported here indicates that IAS officers recruited in the period 1958–64 were shaped by a general process both during initial training and early postings which instilled norms and values in the ICS tradition. The account has inevitably focused quite narrowly on the research findings. The shaping process, however, was a more broadly complex process than has been implied so far. In the final section of this chapter, note is taken in a general way of some of these broader aspects as well as changes since the 1960s.

THE SHAPING PROCESS IN THE EARLY 1980S

Much remained essentially the same at the National Academy of Administration in 1983 (when I went back to Mussoorie for a brief visit in October). It was immediately recognizable for its general ambience of leisured politeness. One could immediately see that for some probationers all this came naturally, while for others one sensed an effort being made. As before, a few found it all a bit 'childish' or 'prim'—one can pick up these attitudes by listening to groups of probationers in places like Hari's shop and café just outside the Academy Gate ('everyone knows Hari's'), where amongst other things, you can buy an IAS tie—almost identical to the old ICS tie. During breaks, some are off to the cafés, some stay in the lounges to talk (called 'lounging about'), a few loners go to the library. On the display shelf of 'light reading' in the library, I found three novels by P. G. Wodehouse, two by Anita Desai, one *Anna Karenina*, one copy of Cronin's *The Citadel*, and several other English novels (the combination of Wodehouse and Anita Desai as preferred items—if this is indeed what they were—seemed to me to catch the peculiar culture of the Academy).

Young IAS officers from Maharashtra who had passed through the Academy in the early 1980s are reported[12] to have referred to it as 'a pretty pip-pip place', 'swanky', and having a '*burra-sahib* atmosphere of bridge and billiard rooms, horse-riding, tennis, and formal dinners'. It provided an opportunity, after years of exam swot, 'to relax and have a good time'. As 'the number of westernized entrants declined, the style

[12] Bakshi, R., 'The Indian Aggrieved Service', *Indian Express*, 21 Mar. 1982.

of the Academy was becoming more and more a new experience for recruits'; 'suddenly,' said one westernized lady officer, 'these guys wake up and find they're in the IAS and they have position, money, facilities, and freedom. They wear their IAS name-tags and strut about the Mussoorie bazaar—you can see the sense of power on their faces.' 'A paid holiday', said another. But no one ran it down. In popular parlance, the Academy was known as 'heaven', district training as 'limbo', work in the field as 'hell'.

The general ambience at the Academy may not have changed much since the 1960s, but the programme and methods of instruction had been substantially revised. In 1969, the district training in a state was placed in the middle of the two years of IAS training rather than at the end—hence the new arrangement became known as the 'sandwich' course. It was still in effect in 1983. 1981 recruits, for example, came straight from success in the examinations to Mussoorie at the end of August, and took the Foundation Course with the other higher services for three months; then they entered immediately on the separate IAS Professional Course: Phase I, also at the Academy, from December to the end of May 1982 (during which they went on a 'Winter Study Tour', the equivalent of the old *Bharat Darshan*); then the probationers dispersed to the states of their allotment for one year of district training organized by each state government; finally, they returned to the Academy at the beginning of June 1983 for the IAS Professional Course: Phase II, which ran until 20 August 1983.

The main objectives of the Foundation Course were the same. The Handbook for the Autumn 1983 Course (mimeo.) summarized them as providing an introduction to the 'constitutional, political, social, economic, legal, historical, cultural, and administrative framework within which the services function', and motivating probationers 'towards developing certain basic professional, administrative, and human values' (p. 3). Different emphases were also evident. One was a deliberate attempt to overcome service exclusiveness by promoting '*esprit de corps* among the probationers of different services emphasizing their interdependence'. Another was a much more aggressive attempt to acquaint probationers with socio-economic conditions in villages, the problems of rural development administration, and the impact of development programmes on the rural poor. All probationers were required to spend more than two weeks of the Foundation Course in a 'backward' district of Uttar Pradesh, studying particular villages and writing reports based on their observations for discussion back at the

Academy. Some of these were then published in the Academy's journal, the *Administrator*. They were usually of high quality, penetrating far into the inadequacies of local administration at the block level, the struggles between upper and lower castes and classes, and so on.[13] Another compulsory feature for all probationers was a 'trekking programme' for about ten days in the mountains 'intended to foster a spirit of adventure and love of nature' (p. 6). This, together with other features like increased emphasis on physical exercise, underlined the greater attention given to discipline and self-confidence. 'Shishtachar' was still in use. The Probationers' Handbook in 1983 told the new IAS recruits quite bluntly: 'The principles and norms outlined in 'Shishtachar' are expected to be followed strictly.'[14] There were other 'dos and don'ts' in the Handbook which were rigorously applied. Attendance at classes, guest lectures, physical training, and so on 'is compulsory' and any absence 'will be treated as dereliction of duty and will be viewed accordingly'. Also 'un-officer-like behaviour is not acceptable' (p. 14). Strict regulations were laid down relating to drinking, smoking, relations with the opposite sex, behaviour in the hostels, and dress. On dress, for instance, apart from formal occasions (when formal dress is required), 'gentlemen probationers should wear shirt/bushshirt/sweaters with or without tie; lady probationers should wear sari/salwar kamiz/regional dress'. The wearing of jeans 'is discouraged' and 'the wearing of *chappals*/slippers as footwear by gentlemen probationers in public places in the Academy is considered casual' (p. 17). Much more attention was also given to language training. The medium of instruction was, of course, English, but Hindi was compulsory for all probationers and an examination in Hindi was held at the end of the Foundation Course. Facilities (including language laboratory) were available to learn Indian languages, and IAS probationers allotted to non-Hindi speaking states were also required to learn the appropriate language.

The methods of instruction at the Academy had also been revised. During the Foundation Course emphasis was being placed less on lectures and more on small group work within larger syndicates, case/studies, simulation exercises, and management games. Small groups of probationers also were assigned a counsellor (a member of

[13] e.g. The excellent Report by Harsh Mander (IAS, MP) from the 1980 batch, published in the *Administrator*, xxvi. 3 (1981), 459–64.

[14] GOI Lal Bahadur Shastri National Academy of Administration, 'Probationers' Handbook: XLII Foundational Course, 29th Aug.–3rd Dec. 1983', mimeo., p. 16.

Faculty) and met regularly with him. Amongst other things, small group work was aimed at developing effective public speaking techniques. Each probationer also had to prepare a term paper and a book review for the counsellor. Such methods were also employed in the IAS Professional Course: Phases I and II. Throughout, there was a steady stream of eminent persons who visited the Academy and addressed the probationers. Senior ICS and IAS officers were prominent amongst the visiting lecturers, as well as distinguished academics and political leaders. Even the Prime Minister appeared at the Academy from time to time.[15]

The IAS Professional Course—Phase I concentrated on development administration and rural economics, general administration (including state and district administration, food and civil supplies, jail administration, law and order, etc.), law (including detailed study of the Indian Penal Code, the Criminal Procedure Code, and the Evidence Act), and constitutional law and political theory. There were attachments during the Winter Study Tour (for about two months) to public enterprises (for example, the Durgapur steel plant), an Agricultural University, and the Bureau of Parliamentary Studies in Delhi. They also lived in, and studied, a tribal village for about eight days. Language training was stressed. Two further matters which were particularly reminiscent of the ICS tradition were also singled out for special mention in the Course Handbook for Phase I.[16] First, 'breadth of interest' is of 'basic importance', while 'mere knowledge of his profession can be a liability in a generalist service in the absence of a high ability to learn and adapt'; hence the Academy stressed the importance of IAS probationers as generalists taking an active interest in 'various clubs and societies, riding, shooting, trekking, hiking, and sports activities' (p. 28). Second, an IAS officer 'is expected to be self-regulating, self-disciplined, and highly responsible; trusting him is axiomatic for his superiors, and close supervision or external discipline are never thought of in his case.' Hence, 'probationers are advised to habitualize ... very high standards of rectitude, responsibility, punctuality, and self-control' (pp. 28–9). After district training, the short Phase II training at the Academy placed similar emphasis on these aspects, while concentrating on helping probationers to relate the

[15] e.g. On 20 June 1974; her address was later published in *Administrative Training Institute Newsletter* (Mysore), 1. 5 (1976), 2–6.

[16] GOI Lal Bahadur Shastri National Academy of Administration, Course Handbook, IAS Professional Course Phase I (1 Dec. 1982–31 May 1983), mimeo.

practical experience they had gained in district training to broader issues of administration.[17] Case-studies were used extensively as a basis for discussion, and considerable attention was given to the situations they could expect to face as SDOs later in the year.

The introduction of the sandwich course meant initially that the National Academy became more involved with the district training in the states. It required that states adjust the length of their district training to one year. The Tamil Nadu Government, for example, had a training programme lasting 57 weeks before 1979, then amended it to fit the sandwich.[18] The National Academy actually laid down the programme reproduced in Table 15 for district training which it urged all states to adopt.[19]

Table 15. *District Training Programme Recommended by the National Academy, 1982*

Nature of training	Duration (weeks)
1. Institutional training	2
2. District Headquarters (including Collectorate, Treasury, judicial work, attachment with district officers)	15
3. Village attachment	2
4. Block attachment	2
5. Revenue attachment	1
6. Subdivisional attachment	2
7. Independent Development charge	16
8. Survey and settlement training	4
9. Independent Revenue charge	4
10. Agricultural training	1
11. Secretariat training	2
Total	51

As of 1983, however, there was still considerable variation in the district training arrangements from state to state.[20] Additional evidence of increasingly centralized control of IAS training was the supervision

[17] GOI Lal Bahadur Shastri National Academy of Administration, 'Course Design, IAS Professional Course: Phase II (Batch 1982–3), 6 June–20 Aug. 1983', mimeo.

[18] Government of Tamil Nadu. *Scheme of Field Training in the Districts for Assistant Collectors*, 1979.

[19] GOI Lal Bahadur Shastri National Academy of Administration, National Training Conference on Training of Civil Servants in India (21–3 Sept. 1982), Recommendations, mimeo., p. 11.

[20] Details are given in the Annexure to the Training Conference document cited above.

exercised by counsellors at the Academy of IAS trainees in the district; for instance, a trainee was supposed to send reports every four weeks to his or her counsellor and the Director at Mussoorie, guide-lines for the village economic study were now provided by the Academy, and the Academy on advice from the Collector, awarded assessment marks for district training. Furthermore, more and more states were opening Training Institutes which, amongst other things, provided IAS institutional training (as urged by the Academy); in 1983 an Association of State Training Institutes was in operation, with the Director of the Rajasthan Institute, M. L. Mehta (IAS), as Secretary. All this tightened IAS control over IAS training. One important consequence of all this was that Collectors were obliged to take more interest in the trainees.

Aspects of the content of the training as a whole have already been mentioned, as they relate to the IAS tradition. One could report endless examples showing clearly the norms and values at the heart of what IAS probationers were exposed to, because much of what was said or discussed at the Academy was reported, run off on a mimeograph machine, or published in the *Administrator* or elsewhere. A few examples must suffice to give further indication of the content of the IAS shaping process. In 1971 L. P. Singh (ICS) informed a group of IAS probationers during a talk at the Academy that in his experience the higher you go in administration, the more prevalent is the political aspect: 'practically all Government is politics—anything you do has political implications'. Also, 'unless you keep on studying political behaviour and problems relating to the political institutions functioning in the country and at least some other countries, I think, you can never make a first-rate civil servant.' Furthermore, 'many of the grievances of the civil servant about the functioning of our political system arise from too idealistic a view of public affairs and in non-recognition of the fact that after all politics is concerned with power.'[21]

The following Summary of a Syndicate Report in 1976 reflects the views of nine IAS probationers and the Director of the Academy, R. Prasad, (ICS, Andhra Pradesh), the staff member working with this particular group. The subject the group worked on was 'Professional, Social and Personal Ethics of the IAS Officer in Contemporary Indian Society.'[22] They began by recognizing that the role of the IAS in a democratic setting was 'very controversial', then indicated the rationale

[21] Singh, L. P., 'Our Civil Service', *Journal of the National Academy of Administration*, xvi. 1 (1971), 12–14.

[22] Published under that title in the *Administrator*, xxi. 2 (1976), 649–64.

for their existence as including the following: (1) the IAS provides top administrators for the central government as well as the states; (2) it enables the centre to be in constant touch with local realities; (3) it facilitates liaison between centre and states; (4) it creates uniform standards of administration throughout the country; (5) it ensures that the services are 'free from communal or petty bias'; (6) it provides administrative leadership for other services, 'ensuring contentment and sense of security' (this, of course, was the IAS view). On ethics, of overriding importance was the value of public service: 'whatever is deemed to be public service by the legitimate representatives of the public or their agents, the public servant must carry out—if he violently disagrees, resignation is the only way out.' What the government expects from an IAS officer, the Syndicate concluded, was efficiency (in executing orders, in prompt handling of unforeseen situations, in aiding government in formulation of policy), loyalty (to the Constitution, etc.), integrity ('honesty, sincerity, probity, no regard to private gain—even the personal life of an IAS officer should be sober and dignified'), impartiality (decisions in accordance with law). What the IAS officer expects from the government is clear authority, security, support, and justice (in promotions, transfers, prize postings, etc.)—'any violations of justice in these fields is sure to have harmful effects on the morale of IAS officers and thereby impair their efficiency'.

The Syndicate then went on to devote all the rest of their report (more than half) to IAS officers' relations with politicians. (This preoccupation with the political dimension was not unusual; one encountered it in other reports and in conversations with IAS officers.) A few examples are sufficient to indicate the general line. IAS and politicians, they say, 'step on each others' toes constantly'. There is a 'wide gulf'. Politicians blame IAS for being 'snobs', IAS 'underestimate the politicians' intelligence and overestimate their own'. So a 'compromise' is necessary, they think. 'The politician is rendered ineffectual without the administrator and the administrator lost without the politician, hence it is in the best interest of both that they meet halfway.' The attitude toward local politicians should not be that their 'only job is interference'. When a politician approaches you as Collector for 'odd jobs like a license for a fair price shop, or an arms license, land allotment, postponement of date of recovery of Government loan, postponement of sale of property for recovery of Government loan, a plea on behalf of some persons to protect them from *goonda* elements, etc.', it is essential 'to examine the pros and cons frankly, with politeness and tact; if you cannot oblige the politician, state clearly the reasons why'. Also, even when politicians come with complaints, 'they are serving a useful function' (as an alternative source of information); 'an administrator who relies on only his subordinates develops a jaundiced view'. There is extensive discussion of relations with ministers, following the standard formulation: 'even in the implementation of policies, the minister is entitled to have a justifiable say—but it is preferable to let the administrator execute it once the guide-lines are laid down.' There is also a section on relations with other civil servants: 'we have to face the concerted criticism levelled against IAS from members of almost every other service.' They close by remarking on the difficulty of living up to 'all these cherished values', but it is 'not impossible'.

A further example is a confidential letter from P. S. Appu (IAS, Bihar), Director of the Academy in the early 1980s, to A. C. Bandyopadhyay (IAS, Orissa), Secretary, Department of Personnel and Administrative Reforms, and dated 26 December 1981. It was leaked to the press on 3 March 1982,[23] when the case to which it refers hit the front pages of the Indian newspapers. It is a very long letter, and the case to which it relates is important from many points of view. Only one aspect is considered here. Briefly, an IAS probationer, V. K. Singh, was a member of a group of about forty probationers on a trekking expedition (as part of their Foundation Course) in October 1981. On the long bus-ride up to Badrinath, where the expedition was to start, Singh and some others were drinking country liquor, and at one point a lady probationer reportedly called Singh 'a drunken stupid Bihari'. When they arrived at Badrinath, Singh apparently abused some lady probationers 'and a number of gentlemen probationers' and threatened them by brandishing a loaded 32-bore revolver. Singh was then taken away by fellow probationers who asked him to behave himself, and the ladies locked themselves up in one room of the *dharamsala* where the group were camping for the night. Word of the incident later reached Appu, and he wrote to the Secretary, Delhi, on 28 October 1981 recommending that Singh be discharged from the Academy. But there was delay, and it is clear that Singh and his political patrons were busy lobbying in Delhi to stop the dismissal. In the letter leaked to the press, Appu summarized the whole case once more, gave a very full account of the reasons why he thought Singh should be discharged, and closed

[23] Letter 3/12/ASP—81, as reported in *Indian Express*, 7 Mar. 1982, 8.

by announcing that if Government did not act immediately to discharge Singh, he could not continue as Director and would seek premature retirement from the IAS. (Appu was actually allowed to retire, but in all the uproar that followed in March the following year, the Prime Minister finally had to step in and Singh was discharged.)

Amongst the series of arguments for Singh's discharge, as noted in the confidential letter, the following are particularly revealing. First, says Appu, Singh's conduct at Badrinath shows 'he is lacking in qualities of mind and character needed for the Service'. For, above all, there is 'need for great self-discipline in the IAS'. This is so because 'there is great scope for discretion in the IAS', and hence for 'misuse of authority'. A man like Singh, lacking in self-discipline, is 'a great risk in the IAS'. Secondly, Appu said that other probationers had been discharged for less serious acts of misconduct. 'If Government takes a lenient view in this case, the only conclusion that one can draw is that probationers with influence in the right quarters can commit every heinous crime with impunity. If he is let off, it will have disastrous effects on discipline and morale in the IAS in general and at the National Academy in particular.' A third argument came straight out of the special role IAS men saw for themselves in a fractious and unruly society. We 'must insist on discipline and impeccable personal conduct for IAS', said Appu. Why? Because we are passing through a difficult period. There are 'declining standards of personal and public conduct', and a 'breakdown of long-cherished values'. Public life is 'in a sorry state'. There is 'a great deal of "violence in the air"'. A tendency to 'take the law into one's own hands is "all pervasive"'. A 'firm nexus has developed between organised crime and some amoral public men with access to levers of power'. 'At the moment our future appears to be rather dark and gloomy', although this is 'probably a passing phase'. But 'until we get past it', the IAS will have to play a crucial role 'in steering us through'. And it can do that only if we insist on 'impeccable conduct and ruthlessly weed out persons lacking in qualities of mind and character needed for the Service'.

One notices the assumption throughout the letter that the Academy is engaged in a deliberate shaping exercise—even attempting to 'weed out' those who don't fit. Gentlemanly norms and values, amongst others, are also very evident from Appu's letter, L. P. Singh's talk, and the Syndicate report. Self-discipline is absolutely essential for IAS officers who are placed in positions with considerable autonomy ('great scope for discretion'). Special qualities of mind and strength of character are needed, reflecting the Service ethics of public service, efficiency, loyalty to superiors, integrity, (including a sober and dignified bearing), and impartiality (in the sense of acting according to the rule of law). When IAS officers rule a district or when they are in other positions of responsibility, they provide leadership, recognizing as they do that everything they do has political implications, being shot through with considerations of power. Also IAS men and women believe they provide a frame of power in a divided and turbulent society. They justify their very existence largely in terms of the importance of such an all-India frame. As for politicians, they serve 'a useful function' and ministers are indispensible in a democracy, but the IAS view is that these relationships are uncertain and can be 'difficult'. Whether or not the two sides can 'compromise', IAS norms assume fundamentally what was always central in the ICS tradition: that the context of the relationship is essentially political, or, as L. P. Singh put it, 'practically all government is politics'.

As suggested earlier, the district training had become more closely integrated with the training at the Academy, and it seems that trainees on arrival at their first SDO posts were better prepared than was the case in the 1960s.[24] But clearly that was not the end of the shaping process. If the culture of the IAS as a whole, which young IAS trainees were entering, was fundamentally different from that of the Academy, then the Academy's values would have died rapidly as young IAS officers worked their way up. Clearly, there are instances of this happening. Dipak Rudra (IAS, West Bengal), who entered in 1963, has referred to 'the temptations of the middle years' and describes how for some, 'early illusions peter out until frustrated civil servants are anxious to make compromises for advancement'.[25] But such abandonment of norms and values learned earlier was probably far less widespread than the critics implied. The tendencies within the IAS have been in the direction of greater tightening up, as it has come increasingly under attack from other services. The general tightening up of the training programme in recent years is one indicator of the trend.

Other features reinforce this tendency. One concerns the work of IAS associations in each state and at the centre. Little is known about

[24] Long-serving faculty members at the Academy like Professor Tewari and others I interviewed in 1983 said the sandwich pattern was a definite improvement.

[25] Rudra, D., 'Gods with Feet of Clay: Temptations of the Middle Years', *Statesman*, 9 Aug. 1980, 6.

them. Indeed, one of the most seasoned IAS watchers in India, an academic in Delhi friendly with many IAS officers, has never been allowed to attend a meeting of the IAS association there, on the grounds that such gatherings are only for 'family'. There were indications in 1983 that an increasing proportion of the Service was maintaining at least some contact with their local association, representing service norms and values. Executive committees of local IAS associations met monthly, and there were annual general meetings. IAS 'weeks' were also held every year in many states, as in ICS days. Chak (ICS, UP) has described in some detail one such IAS week in his autobiography.[26] Back in the 1960s it appears that older officers were less active in such associations than younger ones, and promotees from the state services (also older men) were also not very interested. But this also was changing. Promotees from state services in the IAS formerly received no IAS training (they were, of course, very experienced anyway), but increasingly in the 1970s even they were being inducted into the IAS training set-up, with many being sent after appointment to Mussoorie for short training courses.

This development was related to efforts made increasingly to develop in-service training schemes for IAS officers in mid career. By the early 1980s, a number of IAS officers with six to ten years of service were being sent each year for six weeks of an 'Executive Development Programme' at the Management Development Institute, Gurgaon, and elsewhere; and IAS officers with eleven to sixteen years service were being sent for four weeks of 'Management Development' training either to the National Academy, the IIPA, the Administrative Staff College in Hyderabad, or to one of the Indian Institutes of Management at Ahmedabad, Bangalore, or Calcutta.[27] These and other such in-service programmes were not particularly well articulated or co-ordinated in the early 1980s, but the need to link them all together and to the programmes at the National Academy was recognized and work was in progress to improve the situation.[28] Much of the thrust behind all these initiatives came from the Department of Personnel and Administrative Reforms. The Department was staffed heavily with IAS officers. And it is clear that they saw themselves at least in part, as guardians of service norms and values.[29]

[26] Chak, *Himalayas to Bay Islands*, pp. 121–9.

[27] Details are given in the annual reports of the Department of Personnel and Administrative Reforms.

[28] e.g. National Training Conference at Mussoorie (21–3 Sept. 1982), agenda item 7.

[29] e.g. the essay on Indian civil services by Mattoo, P. K. (IAS, Himachal Pradesh),

Establishing an all-India, co-ordinated process of this kind was uphill work. Individual state cadres differed from each in both their formal training arrangements and in the nuances of their normative codes. Such differences were evident to anyone who travelled from state to state meeting IAS officers. They were part of the folklore of the Service, and provided a topic of endless conversation when IAS officers got together. One published example must suffice here.[30] M. Mukerji (IAS, Rajasthan), who was Chief Secretary in the mid-1970s, once had an IAS friend from Uttar Pradesh come for a short visit, and the friend, after a couple of days, remarked: 'I am amazed by the lack of stiffness in official behaviour in Jaipur; I note that officers who are very junior to you in age or rank behave with a familiarity and express their views with a frankness which would be unthinkable in UP.' Mukerji's response to his friend was that it was 'due to the example set by B. Mehta' (IAS), Chief Secretary from 1958–66. 'When I was a junior', said Mukerji, 'he encouraged me and others to treat him like an affectionate older brother, argue with him on governmental matters with frankness.' Mehta also 'accepted full responsibility for his final decisions and was always lenient to a junior officer who might have made a mistake due to an error of judgement'. In doing all this, 'he laid down norms of office behaviour and we, in turn, have become senior and try to follow his example'. And so, suggested Mukerji to his friend from UP, 'the reputation which Rajasthan has today, of being one of the well-administered states of India, is largely the result of the work done and example set by the late B. Mehta'. The example not only indicates differences of style between different state cadres. It also shows clearly how senior IAS officers can influence more junior officers during the shaping process.

Joint Secretary in the Department of Personnel, GOI, in the early 1970s, in Raksasataya and Siedentopf, *Asian Civil Services*.

[30] Mukerji, M., 'B. Mehta', in Arora, R. (ed.), *People's Participation in Development Process: Essays in Honour of B. Mehta*, Jaipur, HCM Institute of Public Administration, 1979, p. xi.

6

The tradition in the early 1980s

In the 1920s and 1930s the content of the ICS tradition as identified in Chapter 1 centred on location and movement, political work as a characteristic behaviour pattern, and six gentlemanly and service-class norms and values. The purpose of this chapter is to examine briefly the content of the tradition in the early 1980s in relation to these features. The comparison suggests that these central features of Indian administration were still important in the early 1980s, even though various changes had also taken place. The chapter concludes by indicating some of the broader consequences of the tradition affecting the overall character of the Indian state.

LOCATION AND MOVEMENT

IAS structure in 1983 was typified by location in control posts set apart in secretariats and districts from main line departments at each level of government between which IAS persons moved at frequent intervals. Table 16 (together with map 2) indicates the spread of IAS location throughout the country in districts, in every state (and in the Union Territories), and at the centre.

At first glance the data appear to suggest that there had been a major change in terms of overall size. The ICS in 1919 comprised 1,032 persons organized in eight provincial cadres (1,029 persons in 10 cadres in 1938).[1] In 1983, the IAS had 4,092 persons organized in 20 state cadres (plus one for Union Territories). The appearance is deceptive. Relating the figures to growth in the size of the Indian state places the IAS in the appropriate setting. And here, within the state, the overall size of the IAS actually remained more or less constant. The Indian state in terms of numbers of persons in public sector employment roughly quadrupled in size between 1953 and 1983, with growth in the area of public enterprises being most marked.[2] The IAS

[1] Table 1.
[2] Table 13.

Table 16. *IAS Location, 1983*

IAS cadre	District administration	State government	State or central public enterprise	Government of India	Other	Total.
Andhra Pradesh	85	109	35	26	33	288
Assam-Meghalaya	42	63	15	27	12	159
Bihar	85	131	30	53	20	319
Gujarat	47	66	27	27	14	181
Haryana	38	57	29	20	6	150
Himachal Pradesh	21	39	12	12	11	95
Jammu & Kashmir	16	40	8	14	2	80
Karnataka	61	87	35	17	7	207
Kerala	33	62	23	18	7	143
Madhya Pradesh	114	124	29	50	14	331
Maharashtra	98	84	46	45	21	294
Manipur-Tripura	23	42	7	20	5	97
Nagaland	9	24	0	6	3	42
Orissa	35	83	33	32	8	191
Punjab	38	62	28	21	13	162
Rajasthan	67	84	15	32	7	205
Sikkim	5	16	0	4	0	25
Tamil Nadu	55	111	56	26	17	265
Union Territories	26	86	13	24	12	161
Uttar Pradesh	150	172	55	57	19	453
West Bengal	55	102	20	41	26	244
Totals	1,103	1,644	516	572	257	4,092
Per cent	27%	40%	13%	14%	6%	100%

Source: Compiled from individual biographical entries in GOI Ministry of Home Affairs, *Civil List of Indian Administrative Service as on 1.1.1983*, pp. 2–216.

Notes: The category 'other' includes those on foreign assignment (including training abroad), on leave, under suspension, awaiting posting, on deputation to another state, or on whom there is no information. Commissioners of Divisions have been classified under 'District Administration'.

also roughly quadrupled during the same period.[3] Like its predecessor, the IAS remained an utterly minuscule group within the state.

Secondly, the data in Table 16 show the IAS spread throughout the country at different levels, with a few persons from each state cadre making up the IAS contingent working for the Government of India. The overall pattern of IAS location in 1983 was broadly similar to ICS location. Even the proportion of IAS working for the Government of India (14 per cent) was not very different from the ICS pattern (11 per cent) in both 1919 and 1938.

Thirdly, however, the proportions working at district and state levels had changed: 48 per cent of the ICS were in district administration in 1919, compared with 27 per cent of the IAS in 1983. District work thus appeared to be the core experience of the ICS as a whole, whereas for the IAS it centred on the state secretariat. The overall character of IAS location had shifted, although the essential feature of location at all levels of government remained. The main explanation for this shift in proportion is to be found in the changing number of persons, districts, and state secretariats. In 1919, 497 ICS (out of 1,032 altogether) were involved in administering 233 districts, in 1983, 1,103 IAS (out of 4,092) were so involved in 416 districts.[4] There were actually *more* IAS per district in 1983 than ICS per district in 1919. There were, however, more than twice as many states in 1983 (than provinces in 1919), and this together with the huge expansion of the state since the end of the raj accounts for the enlarged representation of the IAS at this level.

Fourthly, Table 16 shows a truly new development: 13 per cent of the IAS in 1983 were working in the public sector of the economy—11 per cent in public enterprises in the states, the other 2 per cent in public enterprises accountable to the Government of India. This new category of posts can be said to have replaced the 'judicial' posts of 1919; with the gradual separation of the executive from the judiciary in the 1950s and 1960s, these judicial posts came to be filled by others. Public enterprise postings for the IAS have grown rapidly since the early 1970s. This change represents a departure in terms of the details of types of posts held. At the same time, it serves to underline the continuing strength and vitality of the ICS tradition. As the state has

[3] According to GOI Planning Commission, *Report on Indian and State Administrative Services and Problems of District Administration* (by V. T. Krishnamachari), Statement, 1, 1962, 68–9, the authorized strength of the IAS in 1953 was 1,314, the actual strength about 975. In 1983 the actual strength was 4,092.

[4] The 1919 district figure is as reported in the 1921 census. The 1983 figure has been compiled from *Times of India Directory and Yearbook, 1983* (Bombay), pp. 148–96.

expanded into the public sector of the economy by either initiating new enterprises or nationalizing existing ones, the IAS has moved in to control them.

Fifthly, a close examination of Table 16 shows certain regional variations, as in 1919, although there are no major surprises nor large deviations from norms. For example, 14 per cent of the IAS as a whole were on deputation to the Government of India in 1983, but IAS men from cadres in southern states were under-represented at this particular date. The data show that Karnataka provided only 8 per cent of their cadre to the Government of India, Andhra Pradesh 9 per cent, Tamil Nadu 10 per cent, and Kerala 12.5 per cent. Uttar Pradesh also provided only 12.5 per cent. On the other hand, Bihar, West Bengal, and Jammu and Kashmir provided somewhat more than the norm (17 per cent). Such variations are not significant in terms of any consistent bias over the years. Similar analyses for other years show that such proportions shift around from time to time. In 1963, for example, all four southern states provided more than the norm to the Government of India, and Uttar Pradesh much more; in 1976 Orissa and Union Territories stood out as providing far more than the norm; and so on.[5]

Also, like its predecessor, IAS people were on top at each level. There were still central and state secretariats, and Collectors, all set apart to some extent from mainline departments and exercising overall supervision and control of the state apparatus as a whole. In the central secretariat in 1983, they held Secretaryships in most of the main secretariat departments (see Table 17). The Secretary to the President of India and the Cabinet Secretary were also IAS. It should be noted that External Affairs, Parliamentary Affairs, and Railways (or their equivalents) had never had ICS Secretaries anyway; most of the other 1983 ministries in that category were very small and highly specialized; and to have both IAS and non-IAS Secretaries in the ministries of Defence and Finance typified the staffing arrangements of the 1930s. On the whole, the evidence suggests some contraction of IAS control of top administrative posts in the central secretariat, but not enough yet to justify calling it a major change in the situation. Figures for 1966 and 1976 on who held the posts of Secretary, Additional Secretary, and Joint Secretary in the Government of India show the IAS holding a majority at both times but with this percentage of the whole declining

[5] The evidence in this paragraph is compiled from IAS Civil Lists for the years mentioned.

by about 10 per cent overall.[6] In state secretariats there was hardly any such contraction. The 1983 Civil List shows all Chief Secretaries as IAS, as well as most important Secretaries. As for Collectors, the IAS was even more fully in control of this post than the ICS was in the 1920s and 1930s. In 1983 in Bihar and Tamil Nadu, for example, all Collectors were IAS; in Rajasthan 24 of the 26 districts had IAS Collectors. The all-India figure for IAS coverage of Collectors' posts was over 90 per cent.[7]

Table 17. *Distribution of IAS Secretaries in Central Ministries, 1983*

Those secretariat ministries where the Secretary (or Secretaries) was (or were) IAS	Those secretariat ministries where one of the two Secretaries was IAS	Those secretariat ministries where the Secretary was non-IAS
1. Agriculture	1. Defence	1. Atomic Energy
2. Civil Supplies and Civil Aviation	2. Energy	2. Chemicals and Fertilisers
3. Commerce	3. Finance (two of three Secretaries)	3. Elections
4. Communications	4. Law, Justice, and Company Affairs	4. Environment
5. Education and Culture	5. Steel and Mines	5. External Affairs
6. Health and Family Welfare		6. Irrigation
7. Home		7. Parliamentary Affairs
8. Industry		8. Petroleum
9. Information and Broadcasting		9. Railways
10. Labour and Rehabilitation		10. Science and Technology
11. Planning		11. Space
12. Rural Development		
13. Shipping and Transport		
14. Social Welfare		
15. Supply and Sports		
16. Tourism		
17. Works and Housing		

Source: Compiled from the *IAS Civil List, 1983*, together with the 1982 Delhi telephone directory (the most recent available at the time the analysis was done).

[6] Gupta, N. P., 'Administrative Reforms: 'How?', *Link*, Aug. 1970, 85, gives the 1966 figures. Dey, B. K., *Bureaucracy, Development and Public Management in India*, New Delhi, 1978, pp. 139–40, gives figures for 1976. The comparison and the percentage are compiled on the basis of these data. The comparison shows, for example, IAS percentage of Additional Secretaryships dropping from 66% to 64%, Joint Secretary from 71% to 60%.

[7] Source: compiled from the *IAS Civil List 1983*, together with district data from the source given in fn. 4 above.

The new growth area in the Indian state, the public sector of the economy, was not dominated by full-time IAS officers in the same way. Of the more than 170 public enterprises accountable to the Government of India in 1981, less than one-third had a full-time IAS Managing Director or (in a few cases) an IAS Chairman of the Board; however, many IAS secretariat officers sat on the Boards of Directors part time and, generally speaking, as one expert put it, 'IAS domination continues to be overwhelming' through this more indirect means.[8] Most public enterprises in India are accountable to a state government, and here also the picture is much the same. In Kerala, for example, of the approximately 53 companies and 22 subsidiaries under the control of various secretariat departments in 1983, only 18 had full-time IAS Managing Directors or Chairmen of Boards of Directors; but in an analysis of the composition of the Boards of Directors in Kerala 46 per cent were found to be government officials (nearly all of them either IAS or from the state administrative service); and it was also found that all major decisions of these public enterprises in such areas as investment plans, annual budgets, major appointments, and large contracts, were taken in the Kerala secretariat.[9] The same study found that one of the principal features of the Kerala Boards was the fast turnover of their memberships. An extreme case was the Board of the Kerala Civil Supplies Corporation in 1979–80: the actual size of the Board was six, yet 43 different Directors had served that year! Such rapid turnover obviously had adverse effects; the study found a direct correlation between the stability of the Board and success of the organization.

Rapid turnover of IAS board members in Kerala or elsewhere is only part of the more general movement of the IAS from post to post; and move they certainly did. An IAS officer 'is always a bird of passage . . . a gypsy', exclaimed Dubhashi (IAS, Karnataka) years ago; 'the whirl or merry (misery)-go-round of transfers goes on continuously'.[10] One unpublished study found that the all-India average tenure of Collectors was 20 months;[11] another study found that the average

[8] Maheshwari, S., 'Ecology of Public Enterprises in India', *IJPA* xxvii. 4 (1981), 1034–42.

[9] Pillai, N. and Balasubramaniam, A., 'The Boards of Directors of Public Sector Companies in Kerala: An Analysis', *Lok Udyog*, 17 (June 1983), 23–33, together with my analysis of the *IAS Civil List, 1983*.

[10] Dubhashi, P. R. (IAS, Karnataka), 'Satisfaction of an Administrative Career', *IJPA* xv. 1 (1969), 116–17.

[11] Gillespie's study, as reported in Dave, P. K. (IAS, MP), 'The Collector, Today and Tomorrow', *IJPA* xi. 3 (1965), 376–88.

tenure of Collectors in Rajasthan was 14 months.[12] That was in the 1950s and 1960s. The pace of the merry-go-round had not slackened by 1983.

Transfer policies in the early 1980s laid down norms calling for postings of three years normally, and certainly not less than two years.[13] Norms at the centre were three years' tenure for an Under Secretary, four years for Deputy Secretary, and five years for Joint Secretary and above.[14] The reality of IAS movement was very different from all this. Table 18 shows that a staggering 80 per cent or more of the entire IAS in the early 1980s actually held their posts for less than two years before moving on.

Table 18. *IAS Movement, 1977–1983*

IAS as of		Length of time in post (% of IAS)			
1 January	Number	Less than 1 year	1–2 years	2–3 years	More than 3 years
1978	3,084	58	26	10	6
1979	3,236	55	30	10	5
1981	3,373	60	22	11	7
1982	3,539	52	31	9	8
1983	3,734	51	29	13	7

Source: Data compiled from the IAS Civil Lists for those years.
Notes: Data on postings of individual officers in the Civil Lists are fairly complete, but not entirely. In two instances, data on as much as ⅓ of a state cadre were missing: Karnataka in the 1982 Civil List and Madhya Pradesh in the 1981 List. For these reasons, the number of IAS on which these percentages are based is somewhat less than the number actually in the IAS at these times. Also IAS under training at the time were excluded, e.g. the 1983 figures exclude the recruits of 1981 and 1982.

The data show that a majority of the IAS stayed in one post for less than one year. Only 20 per cent or less stayed for two years or more. Behind the gross figures in Table 18 are different rates of mobility within different state cadres (although a full analysis of these differences is not to the present purpose here). One point about the all-India figures: there is a consistent discrepancy between the centre and the states. IAS officers on deputation to the centre normally stayed

[12] Bhatnagar, P. and Sharma, G., 'Transfer of Collectors in Rajasthan', *IJPA* xix. 2 (1973), 187–203.

[13] e.g. details of procedure and policies regarding postings, transfers, promotions, etc. in Rajasthan are given in Sogani, *Chief Secretary*.

[14] Transfer policies and procedures at the centre are described in Dubhashi, P. R., 'The Establishment Officer', *IJPA* xxvii. 4 (1981), 975–80.

in one post for two to three years, whereas IAS in state secretariats and districts moved far more frequently. For example, a majority of the Tamil Nadu IAS cadre in central government posts as of 1 January 1983 had been there for more than two years, whereas only 12 per cent of the IAS in the state secretariat and the districts had lasted that long.

The main point is that the IAS were moving around from post to post as rapidly as their predecessors had done in the 1920s and 1930s. The fact of rapid movement—that essential feature of the ICS tradition—is indisputable. But the reasons for it were widely regarded by administrators and others in India as very different from those that operated during the raj. Now, I was informed in 1983, transfers are the result of political interference. There were numerous stories (some of them no doubt true) of IAS officers being transferred because the minister, or some other powerful politician, found the officer's presence inconvenient. And whenever new governments were formed, it was believed that wholesale transfers followed; for the power to influence transfers is the principal means by which a minister could bend an IAS officer to his or her will. The data on IAS movement suggest that all this is overdone. Table 18 shows that IAS movement in the election years of 1977 and 1980 was somewhat higher than in other years, but if one breaks the figures down by state, the gross percentages do not support the idea of wholesale transfers due to changes of governments. In 1977, following the general election which brought Janata to power at the centre, Janata also won elections in a number of states and took over from Congress there as well. In six important states Janata assumed full control, i.e. were not part of a coalition, while in four other states Congress governments remained in power; yet if one compares the percentages of IAS who moved to another post during 1977 (up to 1 January 1978) in these ten states, as shown in Table 19, one finds no consistent pattern of more IAS movement when governments changed.

Apart from Haryana (which is extraordinary), Table 19 suggests that there was rather more IAS movement in states where governments did not change. There certainly is no way to make these comparative data support the view that particularly high rates of IAS transfers accompanied changes of government. In 1980 Congress swept back to power at the centre, and also in most states where elections were held in May that year. It is clear that there was somewhat more IAS movement in states where a Congress Ministry replaced Janata; in five of the six 'Janata states' listed in Table 19, all of which became Congress in 1980, the

Table 19. *Movement of IAS in Election Year 1977*

No change of government in 1977			Change of government in 1977		
State	No. of IAS	% of IAS who moved	State	No. of IAS	% of IAS who moved
Andhra Pradesh	210	69	Bihar	245	64
Assam	117	61	Haryana	114	80
Karnataka	168	68	Madhya Pradesh	258	49
Maharashtra	224	50	Orissa	156	58
			Rajasthan	160	54
			Uttar Pradesh	291	61

(All-India average = 58%, see Table 18)
Source: The data are compiled from the *IAS Civil List, 1978*.
Note: The number of IAS in each cadre excludes the 1976 and 1977 recruits and those for whom no information was available.

percentage of IAS who moved to a new post during that year was above the national average of 60 per cent.[15] At the same time, however, there were two states where IAS movement was most pronounced—Punjab (76 per cent) and Karnataka (73 per cent), but Karnataka was a Congress state where there was no change of government.

High rates of IAS mobility generally, from year to year, are explained by various factors, of which political interference accompanying changes of government is only one. As important are the factors which operated in the 1920s and 1930s—filling leave vacancies (although the consequences of 'home' leave for Europeans had ended), shifting incompetent officers, rewarding others through promotion,[16] replacing others who retired or died—all with the accompanying knock-on effects. Most important, undoubtedly, has been the growth of the state, the consequent opening up of many new and attractive IAS posts, and ambitious IAS men and women scrambling for such posts. 'Wet' posts (from which rupees pour) are preferable to 'dry' posts, urban districts with good schools for the children are preferable to remote rural districts, and so on. As one young IAS man remarked in 1983: 'Nowadays, and I can speak with confidence about the younger members of the Service, we start scheming over postings right from

[15] The 1980 data are compiled from the *IAS Civil List, 1981*.

[16] A candid discussion of IAS upward movement in one state is Mukerji, M. (IAS, Rajasthan), 'Climbing the Civil Service Pyramid Faster than Others', in Mukerji, M. (ed.), *Administrative Innovations in Rajasthan*, New Delhi, 1982, pp. 222–35.

the beginning. We want to go to a particular district, a particular subdivision, and so on.'[17] To get the right posts, IAS men and women lobby senior officials or, on occasion, discuss postings with relevant ministers. Individual IAS initiatives, as a major cause of IAS movement, are not a recent development. Such activity has been a constant feature of the ICS tradition. Rustomji (ICS, Assam) claims that in the days of the raj 'an ICS officer settled down to extracting as much enjoyment as possible from his existing post rather than busying himself angling for a lift'.[18] No doubt some played their career that way. Many others were more energetic. Mason (ICS, UP) reports that ICS men in the United Provinces in the 1930s were encouraged to state their preferences for posts; and without embarrassment he recounts angling for the ICS job in Garhwal.[19]

One final point: the whole issue of frequent transfers is one that does not apply only to the IAS. It affects most higher civil servants in India. Stories about transfers provide the most consistently absorbing topic of conversation when Indian administrators relax together. Everyone in government tends to get caught up in the business. Mukerji (IAS, Rajasthan), for example, called on the state Education Minister one Sunday morning at 11 o'clock. The Minister was in his study and Mukerji was asked to wait upstairs. Soon the Minister came up and said: 'Since 7 o'clock I am listening to requests for transfers without having my bath and breakfast. Thank you for giving me the excuse to get away.'[20]

POLITICAL WORK

The ICS in the 1920s and 1930s worked in secretariats and districts, making authoritative decisions, nursing support structures, and generally being involved in the conflicts in society and the political process in relation to them. Can one say the same of the IAS in the 1980s? Broadly speaking, one can, even though the political context of IAS work appears to have changed considerably. Jain (IAS, Haryana) remarked in 1983 that 'we are now working in a different external environment; greater political interference or let me call it political participation in administration is inherent in the democratic political

[17] Jain, N. K. (IAS, Haryana), 'Political Interference or Political Participation', in Jain, *Public Services*, p. 57.

[18] Rustomji, N., *Statesman*, 21 Oct. 1980, cited in Jain, ibid.

[19] Mason, *A Shaft of Sunlight*, p. 124.

[20] Mukerji, M., *Ham in the Sandwich: Lighter Side of Life in the IAS*, Ghaziabad, 1979, p. 13.

system that we have adopted for the governance of our country.'[21] Yet IAS work in secretariats and districts was not dissimilar to the work ICS administrators faced in the 1920s and 1930s—coping with relevant ministers in the secretariat (under both dyarchy and provincial autonomy) and having to engage directly with political elements in the district. This subject—IAS work within the political process—is an exceedingly large one, and can be treated here only in fairly summary fashion.[22]

As for the districts, the most blindingly obvious facts are perhaps also the most significant: (1) the district was still, in 1983, the basic unit of politics and administration within state government; (2) there were IAS Collectors at the head of the state apparatus in each district; (3) when the main change in district politics and administration was gradually introduced in most states in the late 1950s and 1960s—the creation of a system of interlinked elected local authorities in each district known as *panchayati raj*[23]—the IAS Collector was not made subordinate to these local authorities but instead presided over them from without. Like his ICS predecessor, the IAS Collector had literally thousands of enumerated powers as head of the magistracy, revenue collection, other government departments, and urban and rural local authorities. In exercising these powers, the IAS Collector engaged in a central way in the political process of the district.[24] A prime indicator of this was the fact that every Collector received a steady stream of 'pressure' from local, and not so local, politicians to use his or her powers to allocate scarce resources in a manner beneficial to particular interests. For example:

[21] Jain, N. K., 'Political Interference', p. 55.

[22] For an excellent summary of the Indian political process *c.*1983, see Brass, P., 'National Power and Local Politics in India: A Twenty Year Perspective', *MAS*, 18. 1 (1984), 89–118. One of the best earlier studies on IAS work within the political process, which also gives a number of detailed examples, is Bhambhri, *Bureaucracy and Politics*.

[23] A brief guide to the literature is Mathur, P. C., 'Panchayati Raj Research in India: A Survey of Bibliographic Sources', *Prashasnika*, iv. 3 and 4 (July & Dec. 1975), 64–9. *IJPA* reports on *panchayati raj* regularly.

[24] There is a very large literature on district administration in independent India. One of the best detailed studies is of North Arcot District by Heginbotham, *Cultures in Conflict*. Two other important studies are Desai, N. B., *Report on the Administrative Survey of the Surat District*, Bombay, Indian Society of Agricultural Economics, 1958; and the study of Meerut District by Kothari and Roy, *Relations between Politicians and Administrators*. Excellent studies of district politics are Brass, *Factional Politics* (five districts in UP); Weiner, *Party Building in a New Nation* (five districts in different states); Miller, D. F., *Pervasive Politics: Study of the Indian District*, (Melbourne Politics Monograph), Melbourne, 1972 (two districts in Karnataka—then Mysore). More generally, see Shukla, J. D. (ICS, UP), *State and District Administration in India*, Delhi, 1976.

1. The Collector had power to appoint Class III (or C) and Class IV (or D) public service personnel on a temporary or short-term basis; such powers were especially extensive in Kerala, Tamil Nadu, and Karnataka. Local politicians continually pressed Collectors to allocate jobs in a manner politically beneficial to them, for unemployment was a major problem and all politicians promise at election time to do something about it.

2. The Collector in most states had power over postings and transfers of employees (not just temporary) in Class III and IV services. Decisions in this area were of great personal importance to those involved. The Collector could use this power to reward supporters and punish opponents.

3. In some states the district supply officer was under the control of the Collector, who had authority to issue licences for fair price shops. Having such licences could be very lucrative, and local politicians struggled with the Collector over which influential persons in the district would be allocated such favours.

4. The Collector decided whether or not to evict illegal occupants of government or private land; controlled the allotment of surplus land in rural areas, and house sites and other plots in cities; and ordered the acquisition of private property for public services.

5. The Collector decided whether to proceed or to drop an action against smugglers of essential commodities, particularly food grains in border districts, and against hoarders and blackmarketeers. In some states controlling such illegal movement of commodities from less profitable to more profitable markets was left to subordinate revenue and police officials. In others (for instance, Tamil Nadu and Kerala) the Collector controlled, and once a lorry load of smuggled food grains was detained, political pressure normally was brought to bear on the Collector to free the goods and crew and to shield those involved, for such people were an easy and liberal source of finance for political parties.

6. The Collector was frequently involved in local issues in a district on which political parties took different sides. For example, a Collector had to decide whether or not to withdraw a court case arising from political conflict.

It was actions such as these—and there are innumerable examples—that brought government and top administrators like Collectors into the centre of political life in India far more so than administrators in the West.

More generally, Bayley has argued cogently with reference to the maintenance of law and order that scarcity in India within a democratic framework brings in its train considerable agitation involving militant organizations that government must attept to contain; in such circumstances, those responsible for maintaining law and order in a district, like IAS Collectors and the police, are engaged in an intensely political activity, where order and justice become 'benefits that government must allocate among competing claimants'.[25] The point applies not only to Collectors but also IAS officers in other district posts, for example, SDOs and town commissioners.[26]

In all such examples of allocation of scarce resources in the district, one almost never came across an IAS officer who claimed to be acting simply as a neutral observer, a passive arbiter. Any Collector was continually being pushed by politicians from different groupings to allocate scarce resources in one particular direction or another, and their active engagement in this arena of conflict and pressure involved them in the political process. Some Collectors were more easily pushed than others. Different types of IAS officer were frequently identified in the literature, for example, resisters, accommodators, detractors, promoters.[27] But such differences in style or character do not negate the basic point. This is, however, a rather negative way to put what one learned from talking to IAS Collectors or former Collectors: like their ICS predecessors they took definite *positions* when exercising their powers in the district. These positions varied from individual to individual; one IAS Collector would commit himself to implementing several particular features of a development programme and work to build public support for it; another would be committed to bringing about order in a district hitherto rent by conflict, and used his powers of reward and punishment with that aim in mind; a third would (more unusually) give top priority in his work to bringing about improved conditions for disadvantaged and destitute peoples in the

[25] Bayley, D. H., 'The Police and Political Order in India', *Asian Survey*, xxiii (Apr. 1983), 494–5.

[26] e.g. Bhatt, A., 'Municipal Commissioner in Gujarat: Structure, Process and Style', *Nagarlok*, 10 (1978), 122–37; Mukhopadhaya, A. (IAS, Rajasthan), 'Mr Red Tape is not all Black', *Statesman*, 10 Jan. 1982; the article refers in part to the work of Shri Pankaj (IAS, Rajasthan), an SDO in Alwar District, with whom Mukhopadhaya worked for a time.

[27] Ray, J. K., *Administrators in a Mixed Polity*, Delhi, 1981.

district; another (more usually) would pay more attention to meeting what he considered to be the legitimate demands of the dominant caste and would allocate scarce resources accordingly. Whatever the interest, an IAS Collector acting in the public arena would be continually nursing the base of support needed to assist, or at least not thwart, the pursuit of what he or she wanted done in the district on behalf of government. As in the days of the raj, handing-over notes were still left by departing Collectors to assist the incoming Collector with identifying who were the influential people in the district.

The other main aspect of political work in the district—keeping tabs on the state apparatus—was still performed by IAS Collectors, although the way it was done had changed considerably. An ICS Collector in the 1920s moved about rather grandly like a *raja*; in some regions each major family from villages near where the Collector was passing had to send a representative to attend him. Even in the late 1950s, there was still considerable fuss made over touring Collectors. In the early 1980s this no longer applied; the norm for Collectors was to move about quickly and unobtrusively by jeep. The perks that went with touring had gone. Now the thing to do, perkwise, was to call a small conference and have a 'five-star lunch'. But the purpose of touring the district inspecting subordinate administrators and their activities was similar. As for the changing political context in which ICS Collectors in the 1930s operated, changing political conditions also kept IAS Collectors alert in the 1980s. Whereas in the 1930s the changes related to the mobilization of the Indian National Congress, in the early 1980s it was the changing political complexion of the state government for whom Collectors worked—for example, Congress governments replaced Janata governments in 1980 in Bihar, Haryana, Madhya Pradesh, Orissa, Rajasthan, UP, and elsewhere, and at the beginning of 1983 Congress governments were voted out in Andhra Pradesh and Karnataka, to be replaced by others. Working within a changing political context has been the lot of both ICS and IAS Collectors.

Turning now to political work in the secretariat, in the days of the raj policy making was *shared* between the ICS Secretaries and executive heads, be they either Advisers (or Members) responsible to Governors-in-Council or ministers responsible to Legislative Assemblies. On major policy issues, a minister like Rajagopalachari in Madras or Ambedkar in Delhi could make a major contribution, although normally, on more routine policy decisions, the share-out left most of the power with the

ICS. IAS work in central and state secretariats was similar.[28] IAS Secretaries were at least as powerful as their ICS predecessors. This may appear surprising, given the more democratic context in which they worked. At the same time, however, the secretariat as a policy making arena was more powerful. There were two main reasons for this. First, the state was far more dominant in the life of the country than was the case previously. Second, there had been no corresponding decentralization of policy making power down the line out of the secretariat. And in the secretariat, the share-out still left power over most routine decisions primarily with IAS Secretaries. A minister may have said 'we want more mineral development' or 'get us some more cottage industries', and these were policies, but the numerous policy issues within such guide-lines, and the choices involved, were mostly dealt with by IAS Secretaries and other administrators in the secretariat.

The general picture is supported by evidence from studies of policy making in central government. A survey in 1974–5 of Members of Parliament from both Congress and opposition parties found 'an astonishingly widespread belief in the general ineffectiveness of the political executives as a class and the nearly decisive voice of the bureaucracy in the actual ordering of affairs in the land'. Two examples from these interviews with political leaders illustrate this view:

> Bureaucracy is a permanent fixture in India. A minister who is in conflict with his secretary is liable to forfeit his office. Only those ministers have been successful who know the knack of carrying on with the civil servants. The bureaucrats rule India; they know the politicians can do nothing without them.

> The secretary has a grasp of his subject and so can immediately make up his mind about the matter I take with me. Unless a particular thing goes against the announced policy decisions of the political executive, he can quickly take a

[28] The best accounts of secretariat work that get beyond the standard formal platitudes are in ICS/IAS autobiographies (e.g. in the bibliography). For the central secretariat, a good example is in Mangat Rai, E. (ICS, Punjab), *Commitment my Style*. For a state secretariat, Mukerji, M. (IAS, Rajasthan), *Non-Story of a Chief Secretary during Emergency et cetera*, New Delhi, 1982. More generally Kochanek, S., 'The Politics of Regulation: Rajiv's New Mantras', *Journal of Commonwealth and Comparative Politics*, xxiii. 3 (1985), 189–211; Avasthi, A., *Central Administration*, New Delhi, 1980; Maheshwari, S., 'The Political Executive and the Permanent Executive: An Analysis of the Emerging Role Patterns', *IJPA* xxvi. 3 (1980), 739–49; Maheshwari, S., *State Government in India*, Delhi, 1979; Halappa, G. S., (ed.), *Studies in State Administration*, Dharwar, 1972, which is particularly good on the secretariat in Karnataka (formerly Mysore).

decision. Most ministers don't know their jobs and would like to depend on their civil servants.[29]

Other studies at that time of policy making in the Government of India complement the general position suggested by these MPs. An analysis of the agendas of the Cabinet and its Political Affairs Committee in 1972–3, for example, showed that they were mainly involved with issues for decisions which were (*a*) inherently sensitive, (*b*) nationally urgent, (*c*) related to the work of Parliament and its committees, or (*d*) related to party matters; policy matters in development and other fields received comparatively little attention.[30] An important study of policy making at the centre in the 1970s showed that the ministers and the political leadership generally made a 'limited contribution' to the content of policy as worked out in committees; the political leadership contributed broad goals only.[31] An informed appraisal of policy making in 1983 by one of the authors of this study reached the conclusion that what they had found in the 1970s still broadly applied, with 'the political system still under-represented in the process'.[32] Policy making in more traditional areas like law and order was still dominated by senior administrators and technocrats, with ministers involved in only a general way. As regards security questions, for example, the question of whether or not to impose President's Rule in the Punjab in 1983 was for the political leadership, but all the detailed questions of implementation and political calculation were left almost entirely in the hands of senior administrators and the intelligence agencies; in the Punjab case, the three Advisers sent to rule there were all IAS, and they were briefed before they left for Chandigarh by the Home Secretary and a Cabinet Secretary (both IAS).[33] In the autumn of 1983, it was noticeable that the Prime Minister met with her top civil servants at least as frequently as with her ministers.[34]

Policy making at state level in the early 1980s was similar. An experienced IAS officer from Uttar Pradesh, for example, gave me a

[29] Maheshwari, S., 'Constituency Linkage of National Legislators in India', *Legislative Studies Quarterly*, 1. 3 (1976), 347.

[30] Jain, H. M., 'Decision Making at the Centre', *Journal of the Society for Study of State Governments*, (Jan.–Mar. 1979).

[31] Dayal, I., Mathur, K., et al. *Dynamics of Formulating Policy in Government of India*, Delhi, 1976.

[32] Mathur, K., to the author in a personal interview at IIPA, New Delhi, 1 Dec. 1983.

[33] As reported in *Indian Express*, 8 Oct. 1983, 1.

[34] I am grateful to Professor C. P. Bhambhri of Jawaharlal Nehru University for this observation, made to the author during an interview in New Delhi, 28 Sept. 1983. See also e.g. anon., 'Rule by PM's Secretariat', *EPW*, xvii (13–20 Nov. 1982), 1843, 1845.

very detailed description of policy making in the Hills Development Department of the secretariat at that time.[35] Summarizing, the overall objectives of government in the way of guide-lines were provided each year in the Finance Minister's Budget Speech. Apart from that, he said, the political leadership provided little in the way of policy input. Occasionally, a powerful and resourceful minister would take charge and push hard for clear policies energetically applied, and then things were done. But usually it was difficult for them to have much impact on policy, since their main attraction was directed elsewhere at the political manœuvres in legislature, etc. When they had time, ministers would sit for hours in committee meetings discussing some programme, while IAS Secretaries presented one difficulty after another and continually looked at their watches. Ministers had ideas; 'they are not fools', he said, and they are 'underplayed' in the files. Nevertheless, the detailed content of most programmes was controlled by IAS Secretaries and other administrators in the secretariat. Many policy initiatives came from below, from technical experts like engineers, doctors, and economists, and their problem was to get the senior secretariat officers to move on their proposals. Various stratagems had been developed to this end. Senior Secretaries, he said, may have little in the way of clear objectives or plans, but the ICS tradition had 'elevated them' to the prime position in the middle of the policy process between the political leadership on one side and the people with the expertise on the other.

The ICS tradition continued in the early 1980s in terms of a similar broad share-out of power over policy making between ICS Secretaries and ministers or executive heads. Clearly there were also important differences when one got down to the details of IAS behaviour patterns. There was far more contact between business organizations and IAS Secretaries in certain ministries.[36] Also, the old imperial constraint from London had been replaced by the somewhat different constraint represented by international business and financial institutions working to influence the shape of government policy.[37] This was matched by another new development—increasing numbers of IAS officers being sent abroad for in-service training.[38] Modern IAS officers, when

[35] UP001 to the author in an extended interview with written back-up, New Delhi, 19 and 23 Sept. 1983.

[36] Kochanek, *Business and Politics*, pp. 274–5.

[37] e.g. Posgate, 'Fertilizers', 733–50. Bhambhri, C. P., *The World Bank and India*, New Delhi, 1980.

[38] Ramakrishna, C. S., 'A Preliminary Survey of Exchange Programmes between the United States and India', (July 1983) mimeo. GOI PAR, *Annual Report 1982–83*. '21 IAS men in MP to go for training abroad', *Indian Express*, 17 May 1982.

dealing with political forces, also behaved in certain detailed ways rather differently from the detailed ways of their ICS predecessors. There were, however, some exaggerated notions on this score, principally that IAS officers on the whole tended to bend more when coping with political pressure and that levels of corruption had increased. Increased corruption may be characteristic of the Indian bureaucracy generally (a subject that cannot be pursued here),[39] but seasoned IAS watchers in India in 1983 claimed that such behaviour was uncharacteristic of the IAS. Any successful political administrator must bend to some extent when dealing with politicians, must be resilient and accommodating while holding firmly to the law and basic principles, and there were instances of IAS officers who may have given way too much. Also, there may have been four times as many instances of corruption in the IAS as there were in the ICS (and there were a few between 1919 and 1947), but then there were four times as many IAS in the early 1980s. On the whole, the number of corrupt IAS officers was still very small indeed.

Looking across the range of behaviour patterns in the IAS, one can certainly point to important differences, but that basic feature of central engagement with the political process as part of a particular work pattern in secretariats and districts at all levels of the state had been carried forward from the days of the raj. There was ICS/IAS continuity as regards that general work pattern, and also considerable change within that pattern. It is the general pattern informing IAS work in secretariats and districts that has been of primary concern in this book. As Asok Mitra (ICS, Bengal) remarked in 1981: 'Politics, let there be no mistake, is the senior civil servant's breath and staff of life, whether he perceives it or not in the tasks he performs.'[40]

GENTLEMEN OF THE SERVICE CLASS

The six gentlemanly and service class norms and values singled out for attention in this study were still prominent in 1983 in the administrative tradition carried by the IAS, as the analysis in Chapter 5 has suggested. Several additional points need to be made, however, by way of a broader summing up.

[39] See Gopinath, P. K., 'Corruption in Political and Public Offices: Causes and Cure', *IJPA* xxviii. 4 (1982), 897–918. Hager, L. M., 'Bureaucratic Corruption in India: Legal Control of Maladministration', *Comparative Political Studies*, 6. 2 (1973), 197–219; Kabra, K. N., *The Black Economy in India: Problems and Policies*, Delhi, 1982.

[40] Mitra, A. (ICS, Bengal), 'Guardians of the Law: Reflections on the Indian Administrative Service', *Administrator*, xxvi. 1 (1981), 2.

The first is to notice the composition of the IAS in 1983 in terms of avenues of recruitment. Most members (76.7 per cent) had entered the IAS as a result of the competitive examinations held each year since 1948 (those who had entered through the 1948 exam were on the verge of retirement in 1983), while 23.3 per cent had entered by promotion from another administrative service, or in a few cases, as a result of a 'special' exam or other special scheme.[41] The overall percentage of promotees in 1983 was close to the percentage figure for each individual state cadre, with only a few exceptions.

Table 20. *Promotees to IAS by State, 1983*

IAS cadre	No. of IAS	% of promotees	IAS cadre	No. of IAS	% of promotees
Andhra Pradesh	288	24	Maharashtra	294	23
Assam	159	28	Manipur-Tripura	97	31
Bihar	319	24	Nagaland	42	26
Gujarat	181	9	Orissa	191	25
Haryana	150	24	Punjab	162	23
Himachal Pradesh	95	25	Rajasthan	205	23
Jammu & Kashmir	80	31	Sikkim	25	0
Karnataka	207	23	Tamil Nadu	265	23
Kerala	143	24	Union Territories	161	26
Madhya Pradesh	331	24	Uttar Pradesh	453	24.5
			West Bengal	244	19

All-India average = 23.3%
All-India no. = 4,092
Source: Compiled from individual biographical entries in *IAS Civil List, 1983*, pp. 2–216.

The data in Table 20 show only a few marked deviations from the overall average. The Gujarat cadre had very few promotees (and Sikkim was a special case) whereas Manipur-Tripura and Jammu and Kashmir, each with 31 per cent promotees, were unusual on the other side. Nearly a quarter of the IAS being made up of promotees represented a change from the position under the raj when a substantial number of persons from other administrative services holding listed (ICS) posts were not considered members of the ICS and were not allowed to put ICS after their names. Nevertheless, the distinction within the IAS between promotees and regular recruits should not be exaggerated. It would be misleading, for example, to regard promotees as second-rate, or 'lowering the standard' of the IAS. There were too many instances of promotees who were widely

[41] Figures compiled from *IAS Civil List, 1983*, on the basis of data in Appendix 1.

regarded as outstanding administrators. One consequence of having promotees in the IAS that caused some concern was that it tampered with the all-India character of the Service by increasing the proportion of IAS people working in a state cadre who came from that state. Regular recruits as the dominant element in the IAS continued to be allotted to cadres of states not their own, thereby justifying the IAS as all-India, but there was no doubt that by 1983, with nearly a quarter of the IAS being promotees, the IAS had become somewhat less all-India (in terms of allotment) than its predecessor, even though this was bound to be so because ICS Europeans never had any 'home' province.

In considering the extent to which gentlemanly and service class norms and values persisted in the IAS, it is important to notice that no such research had been done on the promotees—indeed, almost nothing was known about them generally. In Chapter 5 there is an analysis of the regular recruits, and this can be supplemented by the considerable research that has been done on their social background. The general picture this research presents is very clear. Regular recruits up to the early 1980s came overwhelmingly from the service class and were products of the 'better' schools and colleges. Roughly 94 per cent of all the regular recruits up to 1956 were from that class background (50 per cent from civil service families).[42] By the 1980s these early recruits had reached the very top of the IAS. Those recruited between 1957 and 1963 also came mainly from the same background (81 per cent urban professional middle class, 44 per cent of whom were from civil service families), although recruits from rural landowning families began to figure in the data.[43] After 1963 there was a gradual increase in the proportion of regular recruits and promotees from lower classes. Nevertheless, the IAS as a whole still came predominantly from the service class in the 1980s. IAS regular recruits for the years 1980 and 1981 (253 persons) showed 71 per cent from that class, 19 per cent from 'agriculture', and the remaining 10 per cent being in an 'other' category not specified.[44] No one disputed the general class background of the IAS. The main issue was whether the IAS should be more 'representative' of the wider society, which it clearly was not—about 10 per cent of India's work-force was 'middle class'.

There were two definite changes from the ICS tradition in terms of

[42] Subramaniam, *Social Background*, chs. 2 and 7. [43] Ibid.

[44] Singh, S. N., 'A Study of the Recruitment Pattern of the IAS', *Administrator*, xxvii. 2 (1982), 341.

social background. Firstly, a small but growing proportion of people from scheduled castes and scheduled tribes were recruited, helping to give the IAS a less exclusive background than the ICS had. Places had been reserved for such candidates since the 1950s, although the quotas were rarely filled at that time. The government actually set up coaching centres where such candidates could work for a fully supported year to prepare for the examination.[45] By the end of the 1970s quotas were being regularly filled. By 1982 10.1 per cent of IAS were from scheduled castes, 5.4 per cent from scheduled tribes.[46] Secondly, the IAS was not a male preserve as the ICS had been; the first woman entered in 1951; the first female Collector (Sarla Khanna, IAS, Punjab) was appointed in 1956; and since the mid-1960s, 10–15 per cent of IAS recruits each year have been women.[47] As of January 1983, 7 per cent of the IAS as a whole were women.[48]

The other major feature of this steady stream of young men and women into the IAS from mostly professional urban service-class family backgrounds was their facility with the English language. To gain entry to the IAS, it was necessary to speak, read, and write the English language very well indeed. (This had also, of course, been true for ICS Indians.) Until the 1970s English was exclusively the medium of the IAS examination. Also a viva voce was part of the examination process until the 1970s and it is clear, for example, from what Taub's IAS informants told him, that some of the qualities interviewers looked for were 'pleasant manners, facility in English, an attractive appearance and dress (preferably English style) and an authoritative manner'.[49] Even when it became possible in the 1970s to take the examination in any of the languages listed in the Eighth Schedule of the Indian Constitution, only a very few opted for a language other than English. In 1981, for example, 92 per cent of the candidates wrote the examination in English, 5.5 per cent in Hindi, 2.5 per cent in other regional languages.[50] To achieve the standard of English required

[45] Isaacs, H., *India's Ex-untouchables*, New York, 1965, p. 109.

[46] GOI PAR *Annual Report*, 1982–3, (1983), p. 13.

[47] For details, see Vithayathil, T., 'Women in the IAS', *Journal of the National Academy of Administration*, 16, 4 (1971), 91–8; Swarnlata, 'Women in the All India Services', *Prashasnika*, 9, 4 (1982), 39–48; the references to Ms Khanna is in Mangat Rai, *Patterns of Administrative Development*, p. 58.

[48] Compiled from the *IAS Civil List, 1983*.

[49] Taub, *Bureaucrats under Stress*, p. 38. See also, more generally, Mishra, R. K. (IAS, Orissa), *How I Passed the IAS Exams*, Allahabad, 1958.

[50] As reported in Srinath, M., 'Heavy Rush for Central Service Jobs', *Hindustan Times*, 29 May 1982.

meant lengthy preparation, preferably with English the medium of instruction in school (not English learned as a foreign language). A survey made of the 531 IAS recruits who entered between 1974 and 1979 showed that 60.3 per cent had been educated in 'English medium schools'.[51] Such schools were rather special: most of them were affiliated to the Council for the Indian School Certificate Examinations; there were only about 350 such schools in all of India in 1983, including 36 public schools modelled on their counterparts in England.[52] When I asked one well-informed observer of the educational scene in India, who had been associated with the Council for many years, what stood out about these schools apart from English being the medium of instruction, he replied at some length on the following lines:[53] emphasis on (1) discipline and respect for authority; (2) building character, leadership qualities, and what he called 'stature'; (3) 'respect for others'; (4) 'good manners and dress'; (5) competence in games 'but not professionally'—he said the members of the West Indian cricket team touring India at the time of the interview were brilliant, very professional, but 'not gentlemanly'.

Gentlemanly recruits from a broadly similar social class continued to enter the IAS from 1948 to the 1980s. Coming from that background, being shaped by their seniors in the Service, and then working their adult lives in IAS posts at the top of the service class in Indian society, produced in these men and women a strong attachment to service-class values. Three were central to the ICS tradition: (1) the high valuation placed on being a loyal servant of the government under the constitution; (2) in exchange for that loyal service, the importance of trust being reposed in them by the political leadership; (3) as a measure of that trust, the expectation that they be given considerable autonomy and discretion to act appropriately (in accordance with law) for those they served. In addition, the gentlemanly mode emphasized (4) the virtue of public service, (5) the amateur ideal, and (6) the norms of courage, confidence, and self-discipline. The analysis in Chapter 5 suggests that these gentlemanly and service class norms and values were still important ingredients of IAS thinking and behaviour at the National Academy of Administration in Mussoorie and elsewhere, although they were increasingly under attack in the 1970s and early

[51] Saxena, N. C. (IAS, UP), 'The World of the IAS', *Administrator*, xxvi, 1 (1981), 19.

[52] Council for the Indian School Certificate Examinations, *List of Affiliated Schools, 1980*, 1980, privately printed.

[53] To the author in a personal interview, 30 Nov. 1983, New Delhi.

1980s. When talking with IAS people in 1983, the extent to which these 'traditional' norms and values had been undermined proved to be (along with transfers) the subject uppermost in their minds.

I encounted three broad types of position on this issue. One was what amounted to total cynicism. A senior IAS in Tamil Nadu represented the position well.[54] In contrast to 1967 when I first interviewed him, he said that now 'the gentlemanly code and the traditional service values that went with it' were 'no longer relevant' in that 'one doesn't use these ideas in conversation or as a defence of action because doing so makes you look ridiculous'. Political corruption and black money loomed very large in his explanation of these developments. He intimated that most administrators, apart from 'certain exceptions like Appu in Bihar', had become part of this corrupt scene, either becoming actually involved or passively winking at such practices because they had no power to control them. Top administrators as a class had become 'the link between politicians and the business class'. Those IAS holding this point of view were not entirely consistent about it, but generally considered that there had been an emasculation of traditional values which they personally thought was deplorable.

A second position was marked by uncertainty. A senior Secretary in New Delhi, formerly a Chief Secretary in Uttar Pradesh, sketched it this way.[55] Traditional service values 'no longer have the acceptance they once did'. The change began to take place from about 1970 onwards, and there has been 'no settled tradition yet to take its place'. Uncertainty centres on the reward structure. Previously civil servants had clear ideas about the type of behaviour that would be rewarded or punished; furthermore, 'control over that, judgements about it, were in the hands of the civil service itself'. Now, increasingly, 'these standards for reward or punishment can no longer be identified—lip-service is still paid to the old conventions and values but they no longer provide working criteria.' New values had entered in from 'outside', and 'civil servants can no longer define what acceptable and unacceptable behaviour is'. Newer values emphasized 'political loyalty, flexibility, and also merit, but merit is only one amongst others'. Such uncertainty about service norms had been the principal reason for 'low IAS morale'. The position was broadly linked to the view that there had been 'political interference' in the autonomy of the IAS which had hampered

[54] T571 to the author in personal interviews 15 and 22 Nov. 1983, Madras City.
[55] U531 to the author in a personal interview, 27 Sept. 1983, New Delhi.

their ability to act fearlessly (for instance, in advising ministers) in accordance with traditional norms and values.

A third main position was close to the previous one but more confident and certain about the existing reward structure. It was outlined to me by an IAS officer I first got to know well in 1960 when he was a Collector in Rajasthan; in 1983 he had gone to the very top of the civil service in the Government of India.[56] He was not whitewashing the issue by summarizing some 'official' position, because he simply does not operate that way. Certainly (he said) IAS people, on the whole, are less certain now that behaviour in accordance with traditional service norms provide the criteria that really count in assessments about promotion and desirable postings. The main reason for this was the rather more turbulent politics the IAS went through from 1975 to the early 1980s—the Congress (I) Emergency, then Janata, then Congress (I) again, which certainly 'distorted the previous tranquillity' in administration. But many IAS, he claims, overdo the effects of this experience. Moreover, they use it as an 'alibi' for current mistakes or administrative lapses. Despite the worry and uncertainty, which is genuine and widespread, 'rewards still are given to those who follow the traditional values of the civil service'. This is evident to anyone who understands the actual working of the reward structure and the behaviour patterns of those who have done well within it.

All three positions shared at least one common view: that the gentlemanly and service class norms and values identified in this study have been part of the tradition of their service and ought to continue. I did not meet an IAS officer who denied that public service was virtuous, generalists ought to be in charge, behaviour in service should be courageous, confident, and self-disciplined, and that relations between them and their political masters ought to be marked by loyal service, trust, and considerable autonomy. Even the small minority of IAS cynics, who denied that these norms and values were relevant or existed any more in the civil service, were convinced of their worth and lamented their absence.

Although the ICS tradition has changed since 1919, its essentials were still evident in the 1980s in terms of IAS location and movement, engagement in the political process, and the high valuation placed on gentlemanly norms and values. There were many other issues relevant to the IAS in the early 1980s—declining pay scales relative to the

[56] R501 to the author in a personal interview, 29 Nov. 1983, New Delhi.

private sector was one that came to the fore in 1983—but the concern here has been to concentrate on the main features from the raj and to ascertain whether they were still there in the early 1980s. For it was these features that had broader administrative consequences.

SOME BROADER CONSEQUENCES

The content of the ICS tradition was not only the concern of IAS men and women within it, for it has also influenced the behaviour of other administrators and affected the general character of the Indian state structure as a whole. The subject is a large one, and goes beyond the main concerns of this study. To do it justice would require rather different (comparative) research and another book. What follows here, therefore, are hypotheses only, suggesting that three broad features of government in India in the early 1980s were consequences, at least in part, of aspects of the ICS tradition.

The first broad feature of government was the general behaviour pattern of lower-level administrators in India, who tended to be excessively *deferential* to their superiors and excessively *rule-bound*. A study by Mook in Tamil Nadu, published in 1982 illustrates these two orientations.[57] Mook and his four assistants interviewed 344 people in the Education and Agriculture Departments working in four districts—Madras, Chingleput, Thajavur, South Arcot. The bulk of the interviewing was done in 1970–1; there were follow-up studies in 1974 and 1976. Each respondent was interviewed at length, and considerable attention was given to getting beyond the tendency of administrators in India to give what they regard as 'correct' answers. Dilemmas were posed for respondents and the interviewers then probed as to why the respondents took the position they did (and respondents in this study frequently changed their minds after such probing). Another unusual feature of this study was the comparison, deliberately built into the research design, of field administration in a more traditional, inspection-oriented department (Education) with a less traditional, more development-oriented department (Agriculture). This comparison enabled Mook and his associates to address a major issue in studies of Indian administrators—is it culture or structure that determines behaviour and attitudes? The two departments had different structures and procedural norms, and the respondents in

[57] Mook, *World of the Indian Field Administrator.*

each department did differ in their responses to questions; yet respondents in both departments had similar social backgrounds. The analysis suggests that culture (social background) cannot account for the different responses, whereas structure more clearly does so.

The two main categories of field administrators interviewed in the four district were Deputy Inspector of Schools (DI) and Agricultural Extension Officer (AEO). Although they differed in their responses, Mook found that they both shared the following general orientations as regards behaviour and attitudes:

Lack of influence Subordinate officers feel that they cannot do much toward initiating a policy or modifying a programme. One must accept one's place.

Obedience Since one has no resources, one cannot fight.

Paternalism In return for such obedience, superiors should protect subordinates.

Insecurity and hostility Subordinates never know what a superior will demand of them or how he will evaluate them.

Formalism The best way to protect oneself is to stick to rules.

Isolation One has one's job to do. The help of others, either in the organization or outside it, is to be called for only when absolutely necessary.

Emphasis on status Superiors in their department doubt their own competence and knowledge, and therefore demand that subordinates do not threaten them.

Deviations from these basic orientations were more frequent among AEOs than among DIs. For example, AEOs tended to have more interpersonal contact with both the public and other members of their department; in dealing with the frustrations of paperwork, AEOs criticized more, made excuses more, and searched for alibis more; relations between AEOs and their superiors were based more on persuasion, exchange of substantive information, and agreed-upon areas of competence.

Running through these basic orientations was 'the overriding importance which subordinates place on obeying superiors and rules'. Almost without exception, Mook's respondents 'regarded such compliance as their most important duty' (p. 143). The immediate reason why subordinates obeyed superiors was not because of who the superiors were but rather because of what they could do. In an economy marked by unemployment or underemployment, security of position was the most important thing for subordinate administrators. Mook's respondents divulged repeatedly their fear of such things as adverse remarks on their Confidential Reports, being transferred, or being sacked (rare, but when it happened occasionally it completely dominated conversation in administrative offices over a wide area). For most subordinates 'doing one's duty' meant 'pleasing superiors'. No one defied an order openly. If an AEO or DI decided not to obey an order, or (more likely) could not obey, he simply 'cooked up' figures for the superior officer issuing the order or had a plausible excuse ready. Pleasing superiors even extended to doing personal favours for them. Such deference did not normally increase promotion chances because of the widespread system of promotion by seniority, but it helped to insure the subordinate against 'superior capriciousness in personnel matters'.

Looking at such relationships from the other end, Mook reported that 'many superiors who are unsure of their own authority encourage deference and obedience by stressing the symbols and rituals of power'. A widespread practice was not to offer a chair to a subordinate staff member when the latter entered the office. Superiors also encouraged obedience by insisting that rules and regulations had to be observed; such behaviour of course ran with the interest of subordinates, for whom the best way to protect oneself against superiors was to stick to rules.

There is little evidence in Mook's findings that these obedience relationships were resented by subordinates. On the contrary, they were accepted without question for the most part. For Mook, this marked deference was a perfectly 'rational' orientation to the institutional context in which they worked. His research shows that subordinate administrators reasoned as follows: since 'all decisions are taken at the *top* level of one's department . . . things are not in my hands, nor are they in the hands of my superior; only Government knows, and I cannot have any dealings with Government' (p. 146). Furthermore, since real power was so far away, there was no point in criticizing an immediate superior since he was only carrying out decisions made by others. Mook found specifically that both AEOs and DIs were willing to excuse their superiors' lapses; for one thing, their superiors were believed to be close to the centre of decision making and therefore 'they must have many problems with *their* superiors'. In addition, 'because subordinates understand problems of overwork and harrassment, they are reluctant to criticize men whose poor performance may be caused by similar difficulties' (p. 147). The seniority system, which Mook's respondents preferred over promotion by merit, also helps to account for these attitudes. So, docility, deference, obedience, accepting one's place, and sticking to rules characterized the behaviour and attitudes of subordinate field administrators in Tamil Nadu, although there appeared to be certain differences between field administrators in more traditional, regulatory departments as compared with people like AEOs in departments oriented more towards development.

These particular characteristics of administrative life were not peculiar to Tamil Nadu. Mook's findings are convincing because of the thoroughness and care with which the research was carried out, but they are not inconsistent with the main findings of much other research on administrators elsewhere in India. A well-known study of administrators in Meerut District (Uttar Pradesh) found that two norms in particular governed behaviour: follow rules and defer to superiors;[58] interviews with middle-level administrators in four states, including Maharashtra, resulted in a characterization of the spirit of Indian bureaucracy as top-heavy, over-codified, and monopolized by generalists;[59] after working in central government for more than twenty years, Ram framed the following laws of bureaucratic behaviour: never do anything on your own for the first time (i.e. find a precedent), avoid responsibility if you can, pay is a function of the number of hours spent in the office and not that of productivity or achieving results;[60] and there are numerous other examples in the literature on public administration suggesting that an excess of rule-bound deference was common amongst lower-level administrators in India. Why?

To some extent, perhaps, these characteristics are typical of lower-level civil servants everywhere. As McCleery archly remarked years ago, 'the administrative policy of playing it safe, of never deciding anything more than is necessary, of never stirring up the animals or challenging organized interests is as natural as sin . . . as normal as falling down . . .'[61] But to fall back on some supposed human nature of

[58] Kothari and Roy, *Relations between Politicians and Administrators*.

[59] Subhas Rao, K., 'The Unchanging Bureaucracy', *Public Administration* (India), 12 (Apr. 1974), 6–11.

[60] Ram, N. V. R., *Games Bureaucrats Play*, New Delhi, 1978.

[61] McCleery, M., 'On remarks taken out of context', *Public Administration Review*, 103 (Sept. 1964), 162.

civil servants does not provide a convincing explanation. Of the various factors involved it seems that the institutional structure in which these civil servants worked was of major importance. That structure in India in the early 1980s was highly centralized. Administrative power tended to be gathered together into the hands of a small group of élite administrators located strategically in districts and secretariats. This was a broad consequence of the ICS, designed originally to allow a few trusted administrators to oversee a vast apparatus that they felt could not be wholly trusted. In the early 1980s these strategic posts still existed and were, in practice, reserved for the IAS or some other 'superior' service to which lower-level administrators had no hope of access. In consequence, there was an extraordinary distance between the highly structured world of lower-level civil servants and the awesome people in those strategic posts who made the rules that governed that world. In such an extremely stratified structure, deferring to superiors and following rules carefully were sensible things to do. In short, I am suggesting (and further research is needed) that lower-level civil servants in India were not innately deferential and rule-bound; to a large extent, working in an institutional structure organized to accommodate an ICS tradition of administration had made them so.

A second broad characteristic of government in India was referred to by an IAS officer in 1971 as 'those subterranean feelings of mistrust and hostility between the politician and the civil servant, which nobody will dispute often has been harmful to both'.[62] 'It is easy to see', said another commentator in 1978, why the ICS and IAS were 'the prime targets of the politicians from the very beginning', for they controlled other services, ran the administration, and 'had the most intimate contact with politicians at all levels from the District up to the Central Secretariat and were therefore privy to all the secrets of the trade'.[63] Despite instances of civil servants working well with politicians, with basic trust on both sides, the difficulty of such relationships was a problem IAS members wanted to discuss most of all in 1983. Why was it such a problem?

One reason was that, due to the structural aspect of the continuing ICS tradition, the IAS held centralized administrative power at a very high level in the state. This contributed to much misunderstanding

[62] Badrinath (IAS, Tamil Nadu), 'Urban Development of Greater Madras', (report presented to the Government of Tamil Nadu privately, mimeo., 1970), p. 78.

[63] Vohra, 'Anatomy of Mal-administration', 14.

and distrust between the IAS and politicians, both of whom engaged in political work. Equally relevant was the IAS attachment to service-class values as part of their tradition. These values served to suggest a kind of bargain between IAS and politicians: we shall give you loyal service in exchange for you not invading our rightful autonomy in carrying out our responsibilities. Any such invasion of autonomy was bound to be keenly resented. The persistence of these values contributed to the extraordinary preoccupation of IAS people with political *interference* (in what they took to be their legitimate domain). Accusations of interference in the higher reaches of the bureaucracy received far more prominence in the Indian press and academic writings than in other countries. For example, violation of administrative autonomy figured prominently in an analysis by one of India's leading political scientists in 1982 of the enormous danger of the disintegration of the Indian State. 'The culture of violence and thuggery permitted and even nurtured over the last two years, and which has become a substitute for party politics, is now likely to spread upwards,' he argued; and after making various suggestions about what could be done, he concluded by saying that 'above all there is need to strengthen the autonomy of the administration and the Federal process all the way even to the districts with a large measure of autonomy at all levels'.[64]

The whole idea of administrators having the right to be largely autonomous within the state was no doubt bound up with liberal democratic ideology and the 'Rule of Law'. But the notion appeared to be foreign to increasing numbers of politicians being elected to state governments. Their attempts, commendable in many ways, to get a grip on their 'autonomous' administrators adversely affected the working of democratic government in India and the performance of the state.

A third and final broad characteristic was the general orientation of the state bureaucracy as a whole, which found it easier to cope with problems of unity, stability, and order, than with problems requiring innovation, specialist expertise, and responsiveness to local demands. This characteristic was usually couched within a crude dichotomy between the old law-and-order administration and the new development administration, and the need to move from the old to the new. Such a dichotomy must be rejected. The relation between order and development is complex, but surely some order is a prerequisite for

[64] Kothari, R., 'Stemming the Rot', *Indian Express*, 2 June 1982.

development and, over time, some development is a prerequisite for order. Moreover, some areas within the Indian state in the early 1980s were expert, innovative, and responsive; and this was true also in the days of the raj, although to a lesser extent. Nevertheless, that general orientation towards order was built into the overall fabric of administration.

Any explanation of this general characteristic would almost certainly have to identify the continuation of the ICS tradition as a major contributor. Order was of pre-eminent concern for the raj, and central to the ICS tradition. In each district a Collector from an all-India service controlled and co-ordinated. The fact that the Collector was also a magistrate signified the inevitable preoccupation of this controller with public order as a first priority among other priorities. At the state level the secretariat, headed mainly by Secretaries who were shaped in districts, controlled the resources for which other administrators had to bid and directed the work of other administrative departments not directly concerned with maintaining order. The position of the secretariat in central government was similar. In this way, the rest of the bureaucratic structure was more or less locked into this central frame oriented towards order. The value of the frame for political leaders at the centre was repeatedly demonstrated after independence whenever there were political crises, like the temporary breakdown of democratic government in a state and the imposition of President's Rule or of a National Emergency (as in 1975). A single group of political administrators in a national frame controllable from the centre was a most useful mechanism in such circumstances. Through it, the centre had a very long reach, despite federalism, into possible breakaway or rebellious regions. Even in more normal times the value of such a frame for the state leadership had been indisputable. In the years after independence, it helped to hold the polity together and also enabled Indian governments to deliver certain benefits for the voters, as part of a general political process that seemed to work. It certainly seemed to work in contrast to the experience of some other post-colonial countries, where the rapid dissolution of their colonial bureaucracies led to almost total non-performance. Hanson underlined the point at the high noon of decolonization, when he said that the Congress Party in India 'wields the powerful, unpopular, but essential weapon of the IAS, that "steel frame" which was Britain's most valuable legacy to independent

India'.[65] A bureaucracy whose 'natural' orientation day by day was towards problems of unity, stability, order could be said to be both a consequence of the maintenance of the ICS tradition of administration and one of the strengths of the Indian state.

That orientation was also a weakness. It was widely recognized that successful implementation of development programmes initiated by governments required a bureaucracy which (*a*) was innovative, (*b*) could bring to bear on local problems a wide range of specialist expertise, and (*c*) could respond quickly to local demands for such expertise. It was also widely recognized that these characteristics were not 'natural' within the Indian bureaucracy as a whole. Many IAS individuals were staunch proponents of development and gave it a high priority. It was even argued, as Bhatt did forcefully,[66] that an IAS generalist in district or secretariat, when viewed as an individual, could be considered an effective development man or woman. But to make these points about IAS individuals was to miss the broader consequences of the general administrative tradition these individuals sustained. What even the most enlightened IAS officer often failed to see was that their own tradition resulted in a more general orientation throughout the bureaucracy as a whole that de-emphasized these characteristics so important for sustained, successful development administration.

For one thing, the whole posture of the ICS tradition resulted in the celebration of amateur generalists in control at each level, thereby defining specialist expertise and innovation as somewhat peripheral and less rewarding. Any parliamentary democracy requires both generalist and specialist civil servants on tap equally for the political leadership of the day. As for receptiveness to local demands, rapid movement from one type of control post to another, utterly appropriate for gentlemanly amateurs, tended both to produce administrative fragmentation between mobile officers and more stationary civil servants at lower levels and to incline the IAS to identify primarily with the centre, not the locality.[67] Also a highly mobile IAS moving between control posts probably required more elaborate records and paperwork

[65] Hanson, *The Process of Planning*, p. 254. The point is also made forcefully by Tinker, H., *India and Pakistan: A Political Analysis*, New York, 1962, pp. 166–7.

[66] Bhatt, A., 'Colonial Bureaucratic Culture and Development Administration: Portrait of an Old-fashioned Indian Bureaucrat', *Journal of Commonwealth and Comparative Politics*, 17, 2 (1979), 159–75.

[67] The classic study of this administrative phenomenon is Kaufman, H., *The Forest Ranger: A Study in Administrative Behaviour*, Baltimore, 1967.

(red tape) throughout the bureaucracy than was otherwise necessary, adversely affecting the ability of administrators to respond quickly to development initiatives from local groups. It is likely that movement also resulted in less effective administrative leadership; sales tax administration in the early 1980s was identified as one such area where administrative leadership was needed and the IAS could not provide it because they moved too quickly.[68] Behind such particulars was the general proposition found in organization theory—that high rates of turnover are broadly associated with low organizational efficiency. The centrality of rapid movement as a problem in development administration has only recently been recognized. One scholar claimed in 1982: 'Any serious discussion of how India's development administration can be made to work better must put personnel transfers near the top of the agenda for reform.'[69] Another called transfers the 'slipping clutch' of India's efforts to promote development by means of the government bureaucracy.[70] The more one looked at India's bureaucracy, particularly in the districts, the more it appeared a rather blunt instrument for development purposes.[71] Other consequences mentioned earlier are relevant here—including the tendency of subordinate civil servants to be excessively rule-bound and deferential. A good illustration of the problems involved can be found in a study of the administration of economic development programmes at the end of the 1960s in North Arcot District, Tamil Nadu, by Heginbotham.[72] The picture suggested there is one of an enlightened, active IAS Collector, eager to see development programmes succeed, and of administrative subordinates in the district unable to achieve results because of the stultifying structures and procedures within which they had to work.[73]

In sum, the persistence of the ICS tradition resulted in a general

[68] Purohit, M. C., 'Sales Tax Administration in India', *IJPA* xxviii, 4 (1982), 832–9.

[69] Wade, R., 'Corruption: Where does the Money go?', *EPW*, xvii (2 Oct. 1982), 1606.

[70] Chambers, R., 'Economic Development and Cultural Change', 1983, ch. 8, cited in Wade, 'Corruption'. It is not only scholars who were aware of the problem. GOI Planning Commission, *Sixth Five Year Plan* (1981), urged state governments not to transfer able Collectors during the period of the Plan (p. 92); but this was pie in the sky.

[71] There is a large literature on problems of development administration in India; a good introduction is Bhalerao, C. (ed.), *Administration, Politics and Development in India*, Bombay, 1974.

[72] Heginbotham, *Cultures in Conflict*.

[73] Heginbotham also wants to make a lot of the cultural explanation, that the subordinates as Hindus are preoccupied with *dharma* and procedural correctness rather than results (values reminiscent of Krishna's advice to Arjuna in the *Bhagavad Gita*). But I think he makes too much of this aspect.

posture taken by the bureaucratic structure as a whole, giving it strength in the areas of maintaining unity and order while making it less successful in encouraging innovation, specialist expertise, and local demands—all important ingredients in making a development programme work in the districts. Indian revolutionaries perhaps tended to underestimate the strength of the state bureaucracy. Inefficient in implementing development programmes they may have been, but that was never their strong point. What the bureaucratic structures of state power in India continued to be good at, and what the ICS tradition emphasized, was maintaining order and dealing with any serious internal opposition to their rule. The ICS had gone, but that central feature of their tradition lived on in the 1980s.

Conclusion

BROADLY speaking, I have tried in this book to describe central features of the ICS tradition of administration and to explain their persistence from 1919 to 1983. There are several general issues raised by the study that require brief comment by way of conclusion.

The first concerns what the reader may regard as the general line taken on the issue of continuity and change within this particular tradition. Any living tradition ceases to be one if its central features do not continue in recognizable form over time; yet all traditions are also modified as they continue, and certain aspects may indeed change quite markedly. In this study I identified central features of the ICS tradition in 1919 in accordance with what seemed a reasonable conceptual scheme and what the appropriate evidence suggests for the period, and then repeated the examination in 1983. The comparison showed that the central features had survived in modified form although in some respects they had changed substantially. As regards the central feature of location, for example, the distinctive, indeed unique, framework of a single all-India service organized by provincial cadre working at district, provincial, and central levels of the state was still very much in evidence in 1983, yet there were also important differences—increasing numbers of IAS people were working in public enterprises, a new development, and the old 'judicial' aspect of location had largely faded away.

There is no doubt, however, that I have given more attention in this study to continuity than to change. To some extent this may be a consequence of the way the analysis has been framed, and it is best to be clear about it. For one thing, more or less continuity may be found depending on what is being compared. The ICS tradition in the days of the raj has been depicted in many different ways. Roy, for example, identifies its central values as 'efficiency, professionalism, decisiveness';[1] Alexander says they were 'devotion to duty, efficiency, incorruptibility, and impartiality'.[2] If one took these as the central features of the ICS

[1] Roy, W. F., 'The Steel Frame: The Legend of the Indian Civil Service', *New Zealand Journal of Public Administration*, 30, 1 (1967), 50.

[2] Alexander, 'Discarding the "Steel Frame"', 1.

tradition in 1919 and examined their relevance to the IAS in 1983, one might find less continuity and more change than I found using different criteria. My criteria were the actual location of the ICS within the colonial state, their speed of movement from post to post, the nature of their political work as superior generalists in separate secretariats and in the districts, and certain gentlemanly and service-class norms and values that helped to legitimate their location and behaviour patterns. I have gone on to show that *this* tradition, with those particular features, existed in 1919 because of the particular needs and requirements of the colonial ruler in India; and although these features have come under attack and changes have occurred, they have been brought forward in recognizable form to 1983. The evidence suggests clearly that these were central features in 1919, and my emphasis on continuity flows from a 1919–1983 comparison using these criteria.

Another factor that can affect assessment of continuity and change in a tradition is the level of generality at which the analysis is pitched. Hence, if the features of the tradition in 1919 had been stated in a very specific way, for example, Collectors normally tour on horseback, then one is likely to find that there has been massive change by 1983. On the other hand, if they are stated in such general terms that they amount to defining characteristics of administrators at any time, then no change will be found. I have tried to describe the content of the ICS tradition fairly specifically while bearing the problem of level of generality in mind, but anyone who tries to make comparisons across time in this way is likely to be criticized for getting it wrong if the critic disagrees with the conclusions reached.

Perhaps this problem of the level of generality helps to account for the variety of views that have been expressed by those who have attempted a comparative evaluation of the IAS and the ICS. The dominant view has been that the 'quality' of the personnel has changed, and changed for the worse, for example, 'the Indian Civil Service (now Indian Administrative Service) . . . tradition of competence and integrity . . . has become somewhat frayed since independence';[3] 'standards of efficiency and integrity have gone down';[4] 'the quality of the IAS is generally admitted to be somewhat lower than the old ICS';[5]

[3] Lewis, J. P., *Quiet Crisis in India*, Washington, DC, 1962, p. 4.
[4] Khanna, B. S., 'Trends in Public Administration in India since the Transfer of Power', *The Research Bulletin (Arts) of the University of the Punjab*, xvi. 2 (1955), p. 5.
[5] Lamb, B., *India, a World in Transition*, New York, 1966, p. 215.

'the IAS is less qualified, on the whole, than the old ICS group';[6] 'the quality of the IAS recruits are very different than the ICS';[7] 'decline in the standards of [ICS/IAS] administration developed after the attainment of independence';[8] 'there has been a steady deterioration in the calibre of our administrative personnel since independence'.[9] Such judgements have frequently been made in passing, based on an uninformed and romanticized view of the ICS, that view itself the product of some active myth-making. As Stephen Hugh-Jones remarked years ago: 'accepting that imperialism itself is a lost cause, we are mythicizing its administrators, the Indian Civil Service', with the consequence that 'in retrospect these oligarchs have become uniformly incorruptible, far seeing, all competent: stern but devoted servants of India, whose life-work found its fulfilment in Indian independence . . .[10] The general phenomenon of 'a nostalgic distortion of the past by more senior generations'[11] is well known; and it is abundantly clear that the myth has been actively cultivated by ICS people for the IAS. A steady stream of ICS Indians have gone up to Mussoorie over the years and told fresh IAS recruits about how wonderful it all was in 'the good old days'.[12] Occasionally, the judgements have been cruder. The 1962 batch of IAS recruits were apparently greeted at the Academy by a senior ICS Indian with the remark that they had made a mistake in joining their Service.[13] It is unfortunate that the ICS mythology has been so widely accepted, and comparative evaluations affected thereby. Even many IAS people believe it, and consequently have been excessively critical of their own Service.

My own view regarding the comparative 'worth' of the individuals involved, based on the evidence reported in this book and impressions gained when talking to both ICS and IAS people, is that IAS people, on

[6] Palmer, N., *The Indian Political System*, Boston, 1961, p. 147.

[7] Sinha, V. M., 'The Indian Administrative Service', *Political Science Review*, 12. 3–4 (1973), 247.

[8] Misra, B. B., *District Administration and Rural Development in India*, Delhi, 1983, p. 371.

[9] Narain, Govind, 'Bureaucrats Frown upon Authority and Direction', *Sunday*, 14–20 Aug. 1983, 29.

[10] Hugh-Jones, S., 'The ICS Myth', *New Statesman*, 72 (2 Dec. 1966), 842.

[11] Rudolph, L. and Rudolph, S. (eds.), *Education and Politics in India*, Cambridge, Mass., 1972, p. 35.

[12] Many of these talks have been published in the *Administrator*. But there are numerous other examples. A classic instance of ICS myth-making is Chettur, S. K., 'ICS before and after Independence', *Public Administration* (Kanpur), 3. 27 (3 July 1965), 301–2.

[13] B624 to the author in a personal interview, 1966.

the whole, are at least as able as their ICS predecessors. To say this is perhaps unusual, although not unheard of. Mitra (ICS, Bengal), for example, has asserted that 'the best of the IAS begin by being as good material as the best of the ICS', although he goes on to say that 'the system rusts them quickly'.[14] A few others have expressed similar views.[15] There is no need to knock the old ICS to support this claim, although it is necessary to cut through the mythology. In any event, the preoccupation with whether or not IAS individuals 'measure up' to their ICS predecessors is misdirected. What matters is the tradition of administration they carried from generation to generation and its broader structural consequences for other civil servants and the overall performance of the Indian state.

Explaining how and why that tradition has been carried from generation to generation has been the other main preoccupation of this book, and the nature of this explanation raises broader issues that also require brief comment here.

As with most explanations in the social sciences, the one advanced here to explain the persistence of a tradition rests fundamentally on elements both of structure and of agency. Each of the three processes identified as necessary conditions for reproducing the tradition combine elements of both. First, there is the process of obtaining similar successors on a continuing basis. This process represents an agency factor in that, for example, the British Government was frequently required to keep the process going by deliberately intervening in it to change the rules. At the same time, the Government's initiatives were constrained by the existing structure of class and power, which determined that some interventions were possible and others were not. Second, there is the process of shaping successors to the norms, values, and behaviour patterns of the tradition. It has been shown that this can be quite a deliberate process, representing the agency of individual and group initiatives. Yet for the person being shaped, the process represents a powerful structural force. The third process is continuing political support for the

[14] Mitra, A., 'Guardians of the Law: Reflections on the Indian Administrative Service', *Administrator*, xxvi. 1 (1981), 12.

[15] e.g. Mangat Rai, *Commitment my Style*, p. 212. Trivedi, R. K. and Rao, D. N., 'Higher Civil Service in India', *Journal of the National Academy of Administration*, vi. 3 (1961), 63; Shils, E., *The Intellectual between Tradition and Modernity: The Indian Situation* (Comparative Studies in Society and History, Supplement I), The Hague, 1961, p. 92; Rustomji, N., 'Changing the Guard: Unimportance of Being Earnest', *Statesman*, 21 Oct. 1980, 6.

administrative tradition. From the point of view of the administrators, support from the political leadership of the state amounts to a structural 'given' in their universe, on which they know the survival of their tradition ultimately depends. But there are agency aspects at work in this process also, not least by the administrators themselves who from time to time, singly or in groups, actively cultivate that essential support when they sense it is waning.

The question of whether agency or structure has primacy in explanations of the state is one of the major issues on which rival political theories divide—pluralist theories tending to be agency led and Marxist theories tending to give primacy to structural determinations. It is important to emphasize that the explanation advanced in this book has a more limited focus within this wider debate. Rather than trying to explain the Indian state, I have proposed an explanation for how and why a major element *within* the state—the bureaucratic apparatus, more particularly the élite administrative tradition within that—has been reproduced through time despite major political changes in its environment. The particular explanation is situated within a more general perspective on the nature of the Indian state, but has been only indirectly related to it.

Briefly, all three processes involved in the explanation of the ICS tradition were shown to be necessary, but political support stands out as of fundamental importance. Finding and shaping successors are both necessary, but both processes depend on political support. The reverse, however, does not apply. Political support does not depend on the other two processes. Although alone it does not explain bureaucratic reproduction, it does appear to have a more determining affect on the survival of the tradition than the other two. Furthermore, although the process of political support for the administrative tradition involves both structure and agency, it is primarily the continuing *structure* of political support, formally specified in the Constitution and thereafter sustained by the inaction (and occasional action) of the political leadership at the centre, that has ultimately been decisive. There has been reference from time to time in this study to even broader class alignments which to some extent set the agenda for the political leadership and the state as a whole and affect the outcomes of state action, but these relationships have not been systematically examined because, although they are essential to an explanation of the state, they are not directly pertinent to the particular phenomena examined here.

Even though this particular explanation does not engage directly with the major explanations of the state and their attendant debates, it is worth pointing out that it sits more comfortably in some of them. The question for explanation being posed in terms of reproduction through time, for example, probably emerges more easily from a Marxist perspective. The emphasis on continuity also tends to make it consistent with Alavi's on the post-colonial state. But, on the whole, my own position would be that most Marxists do not conceptualize and explain the *Indian state* very well, nor do most pluralists. They both rely too much on external determinants of the state, whether they be the constraints of dominant classes and internal modes of production or the constraints of voters and interest group demands. The Indian state is far less 'dependent' than other 'third world' states. It is also probably not helpful to perceive the Indian state *qua* state as 'post-colonial' (although one can label the bureaucratic apparatus within the Indian state that way more easily). The Indian state may fairly be conceptualized as subsidiary within the world capitalist system, for it has to enter the international arena (e.g. 'go to the World Bank') for resources and in consequence becomes integrated into these networks; but individual voters and interest groups in Indian society are probably becoming more dependent on the Indian state than the state on them. The Indian state may even be said now to rest on its own independent economic base to some extent and to produce portions of the domestic economy. The issue of how one conceptualizes and explains the Indian state lies beyond the confines of this study, and cannot be pursued here. I have touched on it only to indicate that in referring to the political leadership of the state, in the context of the process of political support for the administrative tradition, I have assumed (in view of the conceptualization just mentioned) that political leaders are not merely agents for other groups or classes who really control the destiny of administrative traditions. The political leadership of the Indian state does call the shots *vis-à-vis* the administrative tradition, and therefore it has not been necessary in this study to go beyond them in order to explain the persistence of the tradition.

One other point about the nature of the explanation: I have deliberately avoided making explicit comparisons with other traditions in order to keep the study to manageable length. In consequence, the explanation can only be tentative, resembling a set of hypotheses. In order to convert it into an empirically based set of propositions explaining the reproduction of administrative traditions, a comparative analysis of traditions that survived and others that did not is required.

The particular explanation advanced here seems plausible for the Indian case, but the whole subject cries out for further research and analysis.

In closing, I should like to make clear that I should be surprised if the central features of the ICS tradition recognizable in the IAS in the early 1980s survived into the twenty-first century. In the intense struggle currently going on within the bureaucracy between the IAS and rival services from below demanding greater equality and an enhanced role for specialist expertise, one senses that the IAS and its tradition are becoming increasingly isolated, that more vigorous forces are closing in. The end of the essential political support may not be far behind. Once each IAS person is required to opt for a particular career pattern, a proposal being seriously considered in 1983 (even within the IAS), then the rationale for generalist Collectors, secretariats, the tenure system, and all the rest is gravely weakened. It seems to me that IAS people are beginning to recognize that the heyday of their tradition may be over. They would never admit it, of course, but I did detect in more senior IAS men and women I interviewed in 1983 a rather less confident attitude towards their tradition than I found in similarly placed IAS in the 1960s. They have not succumbed yet. After all, their tradition makes them great survivors, politically adept at moving quickly for advantage in a political struggle. In any new administrative structure, they or others like them will be there as individuals. Even remnants of their tradition may survive. But the tradition as a whole cannot last much longer.

Bibliography

I HAVE made no attempt here to provide a complete inventory of all relevant works. Only those sources that have been of direct use for this book have been listed. For example, numerous ICS memoirs in both the India Office Library and Records (hereafter IOL) and the Centre of South Asian Studies Archive, Cambridge University (hereafter Cambridge Archive) not cited in the text are not listed here. Also, those ICS and IAS people whom I interviewed and who provided substantive content of direct use for this book have been identified here (including the 65 IAS interviewed for the special study reported in Chapter 5), but the date and precise location of each interview are not stated nor are particular interviewees identified by name in the text in order that interview evidence cited in the text cannot be traced to individuals.

I MANUSCRIPTS, PAPERS, INTERVIEWS (BY THE AUTHOR) AND PUBLISHED MEMOIRS OF AN AUTOBIOGRAPHICAL NATURE BY ICS AND IAS OFFICERS

North India

Agarwal, R. K. (IAS, Rajasthan), interview.

Arthur, A. J. V. (ICS, Punjab), IOL MSS Eur. F.180/63.

Baraya, K. L. (IAS, Rajasthan), interview.

Barlow, H. A. (ICS, UP), Cambridge Archive, Papers.

Belcher, R. H. (ICS, Punjab), IOL MSS Eur. F.180/64.

Bhargava, K. N. (IAS, Rajasthan), interview.

Bhatnagar, K. K. (IAS, Rajasthan), interview.

Bonarjee, N. B. (ICS, UP), *Under Two Masters*, London, 1970.

Chak, B. L. (IAS, UP), *Himalayas to Bay Islands: Recollections of a Bureaucrat*, Lucknow, 1978.

Chandra, C. N. (ICS, Punjab), 'Indian Civil Service', in Panjabi, K. L. (ed.), *The Civil Servant in India*, Bombay, 1965 (hereafter Panjabi, *Civil Servant*), pp. 293–301.

Chandra Prakash (IAS, Rajasthan), interview.

Chatterji, A. (IAS, Rajasthan), interview.

Chaturvedi, T. N. (IAS, Rajasthan), interview.

Corfield, C. (ICS, Punjab), *The Princely India I Knew*, Madras, 1975.

Darling, M. (ICS, Punjab), *Apprentice to Power*, London, 1966.

Fletcher, A. L. (ICS, Punjab), 'The Collector in the Nineteen Sixties', *Indian Journal of Public Administration* (hereafter *IJPA*), xi. 3 (1965), 368–75.

Garbett, C. (ICS, Punjab), *Friend of Friend*, London, 1943.
Gill, M. S. (IAS, Punjab), interview.
Gould, B. J. (ICS, Punjab), *The Jewel in the Lotus*, London, 1957.
Gupta, L. N. (IAS, Rajasthan), interview.
Haig, G. A. (ICS, UP), IOL MSS Eur. F.180/75.
—— Cambridge Archive, Papers.
Hume, A. P. (ICS, UP), IOL MSS Eur. D.724, letters.
—— Cambridge Archive, Papers.
Jain, N. K. (IAS, Haryana), 'Political Interference or Political Participation', in Jain, R. (ed.) *Public Services in a Democratic Context*, New Delhi, 1983, pp. 51–8.
Jha, A. N. (ICS, UP), 'Planning, The Federal Principle and Parliamentary Democracy', *IJPA*, xi. 2 (1965), 161–73.
Jhingran, I. G. (IAS, Rajasthan), interview.
Johnson, L. J. (ICS, UP), radio broadcast, BBC 4, 'Plain Tales from the Raj', 15 Dec. 1974.
Johnston, R. H. (ICS, UP), Cambridge Archive, Papers.
Khera, S. S. (ICS, UP), 'Then and Now', *Metcalfe House Journal*, iv. 1 (1959), 31–6.
—— *District Administration in India*, New York, 1964.
Khosla, G. D. (ICS, Punjab), 'My Work in the ICS', in Panjabi, *Civil Servant*, pp. 109–17.
Khosla, R. P. (IAS, UP), interview.
Kumar, A. (IAS, Rajasthan), interview.
Kumar, S. (IAS, Rajasthan), interview.
Ladha, L. N. (IAS, Rajasthan), interview.
Macleod, R. D. (ICS, UP), *Impressions of an Indian Civil Servant*, London, 1938.
Mangat Rai, E. N. (ICS, Punjab), *Commitment My Style: Career in the Indian Civil Service*, Delhi, 1973.
Mason, P. (pseud. Philip Woodruff) (ICS, UP), *A Shaft of Sunlight: Memories of a Varied Life*, London, 1978.
Mehta, B. (IAS, Rajasthan), 'District Administration in the Past and in Future', *IJPA* xvii. 2 (1977), 522–6.
Mehta, D. R. (IAS, Rajasthan), interview.
Mehta, M. L. (IAS, Rajasthan), interview.
Menon, K. P. (IAS, Rajasthan), interview.
Misra, R. L. (IAS, Rajasthan), interview.
Moon, P. (ICS, Punjab), *Divide and Quit*, London, 1964.
—— radio broadcast, BBC 4, 'Plain Tales from the Raj', 17 Nov. 1974.
Muhammad Azim Husain (ICS, Punjab), IOL MSS Eur. F.180/68.
Mukerji, M. (IAS, Rajasthan), *Ham in the Sandwich: Lighter Side of Life in the IAS*, Ghaziabad, 1979.

—— 'Climbing the Civil Service Pyramid Faster than Others', in Mukerji, M. (ed.), *Administrative Innovations in Rajasthan*, New Delhi, 1982, pp. 222–35.
—— *Non-Story of a Chief Secretary during Emergency et cetera*, New Delhi, 1982.
Narain, Govind (ICS, UP), 'Some Stray Thoughts', *Administrator*, xxi, 2 (1976), 593–7.
—— 'Bureaucrats Frown upon Authority and Direction', *Sunday*, 14–20 Aug. 1983,. 29–30.
Nath, V. (IAS, Rajasthan), interview.
Nehru, B. K. (ICS, Punjab), interview.
Noble, T. A. Fraser (ICS, NWFP), interview.
Pandey, H. C. (IAS, Rajasthan), interview.
Pandit, A. D. (ICS, UP), 'Little Gandhis for IAS', *Public Administration* (India), 12. 2 (1974), 52–7.
Penny, J. (ICS, Punjab), Cambridge Archive, Papers.
Prashad, K. (IAS, Rajasthan), interview.
Pullan, A. G. P. (ICS, UP), Cambridge Archive, Papers.
Puri, S. S. (IAS, Punjab), 'Union–State Relationship in Agricultural Administration', *IJPA* xvi. 3 (1970), 352–60.
Rao, C. B. (ICS, UP), 'Local Elections and Politics', *IJPA* xiv. 3 (1968), 533–7.
Rawat, D. S. (IAS, UP), interview.
Roy, A. K. (IAS, Rajasthan), 'The Collector in Rajasthan', *IJPA* xi. 3 (1965), 560–77.
Sahay, Vishnu (ICS, UP), 'What does it mean?' *Seminar*, 168 (1973), 19–23.
Saxena, K. K. (IAS, Rajasthan), interview.
Saxena, N. C. (IAS, UP), 'The World of the IAS', *Administrator*, xxvi. 1 (1981), 15–20.
Shrinagesh, J. M. (ICS, Punjab), 'Administration in Perspective', in Panjabi, *Civil Servant*, pp. 215–21.
Shukla, J. D. (ICS, UP), *Indianization of All-India Services*, New Delhi, 1982.
Skrine, C. (ICS, UP), *World War in Iran*, London, 1962.
Venkatachar, C. S. (ICS, UP), IOL MSS Eur. F.180/85.
Verma, V. S. (IAS, Rajasthan), interview.
—— 'Of Horses and of Law', *Journal of the National Academy of Administration*, v. 4 (1960), 97–103.
Vernede, R. V. (ICS, UP), Cambridge Archive, Papers.
Vira, Dharma (ICS, UP), *Memoirs of a Civil Servant*, Delhi, 1975.
Wakefield, E. (ICS, Punjab), *Past Imperative: My Life in India 1927–1947*, London, 1966.
Wingate, R. E. (ICS, Punjab), *Not in the Limelight*, London, 1959.

West and Central India

Afzulpurkar, D. K. (IAS, Maharashtra), interview.

Bakhle, D. S. (ICS, Bombay), 'The Error of the Government and the Trial of the People', in Panjabi, *Civil Servant*, pp. 233–45.

Banerjee, R. N. (ICS, CP), 'In the Indian Civil Service', in Panjabi, *Civil Servant*, pp. 303–39.

Barty, D. C. (ICS, Sind), IOL MSS Eur. F.180/26.

Batabyal, A. N. (IAS, Maharashtra), interview.

Bedekar, G. V. (ICS, Bombay), 'Not many but much', in Panjabi, *Civil Servant*, pp. 271–7.

Benjamin, S. (IAS, Bombay), *The Hard Way*. Being the experiences of a Revenue Officer, published by the author, 1961.

Bhagwat, B. N. (IAS, Maharashtra), interview.

Chaturvedi, M. K. (IAS, MP), 'Commitment in Civil Service', *IJPA* xvii. 1 (1971), 40–6.

Crofton, R. M. (ICS, CP), Cambridge Archive, Papers (microfilm).

Dave, P. K. (IAS, MP), interview.

Desai, C. C. (ICS, CP), 'My Work in the ICS', in Panjabi, *Civil Servant*, pp. 71–83.

Deshmukh, C. D. (ICS, CP), 'Looking Back on my Service Days', in Panjabi, *Civil Servant*, pp. 3–4.

—— *The Course of my Life*, Bombay, 1974.

Faruqui, M. A. (ICS, Bombay and Sind), IOL MSS Eur. F.180/27.

Fitze, K. (ICS, CP), *Twilight of the Maharajas*, London, 1956.

Gorwala, A. (ICS, Bombay), *Role of Administator: Past, Present and Future*, Bombay, 1957.

Hmingliana, L. (IAS, Maharashtra), interview.

Holt, E. H. (ICS, Bombay), IOL MSS Eur. F.180/30.

Hyde, E. S. (ICS, CP), Cambridge Archive, Papers.

Iengar, H. V. R. (ICS, Bombay), 'My Life in the ICS', in Panjabi, *Civil Servant*, pp. 119–27.

Isvaran, V. (ICS, Bombay, then Gujarat), 'The Indian Civil Servant', in Panjabi, *Civil Servant*, pp. 247–57.

Jayaraman, N. (IAS, Maharashtra), interview.

Joshi, R. C. (ICS, Bombay), interview.

Kakodkar, S. R. (IAS, Maharashtra), interview.

Kale, S. G. (IAS, Maharashtra), interview.

Kelkar, S. M. (IAS, Maharashtra), interview.

Khanna, S. (IAS, MP), 'Case Study of a Regulatory Operation: Simultaneous Raids on 106 Rice Mills', *Administrator*, xxi. 4 (1976), 910–18.

Kincaid, C. A. (ICS, Bombay), *Forty-Four Years a Public Servant*, Edinburgh, 1934.

Kincaid, D. (ICS, Bombay), *British Social Life in India 1608–1937*, London, 1938.
Knight, H. (ICS, Bombay), *Food Administration in India 1939–47*, Stanford, 1954.
Kulkarni, S. B. (IAS, Maharashtra), interview.
Kumar, A. (IAS, Maharashtra), interview.
Lambrick, H. T. (ICS, Bombay and Sind), IOL MSS Eur. F.180/31.
Maconochie, E. (ICS, Bombay), *Life in the Indian Civil Service*, London, 1926.
Makhija, B. N. (IAS, Maharashtra), interview.
Mander, H. (IAS, MP), 'A Report on Pauri District (UP)', *Administrator*, xxvi. 3 (1981), 459–64.
Matthews, V. G. (ICS, CP), IOL MSS Eur. F.180/44.
Maxwell, R. (ICS, Bombay), Cambridge Archive, Papers.
Mitchell, A. N. (ICS, CP), *Life of Sir George Cunningham*, Edinburgh, 1968.
Nadkarni, L. M. (ICS, Bombay), 'Approaches to Administration', *Journal of the National Academy of Administration*, v. 1 (1960), 50–7.
Nair, V. (IAS, Maharashtra), interview.
Natarajan, M. R. (IAS, Maharashtra), interview.
Noronha, R. P. (ICS, CP), *A Tale Told by an Idiot*, New Delhi, 1976.
Padmanabhaiah, K. (IAS, Maharashtra), interview.
Panjabi, K. L. (ICS, Bombay), (ed.) *The Civil Servant in India*, Bombay, 1965.
—— 'My Experiences in the ICS', in Panjabi, *Civil Servant*, pp. 85–107.
Patel, H. M. (ICS, Bombay), 'Cabinet Government in India', in Aiyar, S. and Srinivasan, R. (eds), *Studies in Indian Democracy*, Bombay, 1965.
—— *My Submissions*, (private circulation, no date).
Paterson, N. K. (ICS, CP), IOL MSS Eur. F.180/46.
Paymaster, B. B. (ICS, Bombay), interview.
Pillai, N. R. (ICS, CP), 'The Civil Service as a Profession', in Panjabi, *Civil Servant*, pp. 23–7.
Pimputkar, M. G. (ICS, Bombay), interview.
Pradhan, D. R. (ICS, Bombay), interview.
Radhakrishnan, K. (ICS, CP), 'Introducing ourselves', *Metcalfe House Journal*, i (1956), iii–iv.
Rajagopalan, P. B. (IAS, Maharashtra), interview.
Ramadhyani, R. K. (ICS, CP), 'The Civil Service today', *Journal of the National Academy of Administration*, v. 1 (1960), 23–8.
Ramanujachari, T. C. A. (IAS, MP), 'Secretarial–Executive Department Relationship', *IJPA* xii. 3 (1966), 424–39.
Raza, S. H. (ICS, Bombay and Sind), IOL MSS Eur. F.180/29.
Ridley, S. (ICS, Bombay), IOL MSS Eur. F.180/32.
Sawian, H. A. D. (IAS, Maharashtra), interview.
Shankar, V. (ICS, Bombay), *My Reminiscences of Sardar Patel*, 2 vols., New Delhi, 1975.

Subramanyam, P. (IAS, Maharashtra), interview.
Sukthankar, Y. N. (ICS, CP) 'What makes a Good Administrator', *Journal of the National Academy of Administration*, v. 3 (1960), 4–10.
Sundaram, V. (IAS, Maharashtra), interview.
Symington, D. (pseud. James Halliday) (ICS, Bombay and Sind), *A Special India*, London, 1968.
Varma, R. S. (IAS, MP), *Bureaucracy in India*, Bhopal, 1973.
Venkatesan, V. (IAS, Maharashtra), interview.
Verma, B. P. (IAS, Bihar), interview.
Watson, G. L. (ICS, CP), IOL MSS Eur. F.180/48.
Wiles, G. (ICS, Bombay), Cambridge Archive, Papers.
Yardi, M. R. (ICS, Bombay), 'The Reorganization of the Nasik Collectorate', *IJPA* iii. 1 (1957), 42–52.
Zinkin, M. (ICS, Bombay), *Development for Free Asia*, London, 1963.
—— 'Impressions, 1938–47', in Phillips, C. H. and Wainwright, M. (eds.), *The Partition of India*, London, 1970, pp. 546–50.

Eastern India

Arthanareswaran, K. N. (IAS, Bihar), interview.
Baker, E. B. H. (ICS, Bengal), Cambridge Archive, Papers (microfilm).
Baksi, N. (ICS, Bihar and Orissa), 'In Bihar: The State of My Adoption', in Panjabi, *Civil Servant*, pp. 141–213.
Bapat, S. B. (ICS, Bengal), 'The Training of the Indian Administrative Service', *IJPA* i. 2 (1955), 119–29.
Bell, F. O. (ICS, Bengal), IOL MSS Eur. F.180/8.
Bell, J. M. G. (ICS, Bengal), Cambridge Archive, Papers.
Bhatnagar, S. (IAS, Bihar), interview.
Carritt, M. (ICS, Bengal), *A Mole in the Crown*, Hove (published privately), 1985.
Chatterjee, A. K. (IAS, Bihar), 'Tinkering with the Rule of Law', in Jain R. (ed.), *Public Services in a Democratic Context*, New Delhi, 1983, pp. 23–39.
Chaturvedi, S. K. (IAS, Bihar), interview.
Christie, W. H. J. (ICS, Bengal), IOL MSS Eur. F.180/9.
Das, B. L. (IAS, Bihar), interview.
Das, Nabagopal (ICS, Bengal), 'My life in the ICS', in Panjabi, *Civil Servant*, pp. 254–69.
Das, S, K. (ICS, Bihar and Orissa), radio broadcast, BBC 4, 'Plain Tales from the Raj', 15 Dec. 1974.
Dash, R. N. (IAS, Bihar), interview.
Datta, S. K. (ICS, Assam), 'New Training Programme for Central and State Government Employees', *IJPA* ix. 3 (1965), Supplement, 125–43.

Desai S. P. (ICS, Assam), 'My Thirty-five Years in Assam', in Panjabi, *Civil Servant*, pp. 61–9.

Dhanoa, S. S. (IAS, Bihar), 'The Collector in Bihar', *IJPA*, xi. 3 (1965), 420–44.

Donovan, J. T. (ICS, Bengal), Cambridge Archive, Papers.

Dutt, R. C. (ICS, Bengal), 'Principles of Selection in Public Services', *IJPA* i. 3 (1955), 204–11.

—— 'The Problem' (of a committed civil service), *Seminar*, 168 (Aug. 1973), 10–13.

Flack, A. W. (ICS, Bihar), IOL MSS Eur. F.180/17.

Griffiths, P. J. (ICS, Bengal), *The British In India*, London, 1946.

—— radio interview, BBC 4, 'Plain Tales from the Raj', 15 Dec. 1978.

Gupta, H. C. (ICS, Bengal), 'Administration: In Retrospect', *Public Administration* (India), 12. 3 (1974), 5–9.

Hoda, A. (IAS, Bihar), interview.

Holland, E. W. (ICS, Bengal), Cambridge Archive, Papers.

Hubback, J. A. (ICS, Bengal, then Bihar and Orissa), Cambridge Archive, Papers.

Hughes, A. (ICS, Bengal), interview.

Jha, L. K. (ICS, Bihar), 'Time for New Norms', *Seminar*, 230 (1978), 33.

—— 'The Role of Bureaucracy in a Developing Democracy', Training Abstract No. 2, Training Division, Department of Personnel and Administrative Reforms, GOI mimeo., 1983.

Kemp, A. H. (ICS, Bihar and Orissa), IOL MSS Eur. F.180/18.

Kidwai, A. N. (ICS, Assam), 'The Collector in Assam', *IJPA* xi. 3 (1965), 414–19.

Kirpalani, M. K. (ICS, Bengal), 'My Work in the Indian Civil Service: Some Memories of old Bengal', in Panjabi, *Civil Servant*, pp. 129–39.

Lall, S. (ICS, Bihar and Orissa), 'Civil Service Neutrality', *IJPA* iv. 1 (1958), 1–13.

—— 'An Indian Civil Servant', in Panjabi, *Civil Servant*, pp. 7–21.

Lines, R. N. (ICS, Bihar), IOL MSS Eur. F.180/19a.

Lothian, A. C. (ICS, Bengal), *Kingdoms of Yesterday*, London, 1951.

Lydall, E. (ICS, Assam), *Enough of Action*, London, 1949.

Macdonald, I. H. (ICS, Bihar and Orissa), IOL MSS Eur. F.180/20.

Mansfield, P. T. (ICS, Bihar and Orissa), Cambridge Archive, Papers.

Martin, H. B. (ICS, Bihar), IOL MSS Eur. F.180/21.

Martin, O. M. (ICS, Bengal), Cambridge Archive, Papers.

Mishra, R. K. (IAS, Orissa), *How I Passed the IAS Exams*, Allahabad, 1958.

Mitra, A. (ICS, Bengal), 'Guardians of the Law: Reflections on the Indian Administrative Service', *Administrator*, xxvi. 1 (1981), 1–14.

Noronha, C. (IAS, West Bengal), *My Life* (privately published and printed, 1975). Copy in Stuart Papers, Cambridge Archive.

Orr, J. W. (ICS, Bihar and Orissa), IOL MSS Eur. F.180/22.
Patankar, S. (IAS, Bihar), interview.
Prabhakaran, S. (IAS, Bihar), interview.
Prasad, V. (IAS, Bihar), interview.
Raman, K. (ICS, Bihar and Orissa), interview.
Raman, K. S. V. (ICS, Bihar and Orissa), 'Reminiscences of a Government Officer', *Searchlight* (Patna), 8 Dec. 1966, 4.
Rao, B. G. (ICS, Bengal, later Rajasthan), 'My Work in the ICS', in Panjabi, *Civil Servant*, pp. 274–91.
Ray, G. M. (ICS, Bihar and Orissa), IOL MSS Eur F.180/23.
Reid, R. (ICS, Bengal), *Years of Change in Bengal and Assam*, London, 1966.
Rudra, D. (IAS, West Bengal), 'Gods with Feet of Clay: Temptations of the Middle Years', *Statesman*, 9 Aug. 1980.
Rustomji, N. (ICS, Assam), *Enchanted Frontiers: Sikkim, Bhutan and India's North-Eastern Borderlands*, London, 1971.
—— 'Changing the Guard: Unimportance of Being Earnest', *Statesman*, 21 Oct. 1980.
Saran, K. K. (IAS, Bihar), interview.
Saumarez Smith, W. H. (ICS, Bengal), *A Young Man's Country: Letters of a Subdivisional Officer of the Indian Civil Service, 1936–37*, Salisbury, 1977.
Scott, W. (ICS, Assam), Cambridge Archive, Papers.
Sen Gupta, J. C. (IAS, West Bengal), 'The Collector in West Bengal', *IJPA* xi. 3 (1965), 595–602.
Singh, Abhimanyu (IAS, Bihar), interview.
Singh, B. K. (IAS, Bihar), interview.
Singh, B. P. (IAS, Assam), 'The Emergence of a New Pattern of Administration', *IJPA* xix. 4 (1973), 600–11.
—— 'Political Culture and Public Administration in the National Value System: the Indian Scenario', *IJPA* xxvii. 4 (1981), 1043–54.
Singh, L. P. (ICS, Bihar), 'Talk to some Officers on an In-service Training Course', IIPA mimeo. 7 Mar. 1970.
—— 'Our Civil Service', *Journal of the National Academy of Administration*, xvi. 1 (1971), 12–14.
Singh, N. K. (IAS, Bihar), interview.
Sinha, R. K. (IAS, Bihar), interview.
Sirkar, J. (IAS, West Bengal), 'Professional, Social and Personal Ethics of the IAS Officer in Contemporary Indian Society: Syndicate Report', *Administrator*, xxi. 2 (1976), 649.
Sivaraman, B. (ICS, Bihar), 'Generalists and Specialists in Administration', *IJPA*, xvii. 2 (1971), 383–96.
Solomon, S. (ICS, Bihar and Orissa), IOL, MSS Eur. F.180/24.
—— *Memories with Thoughts on Gandhi*, London (Counter-Point), 1983.
Srivastava, R. K. (IAS, Bihar), interview.

Stuart, M. M. (ICS, Bengal), Cambridge Archive, Papers.
Subarno, M. C. (IAS, Bihar), interview.
Swann, R. S. (ICS, Bihar and Orissa), IOL MSS Eur. F.180/25.
Tripathi, P. K. (IAS, Orissa), *Reminiscences of a Public Servant*, Cuttack, 1960 (?).
Twynam, H. (ICS, Bengal), Cambridge Archive, Papers.
Vaghaiwalla, R. B. (ICS, Assam), 'Instruction in District Administration', *Metcalfe House Journal*, i (1956), 49–59.
Venkataram, C. R. (IAS, Bihar), interview.

South India

Badrinath, (IAS, Tamil Nadu), interview.
Bhoothalingam, S. (ICS, Madras), 'Ends and Means', *Seminar*, 192 (Aug. 1975), 12–15.
Carleston, H. H. (ICS, Madras), IOL MSS Eur. F.180/49a.
Chettur, S. K. (ICS, Madras), *The Steel Frame and I: Life in the ICS*, Bombay, 1962.
—— 'ICS before and after Independence', *Public Administration* (Kanpur), 3. 27 (3 July 1965), 301–2.
Dass, K. K. (ICS, Madras, then UP), 'Rules', *Seminar*, 192 (Aug. 1975).
Dayanand, A. (IAS, Tamil Nadu), interview.
Downing, H. J. (ICS, Madras), IOL MSS Eur. F.180/50.
Dubhashi, P. R. (IAS, Karnataka), interview.
—— 'Satisfaction of an Administrative Career', *IJPA* xv. 1 (1969), 110–17.
—— 'The Establishment Officer', *IJPA* xxvii. 4 (1981), 975–80.
Dunlop, S. W. C. (ICS, Madras), IOL MSS Eur. F.180/51.
Geethakrishnan, K. P. (IAS, Tamil Nadu), interview.
Georgeson, W. W. (ICS, Madras), IOL MSS Eur. F.180/52.
Hope, R. C. (ICS, Madras), IOL MSS Eur. F.180/53.
Hunt, R. C. C. (ICS, Madras), Cambridge Archive, Papers.
Jas, G. (IAS, Tamil Nadu), interview.
Kaiwar, S. R. (ICS, Madras), interview.
Kochukoshy, C. K. (IAS, Kerala), 'All India Services: Their Role and Future', *IJPA* xviii. 1 (1972), 67–77.
Krishnamurthy, N. (IAS, Tamil Nadu), interview.
Lamarque, W. G. (ICS, Madras), IOL MSS Eur. F.180/54.
Lobo Prabhu, J. M. (ICS, Madras), 'My Work in the ICS', in Panjabi, *Civil Servant*, pp. 223–31.
Maher, J. E. (ICS, Madras), IOL MSS Eur. F.180/55.
Masterman, C. (ICS, Madras), Cambridge Archive, Papers.
Menon, K. P. S. (ICS, Madras), *Many Worlds: An Autobiography*, London, 1965.

—— 'My Life and Work in the ICS', in Panjabi, *Civil Servant*, pp. 29–59.

Menon, P. A. (ICS, Madras), 'My Years in the Public Service', *IJPA* xxi. 1 (1975), 53–66.

Narasimhan, C. V. (ICS, Madras), IOL MSS Eur. F.180/56.

Narisimha Rau, N. (IAS, Mysore), 'The Collector in Mysore', *IJPA* xi. 3 (1965), 526–42.

Pai, M. P. (ICS, Madras, then Andhra Pradesh), 'The Emerging Role of the Collector', *IJPA* viii. 4 (1982), 478–88.

Patnaik, N. M. (IAS, Kerala), 'The Collector in Kerala', *IJPA* xi. 3 (1965), 462–81.

Platt, A. J. (ICS, Madras), IOL MSS Eur. F.180/57.

Raghupathy, M. (IAS, Tamil Nadu), interview.

Ramachandran, C. (IAS, Tamil Nadu), interview.

Ramachandran, G. (IAS, Tamil Nadu), 'The Collector in Madras', *IJPA* xi. 3 (1965), 498–515.

Ramakrishnan, C. A. (ICS, Madras), interview.

Ramamurty, S. V. (ICS, Madras), *Looking across Fifty Years*, Bombay, 1964.

Ramdas, C. (IAS, Tamil Nadu), interview.

Ramesh, M. S. (IAS, Tamil Nadu), interview.

Ranga Rao, G. (IAS, Tamil Nadu), interview.

Sathianathan, W. R. S. (ICS, Madras), 'Training Tougher IAS Officers', *Yojana*, vi. 23 (25 Nov. 1967), 23–4.

Shetty, K. J. M. (IAS, Tamil Nadu), interview.

Tottenham, G. R. F. (ICS, Madras), Cambridge Archive, Papers (microfilm).

Trevelyan, H. (ICS, Madras), *The India We Left: Charles Trevelyan 1826–65, Humphrey Trevelyan 1929–47*, London, 1972.

—— *Public and Private*, London, 1980.

Vaz, F. J. (IAS, Tamil Nadu), interview.

Vellodi, M. K. (ICS, Madras), 'The Sardar I knew', *Indian and Foreign Review*, 13. 3 (15 Nov. 1975), 13–14.

Venkatachalam, M. (IAS, Tamil Nadu), interview.

Venkataraman, T. V. (IAS, Tamil Nadu), interview.

Venkatesan, K. (IAS, Tamil Nadu), interview.

Vepa, Ram K. (IAS, Andhra Pradesh), 'The Collector in Andhra Pradesh', *IJPA* xi. 3 (1965), 391–413.

—— 'Administrative Consultation: Formal and Informal', *IJPA* xvi. 3 (1970), 419–29.

—— 'Public Administration: The Challenge of the Seventies', *IJPA* xvii. 1 (1971), 10–32.

Wadsworth, S. (ICS, Madras), Cambridge Archive, Papers.

Westlake, A. R. C. (ICS, Madras), Cambridge Archive, Papers.

2 CIVIL LISTS

The India List and India Office List, 1905 (London, Harrison and Sons, 1905. Also for 1906.

The India Office List, 1907 (London), 1907. Also for each year thereafter to 1937.

The India Office and Burma Office List, 1938 (London), 1938. Also for 1939, 1940, 1945, 1947.

Thacker's Indian Directory, 1919 (Calcutta, Thacker's Directories Ltd.), 1919. Also for each year thereafter to 1936.

Thacker's Indian Directory including Burma and Ceylon, 1937–8 (Calcutta), 1938. Also each year to 1941–2. Also 1943–4, 1944–5, 1947–8, 1948–9, 1949–50.

The Combined Civil List for India and Burma, October–December 1946 (Lahore, Civil and Military Gazette Ltd.), 1947.

All-India Civil List, as on 18th April 1954 (Bombay, Associated Advertisers), 1954.

Government of India (hereafter GOI), Ministry of Home Affairs, *The Civil List: Indian Administrative Service and the Indian Police Service, as on 1st January 1956* (Delhi, Government Press), 1956. Also for 1957, 1958, 1959.

GOI Ministry of Home Affairs, *History of Services: Indian Administrative Service and Indian Police Service, as on 1st January 1957* (Delhi), 1958.

GOI Ministry of Home Affairs, *The Civil List of Indian Administrative Service, as on 1st January 1962* (Delhi), 1962. Also for each year thereafter to 1983.

3 OFFICIAL PRINTED SOURCES

National Archives of India

Unpublished proceedings of the Government of India in the Home Department—

Establishment	Ests.	1919–43
Police	Pol.	1934
Political	Poll.	1940

Government of India

Administrative Reforms Commission, *Report: Personnel Administration* (New Delhi), 1969.

All India Services Act, 1951.

Cabinet Secretariat, *Public Administration in India: Report of a Survey* by Paul Appleby, 1953.

Cabinet Secretariat, *Re-examination of India's Administrative System with Special Reference to Administration of Government's Industrial and Commercial Enterprises* by Paul Appleby, 1956.

Cabinet Secretariat, Organization and Methods Division, *Paper on Measures for Strengthening of Administration*, 1961.

Constituent Assembly (Legislature) Debates, Vol. I (1947).

Constituent Assembly Debates, Vol. ix, Vol. x (1949).

Department of Commercial Intelligence and Statistics, *Statistical Abstract for British India from 1926–27 to 1935–36*, 1938.

Directorate General of Employment and Training, 'Census of Central Government Employees, 1961', mimeo.

Directorate of Labour and Rehabilitation, 'Census of Central Government Employees (as of 31st March 1980)', 1983, mimeo.

Federal Public Service Commission, *Pamphlet for the Competition for the Indian Civil Service held in India in January/February 1941*, 1941.

Legislative Assembly Debates, Vol. 6 (1936).

Ministry of Finance, *Central Pay Commission (Varadachariar) Report*, 1947.

—— *(Das) Commission of Enquiry on Emoluments and Conditions of Service of Central Government Employees, 1957–59*, 1959.

—— *Third Central Pay Commission*, 4 vols., 1973.

—— Economic Division, *Economic Survey, 1973–74*, 1974.

Ministry of Home Affairs, *All-India Services Manual*, 2nd edn. (corrected up to 1.8.1969), 1969.

—— *All-India Services Manual*, 3rd edn. (corrected up to 1.2.1975), 1975.

—— *Report, 1975–76*, 1976.

—— Department of Personnel and Administrative Reform, *Annual Report, 1982–83*, 1983.

—— Special Recruitment Board, *Report*, 1955.

Ministry of States, *White Paper on Indian States*, 1950.

Planning Commission, *First Five Year Plan*, 1951.

—— *Report on Public Administration*, by A. D. Gorwala, 1951.

—— *Second Five Year Plan*, 1956.

—— *Third Five Year Plan*, 1961.

—— *Report on Indian and State Administrative Services and Problems of District Administration* by V. T. Krishnamachari, 1962.

—— *Fourth Five Year Plan, 1969–74*, 1970.

—— *Sixth Five Year Plan*, 1981.

Report of the Government of India Procedure Committee, 1919.

Report of the Government of India Secretariat Committee, 1937.

Report on the Reorganisation of the Central Government, 1945–46, 1946.

Shah Commission of Inquiry, *Interim Report II*, 1978.

—— *Third and Final Report*, 1978.

The Constitution of India, 1949, and reprinted with amendments to the present day.

Other (official printed sources)

Government of Andhra Pradesh. *Report on the Administrative Reforms Committee, 1964–65* (Hyderabad), 1965.

Government of Bengal Province. *Report Regarding the Establishments of Commissioners, Districts and Subdivisional Offices*) (by L. A. (Chapman, ICS) (Alipore), 1938.

—— *Report of the Bengal Administration Enquiry Committee, 1944–45* (A. Rowland) (Alipore), 1945.

Government of Bihar State. Cabinet Secretariat, *Rules of Executive Business* (Patna), 1965.

Government of Bombay State, *Assistant–Collector's Manual* (Bombay), 1951.

—— *Report of the Reorganization of District Revenue Offices*, 1959.

Government of Great Britain. *Report on Indian Constitutional Reforms* (Montagu–Chelmsford Reforms), Cd. 9109, 1918.

—— *Government of India Act, 1919.*

—— *Parliamentary Debates*, HC, 157, 1922; 434, 1946–7.

—— *Report of the Royal (Lee) Commission on the Superior Civil Services in India*, Cmd. 2128, 1924.

—— *Report of the Indian Statutory Commission* (Simon Commission), Cmd. 3568–9, 1930.

—— *Government of India Act, 1935.*

—— *Instrument of Instructions to the Governor-General and Governors* (Under the 1935 Act), Cmd. 4805, 1935.

—— *India. Compensation for the Services*, Cmd. 7116, 1947.

—— *Indian Independence Act, 1947.*

Government of Kerala. *Report of the Administrative Reforms Committee* (Trivandrum), 1958.

Government of Madras Province. *The Indian Civil Service Manual, Madras* (Madras), 1941.

Government of Madras State. *The Indian Administrative Service Manual, Part II, Madras* (Madras), 1957.

Government of Punjab State. *Report on the Reorganization of District Administration in Punjab* (Chandigarh), 1954.

Government of Rajasthan. *Report of the Administrative Reforms Committee* (Jaipur), 1963.

—— *Report of the Rajasthan Pay Commission* by J. S. Ranawat (Jaipur), 1968.

—— *Report of the Rajasthan Pay Commission* by B. P. Beri (Jaipur), 1981.

Government of Tamil Nadu. *Scheme of Field Training in the Districts for Assistant Collectors*, 1979.

Government of United Provinces. *Handbook for the Guidance of Junior Collectors* (Allahabad), 1936.

Government of Uttar Pradesh. *Reorganization of Collectorates* (Lucknow), 1956.

Government of West Bengal. *Report of the Administrative Reforms Committee* (Calcutta), 1983.

Lal Bahadur Shastri National Academy of Administration (Mussoorie, UP), 'Probationers' Handbook: XLII Foundational Course, 29th August–3rd December 1983', mimeo.

—— 'National Training Conference on Training of Civil Servants in India (21–23 September 1982): Recommendations', 1982, mimeo.

—— 'Course Handbook, IAS Professional Course: Phase I (1 December 1982–31 May 1983)', mimeo.

—— 'Course Design, IAS Professional Course: Phase II (1983) (1982–83 Batch) (6 June–20 August 1983)', mimeo.

—— 'Shishtachar' (Handbook on Etiquette and Manners), n.d., mimeo.

Lok Sabha Secretariat, Estimates Committee, *Ninth Report, 1953–54, Administrative, Financial and Other Reforms*, 1954.

—— (1965–6), *Ninety-Third Report (Third Lok Sabha), 1966.*

Mansergh, N. *et al.* (eds.), *Constitutional Relations between Britain and India: The Transfer of Power, 1942–7* (HMSO), Vol. viii (1979), vol. x (1981).

Sardar Patel's Correspondence, 1945–50 (ed. Durga Das), Vol. ix (Ahmedabad, 1973).

The Framing of India's Constitution: Select Documents (ed. B. Shiva Rao), Vol. iv (New Delhi, 1968).

4 SECONDARY SOURCES

Aberbach, J., Putnam, R., and Rockman, B., *Bureaucrats and Politicians in Western Democracies*, Cambridge, Mass., 1981.

Aiyar, S. P., 'Political Context of Indian Administration', *IJPA* xvii. 3 (1971), 337–54.

Alavi, H., 'The State in Post-Colonial Societies', *New Left Review*, 74 (1972), 59–81.

—— 'State and Class under Peripheral Capitalism', in Alavi, H. and Shanin, T. (eds.), *Introduction to the Sociology of the Developing Societies*, London, 1982.

——'Class and State', in Gardezi, H. and Rashid, J. (eds.), *Pakistan: The Roots of Dictatorship*, London, 1983.

Alexander, H. M. L., 'Discarding the "Steel Frame": Changing Images among Indian Civil Servants in the Early Twentieth Century', *South Asia*, New Series, v. 2 (1982), 1–12.

Allen, C., (ed.), *Plain Tales from the Raj: Images of British India in the Twentieth Century*, London, 1975.

Anderson, B. R. O'G., 'Old State, New Society: Indonesia's New Order in Comparative Historical Perspective', *Journal of Asian Studies*, xlii. 3 (1983), 477–96.

Anter Singh, *Development Administration*, Delhi, 1981.

Armstrong, J., *The European Administrative Elite*, Princeton, 1973.

Arnold, D., 'The Armed Police and Colonial Rule in South India, 1914–1947', *MAS* 11. 1 (1977), 101–25.

Austin, G., *The Indian Constitution: Cornerstone of a Nation*, Oxford, 1966.

Avasthi, A., *Central Administration*, New Delhi, 1980.

Ayyangar, M. Ananthasayanam, 'Administration of a State as seen by a Governor', *Management Perspective* (Delhi), vii (Apr.–June 1969), 37–43.

Badrinath, 'Urban Development of Greater Madras', (report presented to the Government of Tamil Nadu privately, mimeo., 1970).

Bagchi, A. K., *Private Investment in India, 1900–1939*, Cambridge, 1972.

Bailey, F. G., 'Parliamentary Government in Orissa, 1947–1959', *Journal of Commonwealth Political Studies*, 1 (May 1962), 112–22.

Baker, C., Johnson, G. and Seal, A. (eds.), *Power, Profit and Politics: Essays on Imperialism, Nationalism and Change in Twentieth-Century India*, Cambridge, 1981.

Bansal, P. L., *Administrative Development in India*, New Delhi, 1974.

Barker, E., *The Future Government of India and the Indian Civil Service*, London, 1919.

Bayley, D. H., 'The Police and Political Order in India', *Asian Survey*, xxiii. 4 (1983), 484–96.

Bayly, C. A., *The Local Roots of Indian Politics, Allahabad, 1880–1920*, Oxford, 1975.

—— *Rulers, Townsmen and Bazaars: North Indian Society in the Age of British Expansion 1770–1870*, Cambridge, 1983.

Beaglehole, T., 'From Rulers to Servants: The Indian Civil Service and the British Demission of Power in India', *MAS* 11. 2 (1977), 237–55.

Bernard, H. C., *The History of English Higher Education*, London, 1947.

Bettelheim, C., *India Independent*, New York, 1968.

Bhalerao, C. (ed.), *Administration, Politics and Development in India*, Bombay, 1974.

Bhambhri, C. P., *Bureaucracy and Politics in India*, Delhi, 1971.

—— *The World Bank and India*, New Delhi, 1980.

Bhatia, L. M., 'Public Service Ethics', *Journal of the Lal Bahadur Shastri National Academy of Administration*, xix. 3 (1974), 441.

Bhatnagar, P. and Sharma, G., 'Transfer of Collectors in Rajasthan', *IJPA* xix. 2 (1973). 187–203.

Bhatt, A., 'Municipal Commissioner in Gujarat: Structure, Process and Style', *Nagarlok*, 10 (1978), 122–37.

—— 'Colonial Bureaucratic Culture and Development Administration: Portrait of an Old-fashioned Indian Bureaucrat', *Journal of Commonwealth and Comparative Politics*, 17. 2 (1979), 159–75.

Blunt, E., *The ICS*, London, 1937.

Bottomore, T. B., 'Modern Elites in India', in Unnithan, T. K. N. *et al.* (eds.), *Towards a Sociology of Culture in India*, New Delhi, 1965, pp. 180–8.

—— 'The Administrative Elite', in Horowitz, I. L. (ed.), *The New Sociology: Essays in Honour of C. Wright Mills*, New York, 1965, pp. 357–69.

—— and Goode, P. (eds.), *Austro Marxism*, Oxford, 1978.

Braibanti, R., 'The Civil Service of Pakistan: A Theoretical Analysis', *South Atlantic Review*, 58 (1959), 258–304.

—— 'Reflections on Bureaucratic Reform in India', in Braibanti, R. and Spengler, J. (eds.), *Administration and Economic Development in India*, Durham, North Carolina, 1963, pp. 3–68.

—— 'The Higher Bureaucracy in Pakistan', in Braibanti, R. and Associates, *Asian Bureaucratic Systems*, pp. 209–353.

—— and Associates, *Asian Bureaucratic Systems emergent from the British Imperial Tradition*, Durham, North Carolina, 1966.

Brass, P., *Factional Politics in an Indian State*, Berkeley, 1965.

—— *Language, Religion and Politics in North India*, Cambridge, 1974.

—— 'National Power and Local Politics in India: A Twenty Year Perspective', *MAS* 18. 1 (1984), 89–118.

Brown, J., 'Imperial Facade: Some Constraints upon and Contradictions in the British Position in India, 1919–1935', *Transactions of the Royal Historical Society*, Vol. 26, Fifth Series, 35–52.

Butani, K. N., 'Personnel Administration: A Muffled Cry for Change by the Administrative Reforms Commission', *IJPA* xv. 1 (1969), 11–31.

Campbell-Johnson, A., *Mission with Mountbatten*, London, 1951.

Capoor, H. K. L., 'The Collector in Gujarat', *IJPA* xi. 3 (1965), 441–52.

Casey, Lord, *Personal Experiences, 1939–46*, London, 1962.

Chanda, A., *Indian Administration*, London, 1958.

Chandra, B., 'Personnel Administration: Time for Action', *IJPA* xv. 2 (1969), 277–87.

Chaturvedi, H. R., *Bureaucracy and the Local Community: Dynamics of Rural Development*, Bombay, Centre for the Study of Developing Societies, Monograph No. 2, 1977.

Chaturvedi, M. K., 'Personnel Administration: The Need for Realism, *IJPA* xv. 1 (1969), 32–73.

Chaturvedi, T. N., 'Commitment in Public Service', *Journal of Constitutional and Parliamentary Studies*, 11 (Jan.–Mar. 1977), 17–29.

Chopra, R. N., 'The Collector in Madhya Pradesh', *IJPA* xi. 3 (1965), 482–97.

Coen, T., *The Indian Political Service*, London, 1971.

'Committed Civil Service: A Symposium', *Seminar*, 168 (Aug. 1973).

Conlon, F., *A Caste in a Changing World: The Chitrapur Saraswat Brahmans 1700–1935*, Berkeley, 1977.

Crozier, M., *The Bureaucratic Phenomenon*, Chicago, 1964.

Council for the Indian School Certificate Examinations, *List of Affiliated Schools, 1980*, 1980, privately printed.

Dave, P. K. 'The Collector, Today and Tomorrow', *IJPA* xi. 3 (1965), 376–88.

Dayal, I., Mathur, K., *et al.*, *Dynamics of Formulating Policy in Government of India*, Delhi, 1976.

De Montmorency, J., *The Indian States and Indian Federation*, Cambridge, 1942.

Desai, N. B., *Report on the Administrative Survey of the Surat District*, Bombay, Indian Society of Agricultural Economics, 1958.

Dey, B. K., *Bureaucracy, Development and Public Management in India*, New Delhi, 1978.

Dogan, M. (ed.), *The New Mandarins of Western Europe: The Political Role of Top Civil Servants*, New York, 1976.

Dubhashi, P. R., 'ARC's Report on Personnel Administration: Faulty Superstructure on False Premises', *IJPA* xv. 4 (1969), 623–34.

—— 'Committed Bureaucracy', *IJPA* xvii. 1 (1971), 33–9.

—— *The Process of Public Administration*, Pune, 1980.

Dwarkadas, R., *Role of Higher Civil Service in India*, Bombay, 1958.

Epstein, S., 'District Officers in Decline: The Erosion of British Authority in the Bombay Countryside, 1919 to 1947', *MAS* 16 (1982), 493–518.

Ewing, A., 'The Indian Civil Service, 1919–1942', unpublished Ph.D. dissertation, Cambridge University, 1980.

—— 'Administering India: The Indian Civil Service', *History Today*, 32 (June 1982), 43–8.

—— 'The Indian Civil Service 1919–1924: Service Discontent and the Response in London and in Delhi', *MAS* 18. 1 (1984), 33–53.

Franda, M., *Bengal and the Federalizing Process in India*, Princeton, 1968.

Frankel, F. R., *India's Political Economy, 1947–1977*, Princeton, 1978.

Frykenberg, R., *Guntur District 1788–1848: A History of Local Influence and Central Authority in South India*, Oxford, 1965.

Gadgil, N. V., *Government from Inside*, Meerut, 1968.

Gallagher, J., Johnson, G., and Seal, A. (eds.), *Locality, Province and Nation: Essays on Indian Politics 1870–1940*, Cambridge, 1973.

—— *The Decline, Revival and Fall of the British Empire*, ed. A. Seal, Cambridge, 1982.

Goldthorpe, J., 'On the Service Class, its Formation and Future', in Giddens, A. and Mackenzie, G. (eds.), *Social Class and the Division of Labour*, Cambridge, 1982, pp. 162–85.

Goodnow, H., *The Civil Service of Pakistan: Bureaucracy in a New Nation*, New Haven, 1964.

Gopinath, P. K., 'Corruption in Political and Public Offices: Causes and Cure', *IJPA* xxviii. 4 (1982), 897–918.

Guha, R. *et al.*, *Subaltern Studies: Writings on South Asian History and Society*, i. ii, iii, Delhi, 1982–4.

Gupta, B. K., 'Some Aspects of Indian Bureaucracy in the Gupta, Mughal and British Empires', *Journal of the National Academy of Administration*, 6. 3 (July 1961), 65–73.

Gupta, D. and Premi, M., *Sources and Nature of Official Statistics of the Indian Union*, Delhi, 1970.

Gupta, N. P., 'Administrative Reforms: How?', *Link* (15 Aug. 1970), 85.

Hager, L. M., 'Bureaucratic Corruption in India: Legal Control of Maladministration', *Comparative Political Studies*, 6. 2 (1973), 197–219.

Halappa, G. S. (ed.), *Studies in State Administration*, Dharwar, 1972.

Hampden-Turner, C., *Gentlemen and Tradesmen: The Values of Economic Catastrophe*, London, 1983.

Hanson, A. H., *The Process of Planning: A Study of India's Five Year Plans, 1950–1964*, London, 1966.

Heginbotham, S. J., *Cultures in Conflict: The Four Faces of Indian Bureaucracy*, New York, 1975.

—— 'The Civil Service and the Emergency' in Hart, H. C. (ed.), *Indira Gandhi's India: A Political System Reappraised*, Boulder, Colorado, 1976, pp. 67–91.

Hejmadi, V. S. and Panandiker, V. A., 'The Public Services: Recruitment and Selection', *IJPA* ix. 3 (1963), 356–69.

Heningham, S., 'Bureaucracy and Control in India's Great Landed Estates: The Raj Darbhanga of Bihar, 1879–1950', *MAS* 17. 1 (1983), 35 –55.

Hodson, H. V., *The Great Divide: Britain, India, Pakistan*, London, 1969.

Hugh-Jones, S., 'The ICS Myth', *New Statesman*, 72, 2 Dec. 1966, 842.

Hunt, R. and Harrison, J., *The District Officer in India, 1930–1947*, London, 1980.

Hutchins, F. G., *Spontaneous Revolution: The Quit India Movement*, Delhi, 1971.

Isaacs, H., *India's Ex-untouchables*, New York, 1965.

Jain, H. M., 'Decision Making at the Centre', *Journal of the Society for Study of State Governments*, (Jan.–Mar. 1979).

Jain, R. B., 'Classification of Services and Pay Structure: Absence of a Rationale' in Jain, R. B., *Contemporary Issues in Indian Administration*, Delhi, 1976, pp. 72–104.

Jilani, S. G., *Anatomy of a State Civil Servant*, Ranchi, 1959.

Kabra, K. N., *The Black Economy in India: Problems and Policies*, Delhi, 1982.

Kaufman, H., *The Forest Ranger: A Study in Administrative Behaviour*, Baltimore, 1967.

Khanna, B. S., 'Trends in Public Administration in India since the Transfer of Power', *The Research Bulletin (Arts) of the University of the Punjab*, xvi. 2 (1955), 5.

Khanna, K., *Behavioural Approach to Bureaucratic Development*, New Delhi, 1983.

Khare, R. S., *The Changing Brahmans*, Chicago, 1970.

Kiernan, V., *The Lords of Human Kind*, London, 1969.

Kirk-Greene, A., 'New Africa's Administrators', *Journal of Modern African Studies*, 10. 1 (1972), 93–107.

Kochanek, S., *The Congress Party of India*, Princeton, 1968.

—— *Business and Politics in India*, Berkeley, 1974.

—— 'The Politics of Regulation: Rajiv's New Mantras', *Journal of Commonwealth and Comparative Politics*, xxiii. 3 (1985), 189–211.

Kothari, R., *Politics in India*, Boston, 1970.

—— 'Stemming the Rot', *Indian Express*, 2 June 1982.

Kothari, S. and Roy, R., *Relations between Politicians and Administrators at the District Level*, New Delhi, 1969.

Kraus, R. and Vanneman, R., 'Bureaucrats versus the State in Capitalist and Socialist Regimes', *Comparative Studies in Society and History*, 27 (1985), 111–22.

Laporte, R., 'Public Administration in South Asia since the British Raj', *Public Administration Review*, 41. 5 (1981), 581–8.

Leonard, K., *Social History of an Indian Caste: The Kayasths of Hyderabad*, Berkeley, 1978.

Letwin, S., 'The Morality of the Gentleman', *Cambridge Review*, xcvii (7 May 1976), 141–5; and (4 June 1976), 168–73.

Lewis, J. P., *Quiet Crisis in India*, Washington DC, 1962.

Limmaye, M., *Why Samyukta Socialist?*, Delhi, 1967.

Low, D. A., 'The Government of India and the First Non-Co-operation Movement: 1920–22', *Journal of Asian Studies*, xxv (1966), 241–59.

—— *Lion Rampant*, London, 1973.

—— (ed.), *Congress and the Raj: Facets of the Indian Struggle, 1917–47*, London, 1977.

Mack, E., *Public Schools and British Opinion since 1860: The Relationship between Contemporary Ideas and the Evolution of an English Institution*, London, 1941.

Madhok, B., *Why Jana Sangh?*, Delhi, 1967.

Maheshwari, S., 'The All-India Services', *Public Administration* (London), 49 (1971), 291–308.

—— *The Administrative Reforms Commission*, Agra, 1972.

—— 'United Civil Services in Pakistan', *Public Administration* (Kanpur), 12 (Nov. 1974), 12.

—— *Indian Administration*, 2nd ed., New Delhi, 1974.

—— 'Constituency Linkage of National Legislators in India', *Legislative Studies Quarterly*, 1. 3 (1976), 331–54.

—— *State Government in India*, Delhi, 1979.

—— 'The Political Executive and the Permanent Executive: An Analysis of the Emerging Role Patterns', *IJPA* xxvi. 3 (1980), 739–49.

—— 'Ecology of Public Enterprises in India', *IJPA*, xxvii. 4 (1981), 1034–42.

Majumdar, A. K., 'Writings on the Transfer of Power', in Nanda, B. R. (ed.), *Essays in Modern Indian History*, New Delhi, 1980, pp. 182–222.

Mangat Rai, E. N., *Patterns of Administrative Development in Independent India*, University of London Institute of Commonwealth Studies, Commonwealth Paper 19, London, 1976.

Mannheim, K., *An Introduction to the Sociology of Education*, London, 1962.

Markovitz, C., *Indian Business and Nationalist Politics, 1931–39: The Indigenous Capitalist Class and the Rise of the Congress Party*, Cambridge, 1985.

Marz, T., 'The National Academy of Administration: Normative Vocabularies and Organizational Reality', in Schaffer, B. (ed.), *Administrative Training and Development: A Comparative Study of East Africa, Zambia, Pakistan, and India*, New York, 1974, pp. 315–82.

Masaldan, P. N., *Planning in Uttar Pradesh*, Bombay, 1962.

Mason, P. (pseud. Philip Woodruff), *The Men who Ruled India: The Founders*, London, 1953.

—— *The Men who Ruled India: The Guardians*, London, 1954.

—— *The English Gentleman*, London, 1982.

Mathur, Kuldeep, *Bureaucratic Response to Development: A Study of Block Development Officers in Rajasthan and Uttar Pradesh*, Delhi 1972.

Mathur, P. C., 'Panchayati Raj Research in India: A Survey of Bibliographic Sources', *Prashasnika*, iv. 3 and 4 (July & Dec. 1975), 64–9.

Mattoo, P. K., 'The Civil Service System in India', in Raksasataya A. and Siedentopf, H. (eds.), *Asian Civil Services: Development and Trends*, Kuala Lumpur, 1980, pp. 47–130.

Mayer, A. C., 'Public Service and Individual Merit in a Town in Central India', in Mayer, A. C. (ed.), *Culture and Morality*, London, 1981, pp. 153–73.

Miller, D. F., *Pervasive Politics: A Study of the Indian District*, Melbourne Politics Monograph, Melbourne, 1972.

Misra, B. B., *The Indian Middle Classes: Their Growth in Modern Times*, London, 1961.

—— 'The Evolution of the Office of Collector', *IJPA* xi. 3 (1965), 355–67.

—— *The Bureaucracy in India: An Historical Analysis up to 1947*, London, 1971.

—— *The Indian Political Parties: An Historical Analysis of Political Behaviour up to 1947*, Delhi, 1976.

—— *District Administration and Rural Development in India*, Delhi, 1983.

Mohanty, N., 'ARC on Personnel Administration: A Study in Bias', *IJPA* xv. 4 (1969), 635–55.

Mommsen, W. and Osterhammel, J. (eds.), *Imperialism and After*, London, 1986.

Mook, B., *The World of the Indian Field Administrator*, New Delhi, 1982.

Moon, P., *Divide and Quit*, London, 1961.

Moore, B., *Social Origins of Dictatorship and Democracy: Lord and Peasant in the Making of the Modern World*, Boston, 1966.

Moore, R. J., 'Recent Historical Writing on the Modern British Empire and Commonwealth: Later Imperial India', *Journal of Imperial and Commonwealth History*, 4. 1 (1975), 55–76.

—— (ed.), *Tradition and Politics in South Asia*, Delhi, 1979.

—— *Escape from Empire: The Attlee Government and the Indian Problem*, Oxford, 1983.

Morris-Jones, W. H., *The Government and Politics of India*, 3rd ed., London, 1971.

—— and Fischer, G. (eds.), *Decolonisation and After: The British and French Experience*, London, 1980.

Mosley, L., *The Last Days of the British Raj*, London, 1961.

Mowat, C., *Britain between the Wars 1918–1940*, London, 1956.

Mukerji, M., 'B. Mehta' in Arora, R. (ed.), *People's Participation in Development Process: Essays in Honour of B. Mehta*, Jaipur, HCM Institute of Public Administration, 1979, p. xi.

Mullick, B. N., *My Years with Nehru*, Bombay, 1971.

Muramatsu, M. and Krauss, E., 'Bureaucrats and Politicians in Policy Making: The Case of Japan', *American Political Science Review*, 78. 1 (1984), 126–46.

Muthayya, B. C. and Gnanakannan, I., *Development Personnel: A Psycho-Social Study across Three States in India*, Hyderabad, National Institute for Community Development, 1973.

Nair, B. N., *The Dynamic Brahmin*, Bombay, 1959.

Narain, I. and Mathur, P. C., 'Union–State Relations in India: A Case Study of Rajasthan', *Journal of Commonwealth Political Studies*, 2 (May 1964), 120–40.

Narula, B. S., 'Administrative Reforms Commission: Perspective and Findings', *IJPA* xvii. 4 (1971), 634–60.

Nehru, J., *An Autobiography*, London, 1936.

—— 'A Word to the Services', *IJPA* i. 4 (1955), 289–302.

Nordlinger, E., *On the Autonomy of the Democratic State*, Cambridge, Mass., 1981.

Ogilvie, V., *The English Public School*, London, 1957.

O'Malley, L., *The Indian Civil Service 1601–1930*, London, 1931.

Palmer, N., *The Indian Political System*, Boston, 1961.

Panna Lal, *Handbook for the Guidance of Junior Collectors*, Allahabad, 1936.

Pannikar, K. M., 'India's Administrative Problems', *Eastern Economist*, 26 (9 Mar. 1956), 408–9.

Paranjape, H. K., 'A Trojan Inheritance', *Seminar*, 84 (Aug. 1966), 32–3.

Patel, H. M., 'Cabinet Government in India', in Aiyar, S. and Srinivasan, R. (eds.), *Studies in Indian Democracy*, Bombay, 1965, pp. 197–215.

Pekin, L. B., *Public Schools*, London, 1932.

Pillai, N. and Balasubramaniam, A., 'The Boards of Directors of Public Sector Companies in Kerala: An Analysis', *Lok Udyog*, 17 (June 1983), 23–33.

Posgate, W. D., 'Fertilizers for India's Green Revolution: The Shaping of Government Policy', *Asian Survey*, xiv (Aug. 1974), 733–50.

Potter, D. C., 'The Relevance of Training for the Indian Administrative Service', *Political Science Review* (Jaipur), 8. 3–4 (1969), 325–46.

—— 'Political Change and Confidential Government Files in India: 1937, 1947, 1967', *Journal of Commonwealth Political Studies*, viii. 2 (1970), 134–46.

—— 'Manpower Shortage and the End of Colonialism: The Case of the Indian Civil Service', *MAS* 7. 1 (1973), 47–73.

—— 'The Shaping of Young Recruits in the Indian Civil Service', *IJPA* xxiii. 4 (1977), 575–89.

Prasad, B., *The Indian Administrative Service*, Delhi, 1968.

Public Schools Yearbook, 1914, London.

Public and Preparatory Schools 1939, London.

Purohit, M. C., 'Sales Tax Administration in India', *IJPA* xxviii. 4 (1982), 832–9.

Ram, N. V. R., *Games Bureaucrats Play*, New Delhi, 1978.

Raven, S., *The English Gentleman*, London, 1961.

Ravi Dhavan Shankardass, *The First Congress Raj: Provincial Autonomy in Bombay*, Delhi, 1982.

Ray, J. K., *Administrators in a Mixed Polity*, Delhi, 1981.

Ray, S., *Indian Bureaucracy at the Crossroads*, New Delhi, 1979.

Riker, W. H., *Federalism*, Boston, 1964.

Rose, J. and Ziman, J., *Camford Observed*, London, 1964.

Rosenthal, D. *The Limited Elite: Politics and Government in Two Indian Cities*, Chicago, 1970.

Rothermund, D., 'Constitutional Reforms versus National Agitation in India, 1900–1950', *Journal of Asian Studies*, xxi. 4 (1962), 505–22.

Roy, R., *Bureaucracy and Development: The Case of Indian Agriculture*, New Delhi, 1975.

Roy, W. F., 'The Steel Frame: The Legend of the Indian Civil Service', *New Zealand Journal of Public Administration*, 30, 1 (1967), 39–51.

Rudolph, L. and Rudolph, S., *The Modernity of Tradition: Political Development in India*, Chicago 1967.

—— (eds.), *Education and Politics in India*, Cambridge, Mass., 1972.

Rumbold, A., *Watershed in India 1914–1922*, London, 1979.

Russell, B., *Selected Papers*, New York, 1927.

Schiff, L. M., *The Present Condition of India: A Study in Social Relationships*, London, 1939.

Scott, P., *Staying On*, London, 1977.

Seal, A., 'Imperialism and Nationalism in India', in Gallagher, J., Johnson, G., and Seal, A. (eds.), *Locality, Province and Nation: Essays on Indian Politics 1870–1940*, Cambridge, 1973, pp. 1–27.

Seminarist, 'Self before Service', *Seminar*, 84 (1966), 13.

Sen, A., *The State, Industrialization and Class Formation in India: A Neo-Marxist Perspective on Colonialism, Underdevelopment and Development*, London, 1982.

Sharma, S. N., 'The Collector in Orissa', *IJPA* xi. 3 (1965), 543–59.

Sharnkar, G., 'Socialist Ideas of Jawaharlal Nehru', *Journal of Indian History*, lvii (Aug.–Dec. 1979), 441–9.

Shils, E., *The Intellectual between Tradition and Modernity: The Indian Situation* (Comparative Studies in Society and History, Supplement I), The Hague, 1961.

—— *Tradition*, London, 1981.

Shukla, J. D., *State and District Administration in India*, Delhi, 1976.

Singer, M., *Traditional India: Structure and Change*, Jaipur, 1975.

Singh, S. N., 'A Study of the Recruitment Pattern of the IAS', *Administrator*, xxvii. 2 (1982), 337–44.

Singh, Tarlok, *India's Development Experience*, London, 1979.

Sinha, N., 'The IAS Academy', *Amrita Bazar Patrika*, 28 Mar. 1982.

Sinha, V.M., 'The Problem of Reorganization of the Superior Civil Services in India', unpublished Ph.D. dissertation, Saugar University, 1957.

—— 'The Indian Administrative Service', *Political Science Review*, 12. 3–4 (1973), 247–56.

Skocpol, T., *States and Social Revolutions: A Comparative Analysis of France, Russia and China*, Cambridge, 1979.

Sogani, M., *The Chief Secretary in India: A Study of his Role in State Administration in Rajasthan*, New Delhi, 1984.

Spangenburg, B., *British Bureaucracy in India: Status, Policy and the ICS in the Late 19th Century*, New Delhi, 1976.

Srinivas, M. N., *Social Change in Modern India*, Berkeley, 1966.

Srivastava, G. P., *The Indian Civil Service*, Delhi, 1965.

Subhas Rao, K., 'The Unchanging Bureaucracy', *Public Administration* (India), 12 (Apr. 1974), 6–11.

Subramaniam, V., *Social Background of India's Administrators*, New Delhi, 1971.

—— *Transplanted Indo-British Administration*, New Delhi, 1977.

Suleiman, E., *Politics, Power and Bureaucracy in France: The Administrative Elite*, Princeton, 1974.

Swarnlata, 'Women in the All India Services', *Prashasnika*, 9. 4 (1982), 39–48.

Taub, R., *Bureaucrats under Stress: Administrators and Administration in an Indian State*, Berkeley, 1969.

Taylor, A. J. P., *English History, 1914–1945*, New York, 1965.

Templewood (Samuel Hoare), *Nine Troubled Years*, London, 1954.

Thakur, R. N., *The All India Services: A Study of their Origin and Growth*, Patna, 1969.

—— *Elite Theory and Administrative System*, New Delhi, 1981.

Therborn, G., *What Does the Ruling Class do when it Rules? State Apparatuses and State Power under Feudalism, Capitalism and Socialism*, London, 1978.

Thorner, A., 'Semi-Feudalism or Capitalism: Contemporary Debate on Classes and Modes of Production in India', *EPW* xvii. 49 (1982), 1961–8; 50 (1982), 1993–9; 51 (1982), 2061–6.

Times of India Directory and Yearbook, 1983, Bombay, 1983.

Tinker, H., *India and Pakistan: A Political Analysis*, New York, 1962.

Tomlinson, B. R., *The Indian National Congress and the Raj, 1929–1942: The Penultimate Phase*, London, 1976.

—— 'Congress and the Raj: Political Mobilization in Late Colonial India' (Review Article), *MAS* 16. 2 (1982), 334–49.

Trivedi, R. K., and Rao, D. N., 'Higher Civil Service in India', *Journal of the National Academy of Administration*, vi. 3 (1961), 31–86.

Tyagi, A., *The Civil Service in a Developing Society*, Delhi, 1969.

Vithayathil, T., 'Women in the IAS', *Journal of the National Academy of Administration*, 16. 4 (1971), 91–8.

Vittachi, T., *The Brown Sahib*, London, 1962.

Vohra, B., 'Anatomy of Mal-administration', *Seminar*, 230 (Oct. 1978), 14.

Wade, R., 'Corruption: Where does the Money go?', *EPW* xvii (2 Oct. 1982), 1606.

Wavell, The Viceroy's Journal, ed. P. Moon, London, 1973.

Webster, F. A. M., *Our Great Public Schools*, London, 1937.

Weiner, M., *Party Politics in India*, Princeton, 1957.

—— *Party Building in a New Nation: The Indian National Congress*, Chicago, 1967.

Weiskopf, T., 'Dependence and Imperialism in India', in Selden, M. (ed.), *Remaking Asia*, New York, 1974, pp. 200–46.

Wheeler-Bennett, J. W., *King George VI: His Life and Reign*, London, 1958.

Wilkinson, R., *Gentlemanly Power*, London, 1964.

Williams, R., *Culture and Society, 1780–1950*, Harmondsworth, 1958.

—— *Culture*, London, 1981.

Wingate, R., *Lord Ismay: A Biography*, London, 1970.

Worsley, T. C., *Barbarians and Philistines: Democracy and the Public Schools*, London, 1940.

5 NEWSPAPERS

Amrita Bazar Patrika (Calcutta)
Guardian (London)
Hindu (Madras)
Hindustan Times (New Delhi)
Indian Express (New Delhi)
Searchlight (Patna)
Statesman (Calcutta)
The Times (London)
Times of India (Bombay)
Tribune (Ambala)

Glossary

aman sabha: local assembly loyal to British rule
ashram: religious retreat
babu: clerk; used by British to describe western-educated Indians
bania: a trader or money-lender belonging to a Hindu (or *Jain*) trading caste
Bhagavad Gita: one of the most sacred books of the Hindus
Bharat Darshan: tour of India for IAS recruits
Brahman, Brahmin: the priestly order in the traditional *Varna* hierarchy of Indian society; also a person belonging to that order
burra-sahib: important man
dharma: religious law or duty, moral order
dharamsala: religious guest-house
goonda: bad character
izzat: prestige
jagir: landed estate granted initially in return for service
jagirdar: holder of a *jagir*
Jain: a separate Indian religion related to Hinduism, involving the veneration of deified mortals; several million adherents, mostly in Western India
jati: caste, endogamous social group with shared rules of commensality
Kanya-Kubja Brahman: a particular *Brahman jati*
karnam: village accountant in south India
kayasth: a Hindu writer and administrative *jati*
khadi: handmade cloth
Kshatriya: The warrior order in the *Varna* hierarchy; also a person belonging to that order
Lok Sabha: lower house of the Indian Parliament
Maharaja: prince, large landlord
Mahatma: honorific title meaning (lit.) 'great soul'
mamlatdar: a subordinate revenue official
mulaqatis: persons visiting a government official on business
namaste: a form of greeting (Hindu)
nawab: Muslim aristocrat, ruler
panchayat: a village council or court
panchayati raj: a system of interlinked elected local authorities within a district, in independent India
pandit, pundit: Hindu scholar, teacher
patwari: local revenue official, mainly North India
peon: messenger
raj: rule; particularly British rule in India

raja: ruler
salaam: a term of greeting (Muslim)
salwar kamiz: women's tunic and trousers
Sardar: chief
swaraj: self-rule, autonomy, or independence
tahsil, tehsil, taluka: administrative division within a district for land revenue
tahsildar, tehsilder: government official in charge of a *tahsil, tehsil*
taluqdar: landowner (particularly in UP)
Vaishya: the third (merchant) order in the *Varna* hierarchy
Varna: one of the four classical orders or divisions in Hindu society
zamindar: landowner
zamindari: a land settlement with a zamindar
Zila parishad: a local authority at district level, in independent India

Index